Multimedia Sound and Music Studio

Multimedia Sound and Music Studio

Jeff Essex

Sponsored by Apple Computer, Inc.,
Entertainment and New Media Division
for the
Apple Multimedia Program

RANDOM
HOUSE

New York   Toronto   London   Syndey   Auckland

Multimedia Sound and Music Studio

Copyright © 1996 by Jeff Essex

Published in the United States by Random House Reference and Information Publishing, Inc., New York, and simultaneously in Canada by Random House of Canada, Limited.

Publisher	Charles Levine
Managing Editor	Jennifer Dowling
Production Editor	Joseph Vella
Copy Editor	Sybil Ihrig, VersaTech Associates
Cover Design	Elektrik Graffiti, Inc.
Interior Design	Nancy Sugihara
Page Composition	Sybil Ihrig, VersaTech Associates
Proofreader	Lorraine Maloney
Apple New Media Library Liaison	Dana De Puy Morgan

Typeset and printed in the United States of America

First Edition

0 9 8 7 6 5 4 3 2 1

ISBN 0-679-76191-8

Visit the Random House Web site at http://www.random.com/

Contents
at a Glance

Contents

PART TWO: TECHNIQUES   129

Foreword

Writing the introduction to a book is a tricky business. Do you take the intellectually rigorous approach, and develop a trenchant critical analysis of the book's contents? Or do you go the savvy, marketing route and trumpet the incredible benefits the book offers to one and all, whether pro or amateur, producer or composer, writer or engineer, lay or clergy? Or do you simply make sure you plug your *own* book (*MIDI for the Professional,* $19.95, Amsco publications, available at fine music and book stores everywhere)?

The answer, of course, is self-evident. As a true Audio Professional (not actually a contradiction in terms, as many would have you believe, but in fact a deeply ironic expression of respect, believed to derive originally from either the *Upanishads* or an early, uncensored version of *Candy),* one naturally avoids the temptation to be self-serving and eschews mention of one's own accomplishments (see above) to do justice to the work at hand.

In this case, all kidding aside, it is not hard to do. Jeff Essex has put together here a frankly amazing lot of very useful information about one of the least-understood, yet most important, aspects of the most heralded Technology of the Nineties: the desktop computer-based production of digital data capable of real-time playback through a range of various sensorially-stimulating devices. This technology is more commonly known by the most overused of all buzzwords: multimedia. (I'm going to try not to use this word again, and I'm also not going to refer to it as the *M* word. It's not going to be easy, but I know you'll appreciate it.) And while most mult&$@#ia brouhaha has been concentrated on the visuals—video, illustration, 3-D modeling, animation—this is only because it's been so hard to figure out how to *do* that part right. (It also looks incredibly cool, but that's another book, probably by Jeff Burger.) The medium Jeff Essex has taken on here had actually been figured out pretty well by the time the m*$%&me@#a frenzy began, but it was forced to swing on a vicious breaking curve when the visuals people developed their own ways of doing things without asking the advice of the audio people—a grave error, but understandable if you've ever met a mixdown engineer.

There are today a few individuals who understand how to produce music, narration, and sound effects and integrate them into a desktop presentation. They're the ones with the vacant expressions, ruined personal lives, and open wounds consistent with spending too much time on the bleeding edge of computer technology. Jeff is one of those grizzled veterans, having been there and done that, and he's poured the fruits of his experience into the book and CD-ROM you're about to read and hear. While creating *Multimedia Sound and Music Studio* may have been originally prescribed for Jeff as therapy by a licensed, if somewhat misguided, "psychoacoustician," it has certainly ended up as an invaluable tool for anyone who actually wants to put *multiple* media in their production. Just about everything is here—from bedrock traditional recording concepts and techniques to the latest way to protect your sound and music when the client decides you have 6 KB of disc space to score a two-hour CD-ROM extravaganza—and your legal options when he screeches out the Client's Credo in a voice resonating in the frequencies of chalk on a blackboard: "An' I want ya to make it sound *good,* too! By tomorrow, Y'unnerstan'?"

This is not only a technical reference, but a how-to book as well, and the music and effects on the CD-ROM provide a great jump start for any production—from a QuickTime video to your next business presentation. It covers both Macintosh and Windows, MIDI and digital audio, and even includes analyses of many of the most popular hardware and software tools you'll be shopping for and using. Whether you do audio yourself, or even just hire it out to "one of those, like, sound guys," the information here can make your life in m@#$%m(*&a a whole lot less annoying. And trust me, you need a tool like that.

Remember the advice my great-aunt Harriet gave me at her knee: "You can flash the lights and show the pictures as long as you want, but the customers don't start dancing until the music plays," she said. Then she pushed me into a snowdrift.

Tim Tully
Menlo Park, California. 1996

Tim Tully has been practicing and preaching music, audio, and MIDI for over twenty years. He has co-written two books, MIDI for the Professional *(Amsco/Music Sales) with Paul D. Lehrman, and* The Audible PC, *(Sybex) with David Rubin. He is the former editor of* Electronic Musician *magazine, the present Digital Media Editor of* NewMedia *magazine, and has con-*

tributed to EQ, Mix, Pro Sound News, Sound on Sound, *and other periodicals. Production credits include Compton's* Grammy Awards *and NewMedia's* ToolGuide Interactive *CD-ROMs, numerous computer games, and more industrial videos than should be allowed. He plays better tenor sax than Bill Clinton.*

Acknowledgments

Although I'm the principal author, this work is brought to you by a cast of hundreds. This book would have been impossible without the efforts of Dana DePuy Morgan and Kelli Richards of Apple Computer. They were involved from start to finish, paving the way with contacts and interviews, giving editorial support, providing lots of encouragement, tracking down content for the CD, and adding good ideas. David Roach, Tech Editor *extraordinaire,* added lots of pertinent details. His experience and depth of knowledge put a real shine on the material. My editors at Random House—Mike Roney, Charles Levine, and Tracy Smith—Managing Editor Jennifer Dowling, and Production Editor Joe Vella, helped me navigate through the entire process. Jeff Burger shoehorned massive amounts of data onto the CD-ROM, and actually got the beast to run on both Mac and Windows; no small feat in this business. Sybil "bite-the-speeding-bullet" Ihrig of VersaTech Associates played the dual roles of page compositor and copy editor, with the assistance of Lorraine Maloney as proofreader. And, of course, thanks go to Eileen LaPorte of the Apple Multimedia Program and Albert Chu, Director of Marketing for the Entertainment and New Media Division, for their support of the project.

Special thanks go to all of the very busy and very talented people who contributed interviews and product examples. Many vendors also were gracious enough to provide sample materials and review copies of products which are discussed in the book. In both categories, thanks for answering my many hours of questions. Kudos to Chuck Surack at Sweetwater Sound (one of the best mail-order sources for audio hardware and software) for helping to arrange loaner hardware.

No one person can possibly learn about multimedia without a network of friends, and I've been fortunate to have learned from some of the best. Many of them are current and former Macromedians, including Mark

Castle, Roger Jones, Bill Schulze, Terry Schussler, and John Ware. I also wouldn't have made it this far without my personal MIDI and Mac gurus, Shof Beavers and Greg Jalbert.

Of course, I *really* wouldn't have made it through the process without my family: Dad, who taught me how to schmooze; Mom, who put songs in my head; Johnny, who held it all together; and of course, my wife and daughter for enduring 15 minutes of quality time per day over the course of six months.

With all these people involved, you'd think there would be enough of them to share the blame for whatever errors and omissions you may find in this work. You would, however, be wrong. That singular honor is mine alone, and may God have mercy on my soul for ever committing information on such rapidly changing technology to the printed page.

Introduction

Welcome to the brave new world of audio for multimedia. You're just in time to stake a claim on one of the industry's last great frontiers. New technologies with great potential are appearing on the market, and audio quality in multimedia is poised for a big leap. This book is designed to help get you up to speed so that you can take advantage of the best audio available.

Seven or eight years ago, few people had even heard the term "multimedia." By now, you probably know that *multimedia* can be defined loosely as an interactive environment that includes many media types: text, graphics, animation, video, and, of course, audio. Of these media types, audio has been one of the last to really capture the attention of the creative community. The production of text, graphics, and animation has been well-served by graphic artists who cut their teeth in desktop publishing. Digital video had a four-year reign as the latest and greatest technology and thousands of people learned to tame the medium in their products. All the while, audio for multimedia has remained largely unchanged, practically since the appearance of the personal computer. This is surprising when one considers the impression high-quality audio can make in a presentation.

Everyone in this business understands that multimedia involves compromises. Graphics are displayed in 8-bit color instead of 24-bit color. Digital video is played at reduced frame rates and at small frame sizes. But it seems that digital audio has suffered through a disproportionate share of compromises. This may be because many people approach multimedia from visual disciplines like graphic design and video. It may be because producers have made the erroneous assumption that people are more willing to suffer through low-resolution sound than low-resolution graphics. Undoubtedly, it's because there haven't been as many tools for delivering high-quality audio from within a multimedia presentation. Now, however, things are changing for the better. Every new computer sports 16-bit audio output, MIDI playback in software is freeing users from expensive hardware and configuration issues, and audio compression schemes are making it easier to deliver high-fidelity sound.

As this field develops, we should see lots of improvement in audio quality—but only if people know how to use the tools to make it happen. That's where you and I come in. As multimedia audio specialists, it's our job to evangelize and demonstrate the benefits of high quality audio.

Why Is Audio Important?

Here are a few points to help you make your case. Studies have shown that people will tolerate poor-quality video as long as it's accompanied by good-quality audio, but they are less tolerant of good video with poor audio. In fact, if you improve the quality of audio playing in conjunction with video, people perceive that the picture quality is enhanced. If the quality argument doesn't work, maybe the financial one will. It's a lot faster and cheaper to create an immersive environment with audio than with graphics. Modeling and rendering three-dimensional graphics can take days, but you can build a compelling audio environment in a few hours. If the end goal of a multimedia production is to immerse the user in a sensory experience, audio provides the most bang for the buck.

The Perception of Sound

When I'm asked to describe why audio is a fundamentally important component of multimedia, I usually think back to the role of audio in the environment and how it affects our perception of the world around us. This is my "we're all still a bunch of monkeys" theory. While most of us spend our days sitting in chairs and staring at computer monitors, we're really designed to be out foraging in the wilderness, stalking prey and avoiding predators. Our senses developed as survival mechanisms; it's the way we're wired. When we hear an animal rustling in the bushes, we need to know if it's something that we could have for lunch or whether we are about to *be* lunch.

One of the traits that set humans on the evolutionary fast track was the ability to process and share information. Before written language existed, information was transferred through sounds and visuals—through the creation of symbolic icons, storytelling, dance, and cave paintings. Then a Phoenician bean-counter got the idea of marking up clay tablets. The first text-based display was born.

Such was the predominant means of information storage until about ten years ago, when computers began moving from text displays back toward graphic interfaces and multimedia data types. It's interesting that the way computers present information to us has actually evolved in reverse of the way we're wired to receive information. The appeal of multimedia lies in its ability to convey information through the channels that are most natural to us.

Who Should Read This Book

The fact that you're reading this book should mean that you already have some appreciation for the value of high-quality audio. This book will help you get the best results from the tools at your disposal. It also will give you guidance in choosing additional tools to expand your capabilities. I've tried to avoid "techno-babble" as much as possible, but we will get dragged into it at a few points along the way, so have some strong coffee nearby. The focus is on practical production techniques, but we'll also talk a lot about the issues you need to consider when dealing with the inevitable compromises that every multimedia producer faces. Above all, I've tried to create the book I wanted to read four years ago when I got seriously involved in multimedia audio.

This book is written for:

❏ Multimedia designers and producers who want to have a better understanding of the audio production process and the capabilities of audio within multimedia

❏ Production staff who need to scramble through an occasional audio job in the course of their work with graphics, video or programming

❏ Musicians and audio engineers eager to tap into the multimedia market

❏ Marketing and sales staff looking to add more impact to presentations

❏ Multimedia enthusiasts and hobbyists who want to improve the audio quality of their efforts

The emphasis for this book is on CD-ROM development, Macintosh-based authoring, and cross-platform delivery. That's been the major creative arena for the past year, and it seems to be carrying into next year as well. "But wait," you say, "isn't CD-ROM dead?" I doubt it. In fact, I think

CD-ROM is just hitting its stride. While there are many new exciting avenues of distribution coming into play (the Internet, for example), the largest market share for the forseeable future will continue to be held by CD-ROM. Even if you're using other channels for distribution, the techniques involved in overcoming CD-ROM bottlenecks apply equally well to playback from the Internet.

Part of my intention in writing this book is to encourage multimedia producers to look at some new approaches to implementing good-quality audio. But if you're just getting into this field from the "traditional" audio world, be prepared to lower your expectations a bit. Musicians and audio pros who aren't used to dealing with the limitations of the medium may be in for a shock when they apply their skills to multimedia.

You see, we've become a bit spoiled. In the past ten years the development of personal computers, digital audio and synthesizer technology has put a staggering amount of power into the hands of serious musicians. CD-quality masters can be produced on the desktop. But this level of quality doesn't necessarily transfer over to multimedia. When push comes to shove, reducing the quality of audio is the first place many developers look to boost performance, save disk storage, or reduce RAM requirements. So while our ability to produce fabulous audio has grown by leaps and bounds, we still have to be prepared to make music listenable at 11 kHz sampling rates.

What's in This Book

This book is divided into four main sections.

Part One— Tools and Technology

Part One has all the background information you need to understand the many different tools required for multimedia audio production.

Chapter 1 introduces basic concepts of digital audio sampling. You'll need this basic knowledge to understand much of the material that follows in later chapters. It also establishes seven basic steps in the audio creation process: planning, recording, capture, editing, output, integration, and playback. These seven steps form the framework for the order in which material is covered in the remainder of the book.

Chapter 2 covers hardware—the tools for recording and capture. We'll look at the basic elements of recording and capturing sound, including both audio and computer equipment. We'll also review how to configure a system.

Chapter 3 takes a side trip into MIDI, the Musical Instrument Digital Interface. We'll see how MIDI equipment can be used to create soundtracks, and how MIDI can be used to play soundtracks at runtime.

Chapter 4 digs into the software side of audio, starting with file formats and system software. Then the discussion turns to the pluses and minuses of various file formats and to strategies you may find useful when you consider what tradeoffs you may have to make.

Chapter 5 provides examples of systems for creating audio, depending on whether your budget and goals are modest or extravagant.

Part Two— Techniques

Now that you understand the tools, we can talk about how to use them. Part Two focuses on hands-on tips for audio production.

Chapters 6 and 7 walk through the entire audio-creation process, from planning through playback, with specific tips for handling each stage of the process. Most of the lessons I've learned through experience can be found in these two chapters.

Chapter 8 looks at creative and aesthetic considerations of sound design. This section will give you ideas about how to use voice, sound effects, and music in your presentations.

Part Three— Product Reviews

There's no substitute for having the right tools for the job. Part Three has reviews of most of the major audio tools that are available, including editors and mixers (Chapter 9), utilities and processors (Chapter 10), and MIDI sequencers that integrate digital audio (Chapter 11).

Part Four— Looking Ahead

Finally, Chapter 12 looks at the major emerging technologies that will be gaining in the market during 1996 and 1997, including Enhanced CD, software synthesis, 3-D sound, and on-line distribution.

Throughout the book, you'll find interviews with leading creative artists talking about their recent projects and their goals in exploring music and technology.

What's on the CD

The CD in the back of the book is packed with goodies, including:

❏ Shareware and freeware sound utilities
❏ Audio system software updates from Apple

- ❏ Clip media samples
- ❏ Demo versions of many products discussed in the book
- ❏ Sample works from the artists that were interviewed
- ❏ A hypertext version of the book
- ❏ Tutorials that illustrate key concepts covered in the book

I especially encourage you to investigate the artist samples and tutorials. Although the text explains certain concepts, you'll gain greater appreciation by actually hearing the examples. Look for the CD-ROM icon throughout the book for pointers to the tutorials.

And Finally . . .

One of the greatest challenges in this industry is keeping up with the technology. This book should give you a jump start, but after that it's up to you to stay on top of the latest trends. No single person or source will have all the answers. You'll have to tap into a network of colleagues, read voraciously, get on-line, and set aside time for your own personal research and experimentation. Keeping up is a full-time job in itself.

But it's not enough just to master the technology. It's equally important that you keep your creative edge. While some aspects of sound work are mundane, others have the potential to really connect with the listener. People can hear the difference when your heart is in your work. So give them the best you have to offer. In return, you'll receive one of life's great rewards: being successful while doing work that you enjoy.

Part One

TOOLS AND TECHNOLOGY

1

Digital Sound Technology

There are plenty of approaches to creating a multimedia product. But the blending of creative talent and technical know-how is a common thread that runs through every successful title. It's not always enough to create great content; you also have to understand how the computer handles the data.

Granted, the creative artist and a programmer working in tandem can share these tasks. But the more the artist knows about the programmer's task, the better the result. A computer is a medium just as oil, watercolor, marble, brass or audiotape is. The challenge is to work within the medium while also pushing its boundaries. To do this well, you need to know which boundaries are flexible and which ones offer the most advantages when stretched to the extreme.

The same is true for audio. We make a lot of tradeoffs when integrating sound into multimedia, but we also have to please listeners who are accustomed to hearing their CD collection. Once you understand some of the basic building blocks of audio and digital sampling technology, you will be better equipped to make intelligent decisions about what sacrifices to make, and when.

Sampling Basics

In this section, we will cover the basics of sampling: how sound is created, the properties of sound waves, and how digital sampling can be used to capture and recreate sounds.

The Physics of Sound

Sound is created by the vibration of an object, as shown in Figure 1.1. The object transmits its vibrations to the air surrounding it, creating waves of air pressure. These waves travel through the air to our eardrums. The eardrums transfer the vibration to our inner ear, which in turn sends signals to the brain, and we interpret the vibration as sound. This basic mechanism is the means by which all sounds are created and perceived; one object causes air to vibrate, and another object captures the vibration.

Frequency and Amplitude

Sound waves have two basic characteristics: the number of times the wave vibrates in a given period of time (called *frequency*) and the strength of the vibrations (called *amplitude*). Figure 1.2 illustrates the relationship between the two.

❏ *Frequency* is directly related to the pitch of a sound. High-pitched sounds are caused by rapid vibrations such as the piercing squeal of a whistle or a high note played on a violin. Low-pitched sounds are caused by slower vibrations such as the rumble of a passing train or a low note played on a piano. We usually measure the frequency of sound in terms of vibrations per second. Sound engineers have adopted the scientific convention of *Hertz* (abbreviated *Hz*), or cycles per second, to describe the frequency of a sound. For example, a common tuning reference on a piano, the note A below middle C, is described as 440 Hz.

Figure 1.1

Waves of air pressure created by a vibrating source travel to our ears and are perceived as sound.

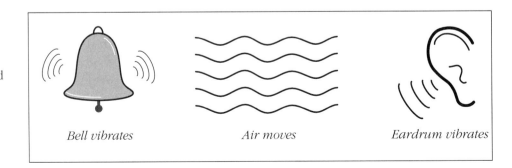

Bell vibrates   *Air moves*   *Eardrum vibrates*

Figure 1.2

The frequency of a sound wave is measured along a horizontal axis that represents time, or the number of waves or vibrations per second. Amplitude is measured on the vertical axis and represents the strength of the wave, which we perceive as volume.

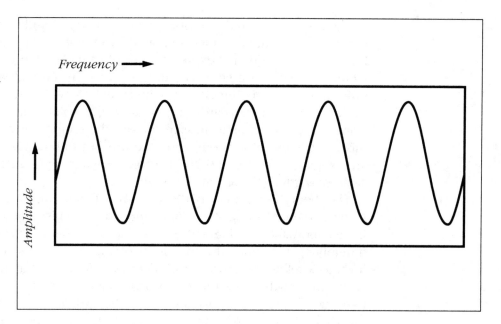

❏ **Amplitude** corresponds to the volume of a sound. The greater the distance between the top and the bottom of a sound wave, the greater the amplitude. A good way to visualize this is to think of a guitar string. If you touch the string gently, it vibrates at a fixed rate (in other words, at a fixed frequency), but the distance between the top and bottom of the area in which it vibrates is small. Give the string a good, strong pluck, and the distance over which the string vibrates increases greatly. As a result, the string moves more air, and the volume is louder.

Amplitude, or loudness, is described in *decibels*. A decibel is abbreviated as *dB*. For you trivia fans, a decibel is one-tenth of a *bel,* a sound pressure level measurement named after Alexander Graham Bell.

We need to clarify the concept of decibels here, because you'll encounter the decibel frequently in the audio world. The dB unit (dBu) is used to measure two related but very different phenomena. One is the *sound pressure level* (SPL), the actual loudness perceived by your ears. This is based on the strength of air pressure changes caused by vibrations or "sound waves" traveling through the air. For purposes of comparison, the ambient background noise of a recording studio registers about 20 dB SPL, regular human speech at a distance of one foot registers 70 dB SPL, and a jet plane engine registers about 130 dB SPL.

The second use of the decibel is the measure of audio signal level as an electrical phenomenon. One real-world example is the strength of a line-level voltage, frequently expressed as –10 dBu. Another example is the dB meters you see on a tape recorder or mixer. In the real world, this is the important thing to remember: when dealing with decibels in terms of cables or connecting hardware, be sure the voltage levels match. When using decibel level as a measure of signal strength (as with volumes in a mixer), it is useful for comparing the level of different signals. The values are expressed relative to 0 dB, the point at which the signal going out is the same strength as the signal coming in.

The theory behind decibel levels can get pretty involved from a mathematical or engineering standpoint, and I did promise not to bog you down in "techno-babble." Here's the basic idea: the decibel level is derived by multiplying ten times the logarithm of the ratio of the measured power level to a reference power level. Frankly, it's not something you'll need to worry too much about unless you're designing circuits (if you really want to wade through an explanation, see the "Suggested Reading" section in the back of the book), but it does illustrate an interesting point. Much of audio measurement involves logarithms and other exponential functions because

❏ these numbers make it easier to express the wide range of values that our ears can detect; and

❏ exponential numbers more closely reflect the way sound works in the real world.

For example, every doubling of frequency is a musical octave. Going back to our friend 440 Hz (the note "A" below Middle C on the piano), we see that 220 Hz is also the note A—but one octave lower—and that 880 Hz is the note A one octave higher. The relative difference between the notes of the lower octave (220 Hz to 440 Hz) and the higher octave (440 Hz to 880 Hz) sounds the same to our ears, but the actual difference in frequency is changing by a ratio of 2:1.

With decibels, we find that doubling the strength of an electrical voltage doesn't double the sound output level. Instead, every doubling produces an increase of 6 dB.

There's one final aspect of how the ear works that affects our perception of sound. We're much less sensitive to low-frequency material at lower volumes. This is why many stereos have a loudness switch to boost the bass when you turn the volume down. It also makes it more difficult for multimedia producers to create material with decent bass response. Unless the listener has a subwoofer or has cranked up the volume through a regular stereo system, it's likely that material mixed in a standard studio setting will sound tinnier when played back on small multimedia speakers.

Capturing and Transmitting Sound

The ability to record sound has been available for just over 100 years. During that brief period, the technology for recording sound has evolved historically from wax cylinders to wire recorders, vinyl records, magnetic tape, and now digital recording. To record sound, you need to capture sound waves. Here's an overview of the basic process for capturing and transmitting sound electronically.

Sound waves traveling through the air can be converted into electrical waveforms using a microphone. Microphones consist of a diaphragm (a thin membrane) and some type of *transducer*, which converts mechanical energy into electrical energy. The membrane moves in response to changes in air pressure, and the transducer converts this movement into a series of voltage variations that represent the sound waveform. The voltage variations are an electrical waveform; the amplitude and frequency of the waveform correspond exactly to the original acoustic waveform. This electrical signal can then be amplified and sent to a loudspeaker. The speaker cone vibrates in response to the electrical signals, creating sound waves that travel to the listener. Figure 1.3 illustrates this process.

Figure 1.3

A microphone converts sound waves into electrical energy. The electric signal can then be sent to a loudspeaker, producing sound that closely matches the sound picked up by the microphone.

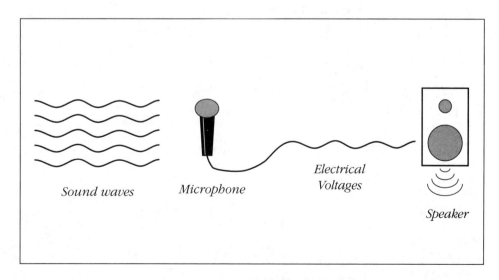

Sound waves   *Microphone*   *Electrical Voltages*   *Speaker*

Digital Sampling

With digital technology, it is now possible to create circuits that can convert electrical waveforms into digital information and vice versa. These are analog-to-digital (A-to-D) or digital-to-analog (D-to-A) converters. The term "analog" stems from the fact that the electrical waveform is analogous to the original, continuous sound waveform. Figure 1.4 shows how this process works.

The conversion of an analog waveform into digital information is called *sampling* because the A-to-D converter samples the status of the electrical signal at regular intervals and assigns a numerical value to represent the waveform. In this process, two main factors determine the quality of the resulting sampled waveform: the *sampling rate,* which defines how often the samples are captured, and the *sampling resolution,* which describes the number of values available to represent the amplitude of the wave.

Sampling Rates

Sounds are sampled several thousand times every second. Sampling rates, like sound wave frequencies, are measured in terms of *Hertz (Hz)*—the number of samples per second—or in terms of *kiloHertz (kHz),* for thousands of samples per second.

The most common sampling rates in use today are 11.025 kHz, 22.050 kHz, and 44.1 kHz. Higher sampling rates result in higher-quality sound.

To understand how a sound is sampled, visualize a wave on a vertically lined piece of paper, as in the example in Figure 1.5. Place dots at each point where the waveform and a line intersect, and then connect the dots. The higher the number of dots, the more closely the dots match the shape of the analog curve.

Figure 1.4

Electrical signals can be converted into digital information using an analog-to-digital converter. Digital information is converted back into electric signals using a digital-to analog converter.

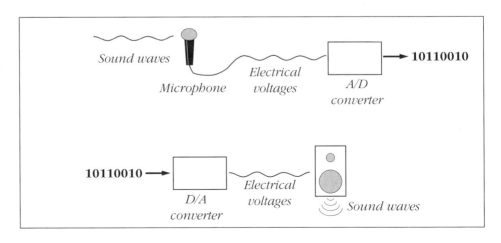

Figure 1.5

Original
waveform,
samples, and
the resulting
digitized
waveform.

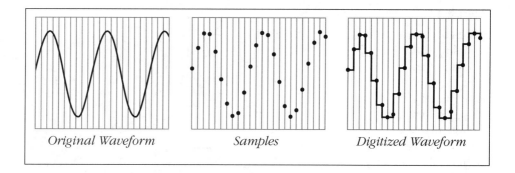

Original Waveform   Samples   Digitized Waveform

Sampling Resolution

As sounds are sampled, they are converted into numbers. Since computers represent numbers using *bits* (binary digits, or ones and zeroes), the numerical values for representing samples are allocated in bits. The most common resolutions in multimedia are 8-bit and 16-bit. With eight bits, you can store 256 discrete values (2^8 = 256), while 16 bits yields 65,536 values (2^{16} = 65,536). To understand sampling resolution, think of a waveform on a horizontally lined piece of paper like the one illustrated in Figure 1.6.

As with sampling rates, higher sampling resolutions result in higher-quality sound, because more information is available with which to represent the original waveform. Figure 1.7 shows an example of how the sampling rate and resolution of 8-bit, 22kHz sound compares to a 16-bit, 44kHz sound.

At this point, you may be thinking to yourself, "Gee, that wave on the top looks pretty rough compared to the nice, smooth wave we started with." Your concern is completely justified. Getting decent sound at low sampling rates and resolutions such as 8-bit 22 kHz or 8-bit 11 kHz is one of the major struggles of multimedia sound designers. That's why we're glad you're reading this!

Figure 1.6

Sampling
resolution
determines the
number of values
available for
measuring the
amplitude of
a wave.

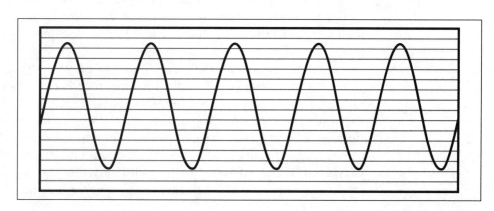

Figure 1.7

Taken together, sampling resolution and sampling rate determine how closely a digitized sample of a wave resembles the original analog waveform.

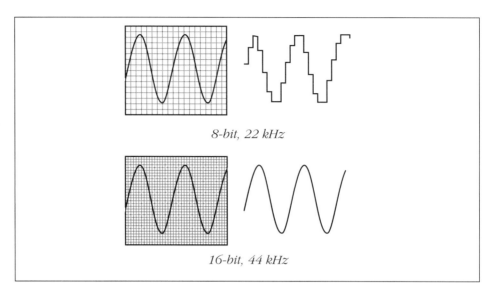

8-bit, 22 kHz

16-bit, 44 kHz

Sampling Rates, Frequency Response, and Aliasing

Ideally, humans can hear sounds that fall within a frequency range of 20 Hz to 20 kHz. As we age, our ability to hear high-frequency sounds diminishes, so it's fair to say that adults can hear sounds as high as 10 kHz to15 kHz. You might think that since we can only hear frequencies up to a certain frequency, a 22 kHz sampling rate would be more than enough. The truth is, unfortunately, a little more complicated.

The physicist H. Nyquist is credited with a very important discovery about the process of sampling points in a waveform. He found that the frequency range of a digitized sound is actually a little less than *one-half* of the sampling rate. Frequencies that are higher than one-half the sampling rate can appear as lower frequencies. We won't get into the math here, but looking at Figure 1.8 will help you understand this concept.

The resulting sampled wave is called an *alias*. It is masquerading as real audio information, even though it was not present in the original waveform. Most digitizers, such as Apple Sound input and the MacRecorder, filter out high frequencies before sampling to prevent aliasing.

For our purposes, the Nyquist theorem means that a sound sampled at a rate of 44 kHz can contain frequencies up to about 20 kHz. This means that only 44 kHz sampling rates can represent the full range of human hearing. In fact, 16-bit 44 kHz is the standard for audio CDs. The Nyquist theorem also means that a 22 kHz sampling rate can represent frequencies only up to about 10 kHz. This is well below the top range of human hearing, and it explains why 22 kHz audio often sounds muddy or muffled.

Figure 1.8

If a waveform is not sampled often enough, it cannot accurately represent the original wave-form. *(a)* A 3 Hz sound sampled at 2 Hz results in an alias frequency of 1 Hz. *(b)* To avoid aliasing, sounds must be sampled at twice the rate of the highest frequency present in the signal.

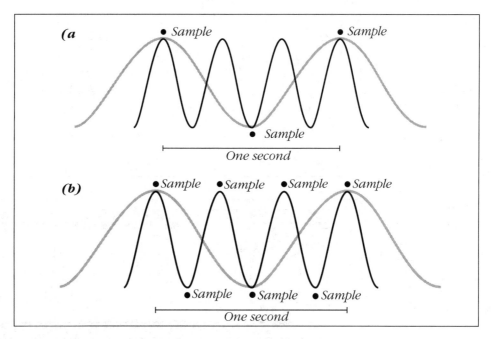

Quantizing and Clipping

When a wave is sampled, especially at low resolutions such as 8-bit, the smooth wave is transformed into a series of discrete steps (refer back to Figure 1.5). As sample resolution decreases, this stair-stepping becomes more pronounced and results in distortion and added noise, called *quantization noise.*

The best way to minimize quantization noise is to be sure that you record your sound at the highest possible input volume without *clipping.* Clipping, illustrated in Figures 1.9 and 1.10, occurs when your sampled waveform amplitude exceeds the maximum possible value, and it creates distortion. You can avoid clipping by reducing your input volume to just below the maximum. Depending on your sound digitizer, some trial and error may be required. Recording sound at the highest possible volume short of clipping ensures that the maximum number of stair-steps are used to represent the sound waves. Once a file has been clipped as in Figure 1.10, there is no way to resurrect the missing data other than returning to an earlier, unclipped version. Digital clipping is a very harsh type of distortion and should be avoided at all costs.

How does input volume affect quantization noise? Think of how digitized sound is represented. In the case of an 8-bit sound, it's an 8-bit number; 256 values are available to represent the maximum amplitude.

Figure 1.9

When the waveform exceeds the maximum amplitude *(a)*, the top and bottom of the wave are clipped *(b)*.

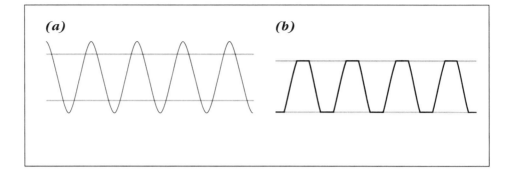

Figure 1.10

An example of a clipped sound file. Notice that the waveform is flattened at the top and bottom.

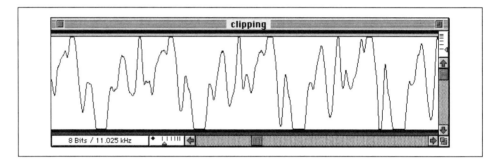

Suppose that you record your sound with a very low input volume, resulting in a wave with very low amplitude. It may only require 64 values of the 256 available. In a sense, you've just recorded a 6-bit sound! Using a sound-editing program to amplify a sound that was recorded at a low level increases the quantization noise along with the sound volume. The sound will be lounder as a result, but it won't sound any better.

Sample Resolution and Dynamic Range

There's another factor tied to sample resolution called *dynamic range.* Dynamic range refers to the range between the loudest possible sound, and the background noise that is always present. Higher dynamic ranges are better, because you can hear more variations in volume without apparent noise or hiss.

We describe dynamic range in terms of decibels (dB). The dynamic range of the human ear is roughly 120 dB. For comparison purposes, recall that the noise level of a jet engine could reach 120 dB SPL, a soft whisper could register 25 dB SPL, and a quiet recording studio might have background noise of 20 dB SPL.

A good rule of thumb in digital sampling is that each bit of sample resolution adds 6 dB of dynamic range. Doing the math, we find that 16-bit samples have 96 dB of dynamic range, and 8-bit sampling has 48 dB of dynamic range. For the purposes of our discussion, this means that it's more difficult to have quiet passages in an 8-bit sample because the noise floor is higher. One of the first places people notice this is when they record speech into their computer. It sounds okay when they're hearing the words, but the gaps between words and sentences are filled with the sound of frying bacon. That sizzle is background noise and is a result of the 48 dB of dynamic range. A 16-bit sample does not have this noise.

Another way to get a feel for the importance of dynamic range is to listen to two common audio devices. An 8-bit sample has about the same dynamic range as a low-quality cassette recorder. A 16-bit sample has the dynamic range of an audio CD. Compare the tape hiss on your old boom box to the clarity of your CD player for a convincing demonstration.

Sampling Theory Meets Multimedia

We now know that the *Nyquist frequency* (the sampling rate divided by two) determines the highest frequency that a digitized sound can represent accurately. We also know that sample resolution is a major factor in the clarity of sound, because greater dynamic range translates into lower background noise. Finally, we know that in the cases of sample rate and sample resolution, higher numbers mean better sound.

Armed with this knowledge, we can begin to put sound into the context of multimedia production. Like practically every other aspect of multimedia, adding audio involves making compromises. The trade-off usually boils down to sound quality versus file size and system *throughput* (in techno-jargon, throughput means the speed with which you can move data through a computer system). That is, better-sounding audio requires more storage and more CPU time. Stereo 16-bit, 44.1 kHz sound requires more than 10 MB of disk storage per minute. Stereo 8-bit, 22.050kHz sound takes up one-eighth that amount of space, but the quality is lower. In cases where storage and throughput are limited, sound data (and sound quality) must be reduced to fit the capabilities of the system. With this in mind, let's review the basic steps involved in adding sound to a multimedia presentation.

Overview of the Audio Creation Process

Adding sound to a presentation can be relatively easy. If you're doing a quick prototype or a simple business presentation, you might record your voice while sitting at the computer. In other circumstances, adding sound can be incredibly complex. A commercial CD-ROM title often involves

Figure 1.11

Basic steps in the audio production process

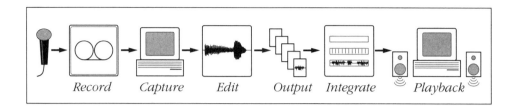

Record   Capture   Edit   Output   Integrate   Playback

voice, sound effects, custom music, and video. Regardless of whether your production is simple or complicated, the process of creating sound usually includes the following steps, illustrated in Figure 1.11:

❏ *Plan*—determine the design for sound as well as its production

❏ *Record*—recording sound on a medium such as tape or computer disk

❏ *Capture*—transfer recorded sound into the computer

❏ *Edit*—use software to cut, mix, and process sound

❏ *Output*—save the finished sound in the desired format

❏ *Integrate*—put the sound into a finished presentation

❏ *Playback*—listen to the final result

Let's take a look at each of these steps, using two examples at opposite ends of the spectrum: a simple presentation and the production cycle for a complex CD-ROM title.

A Basic Presentation

A simple computer-based presentation usually involves a series of "slides," or static screens, containing text and graphics. To enhance the presentation, you could add music and then record voice to emphasize particular points as they are displayed on the screen. Here are the basic steps for creating such a presentation:

1. **Plan** your audio design and requirements. Think about the overall message and mood of your presentation, and decide what style of music will best create that mood and reinforce the content. Write a script that supports the text and graphics on each screen.

2. **Record** your voice into a sound-editing program, such as SoundEdit 16 or Audioshop, using the microphone supplied with the computer. In this case, you can achieve recording and capture of the voiceover in a single step, since your voice is digitized directly into the computer.

3. **Capture** music into the computer. For the sake of accuracy and clarity, I've decided to use the term "capture" rather than "digitize," since

the material may already be in digital form, as in the case of digital audiotape (DAT), CD, or Musical Instrument Digital Interface (MIDI). If you're using a CD music production library, along with a CD-equipped Macintosh, you can take advantage of QuickTime to import the audio directly from the CD. If you're using original music, capture it from tape by running the tape deck's audio output into the computer's audio input.

4. **Edit** the voiceover. If you have recorded several different takes, review them and select the best ones. You may need to break the voiceover into separate segments. Also, remove any unnecessary silence at the beginning or end of the recording. Then mix the voiceover and music into one file.

5. **Output** the finished file in the desired format. This includes *down-sampling*—reducing the sample resolution or rate—and then saving the data in a format that is compatible with your presentation program (usually AIFF or WAV).

6. **Integrate** the sound into the presentation by importing it into the presentation program and instructing the program to launch the sound at the appropriate point.

7. **Playback**—Play the finished presentation in a business meeting. Depending on the size and sophistication of the audience, this may involve a video projector and high-quality speakers.

Basic CD-ROM Development

Creating sound for a CD-ROM title is a much more complex undertaking than the foregoing example, as any developer will attest. However, a simplified version of the major steps involved shows that the process is similar:

1. **Plan** an overall strategy for handling sound throughout the production process. Talk with the production team to get a sense for what types of sounds are required, and determine what tools you need to create that sound. Use *storyboards* (drawings of the main screens and text in the presentation) and scripts to get an idea of what quantity of sounds will be required, and then create a budget based on the scope of the product. Work with the producer and programmers to determine a schedule for creating and delivering the finished audio. You will probably be creating lots of files, so agree now on file naming conventions, file sizes, and resolution. Since your file naming conventions may be severely limited by some operating systems, find out which file formats the target software and hardware platform support.

Think about what other talent you may need to hire, including actors and musicians.

2. **Record** original music using MIDI, live musicians, or both. Also, record character voices onto DAT tape in a professional studio. If you use digital video, record a scratch dialog track (a rough-quality track to use as a reference for laying in better-sounding audio at a later point) on the videotape, but use multiple microphones to simultaneously record high-quality audio to DAT for later "sweetening." Using a portable DAT, create and record sound effects and environmental ambiences.

3. **Capture** all recorded material to the computer using digital audio hardware. Capture additional material from CD production libraries as needed.

4. **Edit** and mix all material to match scenes in the production. For the video, import the sweetened audio and synchronize it using the scratch dialog as a reference; then delete the scratch track and save the new file.

5. **Output** files in the format agreed upon by the producer and members of the production team.

6. **Integrate** the sound into the production, working closely with programmers and graphic artists to assure that sounds are properly implemented.

7. **Playback**—Listen to the sound on a number of different systems to ensure that sound quality and performance are as consistent as possible.

Is it really this simple? Almost never! Every product is different and requires a unique approach. Hardware and software tools are constantly changing, and the tools that work for one job may not be the best solution in another situation. As you go through this process, you will need to draw upon different skills. Most multimedia professionals are used to wearing a few different hats, and audio production is no exception. The job starts from a creative angle, but quickly moves into engineering, production management, and programming. Be flexible.

Summary

In this chapter, you have learned that sound waves are vibrations that are transmitted through the air. These waves can be converted into electrical signals using a microphone and can be converted back into sound waves through a loudspeaker. The electrical signals can also be converted into a digital representation of a sound wave. You also learned that sampling a sound at different rates and resolutions affects the quality of the digital sample. Higher sample rates and resolutions sound better, but they create more data: *lots* of data at high rates, like stereo 16-bit, 44.1 kHz "CD quality." This data consumes massive quantities of storage space and places a heavy load on the computer processor. In multimedia, this usually results in a tradeoff: lower sound quality in exchange for smaller files that take up less room and place fewer demands on the CPU.

Finally, we laid out a seven-step process for producing audio for multimedia: plan, record, capture, edit, output, integrate, and playback. For the remainder of the Tools and Technology section of this book, we will use this model as a template for describing the concepts of audio production and the hardware and software that you need to get the job done.

2

Digital Audio Tools—Hardware

In the previous chapter, we defined seven steps for producing audio for multimedia: plan, record, capture, edit, output, integrate, and playback. This breakdown also provides a good format for discussing the tools and techniques of multimedia audio production, so it will serve as our guide through the next two chapters. We will cover planning in the Techniques section of the book, since it is difficult to understand planning without knowing the process for which you are planning.

This chapter covers the hardware-related issues of producing audio using computers. Each of the tools we discuss here has potential benefits and drawbacks in processing sound, so we should examine these tools in the context of how best to use them.

First, we will review the basic life cycle of an audio signal and the tools of the traditional recording process: microphones, mixers, and recording devices. We also will look at some of the bits and pieces of audio hardware required for multimedia production. These include the cabling, jacks, and adapters needed to transfer audio to and from audio tape, videotape, and the CPU.

Then, we will cover computer hardware as it relates to sound, including the CPU itself, the audio-related hardware and system software of the basic CPU, and associated data storage devices. We will also examine peripheral computer hardware specific to capturing, processing, and editing digital audio.

Recording: The Tools and the Process

As sound is created, recorded, edited, and replayed, it passes through a variety of devices including microphones, cables, connectors, mixers, recorders, amplifiers, and speakers. We often refer to the devices through which an audio signal passes as the *signal chain.* The structure of a signal chain has a major effect on audio quality because it's the pathway through which the audio travels. Whether that pathway is the equivalent of a bumpy dirt road or a new superhighway depends on how you set it up. The bottom line is that your signal chain is only as good as its weakest link, so it's important to know how the links fit together.

How Sound Is Created and Recorded— a Review

Here is a brief review of the basic stages in the life cycle of an audio signal. Refer to Chapter 1 for more details.

❏ Sound is created when an object vibrates, generating variations in air pressure; we refer to these variations as "sound waves." Sound waves travel to our ears, which then translate the pressure variations into signals sent through the nervous system to our brains, and we perceive the information as sound.

❏ A *microphone* functions similarly to our ears. A diaphragm vibrates in response to changes in air pressure, and a transducer translates this vibration into pulses of electrical energy (voltages), which correspond to the strength of the pressure changes. A wire transmits these voltages to a recording device.

❏ The resulting voltages are then recorded. When recorded to an *analog* medium such as magnetic tape, the incoming signal alters the charge of magnetized particles on the tape so that they create an analog record of the original voltages. The strength of the magnetic charge recorded to the tape correpsonds directly to the strength of the original voltage. When recording to a *digital* medium such as the hard disk of a computer, the signal passes through an *analog-to-digital converter,* which measures the strength of the incoming voltages at a fast rate (up to 48,000 times per second) and assigns a numeric value to represent the voltage at a particular instant.

❏ Once material has been recorded, it can be replayed through some type of a loudspeaker. In the case of digital source material, the information must first be translated from the digital domain back into a series of electrical voltages. This is done with a *digital-to-analog converter,* which reads the numeric information and sends out an analog voltage corresponding to that value. At this point, both digital and analog sources exist as a series of voltages. These voltages can be sent through a wire to an *amplifier,* which increases the strength of the voltages so that they have sufficient strength to drive a loudspeaker. A loudspeaker is like a microphone in reverse: an electromagnet attached to a diaphragm causes air to vibrate according to the strength of an electrical signal. The vibrating loudspeaker creates sound waves that reach our ears, and the cycle is complete.

Recording, which is the first step of audio production, requires two pieces of equipment: a sound source (such as a microphone) and a recording device (for example, a tape recorder). In its simplest form, a recording device can be a microphone connected directly to the audio input of a computer. In serious audio production, however, there are a number of other valuable tools that can enhance both sound quality and productivity. These include audio mixers, tape recorders, amplifiers, high-quality speakers, signal processors, and more. Before reviewing how these devices fit into a multimedia production studio, you should become familiar with the basic types of connectors you can expect to encounter (shown in Figure 2.1):

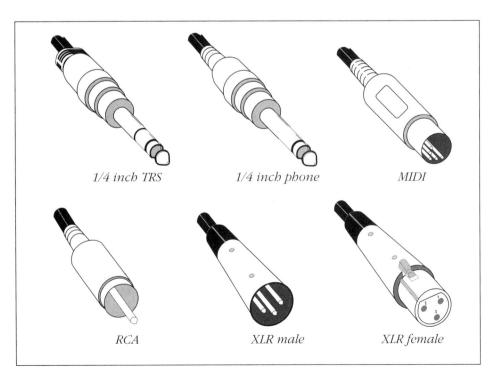

1/4 inch TRS   *1/4 inch phone*   *MIDI*

RCA   *XLR male*   *XLR female*

Figure 2.1

Common types of audio connectors

❏ **RCA**—for audio, video, and S/PDIF digital, also called "phone" connectors. This is the same type of plug used on the back of most stereo equipment. If there is a stereo pair, the right connector is usually colored red.

❏ **XLR**—for most professional microphones and for balanced line audio and AES/EBU digital signals. XLR connectors are the choice of audio professionals.

❏ **1/4 inch**—standard for most musical equipment, often called "phone plugs"

❏ **1/4 inch TRS**—Tip/Ring/Sleeve, either stereo or send/return. This looks like a normal phone plug but has one additional conductor ring in the middle of the plug. Most stereo headphones use this type of connector.

❏ **3.5 mm**—a type of connector found on older digitizers like the MacRecorder

❏ **3.5 mm TRS**—mini-headphone "Walkman-style" connector found on most CPU sound inputs and outputs. The tip is usually the left channel; the ring is the right channel.

❏ **MIDI**—a five-pin DIN plug for MIDI devices

❏ **Optical**—a fiber optic cable for S/PDIF digital transfer

The Basic Classic Recording System

Although multimedia is a relatively recent phenomenon, the fact that this creative form draws from several disciplines works to the advantage of the multimedia producer. In the audio field, the recording industry provides a well-developed infrastructure of technology, talent, and experience upon which to draw. Over the past thirty years, the emergence of the microprocessor, affordable studio electronics, and a booming popular music industry have fueled tremendous growth in the number of people interested in doing professional-quality recording. As a result, someone spending $20,000 on a studio system today has capabilities far beyond a system that would have cost over $100,000 ten years ago. Yet for all the improvements in technology, sound quality, and value for your dollar, the building blocks remain pretty much unchanged.

The following are the basic elements for a recording system, as shown in Figure 2.2:

❏ A **microphone** for recording voice and sound effects

❏ A **compressor** to control the volume of the microphone automatically

❏ A **mixer** for controlling and combining audio inputs and outputs

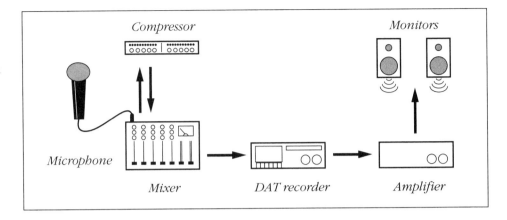

- ❏ A **mixdown recorder** for recording final output to tape (usually DAT)
- ❏ **Amplifier** and **monitors** to check sound quality while recording

Let's look at each of these elements in greater detail.

Microphones

Microphones convert sound waves into electrical signals that can be recorded or amplified. A microphone is like a sonic camera lens. Choose the equivalent of a Hasselblad, and you will have great clarity and detail. Use the equivalent of an inexpensive disposable camera, and the sound you record may differ remarkably from what your ears originally heard. Simply put, a microphone can be one of the most important determinants of the overall quality of recorded sound.

Microphone use for multimedia producers falls into two broad categories: voiceover recording and sound effect recording. Before selecting a microphone for a specific task, think about the types of recording you plan to do and then consider the basic features of microphones, which we discuss next.

The mechanism of a microphone determines whether it is a *dynamic microphone* or a *condenser microphone*. In a dynamic microphone, a diaphragm is attached to a coil of wire, which is suspended around a magnet. When moving air ("sound waves") strikes the diaphragm, the coil slides back and forth along the magnet, producing a series of changing electrical voltages that correspond to the original sound. In condenser microphones, the diaphragm carries an electrical charge. Farther back in the microphone, separated from the diaphragm by a small air chamber, is a charged plate. This combination acts as a capacitor so that as the diaphragm moves, the voltage on the back plate fluctuates accordingly. These voltages are very small, so condenser microphones contain internal amplifiers to increase the level of the sound. As a result, condenser microphones need power sources. For some condenser microphones, the power source can be a built-in battery; other microphones rely on *phantom power*—a small charge sent from a mixer or phantom power device through the microphone cable to the microphone.

Condenser microphones generally boast better response than dynamic microphones because a condenser doesn't have to physically move a voice coil. This means that it can react more quickly to changes in pressure, and it can more accurately represent a signal. As a general rule, dynamic microphones are more rugged, more portable, and less expensive than condensers, but condensers offer superior performance.

Microphones also vary in their responses to sounds coming from different directions. The *directional response* or *pickup pattern* of a microphone describes the area in which a microphone picks up the best sound. The main types are omnidirectional, cardioid, hyper-cardioid, and bidirectional.

❏ *Omnidirectional* microphones are good for picking up sounds from all directions and are therefore useful for recording ambient sound effects.

❏ *Cardioid* microphones are good for recording a single voice, since they capture sounds directly in front, and slightly to the side, of the microphone.

❏ *Hyper-cardioid* microphones are even more directional than cardiods and tend to eliminate sounds originating from the sides of the microphone, at the expense of picking up a little sound directly behind the microphone. This can be helpful when trying to record voice in a noisy environment.

❏ *Bidirectional* microphones can be used to record ambiences or multiple voices on the front and back of the microphone (but not on either side of it).

When selecting a microphone, try to find one with as flat a frequency response rating as possible. *Flat frequency response* means that the microphone responds equally to all frequencies, without enhancing or reducing certain frequency bands. Some vocal microphones, for example, accentuate frequencies in the 5 kHz to 7 kHz band to add "presence" to the voice. If you're only recording voice, this may be desirable, but if you want a microphone to be as flexible as possible, it shouldn't color the sound too much. Besides, you can always add your own equalization later.

If you will be interviewing people for video, you may want a *lavalier* microphone (the small clip-on variety). If most of your recording is for voiceover, an inexpensive dynamic microphone may result in the voice having a thin, nasal tone that lacks presence and clarity. If you only need to record "quick and dirty" voiceover, then you may want the economy and ease of use of a dynamic microphone. Expect to pay at least $50 for a decent dynamic microphone, and at least $200 for a decent condenser microphone. Be aware, though, that professional microphones used in studios average $1,000 apiece and rarely cost less than $300.

Compressors

An audio compressor functions like an automatic volume controller. Passing the microphone signal through a compressor reduces the dynamic range of the signal; that is, it smooths out differences in volume. This can be critical in multimedia applications, because it lets you raise the overall volume of a signal without causing distortion or clipping. As a result, your sounds have more signal and less relative noise, especially after you downsample. Compression is also helpful when recording voiceover, because it makes recording levels much more consistent.

The compressor is usually inserted in the signal chain with the help of a mixer. The incoming microphone signal passes through a small pre-amplifier (which boosts the signal) and then is routed out to the compressor and returned to the mixer. Very few compressors have the ability to handle a microphone directly.

> **Note:** *The type of audio compression we are discussing here has no relation whatsoever to compressed sound file formats or data compression products like Stuffit, CompactPro, or PKZIP.*

Most compressors have five basic controls: threshold, ratio, attack, release, and output gain.

- ❑ *Threshold* is the point at which the incoming signal will be affected by the compressor. Signals below the threshold will not be compressed at all. For example, setting the threshold to –20 dB means that all signals over –20 dB will be affected by the compressor.

- ❑ *Ratio* controls the extent to which the volume will increase after it has passed the threshold. For example, a ratio of 2:1 means that every 2 dB of additional gain beyond the threshold will result in 1 dB of actual gain change. Ratios range from 1:1 (no compression) to ∞:1 (infinity to one). When set to ∞:1, a compressor acts as a *limiter,* because no matter how much the input gain increases, it is limited to the threshold level. This setting can be used to avoid the clipping signal.

❏ *Attack* and *release* control the speed with which the compressor reacts. Gradual attack and release times result in a more natural sound than would be possible if the compressor is activated instantaneously.

❏ *Output gain* lets you increase the volume of the output signal (the term *gain* is used to describe the strength of a signal). The action of the compressor is likely to reduce the loudest peaks of the signal so that the overall level can be quieter. The output gain can boost the signal back up to the desired level.

Finally, many compressors have a separate *noise gate* function. A noise gate is a radical automatic volume controller, and its main control is yet another threshold. When the volume of a signal falls below the threshold, the gate "closes" and no signal is passed through. This can be extremely helpful when recording voiceover, because silences and pauses between speech are completely silenced. Noise gate control can go a long way toward reducing background hiss in downsampled files.

Noise gates often have threshold, ratio, attack, decay, and output gain controls as well, although they function in a manner opposite to the way a compressor works. If a separate compressor and noise gate are to be used together, always put the noise gate first in the signal chain—it will reduce background noise, whereas the compressor will have the effect of increasing background noise in relation to the primary signal. If the noise isn't there because the noise gate already removed it, then the compressor will have no effect on it.

Medium-quality compressors range in price from about $150 to $500. It's possible to spend much more on the new generation of tube compressors, but if you require that level of quality, consider renting time in a professional recording studio.

Mixers

The mixer is the central control area of every studio, letting you adjust the relative volumes of multiple audio sources. Depending on the functions available, a mixer might also let you alter sounds coming through its inputs before they are sent to the outputs to be recorded. For many multimedia producers, the main benefit of a mixer is that it lets you switch easily between multiple sources so that you can audition material from CD, videotape, audio tape, and various computers.

Mixers come in many different sizes, with a variety of features and prices. The main features to look for in a mixer are sound quality and number of channels. An ideal mixer passes sound transparently from the inputs to the outputs without changing the sound's tonal quality or clarity.

The number of channels determines how many different devices you can route through the mixer. When estimating how many channels you will need, keep in mind that stereo devices require two channels each.

A signal usually passes through the following steps on its journey through the mixer. First, the signal enters by way of a cable at an *input*. Most mixers support 1/4 inch inputs for line-level signals and XLR inputs for microphones. The signal is routed from the input to a *channel* (see Figure 2.3). Channels on a mixer are laid out side by side, usually with a *fader* (a volume slider) at the bottom and a series of knobs for controlling various functions within that particular channel. There are some common controls found within a channel:

❑ **Gain adjustment** to add additional input volume for low-voltage signals (particularly microphones).

❑ **Equalization (EQ)** for adjusting the strength of bands of differing frequencies. Most mixers offer high and low shelving EQ (just like the bass and treble knobs on a home stereo system). More advanced mixers offer parametric EQ, which lets you adjust the bandwidth of the EQ as well as the amount of cut or boost (for more information, see the "Equalization (EQ) for Multimedia" section of Chapter 6).

❑ **Pan** for controlling the position of the signal within a 180° stereo field. Panning allows a signal to be routed to the left channel, the right channel, or anywhere in between.

Because mixers feature a modular, channel-based layout, you can comprehend every channel on the mixing board once you understand the functions of a particular channel.

After the signal within a channel has been adjusted, the combined output of the channels is sent to a *master output* section. As its name implies, the master output controls the total output volume from the mixer. This output can be sent to an amplifier or recording device.

DAT Recorder

Digital Audio Tape (DAT) is the standard mastering medium for multimedia audio. A DAT recorder is a must, simply because DAT offers the best sound quality for the money. DAT delivers the same fidelity as CD in a recordable format. Voiceover recordings are frequently made directly to DAT because the medium is high in quality, portable, and inexpensive. DAT recorders have become affordable in recent years. Consumer units are available for about $500, and entry-level professional units start at just over $1,000. Portable DAT recorders are also extremely handy for location work.

Figure 2.3

A mixer channel usually includes a fader for setting volumes, a gain adjustment control for setting input volume, an equalization control for tonal manipulation, and pan controls for controlling the placement of the signal in a stereo field.

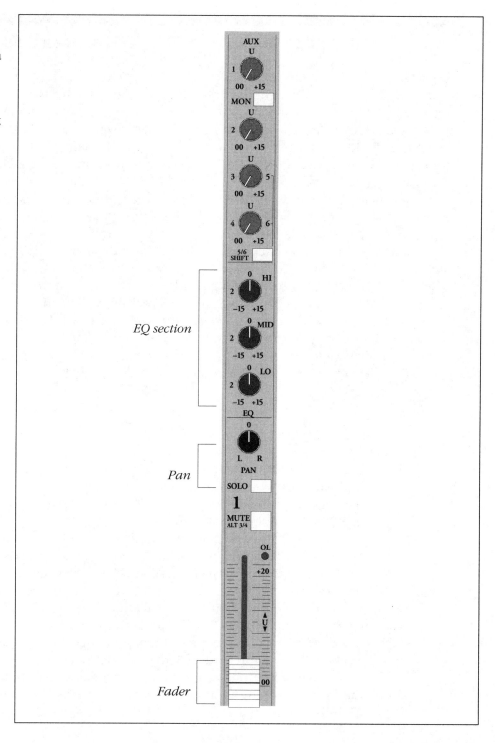

ABOUT DIGITAL INTERFACE STANDARDS

Digital audio professionals have learned to live with two competing "standard" formats: AES/EBU and S/PDIF. These acronyms derive from the agencies responsible for creating the standards: the Audio Engineering Society/European Broadcast Union and Sony/Phillips Digital Interchange Format, respectively. S/PDIF is a subset of the AES/EBU format intended for consumer use. It's important to know which format your equipment supports. You can tell the formats apart by the connectors they use. AES/EBU data is transferred through XLR cables, and S/PDIF is transferred through either RCA cables (S/PDIF RCA jacks are usually orange to differentiate them from the red or white standard RCA audio connectors) or fiber optic cables. Because the data is digital, all the signal information can be carried on one cable. For example, there is no need for two cables to carry the left and right portions of a stereo signal.

Professional-grade DAT recorders and audio interfaces usually support both AES/EBU and S/PDIF. Less expensive models have only S/PDIF inputs. To convert between digital formats, you need a *digital translator box,* such as the Alesis A1. You can't simply use Radio Shack adapters to adapt an XLR to an RCA jack and expect an S/PDIF input to read your AES/EBU signal. (Actually, it *is* possible to splice a conversion cable together, but this isn't recommended.)

There are several things to look for when selecting a DAT recorder. First, find out what types of digital inputs and outputs it supports. If you plan to transfer lots of digital audio, be sure your devices support either AES/EBU or S/PDIF encoding.

Second, find out whether the deck is fettered by *SCMS,* the Serial Copy Management System. Unfortunately, most consumer-grade DATs have this "feature." SCMS is a copy-protection scheme that embeds coded information into the digital signal during recording. If you make a digital copy of an SCMS DAT, and then try to make another digital copy from that copy, an SCMS-equipped DAT will refuse to go into record mode. You will be unable to make digital copies of the second-generation master. Apparently, SCMS delivers the recording industry from potential DAT piracy, but only on consumer-level machines. Professional-grade DAT decks let you defeat the SCMS encoding. You can also bypass SCMS altogether by using only AES/EBU interfaces.

Third, be sure the DAT supports recording at sample rates of 44.1 kHz (the standard audio CD sample rate) and 48 kHz (the DAT standard). Some machines will play tapes at either rate but can record only at 48 kHz. If you plan to produce a CD master using the DAT deck, you must work at the CD standard rate. Also, if your audio is destined for the lower sample rates of multimedia (22.050 kHz, for example), recording your audio at the 44.1 kHz rate will make sample rate conversion better and easier with certain popular tools like Digidesign's Sound Designer II. When the sample rate conversion is a simple divide-by-two operation (going from 44.1 kHz to 22.050 kHz), the result sounds better than a complete mathematical conversion.

Finally, if you plan to do lots of video work, it may be worthwhile to spend more on a DAT that supports SMPTE time code. (For a more complete discussion of SMPTE time code, see Chapter 5.) SMPTE-compatible DATs often cost at least $1,000 more than non-SMPTE DATs, but the ability to lock your DAT to SMPTE could be a necessary requirement in certain situations. Otherwise, you may experience drift between the video and audio signals, resulting in bad lip synchronization. If you use SMPTE time code, be sure to record and play back while in sync with the video to avoid problems down the road.

Amplifier and Monitors

One of the primary determinants of sound quality is the system that delivers the final product to your ears. It is extremely important that your audio monitoring system let you hear exactly what's going on. Studio reference monitors and a high-quality amplifier are an excellent investment. As with microphones, the ideal monitoring system should have a flat frequency response and should not alter the frequency content of the sound in any way. Of course, that's the ideal. In the real world, every system sounds slightly different. The goal is to minimize these differences, or at least to be aware of them so that you can compensate.

For example, most multimedia audio is played back either through the computer speaker or through a pair of inexpensive "multimedia" speakers. For the audio purist, hearing their pristine creations played back on these systems is nothing short of a tragedy. As a general rule, these playback devices have a greatly reduced bass response. They cannot deliver booming bass because delivering low-frequency content requires moving lots of air, and that requires larger speakers. If you mix your audio on a system with a subwoofer, it may sound great to you, but people listening to your music on three-inch speakers may not be so impressed.

On the other hand, if your monitors have poor high-frequency response, you may be boosting the high frequencies to make the mix sound good on your system. It's likely that others will listen to your work and wonder what's making that loud hissing noise.

A major trend in studios today is to use *near-field* monitors, so named because they are designed for listening up close, at a range of three to five feet in front of the speaker. You don't need to turn them up very loud, so they are easier on your ears during longer sessions. Near-field monitors also minimize reflected room noise so that you hear the sound as it comes directly from the speaker, rather than muddled sound that has bounced off walls and ceilings.

A high-quality pair of headphones can also be invaluable. Be sure to get the "closed-ear" variety that reduces outside noise. This can be especially helpful if you produce audio in a noisy production environment. Good headphones are like microscopes for your ears. You hear every bit of noise, especially when working at lower sample rates and bit depths such as 8-bit 22 kHz.

Finally, the best defense is to know your enemy. Use the highest-quality monitors you can afford, but also keep a pair of cheesy computer speakers on hand for comparison purposes.

Other Items to Consider

The items covered above are by no means the only elements you might want to include in your basic setup. Let the type of content you plan to work with guide you. Some other helpful additions might include the following:

❏ **Multitrack tape recorders** for recording multiple layers of sound. Multitrack decks may be especially valuable for musicians who want to record real-time performances on acoustic instruments such as guitars, woodwinds, drums, or vocals (rather than computer-driven synthesizers). In the past few years, eight-track digital recorders have become available in the $3,000 to $4,000 price range. These recorders digitize incoming audio signals and store them on standard videotape formats, such as SVHS and Hi 8.

❏ **MIDI-controlled synthesizers** for creating and editing music. For an in-depth discussion of MIDI, refer to Chapter 3.

❏ **Multi-effects units** for adding ambience or other sound-processing effects to audio signals. Most of these units offer standard effects— reverb and delay, for example—which are very useful for placing sound effects or voices within ambient spaces (rooms, hallways, caves, and so on). They also have pitch-altering effects, which you can adjust to produce eerie, futuristic sounds. Some newer effects units allow localization within a 3-D space in the user's environment, including up/down and forward/back localization, in addition to the left/right placement typical of stereo.

❑ **Videotape decks** and **video monitors** for those who will be adding, editing, or processing ("sweetening") sound for video.

Making It Work

So, you have taken out a second mortgage to buy all the equipment you need. How do you put it all together to obtain the quality of sound you hear on a professionally produced recording? It doesn't happen overnight, but you can reach that stage by following these steps:

1. Ensure that the equipment is properly connected.
2. Balance the levels on all the devices in the signal chain.
3. Practice your mixing skills and compare your mixes to other recordings.

These topics have been covered in numerous books and could easily fill an entire chapter, but we will touch on the high points here. Please see the "Suggested Reading" section of this book for more complete references.

Connecting Equipment

If you think multimedia requires tons of cables, wait until you throw an audio system into the equation! You can *never* have too many types of cables and adapters, because you must constantly deal with a cornucopia of devices, each with different types of inputs and outputs. Understanding how these cables and connectors work is fundamentally important to achieving good sound quality, because cables are the lifeline of an audio signal.

Voltage Levels

The first thing you should know about your equipment is that the audio signals of different devices can have different levels of voltage. If you connect a low-voltage signal (such as a microphone) to an input that expects a higher voltage signal (the "line in" jack on a tape deck, for example), the signal will not be adequate. When the power of the electrical signal is lower than expected, the result sounds as though someone has turned down the volume. However, simply turning the volume up to the desired level adds an unacceptable amount of noise. The solution to this potential problem is to match the voltage levels of all your signals.

Audio voltages are usually measured in units of *dBm* or *dBv;* 0 dBm and 0 dBv are .775 volts. Signals at lower levels than this are referred to as minus dB and signals at greater levels are measured in plus dB. With modern audio equipment, the differences between dBm and dBv can be ignored for the most part. Interfacing to older equipment may require special attention to impedance matching and level conversions.

There are several voltages you can expect to encounter. The most commonly used *line level* is –10 dBv. This signal is the one found at the "line out" or "line in" connectors of most home stereo equipment, as well as VCRs, the audio outputs on the backs of CD-ROM players, the inputs and outputs of line mixers, and the outputs of most synthesizers.

Another standard line level voltage is +4 dBm, usually found in professional audio equipment. This higher level is desirable in professional applications because it provides a higher quality signal. You can convert signal levels between +4 dB and –10 dB using a *direct box*. These devices are available from most professional audio equipment dealers.

The final type of voltage you are likely to encounter is sometimes called "mic level." This nomenclature groups many low-voltage signals into a single category. Many microphones operate in the –40 dBm to –60 dBm range. If you plan to record a microphone into a line-level device, you will have to use a device that can boost the gain of the microphone before the signal reaches the line input. An audio mixer is usually the tool for this task. An XLR plug is a good clue that a piece of equipment is either +4 dBm or mic level. A phone or phono plug is a clue that the equipment is line level.

Balanced and Unbalanced Cables

Now that we understand a bit about voltages, we can consider the two main types of cable: *balanced* and *unbalanced*. Balanced cables have three wires, while unbalanced cables have two wires. Balanced cables eliminate the potential of a wire picking up noise from outside sources. Long audio cables act just like antennas; they can pick up unwanted electromagnetic energy or *radio frequency interference* (RFI). RFI, generated by electrical currents and strong magnetic fields, creates noise and hum in audio signals. Keeping audio cables away from power cables, power transformers, and computers helps reduce RFI. You can also reduce RFI by using balanced cables.

In a balanced cable, one line serves as both a shield and a ground (see Figure 2.4). A wire mesh is wrapped around the inner cables to help shield them from interference and is grounded at either end. The two inner wires

Figure 2.4

A balanced line eliminates noise by sending the same signal through two lines with opposite polarity. Summing the signals automatically removes the noise picked up by the cable itself.

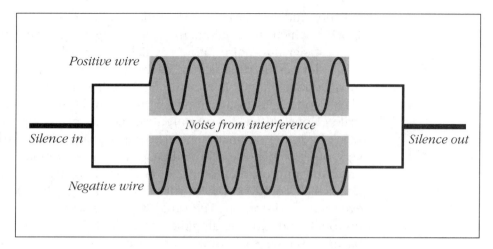

carry an identical signal, but each wire has opposite polarity: one is positive, the other negative. When the signals arrive at their destination, they are recombined. Because the signals were identical when they started out, any differences between the two signals is noise that was picked up along the cable. Since the polarities of the two signals are opposite, they cancel out when added together. Voilà, the noise is gone!

Because of their noise-reducing capability, balanced cables are usually used for low-level signals (such as microphones) or for extended cable runs. You can spot a balanced line by its three-pin connector (also referred to as XLR connectors). Balanced cable runs of 1,000 feet or longer are usually acceptable.

Unbalanced cables are far more common. These cables have just two wires, one for the signal and the other for ground. Quality unbalanced cables use the same shielding ground wire scheme as balanced lines to help reduce interference, but because there is only one signal wire, unbalanced lines can't perform the noise cancellation function of their balanced cousins. Typical unbalanced connectors are the RCA and 1/4 inch variety. Unbalanced cable runs of more than 20 or 30 feet should be avoided.

Gain Staging

In audio terminology, *gain* refers to the strength of an audio signal. For our purposes, this term is interchangeable with volume or loudness. *Gain staging* involves the processes of connecting the devices at a proper level and adjusting the input and output volumes of audio equipment so that each device makes the least possible amount of noise.

Every audio device has an optimal operating range. This is a "sweet spot" at which the equipment is operating most efficiently and delivering the best signal-to-noise ratio of which it is capable. When you use several audio devices in conjunction, each device should be operating within its own optimal range. For example, imagine that you have an audio CD player connected to an amplifier, and they both can output volume on a scale of one to ten. If you only turn the CD player up to 1, you probably won't be in the optimal range. The signal that reaches the amplifier will be very quiet, and noise will make up a greater proportion of the signal. In order to bring up the volume, you might have to turn the amplifier up to ten, which could be beyond its optimal range, thereby adding noise or, even worse, distortion. The same would be true if you turn the CD player up to ten and turn the amplifier down to 1. The best solution is to strike a balance, setting each device as close as possible to its optimal range to obtain the best possible signal-to-noise ratio from each. A good rule of thumb is to operate each device at about 70 percent of its maximum range (although this isn't always possible). Better-quality audio mixers have a gray area between 70 and 80 percent underneath the volume slider to remind you of this.

Listen, Learn, and Practice Mixing

Once your equipment is working as well as it can, it's up to you to squeeze the best possible sound out of it. If you are composing and mixing your own music, you can draw upon a wide range of mixing techniques and styles, depending on the type of music you are creating. For example, if you want to recreate the sound of a symphony orchestra, you might want to use reverb to simulate the sound of a concert hall. If you are mixing rap or techno, you may want a big, fat bass drum sound. One good way to approach mixing music is to listen to other recordings for comparison. Choose a few commercial recordings that you feel are well-engineered, and compare them side-by-side with your own mixes. Surprisingly, the ear's audio memory is quite short, on the order of a second or two. The best way to compare mixes side-by-side is to set each mix to the same relative level and rapidly switch back and forth between them. This is also a useful technique when comparing your mix on several different speaker systems.

If you are not mixing music from scratch, you may not need to worry about music production, but you can still learn a lot by listening to video and film sound work. Notice, for example, that the voices of radio and TV announcers are almost never processed with ambient effects like reverb (unless, of course, your radio station is advertising for the next Monster Truck show). Few people realize it, but almost all the sound you hear in a movie is added in post-production. Listening to how voice, ambient sound, foreground sound effects, and music are blended together in film is a great way to learn about mixing audio elements for multimedia. (Of course, first we need four simultaneous audio channels . . . oh well.)

Capture—Computer-Specific Hardware

Now that you have a basic understanding of the recording process, it's time to look at the integration of computer hardware with audio hardware. One of the most exciting developments of the past few years has been the growth of direct-to-disk digital audio recording technology. Thanks to the computer, hard disks are replacing magnetic tape as a recording medium. Disk-based recording has tremendous advantages over tape-based systems. With digital audio on disk, you can easily edit with cut and paste functions and instantly access any portion of a recording without shuttling through the tape. This type of recording also places new demands on the computer, particularly in the areas of data storage and CPU power. So it's important to evaluate the costs and benefits of tape versus disk-based recording before you decide on a system.

While advances in hardware have made disk-based recording possible, new software is taking advantage of Digital Signal Processor (DSP) functions to replace dedicated external signal processors such as compressors, equalizers, reverbs, and noise-reduction systems. Audio engineers have a fabulous array of powerful new tools at their disposal. The distinction between computer hardware and audio hardware is blurring, and computers are becoming an integral part of a recording studio.

The Macintosh Versus Windows Debate

Systems for creating and editing digital audio for multimedia usually have a computer as their central component. Currently, the majority of multimedia producers author their creations on the Macintosh, then port their presentations to Windows-based PCs. Given that configuring a stable multimedia authoring system on the PC is still a daunting proposition, this is not too surprising. But considering the number of Windows-based PCs in the market, most developers have learned that having a PC on hand for compatibility testing during the development cycle is crucial.

On the other hand, the Macintosh has lagged behind Windows PCs in several areas of sound playback technology. Windows sound cards had built-in MIDI playback capability and 16-bit sound several years before the

Macintosh caught up. This is undoubtedly the result of market forces. PC sound card manufacturers had to add and improve features in order to stay competitive.

For the record, I should state that the Macintosh is my primary authoring system, but I have a Windows PC mainly to convert and audition sound files. This is a typical state of affairs among multimedia sound designers, which is why this book is oriented toward Macintosh users. The Macintosh has enjoyed an advantage thanks to several strong companies in the area of sound, music, and multimedia authoring tools—notably Digidesign, Opcode, Mark of the Unicorn, Passport, and Macromedia. The tools that are currently available for the Macintosh are better developed than those available for Windows. But Windows has been catching up in the past few years. With the advent of Windows 3.1, multimedia capabilities such as device control and sound playback were built into the environment. As these capabilities became available, tools developers began to create Windows versions of products that previously had been Macintosh-only. At this stage, however, for the foreseeable future, the best integration and selection of sound and MIDI tools remains on the Macintosh platform.

Sound and Macintosh Hardware

A knowledge of the sound capabilities of the Macintosh can assist you both in creating sound and in playing it back. Macintosh models vary in their sound capabilities. We will not present an exhaustive review of the development of sound capabilities throughout the entire history of the Macintosh line; at this point, anyone creating or viewing multimedia presentations on the Macintosh should have at least a Macintosh II. Also, unless you are developing your presentation for one specific Macintosh model, you have to prepare your audio for playback on a range of models. Here is a quick summation of developments.

Macintosh Sound Input and Output

The Macintosh has had the ability to play sound since its inception, and its graphic interface and built-in serial ports were attractive to both developers and users of MIDI software. As a result, the Macintosh has had a loyal following among the music community. Early Macintoshes had no built-in sound input and were capable only of playing 8-bit, 22.254 kHz monaural sound. Beginning with the Macintosh II, however, Macintoshes supported stereo output as well. Capturing audio on these older Macintoshes (including the II, IIx, IIcx, IIci and IIfx) requires a third-party digitizer such as Macromedia's MacRecorder or Articulate Systems' Voice Impact Pro. These digitizers include built-in microphones and line-level input jacks. The sound is digitized within the external unit and is then sent to the Macintosh by way of the serial port.

Since the introduction of the IIsi and the LC series, Macintoshes have had audio input jacks. Unfortunately, there are two different types of inputs depending on which model you have, which can be confusing. The older "input-friendly" Macs accept a mic-level input from Apple's first microphone, often called the "Silver Dollar" because of its round shape. Recording a line-level signal through the mic-level input causes distortion. An adapter is required for recording line-level signals. The adapter converts two RCA line-level inputs into one mono signal and is available from Apple or Radio Shack (cord #42-24651 and adapter #42-2435).

In 1993, Apple introduced another audio input standard with the advent of the PlainTalk microphone. A higher-quality audio signal was desirable for PlainTalk, Apple's speech-recognition technology. PlainTalk inputs can accept a line-level source because the PlainTalk microphone internally amplifies the signal to line level before sending it to the Macintosh.

Both the PlainTalk and the Silver Dollar microphones have what appear to be mini-headphone (stereo 3.5 mm) plugs. These *tip-ring-sleeve connectors* are actually mono, however, with the ring supplying power to the condenser microphone. The Silver Dollar-style input accepts only mono signals (for a great discussion of Apple's different inputs and microphones, check out Chapter 17 of Craig O'Donnell's *Cool Mac Sounds*, listed in Suggested Reading*)*.

The PlainTalk microphone plug is a special, extra-long 3.5 mm connector that is only used on the PlainTalk microphone and the JABRA EarPHONE. The tip carries the power for the condenser microphone. The special longer ring connects to both the left and right inputs, so the that the mono mic signal can be recorded in stereo.

If a normal 3.5 mm plug carrying a stereo line level is plugged into the input on the back of the Macintosh, it connects the tip to the left channel and the ring to the right channel. It is not long enough to contact the power terminal. Don't try to force the PlainTalk microphone plug into any other connector than the microphone jack on the back of a Quadra AV or Power Mac, as you will almost certainly break the jack (Silver Dollar microphones don't work on Macs built for PlainTalk microphones either). As weird as it may seem, this is actually a pretty elegant scheme for powering a microphone from a computer while still allowing line-level stereo input that doesn't conflict with the power terminal.

The Quadra 840AV and 660AV ushered in the age of 16-bit 44.1 kHz stereo audio input and output. All Macintoshes in the Power Macintosh line support 16-bit audio, with playback at either 22.050 kHz or 44.100 kHz.

This also includes Performas built with the PowerPC chip and the Powerbook 500 series. The Macintosh Quadra 840AV and 660AV also support 24 kHz rates for speech recognition and the playback of speech synthesis, as well as 48 kHz for compatibility with DAT machines.

With the advent of the Power Macintosh, sound playback capabilities on the Macintosh have increased tremendously. Macromedia's Deck II supports more than 20 simultaneous tracks of 16/44 audio on the PowerMacintosh 8100/110. Before the PowerMacintosh and AV Quadras, the only way to achieve reasonable performance playing 16-bit, 44.1 kHz files was through NuBus hardware using DSP chips.

When using the Macintosh's sound input (except for PowerMac models), be aware of the presence of an Automatic Gain Control (AGC) circuit. This functions like a compressor/limiter to keep the incoming signal at an acceptable level. Some applications, such as SoundEdit 16, let you defeat the circuit. If you're digitizing directly into the Macintosh without an external compressor, you may wish to leave it on.

Why All the Different Sampling Rates?

Standard sample rates have changed over the course of Macintosh development. Engineers arrived at the first standard sample rate (22.254 kHz) using the horizontal scan rate from the video display of the first Macintosh model. One sample was output each time the electron beam finished a horizontal line. With the Macintosh II, a specialized audio chip was added and the scan rate became historical, but the sample rates weren't changed until the AV Macintosh models arrived. The other Macintosh sample rates—11.127, 7.415, and 5.564—were derived by dividing 22.254 by 2, 3 and 4, respectively. The Macintosh is the only computer platform that supports these sample rates.

The newer rates of 44.1 kHz and 22.050 kHz (along with their lower-fidelity cousins, 11.025, 7.350, and 5.512) are standard on Windows PCs and are also in line with the standard audio CD format (16-bit 44.1 kHz). They're derived by dividing 44.1 kHz by 2, 4, 6, and 8. A sample rate of 8 kHz is also commonly used in older Sega game players, telephone equipment, and telephony software attached to the computer. Answering machine software will often run at 8 kHz, for instance, because telephone bandwidth is 4 kHz.

Also, speaking of Windows, be aware that some popular Windows sound cards do not run at the advertised rates, but rather at some frequency which is reasonably close. If you're relying on accurate pitches or timing on the Windows platform, make sure you listen to, and time, your samples on several of the most popular sound cards.

Why Different Rates Matter—and Why They Don't

This divergence from standard sample rates can be a problem when you are creating sounds that may be played back on any Macintosh or Windows computer. Some PC sound cards will not play sounds at rates other than 22.050 kHz or 44.1 kHz. Others play the sound at a slightly altered pitch, since they must lower the playback rate of the file from 22.254 to 22.050.

Fortunately, Apple addressed the situation starting with SoundManager 3.0. This system-level software automatically converts sample rates on the fly to match the capablities of the available hardware. This means that 22.254 kHz files will play back at the proper pitch on a Macintosh that supports only 22.050 rates. For this reason, it makes no sense to use the older 22.254 rate, unless you are developing your presentation specifically for playback on older Macintosh models.

There is a penalty for letting SoundManager handle sample rate conversion. If you are creating 22.050 files on a 22.254 Macintosh or vice versa, you will hear some aliasing noise as the SoundManager performs its sample rate conversion. To double-check that the noise you hear is due solely to SoundManager, copy your 22.050 data and paste it into a 22.254 file. The audio quality should improve a bit. The CPU also has to work much harder when converting sample rates on the fly; this should be avoided whenever possible. We will cover SoundManager in greater detail in Chapter 4, "Digital Audio Software."

Computer Peripherals for Audio Developers

Having touched on the CPU, it's time to look at the basic peripherals for audio recording jobs. Aside from the computer itself, they include the following:

1. A big, fast hard disk
2. A CD-ROM player
3. A removable drive and removable backup system
4. Large display monitors

These components have a major impact on your productivity as you edit and manipulate audio files. By carefully considering your options when creating or adding onto your system, you can improve both the quality and the quantity of your work. Another obvious element in building a digital audio hardware system is dedicated audio digitizing and input/output hardware (such as the Digidesign and NuMedia cards). We will cover these in another section, "Audio Input/Digitizing Hardware."

Why You Need a Fast CPU

In this area, as in most others where computers are pushed to the limit, it's advisable to use the fastest machine you can possibly afford, while also paying attention to the stability and expandability of the system. A digital audio-oriented computer places many demands on hardware:

❏ Processor-intensive operations such as sample-rate conversion and batch processing place high demands on the CPU.

❏ Fast SCSI throughput and disk access are necessary to record and play digital audio.

❏ Massive amounts of disk storage are required.

❏ Sufficient RAM is required to run multiple applications at once, or to allow certain programs (Opcode's OMS or Digidesign's DAE, for example) to run in the background.

❏ Consistent serial port timing is crucial for MIDI recording and playback (this can be a problem, especially on portable computers with integrated power management).

If you plan to use an audio card, either now or at any point in the future, be sure your CPU has enough slots. I suggest a minimum of three, to allow room for a video capture card or a SCSI accelerator card. Also, the newest Macintosh models use a PCI bus, rather than NuBus. While PCI is technically superior, it precludes the newest Macs from using existing digital audio add-in boards, not to mention other existing add-in boards.

Why You Need a Big Drive

In addition to a speedy CPU, it's very important to have plenty of disk space. Consider that one minute of stereo 16/44 (16-bit, 44.1 kHz) audio requires over 10 megabytes of storage. If you transfer an hour of material from tape to the hard disk, you will use roughly 625 megabytes. If you plan to process that file to a mono copy and then downsample it to 16/22, you will have used over a gigabyte for all three files. With hard drive prices constantly dropping, plan on having at least a gigabyte of disk space dedicated to audio alone.

You might think, "I can get away with a smaller drive by capturing smaller segments." This is true for the occasional user, but it isn't practicable in a production environment. You will waste valuable time with each repetition of the capturing and editing process.

In addition to sheer volume, look for a disk with a fast seek time and a high sustained transfer rate. Most hard drives today are sufficient for recording mono audio files. In fact, some removable media, such as Syquest drives, are fast enough to do the job. But if your plans include multitrack recording and playback, or the recording of long, continuous files, sustained transfer rates are critical.

AV drives are ideal for multitrack audio. Hard drives must perform certain housekeeping chores regularly during use. For example, as a drive heats up, it has to compensate for the expansion of the disk media. The drive automatically stops from time to time to adjust the read/write mechanism through a process called *thermal calibration*. It's no problem if you're saving a text document, but this could create a gap in your audio if you happen to be recording to disk. You can avoid this with an AV drive; its priority is maintaining data rates until those times when the drive isn't actively reading or writing data.

If possible, use a dedicated drive for your audio, and a separate drive for your system, applications, and documents. If you do need to use your big drive for tasks other than audio, you should consider partitioning the drive—creating a small partition for general tasks and a large partition for audio. The size of the partition determines the smallest possible file size, since the Macintosh file system can address only a specific number of files on any one partition. For example, on my 1.6 GB drive, the smallest possible file uses 26 KB of storage even though it takes up only 4 KB when copied to a floppy disk. This unusable space can add up pretty quickly, especially if you have folders filled with lots of small documents, such as Photoshop filters or modem set-up files.

Why You Need Plenty of Backup

When you constantly create files that are hundreds of megabytes in size, you need lots of backup space. Create a good backup system, and invest in a good high-capacity storage medium such as SCSI DAT, recordable CD, a magneto-optical drive, or a removable cartridge drive. If you have an audio DAT deck and digital output hardware in your computer, you can make digital transfers and back your sound up on regular DAT tape.

Make sure your backup device is large enough to hold an entire audio session. It doesn't do any good if you can't back up everything in one pass. If you use the right software (such as Dantz' Retrospect), you can back up to multiple data tapes, but you have to feed the tapes in as they fill up and keep them together as a set. Since this is already a time-consuming process, it's better to use one tape (or recordable CD) per session.

CD-ROM Drive

A CD-ROM drive is a very important component of a multimedia audio system. Many high-quality sound effect and music libraries are available on

Look to the
CD-ROM

audio CD. If you have at least a double-speed drive (preferably quad-speed), QuickTime 1.6.1, and Sound Manager 3.0, you can import digital audio directly from an audio CD and save it as a digitized sound file. (The most recent versions of QuickTime and Sound Manager are included on the CD packaged with this book.) A number of programs, including Audioshop, Disc-to-Disk, Interval Music's Transfer Station, Movie Player, SoundEdit 16 version 2.0, and Gallery Software's CD Studio support this feature.

If you plan to do lots of sound effects and have invested in an audio CD production library, consider using a multi-disc player. Players capable of handling up to seven discs are now available for less than $1,000.

Removable Storage

For transferring digital audio files to coworkers or clients, you should have a high-capacity removable storage device, such as those available from SyQuest and Iomega. Another advantage of removable storage is that archived sessions can be mounted and dismounted much more quickly than with data tapes. The preferred removable format is constantly in a state of flux, so base your choice of drive on the models most widely used by vendors and clients with whom you expect to deal.

Practice Safe SCSI

If you have taken the above advice to heart, congratulations! You now have at least four devices on your SCSI chain, not counting the CPU. You are probably battling your way through "SCSI hell," the condition of instability brought about by connecting one too many SCSI devices to your system. Do yourself a favor: invest in the best SCSI cables you can find, and keep your SCSI chain as short as possible.

Make sure that your SCSI devices are all set to different ID numbers. The Macintosh CPU is always number seven, and the internal hard drive is usually set to zero. Also remember to use a terminator at the end of the SCSI chain. An active terminator, like the ones sold by APS, is an especially good investment. If you find yourself constantly shutting down your machine to move or connect SCSI devices, consider buying a SCSI adapter that permits *hot swapping*—the moving of SCSI cables while the CPU is running. Finally, if you have a Macintosh IIfx, remember that it needs its own special type of terminator (they're usually black instead of gray).

Getting the Big Picture

You also can benefit from having a large display monitor. Editing sound files in a graphic environment is similar to editing graphics; your productivity is proportional to the amount of information you can see at once. This is especially true with programs that are "window-rich," such as Deck II, Session, and just about any MIDI sequencing application.

Audio Input/ Digitizing Hardware

If you are serious about the quality of your audio, hardware for inputting and digitizing audio is a necessity rather than an option. Audio hardware is the main gateway between your computer and your audio system. It pays to consider your options carefully and to choose wisely.

These are the main benefits of dedicated audio hardware:

❑ Digital inputs and outputs
❑ High-quality digital-to-analog and analog-to-digital converters
❑ Better connectors, including balanced inputs and outputs
❑ Access to DSP functions
❑ Access to powerful software features that are hardware-dependent

We can divide audio digitizers into two main groups: audio digitizers included as part of video capture, and dedicated audio-only digitizers.

Audio Digitizing with Video Capture Hardware

Those of you capturing video may find that your video card also meets all of your audio needs. Macintosh video digitizers that can capture audio include Radius VideoVision, Truevision Targa 2000, and the discontinued SuperMac Digital Film and RasterOps MediaTime. All of these products are capable of digitizing 16/44 audio, with the exception of the VideoVision (8/22). Just because a card supports the highest rates, however, doesn't necessarily mean it will deliver true audio CD quality. For the serious audio pro, there are several drawbacks to using video cards for audio digitizing. First, they don't support digital transfer of audio with S/PDIF or AES/EBU connections. Second, the quality of the A-to-D and D-to-A converters is likely to be less than that of a dedicated audio digitizer. Third, these cards don't include dedicated DSPs, which are necessary for running a number of powerful audio processing programs.

High-end video systems such as the Avid, Data Translation Media 100, and Radius VideoVision Telecast have better audio support, including balanced line connectors and (except for the Media 100) digital input and output.

Dedicated Digital Audio Hardware

Dedicated audio digitizers come in two main flavors (actually three, but we're not going to discuss 8-bit serial port digitizers like MacRecorder and Voice Impact at this level). One flavor is the all-in-one card on the example of Digidesign's Audiomedia II and Spectral Innovations NuMedia. The second variety includes systems that combine an external rack-mountable interface with an internal card, as in the products from Sonic Solutions and Digidesign.

Each approach has advantages. Self-contained cards are much less expensive (at this time, the NuMedia card runs around $600, and Audiomedia II is about $1,200). Because they are less complicated, they are easier for the casual user to configure. They also offer some degree of portability. If you work on location or move around a lot, it's nice to have a self-contained unit inside your CPU.

Now for the drawbacks. There's only so much room to put jacks on the card, so you have fewer options for connectors. Neither of the products just mentioned has room for an XLR connector on the back, so balanced analog lines can't be connected directly to the card. Also, neither card supports AES/EBU input, since AES/EBU connectors are XLR. The NuMedia card has an optical digital input, so you need a digital translating adapter to use S/PDIF. The Audiomedia II has S/PDIF, but you need a digital translator for AES/EBU. (This multiplicity of standards is starting to make Macintosh to Windows translation look like a cakewalk!) Actually, these problems can be overcome by bouncing your audio to (or through) a DAT deck that supports both S/PDIF and AES/EBU.

Finally, the self-contained cards are more likely to add noise when you are using the card to digitize an analog signal. Consider that your unbalanced lines are going straight into a buzzing den of radio frequency interference—your computer. You can minimize this potential for noise by first recording to DAT and then doing a digital transfer to the card, or by setting the DAT to record/pause mode and using the DAT's A-to-D converters, then recording straight to the hard disk from a digital source.

Then again, you could opt for the high-end solution, with the audio interface separate from the internal card. The advantages of this approach are flexibility, expandability, and higher quality. The interface, which contains the A-to-D and D-to-A converters and connectors, usually resides in a rack with other audio equipment. This reduces the length of audio cabling and keeps audio cables further away from the CPU. Both of these features reduce the potential for audio cables to pick up interference and noise. Once audio has been digitized, it is transferred to a card in the CPU as a digital signal. A second advantage is that an external interface provides more room for connectors, so most interfaces support multiple audio channels. XLR inputs are too large to fit on a NuBus or PCI card, but when mounted on a separate interface, they provide support for several balanced audio cables and AES/EBU as well as S/PDIF digital input and output.

DIGITAL RECORDING OPTIONS

The digital revolution has taken the professional audio recording industry by storm. Many hardware digitizing systems are on the market. High-end professional systems, often called *digital audio workstations* (*DAWs*), are replacing tape-based recording systems in many recording studios and can cost well over $50,000. Very few multimedia production facilities can make this kind of investment for audio. When a situation arises that requires this level of sophistication, it's probably best to rent time in a studio. This book therefore covers systems that are available for less than $10,000.

There are three main approaches to digital audio in the recording industry: Modular Digital Multitrack (MDM) systems such as the Alesis ADAT or Tascam DA-88; dedicated standalone hard-disk recorders such as the Akai DR8, Roland DM-800, and Emu Darwin; and computer-based recording systems such as Deck II, Sonic Solutions, DAWN, and Digidesign systems. For multimedia producers, computer-based recording systems are usually the best solution, since the heart of the system—the computer—is already in place. Since the finished audio will end up on a computer, it makes sense to stay within one system.

Exception: *If you need multitrack recording capability and plan to record for extended periods of time in different locations, consider a standalone disk recorder or an MDM system. For example, if a project involves lots of location video with multiple actors, it could be desirable to isolate their dialog onto separate tracks that can be processed and edited individually at a later date. With the right equipment, it's also possible to digitally transfer ADAT tracks, for example, into a Digidesign-equipped Macintosh for extensive editing, and then transfer the results back to the ADAT.*

Having multiple input and output channels can be helpful in some situations; you can record several sources at the same time, but record them into separate tracks within the computer so that they can be processed independently at a later time. This comes at a price, of course, starting at around $3,000 and ranging up to $10,000.

Hardware Lust—Is More Always Better?

As CPUs become increasingly powerful, software developers are finding they can do much more with a plain-vanilla PowerPC- or Pentium-based CPU, rather than having to rely on hardware assists from added DSPs. Notable examples of this trend include Macromedia's Deck II, Alaska

Software's Digitrax, and plug-ins for Adobe Premiere from companies such as Waves and InVision Interactive. While it is increasingly possible to do studio-quality audio engineering on a stock Macintosh, a crucial bottleneck remains: the Macintosh's built-in analog audio hardware. One cure would be a basic, inexpensive digital audio interface on a card: no DSPs, no A-to-D or D-to-A converters, just something that lets you transfer from audio DAT to the CPU.

Given the Mac's recent move to PCI architecture and the increasing market for PCI peripheral vendors, it is probable that such a product will become available. Such a product would have the potential to make powerful audio editing tools even more widely available, at a significantly lower cost than the proprietary systems currently in use.

For multimedia developers who have huge budgets for audio, this may not be big news. Then again, I've never met one of these people, and I'm beginning to doubt their existence!

Summary

This chapter has covered a lot of ground concerning the hardware requirements for multimedia audio production. We began by looking at the signal chain and at a basic recording system: microphone, compressor, mixer, DAT recorder, amplifier, and monitors. We then discussed Macintosh hardware, its audio inputs and outputs, and the changing sample rates and microphones through the history of the platform. We emphasized the importance of having the right computer peripherals and examined the basic types of audio digitizing and capture products available on the market.

Now that you have a better understanding of audio and computer hardware, we're almost ready to delve into the software tools that make digital audio editing possible. But first, we will veer off on a side trip to a subject that's a little bit hardware, a little bit software, and all about music. It's time to strap on your breath controller and enter the rarefied atmosphere of MIDI: the Musical Instrument Digital Interface.

3

All About MIDI

If you use a computer to create digital audio, sooner or later you will run into MIDI—the Musical Instrument Digital Interface. We have chosen to introduce MIDI here because you may want MIDI hardware in your audio production system. Even if you aren't creating music, you will find that a great deal of audio hardware supports MIDI, and you can use this fact to your advantage. Whatever you do with digital audio, you should know about MIDI, because it has many potential advantages over digitized sound.

This chapter discusses the fundamentals of how MIDI works and how you can use it in a practical sense. We will cover aspects of MIDI that are of particular interest to multimedia developers, including the General MIDI specification. We will also discuss how MIDI works at the system level, examine cross-platform issues, and briefly review the history of electronic synthesis to its present incarnations in modern synthesizers, sound cards, and system software.

MIDI Basics

MIDI is a communication protocol that allows electronic musical instruments to share information with other instruments or computers. If you are new to MIDI, imagine it as the musical equivalent of word processing.

Here is a simple example that illustrates the most basic rudiments of how MIDI works. Imagine yourself playing music on a synthesizer keyboard that is connected to a computer running a MIDI sequencing program (programs for creating and editing MIDI are commonly called *sequencers,* because they work with sequences of musical notes and other MIDI information). As you play, the sequencing program records the details of your performance: which keys you strike and when, how hard or soft you strike each key, and how long you hold each note. This process is similar to typing, except that you are recording notes instead of letters.

When you finish playing, you can have the computer send the musical information back to your synthesizer, duplicating your performance perfectly. In this process, the synthesizer acts like a musical "printer" as it replays the notes.

If you make a mistake while playing, fixing it can be as simple as changing a typo in a string of text. Using MIDI sequencing software, you can change almost any attribute of the recorded notes, including pitch, starting time, and duration.

This brings us to a common misconception about MIDI, one that should be corrected up front: *MIDI data is performance data, not digitized sound data.* Many people confuse MIDI information with any digitized sound. But MIDI has nothing to do with capturing sound; rather, MIDI tells devices how to recreate the sound. In this sense, MIDI is much more like a player piano than a tape recorder.

This key distinction is one of the main advantages of MIDI over digitized sound. Because MIDI files contain only performance data, they can be very small. A MIDI file that tells a synthesizer to play a one-minute piece of music might take 15 KB of disk space. The same file as 16/44 stereo digitized audio would require more than 10 MB.

This advantage also has a downside: the quality of the audio playback is dependent on the playback device. If you write a piece of music that sounds wonderful on your $4,000 synthesizer, you may not be pleased when you hear it playing back on a $200 sound card.

16 MIDI Channels

MIDI is a serial protocol that transmits data on 16 independent channels. Think of it as a 16-track tape deck. Each channel is capable of playing multiple notes (in other words, chords), and usually each channel is assigned to a particular instrument. This allows one channel to play a bass part, another channel to play drums, and so forth.

One part of the MIDI specification makes it possible to select a specific sound you want from a group of sounds stored in an instrument. In MIDI parlance, specific sounds are called *programs* or *patches,* and the messages that MIDI sends to change these settings are called *program changes.* Most synthesizers arrange sounds in groups (often called *banks)* of 128, since that represents the largest number of sounds that can be accessed through one MIDI channel at any given time. Get used to these numbers: many MIDI values range from 0 to 127, offering 128 actual values.

Almost all synthesizers produced today can play different sounds simultaneously on multiple MIDI channels. These multichannel-capable synthesizers are called *multi-timbral,* because different sounds (also called *timbres)* can be played on them at the same time. A multi-timbral synthesizer can play drum, bass, guitar, and piano sounds all at the same time to create a fully orchestrated performance.

Lest you assume that a machine is poised to replace the Rolling Stones and the Chicago Symphony, you should know that there are some limitations. A synthesizer can play only a certain maximum number of notes simultaneously, due to the limitations of the processors that generate sound. Individual notes are often called *voices.* It's not uncommon for synthesizers to have 16 to 32 voices. Most synthesizers feature *dynamic voice allocation*—each channel gets as many voices as it needs at a given instant until the number of voices has been exhausted. For a simple example, imagine a 24-voice synthesizer playing a piece of music using two different instrument sounds: piano and harp. At some points in the music, the piano might require 15 voices, leaving nine for the harp. At other points the harp might use 16 voices, leaving eight for the piano. If all 24 voices are being used, playing an additional note results in stealing a voice; one of the currently active voices is cut off to allow the new note to play.

A Quick Look at a MIDI Sequencer

Look to the
CD-ROM

Let's look at some of the features within a MIDI sequencing program to get a better idea of how you can work with MIDI. There are many good MIDI sequencing products available, from entry level to hard-core professional (check the reviews in Chapter 11 and the turorials on the CD for more details). Just to give you a glimpse of MIDI's power and flexibility, we will take a quick walk through Opcode's StudioVision.

Many sequencers use the metaphor of a multitrack tape recorder. You can record MIDI data onto several different tracks and then play all the tracks back at the same time. It's not uncommon to have 64 or more tracks available at any time. You can think of tracks as similar to layers in a drawing program or alpha channels in an image-editing program. They let you stack multiple elements on top of each other while still having the flexibility to change data within a particular track. Figure 3.1 shows the Tracks window from StudioVision.

In this example you can see multiple synthesizer tracks, with each track playing data on a separate MIDI channel. At the left of the window are toggle buttons for selecting tracks to record, mute, or solo.

Figure 3.1

The Tracks window in StudioVision shows MIDI tracks that have been recorded into the program and indicates which synthesizers and MIDI channels are assigned to play back the data within each track.

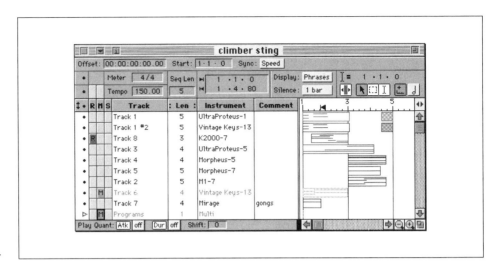

Most sequencers have a main window that lets you control playback, recording, and navigation through the data. In the case of StudioVision, many functions are grouped together on the Control Bar (Figure 3.2). There are play, stop, and record buttons; below them are fast-forward and rewind buttons with a *scrubbing shuttle* in the middle. A scrubber, or shuttle, allows you to fast-forward or rewind at various speeds while also hearing the material. The numbers one through eight below the shuttle let you set *autolocation points* in memory; autolocation lets you set a marker at a particular time, so you can click on a number to jump instantly to a particular point in the file. The time is displayed in bars:beats:units (1.1.0) as well as in *SMPTE code* (Hours:Minutes:Seconds:Frames). Most professional-level sequencers have extensive support for synchronizing MIDI data to SMPTE time code. The text buttons on the left side of the window let you access pop-up lists to switch between the sequences or tracks within a file, set the currently active instrument and MIDI channel within your MIDI setup, or select the program to play a particular sound.

There are many different ways to view MIDI data within a track. Most sequencing programs offer a "piano roll" view (dots and dashes, indicating

Figure 3.2

The Control Bar in Studio Vision

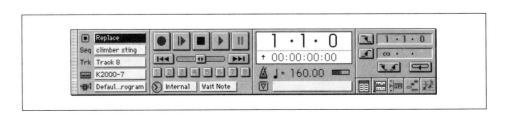

note pitch and length), a list view (text describing the MIDI data), and a notation view (notes placed on a musical staff, much like sheet music). Figure 3.3 shows examples of each type of view.

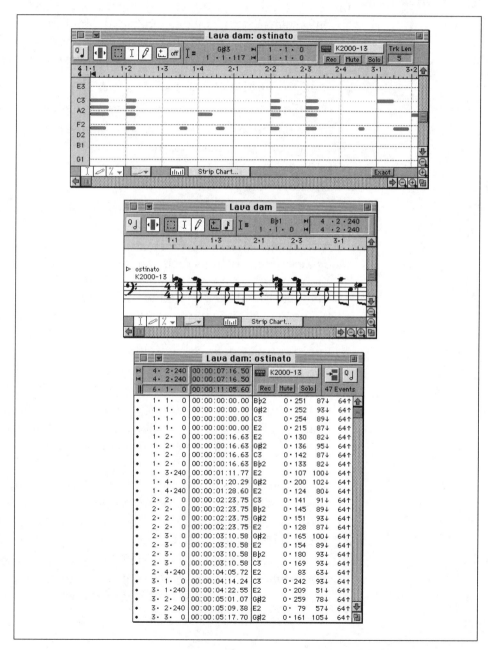

Figure 3.3

Three ways to view MIDI data. ***Top:*** In a typical piano-roll view, notes displayed in the window can be dragged up or down to change pitch, dragged back or forth to change timing, or dragged from the endpoint to change length. ***Center:*** A standard notation view can be printed to create sheet music. ***Bottom:*** A list view shows the timing for each note as well as its pitch and key velocity.

MIDI Message Types and How They Work

There are many different types of MIDI messages, but since the subject is covered in a number of good MIDI reference books, we do not need to discuss each of them in detail here. (For more information on programming with MIDI, refer to the "Suggested Reading" appendix for other sources.) Instead of leading you through a potentially confusing thicket of stop bits, status bytes, and hexadecimal numbers, we will describe the messages in more general terms. For example, here are the messages that a synthesizer might send when a MIDI note is played on its keyboard.

1. Someone just hit Middle C.

    (A MIDI note on message for C3, note number 60)

    Notes on the keyboard are assigned values from 0 to 127. If we assign a value of C3 to Middle C, the Note messages cover a range from C-2 through G8.

2. The note was struck very hard.

    (The "note on" message contains a velocity value of 125 out of a range from 0-127)

    With synthesizers, velocity measures the speed at which a key descends after being struck. Velocity data can be used to change the sound generated by the synthesizer—an increase in velocity, for example, might be assigned to increase the volume or brightness of the note, in the same way that the sound of most acoustic instruments grows louder when the instrument is struck more forcefully. Most synthesizers today are velocity-sensitive.

3. The note is still being held down, and now the modulation wheel is moving.

    (A continuous controller value, in this case modulation wheel, is changing. Continuous controllers are so named because their values change in a smooth, continuous manner, similar to turning a knob or moving a slider.)

    Most synthesizers have real-time control over certain performance attributes. These include the following:

    - ■ *Pitch bender*—a spring-loaded wheel or joystick which can be moved back and forth to "bend" pitch up or down in much the same way guitarists can bend the pitch of a note

    - ■ *Modulation wheels*, often called "mod wheels"—similar to a pitch wheel, but programmable to add vibrato or "wah-wah" types of effects

■ *Pressure sensitivity* or *aftertouch*—In addition to velocity, most synthesizer keyboards can sense changes in applied pressure while a key is held down. Routing this data can create effects similar to those of a modulation wheel.

4. The note has been released.

    (A note off message for C3)

    The note stops playing. Depending on the synthesizer parameters set for that particular sound, the note may stop abruptly or may fade away slowly after being released.

MIDI supports many different types of controllers. As mentioned above, these can include aftertouch, modulation, and pitch bend. Other messages that can be sent in real time include:

❑ Pan (0 through 127, with 0 panning the signal all the way to the left channel in a stereo field, 64 in the center, and 127 panning to the right channel of a stereo field)

❑ Volume (0 through 127, with 0 being silence and 127 maximum volume)

❑ Sustain pedal on/off

❑ Reset Controllers

❑ All Notes Off

The last two messages are particularly useful to return a synthesizer to its normal state if a transmission error occurs. If the All Notes Off message were not available, a transmission error occurring while a note is being played would prevent the synthesizer from receiving a note off message, and the note would sustain indefinitely. Similarly, if the pitch wheel of a controller moved and the pitch went up, the synthesizer would continue to play at the altered pitch until the pitch value returned to zero. Without the Reset Controllers message, if an interruption occurred and the synthesizer never reset the pitch wheel, every note would play at a shifted pitch. Although most newer synthesizers support these last two messages, there is no guarantee that every synthesizer will undestand them. In fact, some of the earliest MIDI synthesizers support only Note On and Note Off on channel 12 alone.

The possibility of transmission errors should come as no surprise to anyone who has ever used a modem. On the whole, MIDI transmission is relatively stable and reliable, but problems can occur if you send too much MIDI data at once, if cables are faulty, or if the CPU is being forced to do too many things at once.

Hooking Up

On the Macintosh, you need a MIDI interface in order to send MIDI data between the computer and a synthesizer. The interface connects to the Macintosh through standard 9-pin serial cables and can be hooked up to the modem port, the printer port, or both.

MIDI cables are 5-pin DIN connectors and are designed in lengths of up to 50 feet. MIDI devices usually have three MIDI jacks: MIDI In, MIDI Out, and MIDI Thru. The MIDI Out jack of the synthesizer should be connected to the MIDI In jack of a MIDI interface. The MIDI Out jack on the interface should be connected to the MIDI In jack of the synthesizer. The MIDI Thru jack can be used to daisy-chain multiple MIDI devices together (see Figure 3.4). To reduce cost or save space on the back panel, some devices have only two MIDI jacks: a MIDI In and a MIDI Out/Thru. You may have to push buttons and search the menus on a MIDI device to set the Out/Thru jack to the desired state.

MIDI Interfaces

The simplest MIDI interfaces for the Macintosh connect to either the printer or the modem port of the computer using one serial cable; they have one MIDI In jack and two MIDI Out jacks. If you are building a MIDI setup for basic music creation and playback and plan to use only one or two synthesizers, a basic interface like this may be adequate for your needs (see Figure 3.5). If you already have a modem or printer, don't worry about losing one of your cherished serial ports. Most MIDI interfaces have a *pass through* jack, which passes the modem or printer data transparently

Figure 3.4

MIDI devices are connected to the computer through a MIDI interface. Multiple MIDI devices can be daisy-chained together using MIDI Thru jacks.

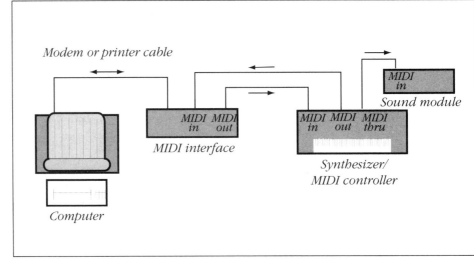

Figure 3.5

Opcode MIDI
interfaces

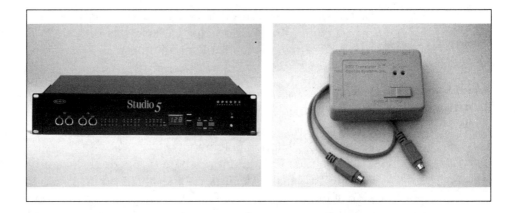

through the MIDI interface. You can hook a modem or printer to the MIDI
interface and access the device by flipping a switch.

As MIDI systems have become more complex, manufacturers have
developed interfaces to address more than the standard 16 MIDI channels.
An early innovation treated the modem and printer ports as independent
data streams, sending 16 channels to both ports at once for a total of 32
channels. More recent innovations have divided the data stream into
smaller packets. By sending information to the interface at a rate 16 times
faster than MIDI's normal speed, the computer can address 16 separate
channels on each of 32 channels, for a total of 512 MIDI channels.

These newer, more complex interfaces (such as Opcode's Studio 5 in
Figure 3.5, for example) function as MIDI *patch bays,* with multiple MIDI
inputs and outputs, so that MIDI data can be routed in many different
ways. They also support SMPTE synchronization, with tape inputs and outputs for writing and reading SMPTE data from audio or videotape. The
incoming SMPTE data can synchronize a MIDI sequencer to an external
videotape deck.

It's not surprising that the two most popular MIDI interface manufacturers are also the two most popular MIDI software developers, namely
Opcode Systems and Mark of the Unicorn.

You may wonder why anyone would need hundreds of MIDI channels.
Most synthesizers made today are multi-timbral and can simultaneously
play different sounds on separate MIDI channels. If you hook up 10 synthesizers, each capable of using 16 channels, you can tie up 160 channels.
This may lead some readers to a second question: If a synthesizer can create any type of sound, why would anyone need ten synthesizers? For the
same reason that a graphic artist needs a paintbrush as well as a pencil.
Different synthesizers have their own tonal colors, and some sounds are

better for certain styles of music than for others. When you need to cover a broad range of styles, it helps to have lots of sounds at your disposal and to have them easily available at all times.

Connection Tips

If you are connecting multiple synthesizers to a basic interface that supports 16 MIDI channels, be sure that the synthesizers are using different MIDI channels. Check the synthesizer's documentation to find out how to select MIDI channel assignments.

Don't daisy-chain more than three devices using MIDI Thru jacks. Having two many devices on the chain could cause a degradation of the signal and ultimately confuse the synthesizer if the connection is poor.

Several synthesizer manufacturers offer sound modules that can connect directly to a modem or printer port, thus removing the need for a MIDI interface. This can be useful if you're creating a presentation to play back on a particular machine—a kiosk or a speaker support situation, for example.

Major Features of the MIDI Specification

MIDI is a shining example of what can be accomplished when manufacturers set aside their differences and concentrate on the greater good of building devices that work well together. Users are more productive, and the overall market is much stronger. The MIDI specification is administered by a group called the MIDI Manufacturer's Association (MMA). As technology has changed over the 12 years since the inception of MIDI, various additions and new specifications have been added, and many of them are directly aimed at the needs of multimedia producers.

Standard MIDI Files

When MIDI-equipped synthesizers hit the scene, MIDI sequencing software wasn't far behind. In 1983, the personal computer industry and the MIDI standard were just getting off the ground. The timing created a synergy between these two technologies, which fueled a growing market for MIDI software.

Today there are many popular MIDI sequencing applications. The Standard MIDI File (SMF) format was created to facilitate the transfer and sharing of MIDI file data between different programs. There are two types of SMFs: Type 1 and Type 0. Type 1 files are multitrack; the data from each channel is assigned to its own track. Type 0 combines all the data into a single "track." When you import a Type 0 file for editing in another program, you may want to separate the data back out into separate tracks. Most MIDI sequencing programs let you select specific types of data (in this case, all the data on our particular MIDI channel) for editing operations. This is analogous to the Magic Wand tool in image editors like Adobe Photoshop.

General MIDI

Thanks to MIDI, musicians and composers have lots of flexibility. A person can play a part using a piano sound, then easily change the piano to a flute, guitar, or violin. It allows many opportunities for experimentation, but it also can be dangerous. If my programs are organized so that programs 10 through 20 are piano sounds, and your synthesizer uses programs 10 through 20 for string sounds, my MIDI file won't sound right on your synthesizer. Looking at the problem this creates for distributing MIDI files, the growth of the multimedia markets, and the need for "plug and play" solutions, certain hardware and software manufacturers lobbied for a "base platform" for MIDI playback. The MMA created the General MIDI specification to address this issue. General MIDI establishes a standard set of sounds and capabilities for MIDI playback modules.

General MIDI declares a bank of 128 sounds in which sounds are assigned to specific program numbers. In MIDI nomenclature, this is called a *patch map*—certain patches (sounds) are *mapped,* or assigned, to specific program numbers. For example, Program 1 is an Acoustic Piano, Program 33 is an Acoustic Bass, and Program 57 is a Trumpet. Unlike the settings on a general-purpose synthesizer, these program assignments never change. Mapping allows a composer to create a song with specific instruments. Program changes are embedded into the start of the MIDI file, allowing instrumentation assignments to be recreated on the listener's sound module, so the user will hear something close to what the composer intended. General MIDI also defines a *Percussion Key Map,* which maps drum and percussion sounds to the proper key values. Percussion always plays on MIDI Channel 10. General MIDI also defines the basic capabilities a synthesizer should have for the playback of General MIDI files (see Table 3.1).

Here are a few tips for creating MIDI files to be distributed for playback through a General MIDI device. If your sequence absolutely has to play on sound cards using older FM synthesis, as well as on newer cards with wavetable synthesis, create two different versions of the sequence: one that sounds good using wavetable instruments, and another that sounds good just using FM synthesis. Use MIDI channels 13 through 16 for the FM version of the sequence, with percussion on channel 16. Use channels 1 through 10 for the wavetable version, with percussion on channel 10. Always initialize your sequences properly by placing program changes at

Table 3.1

Basic synthesizer capabilities required by the General MIDI specification

Voices	A minimum of either 24 fully dynamically allocated voices available simultaneously for both melodic and percussive sounds, or 16 dynamically allocated voices for melody plus eight for percussion.
Channels	General MIDI mode supports sixteen MIDI channels. Each channel can play a variable number of voices (polyphony). Each channel can play a different instrument (timbre). Key-based percussion is always on Channel 10.
Instruments	A minimum of sixteen different timbres playing various instrument sounds. A minimum of 128 presets for Instruments (MIDI program numbers)
Note on/Note off	Octave Registration: Middle C(C3) = MIDI key 60. All Voices including percussion respond to velocity.

Controllers	Controller #	Description
	1	Modulation
	7	Main Volume
	10	Pan
	11	Expression
	64	Sustain
	121	Reset All Controllers
	123	All Notes Off

Registered Parameter Number	**Description**
0	Pitch Bend Sensitivity
1	Fine Tuning
2	Coarse Tuning
Additional Channel Messages:	Channel Pressure (Aftertouch) Pitch Bend

the very beginning, along with your desired settings for volume and pan on each channel.

Supersets of General MIDI—GS and GX

Like most standards, General MIDI has been stretched a bit by those who found the requirements too limiting. The first company to step over the line was Roland Corporation, creators of the first General MIDI module, the Sound Canvas. Roland created a superset of General MIDI, which they dubbed the GS Standard. Roland GS follows all the provisions of plain-vanilla General MIDI, but it adds some extra MIDI control parameters and several new sounds (including sound effects such as footsteps, applause, and doors closing). Some of the controllers take advantage of an extensible backdoor in MIDI's continuous controller table called *Non-Registered Parameter Numbers (NRPNs)* to allow control of synthesizer parameters such as envelope attack and decay rates. *Envelopes* are curves that describe the shape of a waveform's amplitude or frequency characteristics. See Figure 3.6 for an example.

Roland GS also added a new *MIDI Bank Select* message to provide access to eight separate banks of 128 sounds each. The programs in each bank are variations of the stock General MIDI set. This gives users the ability to use customized banks for different tone colors while still working within a General MIDI framework.

While the seven additional banks of 128 sounds provide sonic flavoring, the multiple drum sets are more significant. The jazz drum kit, for example, uses brushed snare instead of regular snare on some keys. This means that sequences composed for GS will play back instrumental voices reasonably accurately, but they may get really confused on the drums.

Not to be outdone by Roland, Yamaha Corporation created its own proprietary sound banks as well with the GX (extended) extension to General MIDI. We can now say, "What we love about General MIDI is that there are so many standards to choose from!" The best advice to composers is to use plain-vanilla General MIDI rather than the GS or GX extensions, since the extensions are not guaranteed for playback. Instead, write for the Microsoft Extended synthesizer described next.

Microsoft Base-Level and Extended Synthesizers

To accomodate the preponderance of first-generation SoundBlaster cards with 11-voice FM synthesizers, Microsoft defined Base-Level and Extended Synthesizers as a part of the Multimedia PC standard for Intel-based PCs. Composers were encouraged to create General MIDI files that use the normal General MIDI patch assignments but have special channel assignments.

In the official General MIDI specification, Channel 10 is for percussion, and all other channels are for instruments. Microsoft's MPC specification, however, defined more specific MIDI channel assignments. Extended synthesizers are expected to respond to up to 22 voices on channels 1 through 10, with 10 still assigned to percussion. Base-level synthesizers are expected to respond to 11 voices on channels 13 through 15 for instruments and to channel 16 for percussion. Composers were encouraged to put a simplified version of the sequence on channels 13 through 16 and a more complex version on channels 1 thru 10. Predictably, this sounds pretty bad when played on a full General MIDI synthesizer—whatever instrument is assigned to channel 16 starts playing a non-tonal rhythm pattern.

Microsoft is no longer encouraging this distinction due to the improved quality of current-model sound cards now on the market, but it is still prudent to keep General MIDI files restricted to channels 1 through 10 whenever possible. This way they will play on both General MIDI and Extended synthesizers and will not play at all on Base-Level FM synthesizers, where they probably would sound horrible in any case.

System Exclusive

One of the benefits of MIDI is that devices are relatively interchangeable. That is, a MIDI message that plays a specific note of a specific duration on one synthesizer will play that same note for the same duration on a different synthesizer, in the same way that two different printers will print relatively similar copies of the same document.

This level of standardization is helpful, but it would be even more convenient to be able take advantage of functions specific to one particular type of synthesizer. One way to handle this would be to give each model of synthesizer its own unique code, somewhat like a telephone number. Then, if your synthesizer receives a message containing that code, it would "know" that a special message is coming. That's the idea behind *MIDI System Exclusive (SysEx)* messages.

SysEx lets computers talk to MIDI devices in their own language. With SysEx, you can control or change practically any function or setting on a MIDI device, as long as both the computer software and the MIDI device support the transmission of SysEx data. The greatest benefit of SysEx is that it has facilitated the development of software that lets you edit synthesizer functions and catalog groups of sounds using a computer. These programs are usually called *editor/ librarians*.

In recent years, synthesizer functions have become increasingly complex and powerful, but user interfaces on synthesizers have been scaled down to limit production costs. Fifteen years ago, synthesizers had such limited functions that you could adjust the sound simply by turning a few knobs.

Figure 3.6

This single editor window from Opcode's Galaxy Plus lets you visualize many types of synthesizer data graphically—oscillator settings, velocity settings, and data for filters, amplifiers, and envelopes.

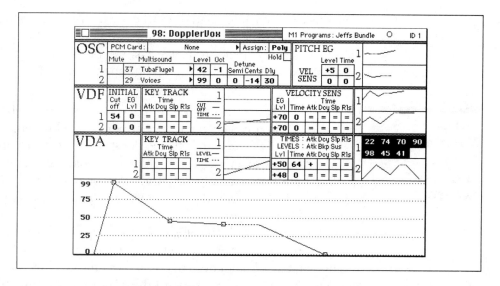

Today, many more features are built into synthesizers, but most products let you access these only by paging through small LED displays and entering numbers on a keypad. Editor/librarians use a computer to create "virtual" knobs, sliders, and envelope controllers, so that editing of functions is faster and more intuitive. The library functions also let you arrange sounds into groups, store multiple sets of sounds, and send and retrieve sounds from a synthesizer's RAM. Most librarians include keyword searching functions that let you locate sounds with specific attributes. Figure 3.6 shows an editor window from Opcode's Galaxy Plus, a popular editor/librarian package.

Sending Sample Data

Digital sampling synthesizers (often called *samplers* or *sampling keyboards)* have become an important and valued component for many MIDI musicians. Samplers capture and digitize audio, then let you control the playback of the audio through the architecture of a synthesizer. This can be useful for imitating the performance of certain instruments like horns or strings. But you can also create tonal palettes built from industrial sounds and use them in a musical way.

As samplers became more affordable and popular in the marketplace, sound editing applications such as Passport's Alchemy were developed to harness the processing power and graphic interface of the computer for sound editing and manipulation. The Sample Dump Standard was developed as an extension of the original MIDI specification, to provide for the transfer of digitized sample data through MIDI. In the past few years, most samplers have begun sporting SCSI interfaces and support a newer standard,

SCSI Musical Data Interchange (SMDI), which lets users transfer data more easily and at faster rates. For older samplers without SCSI, however, the Sample Dump Standard remains a slow, but reliable gateway for sharing sounds between a sampler and a computer.

MIDI Machine Control and Show Control

Once MIDI became firmly entrenched among synthesizer manufacturers and users, companies such as J.L. Cooper began building products for controlling MIDI data, of which the FaderMaster and CS10 are examples. The FaderMaster, for example, has eight sliders that can be assigned to control any MIDI attribute, such as MIDI volume or pan. The CS10 has assignable faders and adds standard tape-transport style controls (play, pause, etc.) and a jog/shuttle wheel.

As these types of controllers became popular, the MIDI Manufacturers Association, the keepers of the MIDI specification, took the next step by adding standard guidelines for implementing machine control. Using MIDI Machine Control, you can control the playback of compatible devices (usually analog and digital recording decks) from within a MIDI sequencing application or any device capable of sending MIDI Machine Control data. This is also a boon for people who need to control equipment located on the other side of the room. Another similar enhancement is MIDI Show Control, which provides for real-time control of stage and lighting equipment. In ten short years, MIDI has evolved from a basic remote control system into a complete musical and theatrical performance network.

A Brief History of Synthesizers

To better understand the capabilities of MIDI and MIDI musicians, it helps to know a bit about the capabilities of synthesis. After all, a MIDI file sounds only as good as the synthesizer playing it back. A deep exploration of the development of synthesis and electronic music is a bit beyond the scope of this discussion (for more information, refer to the "Suggested Reading" section in the back of this book), but here is a brief summary.

Electronic music has been developing since the early 1900s. The big break came in the 1960s with the development of synthesizers from pioneers like Robert Moog. Early synthesizers were capable of creating a few basic waveforms that could then be modified and filtered in various ways to produce different tones.

The development of powerful microprocessors brought about the first digital samplers in the mid-1970s. These were the first synthesizers to allow the recording, manipulation and playback of digitized sound. In the early 1980s, Yamaha brought *FM synthesis* to market. FM used *frequency modulation,* in which one waveform modifies another. Theoretically, given enough processing power, this technique can be used to produce any waveform imaginable.

Another interesting technique is *wavetable synthesis,* popularized by the Korg Wavestation. These synthesizers string together a series of different waveforms to create sounds that evolve over time. This overcomes one of the weaknesses of synthesis techniques such as sampling, which make heavy use of waveforms that loop repeatedly and lack the expressive nature of real instruments.

Speaking of real instruments, a new force on the synthesis scene is *physical modeling.* This approach attempts to use mathematical models to describe the physical and tonal properties of a "virtual" instrument. What is the sound of a 30-foot violin made of brass? We should find out soon as these synthesizers take hold in the market.

The most popular current-model synthesizers combine samples and waveforms stored in *ROM* (*read-only memory*) chips. This includes the wavetable synthesizers found on many General MIDI PC sound cards. Wavetable synthesizers provide reasonably good quality at a good price.

Look to the CD-ROM

MIDI's appearance at about the same time as programmable synthesizers was fortuitous. (In fact, they're both brought to you by Dave Smith, who skipped from Sequential Circuits to Yamaha to Korg.) It drove many musicians into the realm of dealing with programming concepts and using computers in conjunction with music. As a result, there is now a large pool of computer-savvy musicians. For the musician, the use of MIDI sometimes involves pulling away from the concept of using musical phrases and thinking instead about musical data streams. For example, a part played using a piano tone may sound surprisingly musical when you send the data to a drum machine (see the tutorials on the CD for an example). It could sound awful, too, but MIDI gives you the flexibility to change the data until you like the result.

MIDI at the System Level

MIDI support is not built into the Macintosh operating system. For MIDI to work on the Macintosh, system-level drivers (called *system extensions)* have to load into the system while the computer is booting up. These extensions handle the transfer of MIDI data between MIDI programs (such as sequencers and editors) and the Macintosh serial ports. As of this writing, there are three products you can use to manage your MIDI traffic: Apple's MIDI Manager, Opcode's OMS, and Mark of the Unicorn's FreeMIDI.

Apple's MIDI Manager was the first standard for controlling MIDI on the Macintosh. It's no longer supported by Apple, but it still works in most cases. Programs that require MIDI Manager usually provide it as part of the installation process. To use MIDI Manager, you need three files: the MIDI Manager extension, the Apple MIDI Driver, and PatchBay. MIDI Manager runs in the background; it is an environment that lets MIDI Manager-aware applications share data. Access to the MIDI Manager is controlled through an Apple utility, PatchBay, which lets you route data between different MIDI Manager-aware applications and the Apple MIDI Driver. In Figure 3.7, for example, the MIDI Driver's output is connected to the input of Passport's MasterTracks Pro, and the MasterTracks output is connected to the input of the MIDI Driver.

MIDI Manager worked well enough for basic tasks, but over the years MIDI applications became increasingly powerful and complex. Programs such as Opcode's Vision and Mark of the Unicorn's Performer were breaking the 16-channel limit of the MIDI specification and adding sophisticated synchronization features using MIDI Time Code. These developments, along with efforts to achieve synchronization to external sources such as SMPTE, began to push the limits of MIDI Manager.

To enhance MIDI performance, Opcode Systems created its own system-level MIDI architecture, OMS (first called the Opcode MIDI System, later changed to Open Music System), and Mark of the Unicorn created FreeMIDI. These systems took a similar approach to handling traffic on a MIDI network. You create a setup document that describes the configuration of your equipment, and every compatible program refers to that setup to move data around the network (see Figure 3.8). For users, this is a powerful advance. You can pass data between multiple programs running at

Figure 3.7

Apple's Patch-Bay utility showing connections between the Apple MIDI Driver and MasterTracks Pro

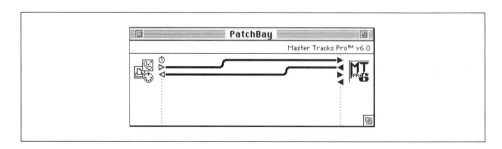

Figure 3.8

This OMS Setup document shows the configuration of devices in a MIDI setup. A MIDI fader box (FaderMaster), percussion controller (drumKAT), MIDI-controllable digital effects (SE-50, Quadraverb and LXP-1), and a MIDI patchbay (MX-8) are integrated into the system.

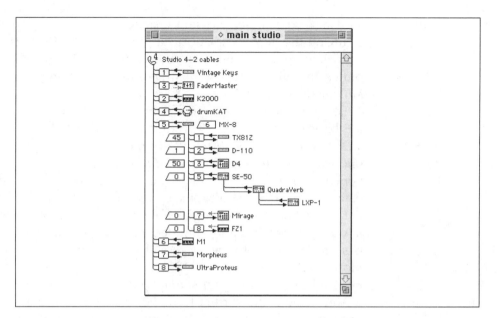

the same time to handle tasks such as MIDI sequencing, patch editing, digital audio editing, and synchronization to video all within the same system.

These two industry leaders have continued their struggle for dominance by trying to attract other MIDI and music software vendors to support their standards. At this point, it appears that OMS has the upper hand, as its technology has been licensed to both Apple and Microsoft for inclusion in future versions of QuickTime and Windows 95.

MIDI and Windows-Based PCs

Most PC sound cards have MIDI interfaces that allow you to connect external synthesizers. The MIDI port often doubles as a joystick port, and a special adapter cable is needed. Depending on the sound card, you may not need an external synthesizer. Almost all PC sound cards have a synthesizer right on the card. MIDI on sound cards is limited to 16 channels, but dedicated MIDI interfaces that extend the number of channels are available for the PC.

In Windows 3.1, the system-level approach to dealing with MIDI is the MIDI Mapper. You can find it in the Windows Control Panel. MIDI Mapper lets you configure and modify the MIDI setup to select whether MIDI data will be sent to a synthesizer on the sound card (you can select FM or Wavetable if your card supports both) or an external MIDI port. You can also create custom patch maps that alter the program change assignments so that, for example, program change 1 could be mapped to program 25, changing the acoustic piano to a guitar. Finally, there is a *key mapper* for changing key assignments in the drum kits. Fortunately, Windows 95 simplifies this approach, with MIDI functions being handled through the Multimedia Control Panel.

For multimedia developers delivering MIDI products on the PC, there are basically two types of synthesis available: FM and wavetable. FM creates waveforms through frequency modulation. This is the process of using one waveform to alter (or *modulate)* the shape of another waveform. The benefit of FM is that it can create complex waves, but there is no sound data to store because the wave is generated from mathematical formulas. FM was made popular on the SoundBlaster series of sound cards because it was inexpensive and sounded marginally reasonable. It was also the basis for a series of very successful synthesizers from Yamaha Corporation, most notably the Yamaha DX7 (the FM synthesizer on the DX7 is much more advanced and better-sounding than most sound cards).

Wavetable is the current format of choice because it uses actual sampled waveforms to produce a sound, resulting in more natural tone. But as you saw in the previous chapter, sound quality is determined by the sampling rate and sample resolution. Most of these cards profess to be 16/44, but the amount of ROM memory allocated to storing the sample data varies from card to card. One megabyte of ROM is barely sufficient to hold all the sample data for a General MIDI bank.

Summary

In a world of changing and competing "standards," MIDI has remained more or less intact for more than ten years—an astonishing record in light of the technological changes that have occurred over the same period, and an indication of the foresight of the founders of the MIDI specification.

We barely managed to brush the surface of MIDI in this chapter, but we did introduce basic concepts of how MIDI works, how sequencing programs deal with MIDI data, how MIDI systems are configured, and how the MIDI specification has evolved to meet changing needs. For creators of multimedia, MIDI has led to powerful tools for creating music, and the General MIDI specification has established a base system for delivering MIDI data.

In the next chapter, we will delve back into the world of audio software. As you read, though, keep an eye peeled for a discussion of the next great advance of MIDI for multimedia: synthesis in software. Technologies such as QuickTime 2.0's Music Tracks and software synthesizer from Seer Systems and InVision Interactive promise to increase the amount of music you can pack into a product, at the same time that they reduce file sizes to a tiny speck. We are on the verge of eliminating another of those nasty multimedia trade-offs, and not a moment too soon.

4
Digital Audio Software

How many times have you found yourself in this situation? Your uncle/neighbor/sister/coworker, a digital neophyte, is about to buy his or her first computer system. He or she pins you in a corner and asks, "Which computer should I get?" The time-tested advice that can almost always rescue you is to turn the tables by asking, "Well, what kind of software do you want to run?" Twelve years ago, the choices would have boiled down to a word processor, database, or one of those newfangled spreadsheets. Then again, twelve years ago, audio editing could only be done with hardware—a razor blade and a splicing block.

Thank goodness for progress! Today, many different sound-editing packages are available, ranging from basic waveform editors to high-end digital workstations that have all the features you would expect to find in a fully-equipped recording studio. And as with any software package, you will obtain the best results if you first figure out what kinds of audio jobs you need to tackle, and then get the program that can best handle those jobs. When creating sound for multimedia (remember our seven-stage process?), you will need software for capture, editing, processing, and output.

In this chapter, we will look at how you can handle these different tasks using the software tools that are currently available (for brief reviews of software products, see Part Three, *Product Reviews*). Our first step will be to examine the processes involved in sound editing. Then, we will delve into a technical discussion of file formats and sound within the Macintosh operating system, because it's important for you to know the nuts and bolts of how sounds are packaged and handled. Choosing the right file format for your needs can give you added flexibility in the playing and distribution of your sounds.

Four Stages of Sound in Software

If you are a new user trying out audio-editing software for the first time, follow this section closely. A basic understanding of how sound programs work will help you as we explore other software-related issues in the book. Here, we will examine how various software products handle four stages of the sound creation cycle: the capture, editing, processing, and output of sound files. Even if you don't use any of the programs we discuss here (new ones are shipping all the time!), the basic features should be relevant to the task at hand.

Most classes of software have settled into a variety of standard paradigms for creating and editing data and displaying it to the user. Anyone familiar with a word processor, for example, knows how to cut and paste. Users of graphics programs know what paint buckets, erasers, and beziér control points do, even in a program they have never used before.

Sound-editing software is no different. As sound-editing programs developed, the paradigm to borrow was—you guessed it—the recording industry. You can see play, stop, and pause buttons in nearly every package. Sliders (usually called *faders)* often control volume, and rows of blinking lights (reminiscent of the meters on a mixing board or tape player) show the current volume of a sound.

It's helpful to know the basic interface used in most sound-editing programs. It's even more important to know how your use of the editor affects the data and, eventually, the final product. Before we lose ourselves in the realms of file formats and data handling, we should look first at how sound-editing packages process the audio itself.

Capture

Many sound programs (including all the sound-editing products) let you record in real time or transfer existing material from tape or audio CD. When recording in real time, expect to see the studio/tape recorder metaphor.

Figures 4.1 through 4.3 show interface examples of several sound programs. Figure 4.1 shows the Macintosh's standard recording dialog box, which also appears within programs that rely on Apple's standard routines for recording sound. The sound waves emanating from the speaker icon indicate that audio is present. The vertical line to the right of the waves indicates that the maximum input volume has been exceeded—in other words, that clipping has occurred and that you are now recording distorted audio. The available recording time appears at the bottom of the dialog box. Figure 4.2 shows the recording panel for Macromedia's SoundEdit 16,

Figure 4.1

The Macintosh's standard recording dialog box, shown here in the Sound Control Panel

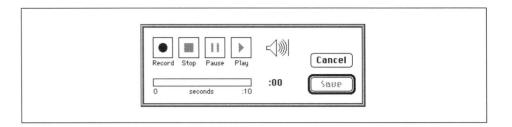

Figure 4.2

The recording panel for Macromedia's SoundEdit 16, version 2.0

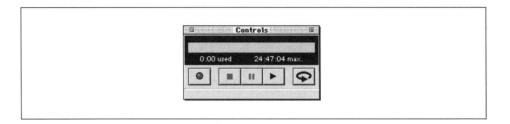

Figure 4.3

The recording panel for Digidesign's Sound Designer II

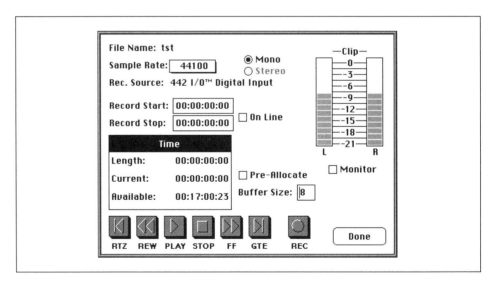

version 2.0. It is strikingly similar to Apple's, but note the addition of a toggle button for selecting looping playback of sounds. SoundEdit records directly to disk rather than to RAM; a 2 GB drive can store almost 24 hours of audio that has been recorded at an 8/22 sampling rate. The recording panel for Digidesign's Sound Designer II (Figure 4.3) still includes the same old Play/Stop buttons, even though it otherwise represents a radical departure from the original Apple design. Digidesign has added Return to Zero

(RTZ) and Go to End (GTE) buttons as well as input meters and SMPTE-compatible start and stop points (see the "DAT and Audiomedia" tutorial on the CD).

Before capturing, you need to select a sample rate and a sampling bit depth. It's always best to capture at the highest possible quality (for example, 16-bit, 44.1 kHz), and to work with your audio at that level until the last possible moment before downsampling. Most programs also give you some indication of how much time you have available for recording before your hard drive fills up or RAM is exhausted.

Editing

Once you have captured some audio, you probably will want to do some editing. At the least, this might involve cutting out excess silence at the beginning or end, or editing out bad takes of a voiceover. Most programs display sound as a waveform. You can select parts of the wave and cut, copy, or paste data as needed (refer to the "Basic Editing" tutorial on the CD).

Figures 4.4 and 4.5 show examples of how leading sound-editing programs display audio waveform data. Figure 4.4 shows two different views of the same sound wave in SoundEdit 16—the entire audio file and a closeup of waveforms within the file. The experienced eye recognizes the file as a piece of music because the peaks are evenly spaced to a rhythm. In the close-up view, notice that the file begins with silence and then—goodness, here are our old friends, Frequency and Amplitude, from Chapter 1! In Figure 4.5, we see the main edit window in Sound Designer II, which shows both an overview of the entire file and a closeup of a selected region. The irregular jumps in timing and amplitude reveal that this file contains voiceover data. The slight spike at the end of the region is probably a "t" or a "k" at the end of a word. With practice, you can learn to edit sound visually, rather than having to preview every single selection.

There are two main metaphors for sound editing: destructive and non-destructive. With destructive editors such as SoundEdit 16, you actually change the file data as you cut, copy, and paste. In non-destructive editing programs on the model of Digidesign's Sound Designer II or Macromedia's Deck II (see Figures 4.6 and 4.7), you define regions within the file and then play the selected data in the order you specify. The software knows how to glue the various sections together so that they play back seamlessly. This is possible because the computer can jump around in the audio on your hard disk, something that can't be done with audio tape. Some software packages can even crossfade from one audio segment to another, allowing the old segment to fade out while the new one fades in (see the "Non-Destructive Editing" tutorial on the CD).

Look to the
CD-ROM

Figure 4.4

These two views of the same sound wave in SoundEdit 16 show the entire audio file (top) and a closeup of waveforms within the file (bottom).

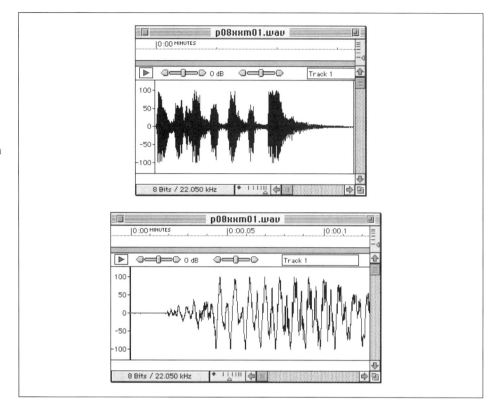

Figure 4.5

The main edit window in Sound Designer II shows an overview of the entire file in the topmost area and a closeup of a selected region in the main part of the window.

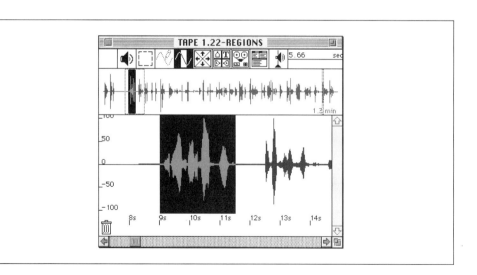

Figure 4.6

The Playlist window in Sound Designer II functions according to a non-destructive editing metaphor.

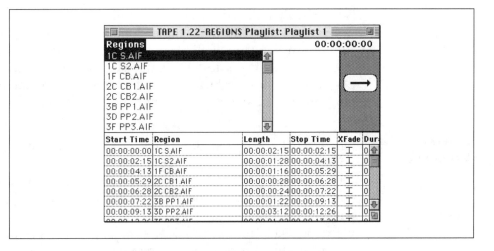

Figure 4.7

The Tracks window in Macromedia's Deck II shows another example of non-destructive editing principles.

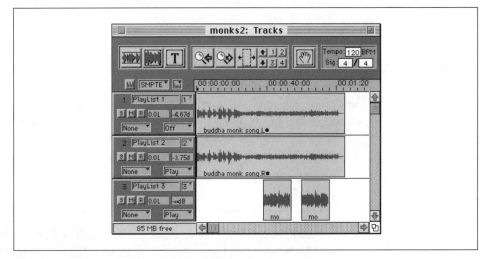

Figure 4.6 shows the Playlist window in Sound Designer II. When a previously defined region is selected in the top half of the window, it also is highlighted automatically in the waveform display (refer back to Figure 4.5). You can drag regions in any order into the playlist area in the bottom half of the window, where they are played sequentially. In the Tracks window of Macromedia's Deck II (Figure 4.7), the two regions in Track 3 have been drawn from the same sound file. Region start and stop points can be easily adjusted by clicking and dragging, and the entire region can be dragged forward or backward.

There are some advantages to non-destructive editing. The first is obvious: you don't irreversibly alter the data when you cut and paste. Another is potentially reduced file size: you can reference the same copy of data as many times as you like without doubling or tripling the size of the file. Non-destructive editing also requires that the hard disk be capable of near-instantaneous access to various areas of the file to avoid gaps in sound playback. It's not hard to see why fast SCSI throughput and peak hard disk performance are critical for this type of application.

Processing

Once you have edited down a raw sound data file to include only the good stuff, you are ready to begin processing the sound. Processing often involves mixing multiple files together or using digital effects to alter or enhance sound quality. To alter sound, you might, for example, use ambient effects such as delay (echo) to lend a dreamy or ghost-like quality to a voice, or to add reverb to a door slam, so it sounds as though it occurred in a gymnasium. Enhancing sound requires a bit more care and often involves adjusting *equalization* (increasing or reducing the level of various frequencies in the signal, popularly abbreviated as *EQ)* or using a *dynamics compressor* to smooth out changes in volume.

Nearly every sound-editing package lets you do some type of mixing. Some programs, such as Deck II and SoundEdit 16, have an intuitive mixing interface. Others, such as Sound Designer II and Opcode's Audioshop (a demo is on the accompanying CD), are less straightforward. Most packages also include effects, sometimes through third-party *plug-ins* such as the one in Figure 4.8. Plug-ins are software programs that can add new features or functions to an existing program.

Figure 4.8

The Voice Processor from AnTares Systems, a plug-in for Sound Designer II, combines EQ, dynamic compression, and effects to improve the quality of voiceover.

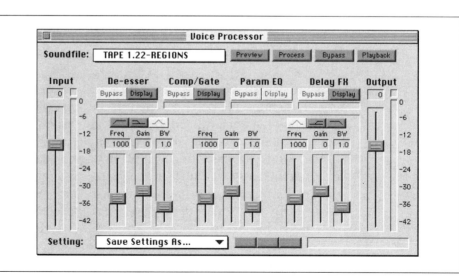

Output

After you have completed processing, it's time to export the sound files in the proper format so that they can be integrated into your presentation. This usually involves downsampling to lower bit-depths and sample rates and saving the file in a particular format such as AIFF or WAV.

System-Level Aspects of Audio

The system is your friend; the system is also your enemy. It lets you create great multimedia content. It also has to be dragged kicking and screaming through the process of creating great multimedia content. The love-hate relationship many of us have with our computers is great fodder for day-time talk shows.

Once again, the best use of the tools comes from knowing the advantages and disadvantages of a multitude of options, and then selecting a strategy that makes the best compromise. Let's examine some of the options (and their ramifications) in the following sections.

Audio File Types

As a general rule, multimedia computers have three basic schemes for playing sound:

❑ **Digitize audio and play recorded samples from memory or disc storage.** The most common example is playback of a sound file from CD-ROM or a hard drive.

❑ **Send device control information** to control an external hardware device, and make that device do most of the work. Examples include a MIDI synthesizer or standard (*RedBook*) CD audio streaming from a CD-ROM player.

❑ **Send commands to a software-based "virtual" device to trigger a series of samples or synthesized sounds.** This third strategy, a hybrid of the first two, is just beginning to emerge. Examples include the MusicTrack interface in QuickTime 2.0 and the MOD file format.

In this section we will discuss all three approaches and the benefits and drawbacks of each.

Why Are Sound File Types Important?

For multimedia sound developers, each file type is like a different type of tool. Depending on the job, you may need sounds to perform one way instead of another. Some file types are cross-platform, but others aren't.

Some are supported by a range of multimedia authoring and editing tools, but others aren't. Each file type provides a different level of performance in terms of how it affects memory usage and disk performance during authoring and playback.

For example, snd resources are Macintosh-specific and can be saved right into a document. This can be an advantage if you are creating a HyperCard stack for students to share with one another at school, but it will cause trouble if your presentation is destined for a Windows PC. Choosing the right file format for the job can have a significant impact on the performance of your presentation.

Recorded Sample Data

This category encompasses the standard sound files with which most of us are familiar. There are many, many sound file formats in use today. Each computer platform has its own collection; there are at least four or five file types for each. Macintosh file formats, for example, include AIFF, AIFC, snd resources, QuickTime, SoundEdit, and Sound Designer. There are at least three or four additional formats as well, but we will not cover them because they are rarely seen in multimedia production.

Why are there so many types of files? A major reason is that some file types have properties or features that make them particularly useful or manageable. Some file formats, such as the Instrument format used in Deluxe Music Construction Set, have been created for specific sound-oriented programs. Others, including AIFC, MPEG, and IMA, have been created to optimize various properties of data compression.

Another reason for the proliferation of file formats is the fact that once sought-after features have outlived their useful life. One way to correct the shortcomings is to define a new file type with the desired features. For example, the AIFF file format has become increasingly popular because it is cross-platform and works for both Macintosh and Windows development. The RIFF format is used on Windows machines for both Wave and MIDI files. Snd files, which used to be the standard for Macintosh, are limiting in cross-platform applications because the PC file architecture has no allowance for a resource fork. For information about resource forks, see the "Macintosh Resources" sidebar on page 79.

A third reason behind the large number of file formats is that certain sound-editing applications have become standards. As of this writing, two of the most popular sound-editing programs on the Macintosh are SoundEdit 16 from Macromedia and Sound Designer II from Digidesign (you will meet some of the many other editors with excellent features in

Chapter 9). Because these two applications are widely used, many other sound applications support their file formats.

Considering the plethora of sound file types, one might wonder why we aren't completely mired in file format anarchy. One restricting factor is the limited number of formats that the most popular sound-editing and multimedia authoring tools support. The six most popular formats in use are AIFF, snd Resource, QuickTime, SoundEdit, Sound Designer II, and Microsoft Wave. Table 4.1 summarizes the characteristics of each format.

Audio Interchange File Format (AIFF)   AIFF (also called Audio IFF) was created by Apple in 1988. It grew out of a proprietary file format (called *IFF*) developed by Electronic Arts and was designed as an *interchange format*—intended to facilitate the transferral of data between platforms. To this extent it has succeeded, and today AIFF files are supported on the Macintosh, UNIX, and Windows platforms. AIFF is the most widely supported sound format on the Macintosh.

File Type	Extension (PC)	Supported Platforms	Plays from RAM	Plays from Disk
Audio Interchange File Format	.AIF	Mac, PC, Unix	Yes	Yes
snd Resource		Mac	Yes	No
QuickTime	.MOV	Mac, PC	Yes[1]	Yes
Sound Designer II		Mac, PC[2]	Yes[3]	Yes
SoundEdit		Mac	Yes	No
Microsoft Wave	.WAV	PC, Mac[4]	Yes	Yes

Table 4.1

A summary of the main audio file types encountered in multimedia production

[1] On the PC, QuickTime movies cannot be preloaded into RAM.

[2] On the PC, Sound Designer files are supported by Sonic Foundry's Sound Forge and Digidesign's Session 8.

[3] Sound Designer files can be previewed from RAM in some cases, but they usually play from disk.

[4] Wave files are supported by many sound editors on the Macintosh, but they aren't supported by Macintosh multimedia authoring tools.

An AIFF file is designed to hold an unlimited number of audio channels. As commonly implemented, however, AIFFs usually contain either one channel (mono) or two channels (stereo). While the format supports up to 32 bits of sample data, 8-and 16-bit files are the most common. AIFF is an *interleaved* file format, which means that the data for multichannel files is written in alternating chunks (somewhat like the teeth of a zipper coming together). To facilitate cross-platform exchange, AIFF files have no resource fork; they contain only data.

AIFF really includes two formats: AIFF and AIFC (the *C* stands for "compressed"). The compressed format supports Apple's MACE compression ratios of 3:1 and 6:1.

AIFF is an ideal format for playing long segments of audio. Thanks to the Apple Sound Manager, AIFF files can play directly from disk rather than having to load completely into RAM before playback. The Sound Manager achieves this through a buffering scheme. Data from disk fills a small RAM buffer. As the sound plays from the buffer, the disk can be accessing and loading the next segment of audio. This "bucket brigade" approach is a very efficient way to obtain fast performance (i.e., the load time is limited to the first seek/buffer operation) with minimal impact on available RAM.

snd resource The snd resource format was one of the first created for the Macintosh and still exists only on the Mac. All system beeps and System 7 sound files are resource files (see the "Macintosh Resources" sidebar).

There are two types of sound resources, creatively named Type 1 and Type 2. Type 1 resources are used exclusively by HyperCard; when you paste a sound resource into a HyperCard stack, it becomes a Type 1 resource.

Originally, it probably made more sense to store sounds as resources because they were part of the interface; they were not edited and embedded into many documents other than sound files and HyperCard stacks. Snds are the traditional format of choice for HyperCard developers and have the advantage of being contained within the HyperCard stack, so developers never have to worry about the sound file becoming detached from the document that plays the sound.

Snd resources have several important characteristics of interest to multimedia developers. First, as previously mentioned, you can embed many snds into one file, which is useful for creating self-contained documents. In addition, snd resources load into RAM and play back from RAM. This characteristic can be a benefit or a drawback and has important ramifications (ahem!) for planning how sound playback might affect the performance of your multimedia presentations on different machines. We'll discuss some of

MACINTOSH RESOURCES

Resources are a special part of the Macintosh file format. The Macintosh file structure is made up of two parts; a *data fork* and a *resource fork*. The data fork is designed to contain data that changes frequently within a file—for example, text in a word processing document or numbers in a spreadsheet. The resource fork is designed to contain interface items that are commonly used by the program, such as menus, dialog boxes, icons, and windows. Figure 4.9 shows some typical resources.

Figure 4.9

A sample of standard resource types: alerts, cursors, dialog boxes, fonts, icons, patterns, sounds, windows, XCMDs, and XFCNs (pronounced "X-commands" and "X-functions")

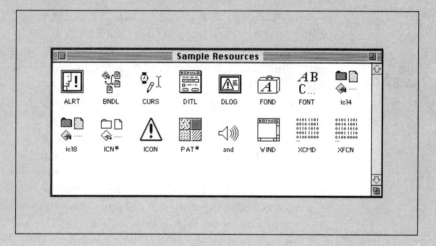

the performance aspects of different file types in the "Audio Files: Things to Consider" section of this chapter.

QuickTime Apple's QuickTime technology is a powerful tool for multimedia developers. For sound designers, the appeal of QuickTime is a bit more pragmatic: QuickTime was the first system-level technology for synchronizing sound to graphics. Best of all, QuickTime gives first priority to preserving the playback of audio, even if it means dropping frames of video.

People usually think of QuickTime movies as digital video tracks that also happen to contain audio. But you also can create QuickTime movies that contain only audio. At their most basic, audio-only QuickTime movies can serve as pointers to an external AIFF file, but you also can integrate the AIFF data into the file by saving the movie as a self-contained document.

QuickTime's time-based architecture brings some special features to sounds that are played as QuickTime documents, so it deserves particular attention. For example, QuickTime lets you change the playback rate of sounds on the fly. The controller bar provides an interface for changing volume or skipping around through a sound. Finally, the new Music Tracks and QuickTime Musical Instruments introduced in QuickTime version 2.0 provide a software-based synthesizer for playing music. This points the way to some exciting new possibilities, which will lead to smaller file sizes and enhanced interactive potentials in music for multimedia.

One of the most promising audio-related QuickTime innovations introduced with version 2.0 is support for the 4:1 *IMA* compressed audio format established by the Interactive Multimedia Association (IMA). The IMA compressor works in two stages. Files are compressed using the MoviePlayer utility, included in the Utilities folder on the CD that accompanies this book (SoundEdit 16 version 2.0 can also save sound data in the IMA format). Then Sound Manager 3.1 automatically decompresses the audio at playback. With the IMA compressor, you can compress a 16/44 file to the same size as an 8/22 file, yet the fidelity is much closer to the 16/44 original. It sounds fantastic in comparison to 8/22. You can also compress 16/22 material to the same size as an 8/11 file. The IMA compressor's magic won't compress 8-bit files at a 4:1 ratio; it works only with 16-bit data. If you try to compress an 8/22 document, the material will automatically be upsampled to 16/22 before compression takes place, so your savings will actually be only 2:1. Always start with 16-bit source material for the best results using IMA compression.

There are two other performance considerations when using IMA compressed files. First, IMA files place a greater load on the CPU during playback, since decompression happens on the fly. Second, IMA is designed to play from the hard disk rather than from RAM, so looping playback of music tracks isn't as seamless as it could be.

Look to the
CD-ROM

SoundEdit   This format was created by Farallon Computing for their sound-recording and -editing program, SoundEdit. SoundEdit was probably the first well-known sound-editing program for the Macintosh.

Macromedia purchased SoundEdit from Farallon in 1991 and upgraded the product first to SoundEdit Pro and then to SoundEdit 16. The newer versions added multitrack mixing features to the product and used a new, proprietary file format. As a result, SoundEdit Pro and SoundEdit 16 files can be opened and edited only in their respective applications. The updates retain the ability to save finished files as standard SoundEdit, however, to maintain compatibility with the wide variety of programs that support the original SoundEdit format.

Standard SoundEdit files are 8-bit 22.254 kHz. The original SoundEdit software could perform basic functions on 16-bit files created with other applications but was designed primarily as an 8-bit environment. One of SoundEdit's most useful functions was its ability to create *looping sound files* so that segments of audio (usually music or background sound-effect ambiences) could play repeatedly. SoundEdit could also open and edit snd resources and AIFF files and was a good tool for converting files into different formats.

SoundEdit (as well as SoundEdit Pro and SoundEdit 16) had proprietary 4:1 and 8:1 compression options that preceded the Apple standard, MACE. These proprietary schemes aren't supported by other applications and are therefore of limited usefulness.

In the days before the Macintosh offered built-in sound input jacks, the MacRecorder digitizer was an integral part of SoundEdit. This device connected to a serial port and contained a small microphone and a line input jack. If you have an older Macintosh without an audio jack, the MacRecorder is still a good, cost-effective method for digitizing sound into the computer.

Sound Designer At about the same time that Farallon was leading the charge for simple Macintosh-based sound editing, Digidesign was pioneering in the professional audio market. Their sound-editing programs, Sound Designer and Sound Designer II, worked in conjunction with Digidesign's proprietary DSP-based hardware: Audiomedia, SoundTools, and ProTools. This hardware provided substantially faster performance for playing and editing large, high-quality 16/44 stereo files.

Sound Designer was the first Macintosh sound-editing program to introduce the concept of non-destructive editing. Destructive editing, the only technique available prior to the advent of Sound Designer, can be slow for large audio files, since the disk is constantly reading and writing large chunks of data. When files are in 16/44 stereo format, for example, they can quickly expand beyond several hundred megabytes.

Look to the
CD-ROM

Rather than change the data on the disk, Sound Designer uses *regions* and *playlists* to edit and rearrange sound data. Users define specific regions within the sound file—for example, a single word, a sentence, or a section of a song. Then they can arrange regions within a playlist so that sounds play in the desired order.

Most high-end audio-editing programs, including Macromedia's Deck II, Passport's Alchemy, SoundEdit 16, Opcode's Audioshop and Studio Vision, and Mark of the Unicorn's Digital Performer, support the Sound Designer II format. Some programs support regions and playlists within Sound Designer

II files as well; users have the option of either importing any number of regions or playlists within a file, or importing the entire file in one piece.

Microsoft Wave The Wave (.WAV) file format is the standard for Windows-based PCs. The format supports multiple bit depths (8 and 16), multiple sampling rates (44.1, 22.050, and 11.025) and both stereo and mono sound. To facilitate the transfer of files between Macs and PCs, several sound-editing applications, including SoundEdit 16, Audioshop, Alchemy, Sound Designer II, and Session support the Wave format.

The Wave file format is actually a type of RIFF file. Also, there are special compressed formats for Wave files that are less standard and not fully supported in a cross-platform environment. Microsoft ADPCM (similar in functionality to the IMA compressed format) and DSP Group's TrueSpeech are two compressed file formats that fall within the Wave category.

Hybrids

So far, we've looked at two sound playback strategies: digital audio and MIDI (if you missed the MIDI part, check Chapter 3). These approaches have been in use for more than ten years, ever since the personal computer market hit its stride in the early 1980s. In the past few years, however, a new method for sound playback has emerged—one which combines the two approaches, taking advantage of the strengths of each. For lack of a standard term, we will call them hybrids.

Like MIDI, a hybrid uses a data stream of events to trigger sounds, thereby duplicating a musical performance. But rather than sending that data to an external device such as a MIDI synthesizer, hybrids trigger digitally sampled sounds stored in a computer's RAM. This frees the user from dependence on external MIDI hardware.

Think of playing back a one-minute selection of piano music. As digitized sound, this amount of music would constitute a fairly large file. A MIDI file would be much smaller, but you would need a synthesizer to hear the music. However, if you had 88 separate samples (one for each note on the piano) triggered in the proper sequence, you could play long segments of music that sound just like a piano. The file would be smaller because the same sample is used each time a particular note is played.

To the best of our knowledge, there are currently three technologies that fit in the hybrid category: Apple's QuickTime Music Architecture (QTMA), software synthesis from Seer Systems and InVision Interactive, and the MOD file format.

QuickTime Music Tracks With the release of QuickTime version 2.0, Apple added a Music Track to the QuickTime specification. You create a Music Track by importing a standard MIDI file into a QuickTime document. The MIDI data is converted into a QuickTime-specific format and is played through the QuickTime Musical Instruments system extension. The extension, which loads into memory during startup, contains samples licensed from Roland Corporation (Roland was one of the original movers behind the General MIDI specification, and their Sound Canvas MIDI module was the first standard General MIDI playback device). The samples included in the Musical Instruments extension are 12-bit compressed files.

In QuickTime version 2.2, Apple has opened the QTMA to allow third-party developers to create custom instrument sets and instrument editors. Sounds can also be stored directly in a movie, with the result that developers will have better opportunities to customize their musical scores.

The MIDI, synthesizer, and sampler markets have long been supported by many companies that create custom samples and synthesizer patches. At least one of these, InVision Interactive, is creating custom instruments for software synthesis. These promise to be a tremendous improvement over the marginal Roland samples shipped with QuickTime.

Software synthesis Seer Systems has developed a software synthesis engine for Intel-based PCs. It is somewhat similar to QTMA in that both approaches send MIDI data to a software synthesizer that resides in RAM. This technology was conceived by Stanley Jungleib and Dave Smith, founding members of both the MIDI Manufacturer's Association and Sequential Systems (makers of the Prophet series of synthesizers). The synthesizer engine was written by David Roach (our heroic technical editor) and Frank Kurzawa. The software synthesizer takes advantage of the sound card's D-to-A converter to play significantly higher-quality sound than would be possible through FM. Software synthesis requires a fairly hefty processor—at least a fast 486 DX machine. Many of the new Pentiums now come with a 16-bit sound chip on the motherboard.

Even on fast Pentiums, this software synthesizer can gobble up anywhere from 0.5 to 3 percent of the available CPU time per voice. An advanced voice-stealing algorithm allows up to 32 voices to play simultaneously along with reverberation while the machine goes about its daily chores, even playing movies. As CPU horsepower increases in general, these techniques will become more and more commonplace.

A similar software synthesis engine is CyberSound VS from InVision Interactive. CyberSound VS has the added advantage of being cross-platform.

One question that remains to be resolved with both of these technologies, however, is their method of distribution. Multimedia developers may be required to pay licensing fees or royalties for the privilege of distributing the synthesis engine with their presentations. On the other hand, hardware manufacturers or computer distributors and resellers may license the technology directly and include it as part of the purchase price of a new computer. In either case, software synthesis is an extremely promising development for music composers working in multimedia.

MOD files The MOD file format is one of the more interesting formats to emerge in recent years. MOD files combine sampled audio data with performance data. The samples are loaded into RAM at the start of playback, and the performance data stream triggers the samples at the proper time and at the proper pitch. One small sample—say, a bass synthesizer tone—can be pitch-shifted on the fly to create a complex bass pattern.

Although MOD files are usually created on the Amiga, they can be played back on a Macintosh through MOD players or the PlayMOD XCMD. XCMDs are segments of code that can add new capabilities to multimedia authoring tools like HyperCard, SuperCard, Director, and Authorware. They're somewhat analogous to Photoshop plug-ins.) Most MOD files distributed on-line are very much in the "techno" vein. The format lends itself to the repetitive bass lines and drumbeats associated with techno music. (But that doesn't mean that it couldn't be used for Bach!)

System Software

Now that you know more about file formats, we're ready to review how audio is handled by the Macintosh operating system.

Sound Manager

Apple's Sound Manager made its first appearance with System 4. It became really useful with the release of System 6.0.7. For the first time, users could play multiple sound files simultaneously. Interactive developers often want to use continuous sound such as music, voice, or ambience, but they also want to be able to mix in new sounds on the fly as the user interacts with the material—clicking on a button, for example. Sound Manager took care of mixing these sound channels into a single audio stream. Sound input was also added in System 6.0.7.

Version 3.0 of the Sound Manager sported an improved sound control panel and was more efficient in handling audio playback. Sound Manager 3.1 has improved the efficiency of sound playback on Power Macintosh computers, and added support for two compressed file formats, IMA and *µLaw* (pronounced "mu-Law," a format used by Sun computers and commonly found on the Internet). Version 3.1 also lets alert sounds play *asynchronously* (whenever available time in the CPU permits). When sound is played synchronously, it takes over the CPU until playback is completed. Before Sound Manager 3.1, the playback of a Macintosh alert sound would tie up the computer until the sound ended. With asynchronous alert sounds, other events (keyboard and mouse events, for example) can occur while an alert sound plays.

But starting with version 3.0, the Sound Manager added some new features that are of special interest to multimedia developers, including support for third-party sound hardware and for automatic sample rate conversion. Versions 3.0 and later also provide better handling of the process for opening and closing sound channels. Let's examine these improvements in greater detail.

Sound Manager's sample rate conversion   Probably the most significant improvement for ease of use is the ability of Sound Manager version 3.*x* to perform sample rate conversion during playback. If Sound Manager receives a sound at a sample rate other than the one that the sound playback hardware supports, Sound Manager automatically resamples the sound to the correct rate. This is important when you consider that different Macintosh models play sounds at different rates (refer back to Chapter 2). Older Macintosh models have a sample rate of 22.254 kHz, while newer models (mainly the Power Macintoshes, the PowerBook 500 series, and the Quadra AV series) play sounds at 22.050 kHz. The 22.050 rate is also standard for sound cards in Windows PCs.

Imagine what happens when you play a 22.050 sound through 22.254 hardware without resampling. A sound that should play using 22,050 samples every second is being sent at a slightly faster rate: an extra 204 samples are played every second. The sound plays at a slightly higher pitch, because the data is playing one percent faster. This is the same effect you get from speeding up a tape recorder. In its more pronounced form, this is affectionately known as "chipmunking." For most people chipmunking would not be a problem, but imagine the ramifications if you are creating a five-minute QuickTime movie. Your sound would be out of synchronization by three seconds by the time you reach the end. Anyone making a CD-ROM spoof of poorly dubbed foreign films will find this to be a great feature, but otherwise it's big trouble.

Thanks to Sound Manager's transparent handling of this issue, you need not worry about the playback rate of your Macintosh or the rate of the sample you are trying to play. It's already being taken care of—although the results aren't always pretty.

Here's the bad news. As anyone who has ever played 22.050 kHz sound back on a 22.254 kHz Macintosh will attest, the sound quality of Sound Manager's resampled audio is not as good as sounds that are sampled at a rate that matches the built-in hardware of that particular machine. If you recall the discussion of quantization noise from Chapter 1, Sound Manager's resampling tends to introduce grainy, crackling noise into a sound. This happens because Sound Manager must either add new bits or throw bits away during the automatic resampling process. If you ever have used a program like SoundEdit or Sound Designer to resample audio, you probably have spent at least a few seconds (even minutes, perhaps) watching a progress bar while the resampling takes place. Pity the poor Sound Manager struggling to handle this in real time! It does an admirable job considering the task, but there is certainly room for improvement. As with most things in the land of CPU bottlenecks, one looks hopefully to faster hardware running faster operating systems. In fact, 22.254 kHz played on Power Macs sounds much better than 22.050 kHz audio played on a Macintosh IIci.

We have two suggestions for those who must create sounds in 22.050 kHz format but are working on a 22.254 kHz machine. First, if possible, try to have a 22.050 kHz machine on hand—preferably a PC—for testing sounds. If that isn't possible, you can check any horrific-sounding 22.050 kHz files simply by converting them to 22.254 kHz. If the noise is still present at 22.254 kHz, don't blame it on Sound Manager. If it sounds great at 22.254 kHz but crummy at 22.050 kHz, hold your nose (and your ears) and press onward; it should sound acceptable on a 22.050 kHz machine.

Sound Manager's hardware driver support   With the advent of version 3.0, Sound Manager supports third-party sound playback hardware, as long as a software driver is present. Companies like Digidesign, Radius, TrueVision, and Spectral Innovations take advantage of this feature to let users channel their sound output to a device other than the Macintosh's built-in speaker or rear audio jack. Figure 4.10 shows the Macintosh's built-in audio output selected for playback using version 8.0 of the Sound Control Panel; note that the playback rate of 22.254 kHz 8-bit stereo is the only option available for a Macintosh IIci. Figure 4.11 shows an example of Sound Manager's support for third-party software drivers in version 3.*x* and later. The Digidesign sound driver is selected as the playback device. The only available playback rate is 44.1 kHz, but the user can select 8- or 16-bit

Figure 4.10

The Macintosh's built-in audio output selected for playback in the Sound Control Panel

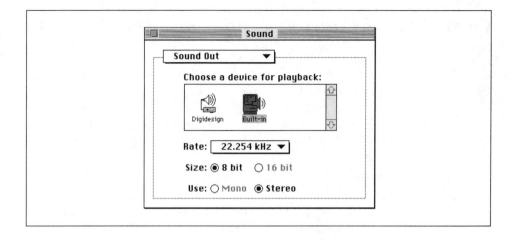

Figure 4.11

The Digidesign Sound Driver selected as the playback device in the the Sound Control Panel

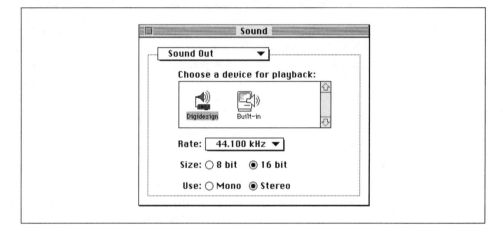

sample depth and mono or stereo. Thanks to the Sound Manager's automatic conversion, this setting plays 22.050 kHz files at the proper rate.

As you may recall from Chapter 2, the Macintosh actually has eight sound channels, and Sound Manager lets you play all eight of them at the same time using programs such as Macromedia Director (of course, don't expect your animation to be zipping across the screen at that point).

In a nutshell, if you plan to distribute your sounds to a broad audience, you should use only the new standard rates of 44.1 kHz, 22.050 kHz, or 11.025 kHz. The only time you should use the older sample rate is if you plan to show your presentation on a specific Macintosh model that supports the old rate.

Overview of Current Frequently-Used Formats

By now you may be wondering, "It's great to know about all these file formats, but which one should I be using?" The answer, as with most aspects of multimedia, is—it depends.

The majority of CD-ROM titles currently in circulation use 8-bit AIFF audio at sample rates of 11.025 kHz or 22.050 kHz. This is due to a combination of performance limitations:

❏ The amount of storage available for sound (as opposed to the storage available for graphics or digital video)

❏ The speed at which data can be read from CD-ROM (with double-speed drives, rates of 120 KB to 150 KB per second are common)

❏ The amount of RAM available for sound and graphics

Working with computers is an exercise in bottleneck management. Most often, you will face a tradeoff between quality and performance. Every increase in speed and capacity is instantly pushed to the maximum. File formats that generate larger files require more storage space and more processor time at playback. At the same time, most developers need to create material for an installed base of older, slower machines. Here are some important things to consider when deciding how and when to make tradeoffs.

> **Note:** *By the end of 1996, we hope to see most CD-ROM titles incorporating IMA compressed audio, with playback from PowerMacs or Pentiums that have quad-speed drives.*

Audio Files: Things to Consider

Computer platforms have become increasingly powerful, but we haven't quite reached the point where viewing a multimedia presentation is as seamless or engaging as viewing a video or film. Consider that a film contains music, dialog, and sound effects—that requires at least three stereo tracks of CD-quality audio! Some sound-editing applications are able to play over eight tracks of simultaneous 16/44 sound if a fast processor is available, but only if not much else is happening on the screen during playback. If you throw some animation or QuickTime video into the stew and then try to play the whole thing back from CD-ROM, performance will slow to a crawl.

The solution involves compromise that balances the quality of the content with the capabilities of the platform. Most graphics are dithered from

24 to 8 bits. QuickTime movies are heavily compressed. Audio files are often downsampled to the lowest acceptable level of fidelity. What's the best trade-off?

Quality Versus File Size

From our earlier discussion of sample rates and bit depths (see Chapter 1), you will recall that a sound sampled at 16 bits of resolution at a rate of 44.1 kHz results in a digitized sound file that is as good a representation of the original sound as the human ear can detect. When you reduce bit depth from 16 to 8, you reduce dynamic range by one-half, and background noise becomes much more of a problem. Similarly, as the sample rate drops from 44.1 kHz to 22 kHz to 11 kHz, the highest frequency we can represent drops from 22 kHz to 11 kHz to 5.5 kHz. This is well below the top range of human hearing, so the listener notices that the sound lacks clarity and presence.

We have reviewed all of the above to emphasize a basic rule of digitized sound: as sample rate and bit depth increase, sound quality and file size increase as well.

The converse is also true. For the multimedia producer, there is one important benefit to using sounds digitized at lower bit depths and lower sample rates: file size is significantly reduced. The trick is to know when you can get away with using lower-fidelity files (refer to Chapters 6 and 7).

You can use frequency analysis tools to determine which frequencies are present in a sound file and then process the file accordingly. Macromedia Sound Edit 16, Digidesign's Sound Designer II, and Passport's Alchemy all offer graphic displays of the frequency content in a sound. Use equalization to remove any frequencies that might accidentally create aliasing (remember, any frequencies higher than just under half of two times the sample rate could cause trouble).

File size has additional ramifications beyond storage space on disk. Smaller files use less memory, so they load more quickly into RAM and leave more room for graphics and other data. Small files also transfer more quickly from CD. During playback, smaller files require less processor time, leaving the CPU free for other tasks.

Calculating Size Requirements

File size calculation actually includes two issues: size on disk and size in RAM. In most cases, available RAM is the more pressing concern. The size rquirement is a function of sample resolution, sample rate and—for compressed audio—the compression ratio. Knowing the sample resolution and rate of a file, one can quickly do the math to see how much space a file will require on disk or in memory.

Calculating file sizes for 8-bit files is easy. Each sample uses one byte. Just multiply the sample rate times the number of seconds in file. For example, one second of 8-bit 22 kHz sound requires 22 KB of storage space or RAM. One minute of 8/22 sound requires 1320 KB, or 1.3 MB. Double these numbers for stereo data. A good rough measurement for 8/22 audio is to count on a little more than 1 MB per minute, or 2 MB per minute for stereo data.

For 16-bit files, multiply the sample rate by the number of seconds, and then double the result. One second of 16/44 sound requires 88 KB of storage space or RAM. One minute of 16/44 sound uses 5280 KB, or 5.2 MB. A good rule of thumb for 16/44 audio, then, is 5 MB per minute, or 10 MB for stereo data.

Silence takes up as much room as music. It may not seem obvious at first, but one second of silence has the same number of samples as one second of sound.

Disk throughput is also a factor in determining file size. Let's assume that the CD is a double-speed drive capable of a sustained data transfer rate of 150 KB per second. In cases where the sound is spooling from disc, a stereo 8/22 file will claim almost a third of the bandwidth. Similarly, loading a 600 KB sound into memory will take four seconds. Some developers choose to reduce sound file sample rates just to speed the load times of a presentation.

RAM-Based Versus Disc-Based Playback

There are two main ways to play back sound files: load them into RAM prior to playback, or stream the audio data from the disc as it plays. Each strategy has advantages and disadvantages.

Sounds played from RAM are often more responsive. This is especially true for CD-ROM, unless great care is taken to optimize the CD so that the sound files are written close to the document calling the sound, thereby minimizing the seek time of the CD drive's data-reading mechanism. Playing sounds from RAM also reduces the risk that sound playback might be interrupted if new graphics are loaded from the disc while sound is playing. Finally, looped sounds *must* be played from RAM in order to loop smoothly.

The main drawback of playing sound from RAM is that sound can take up lots of room. As we just saw, one minute of stereo 16/44 sound would need more than 10 MB of RAM to play back from memory. Even thirty seconds of 8/22 mono uses over 650 KB. The memory needed for an authoring or playback application and a screenful of graphics is often at least 2 MB. If animation is occuring, additional graphics will be waiting in RAM,

THE THREE FACES OF COMPRESSION

You may be thinking, "If file sizes get so large, why not use compression?" Just to clarify what we can and cannot do with compression, let's take a minute to discuss the three faces of compression in audio. They are:

- ❏ *File compression,* using standard utilities such as Stuffit, Compact Pro, or PKZIP. This type of compression is often called *lossless compression,* since no data is lost in the compression process.
- ❏ *Compressed audio,* as in the MACE and IMA standards. Compressed audio takes advantage of the audio nature of the file format being compressed and is often referred to as *lossy compression,* since some of the data is permanently lost in the compression process.
- ❏ *Dynamic compression* (and its digital incarnations), which controls or limits the amplitude of sound waves

File compression reduces the amount of data in a file by reducing the amount of uniform, or *redundant,* data. With sound waveforms, however, the data often changes dramatically and unpredictably. Because much of the information is important, little is gained through file compression. Sound files with quiet levels compress smaller than files with loud levels because fewer bits are used to store data (a soundwave of maximum amplitude has a value of 255 and needs all 8 bits to store the data, whereas a low amplitude like 32 uses only 5 bits). But as we will see in later chapters, the low signal-to-noise ratio of 8-bit files behooves us to make the overall volume as high as possible.

Sound files containing many perfectly silent sections will also compress well, but finished sound files shouldn't contain much silence. When using file compression on audio, you'll rarely save more than 15 to 20 percent of the original file size. In most cases, it's not worth the time it takes to compress and decompress the file.

Compressed audio includes two main formats. The first and best-known—but not the best-sounding—is Apple's Macintosh Audio Compression and Expansion (*MACE*), which supports compression ratios of 3:1 and 6:1. Files compressed at 3:1 are one-third the size of the original file, but the data is lost forever. The sound quality is markedly noisier than the original, but if the original is dense material (loud rock and roll, for example), 3:1 compression is tolerable. MACE 6:1 compressed audio should be used only for voice in circumstances where storage requirements are critical. The 6:1 compressor filters high-frequency noise from the signal, and quality suffers as a result.

(continued)

A newer, higher-quality compression scheme was released as part of QuickTime 2.0. The IMA compressor works on 16-bit files and achieves a 4:1 compression ratio. The result sounds superior to 8-bit audio when you play it back on 16-bit hardware. The compressor is built into QuickTime 2.1 and can be accessed it using Movie-Player, which is on the CD that accompanies this book. The decompressor is built into Sound Manager 3.1, so this system extension must be present for sound play-back. This compressor is supported on both the Macintosh and Windows platforms.

Dynamic compression uses a standalone audio processor called a *compressor* (sometimes also called a *compressor/limiter* or *compressor/gate*—see Chapter 2). As analog audio signals enter the compressor, a circuit measures the amplitude (the volume) of the signal. When the signal exceeds a specified level, an amplifier automatically kicks in to reduce the volume of the signal. It's almost like having a box with a little man inside, sitting at a mixing board, turning the volume down when needed. Compressors are an important part of obtaining good sound at lower bit depths such as 8/22 because, by limiting or reducing the peaks in the amplitude of a signal, you can increase the overall volume without introducing distortion or clipping. This lets you capture samples at a louder volume, which provides a better signal-to-noise ratio.

Look to the
CD-ROM

leaving precious little room for long segments of audio. But short sounds that are used frequently and need to be very responsive (either to user actions or synchronized graphics) may be good candidates for RAM-based playback. Formats that play from RAM include snd resources, AIFF, and WAV files.

Sounds played from the disc require very little RAM because the sound is played continuously through a small buffer used by Sound Manager. When you need to play several minutes of continuous audio, disc playback is the best approach to take. As mentioned previously, the main drawback is that sound playback may stutter if the disc needs to access other information while the audio is playing. Formats that play from disc include AIFF and QuickTime audio.

Playback Platform

When selecting an audio file format, also keep in mind the strengths and weaknesses of the playback platform. For many developers this translates as, "What can I get away with on a 486 Windows PC with a double-speed drive?" One shortcoming of the Windows PC multimedia setup is that the

CD-ROM drive is usually accessed through, of all places, the *sound card!* When you are trying to play sound and are simultaneously grabbing data from the disc, all the information has to pass through the sound card's bus. Select RAM-based versus disc-based playback with care, and leave yourself some leeway when projecting the sustained data transfer rate from the disc.

Almost always, sound problems arise on the PC rather than on the Macintosh. For this reason, it's important to test on both platforms during development. The integration of Macintosh system software with audio playback hardware makes it easy to obtain predictable results with sound. On the PC, unfortunately, the variety of sound cards and drivers can cause nightmares during testing. Try to check playback on several different models of PC sound cards, as differences abound.

Summary

In this chapter we described sound data from the software perspective, starting with a review of basic sound-editing features. We then proceeded through a thicket of file formats to gain a better understanding of how different file types can affect performance. Eventually, all these sounds are passed to the Sound Manager, which has some potential plusses and minuses of its own, and we learned how to take the good with the bad. Finally, we put this information into the context of current usage, discussing the issues to consider when one must make the invariable compromises that confront every multimedia producer.

Congratulations! By now you should have enough background information to move into Part II, "Techniques." The dry discourse of techno-babble is behind you. From here on, we will be exploring multimedia audio production in the real world—at least, to the extent that multimedia production and the real world bear some resemblance to each other!

5

Configuring Your System

Here's a worn-out phrase for you: "the right tool for the job." It seems in this business that the right tool for the job is the one that won't be shipping for a few more months (that's why we have beta programs!). When you're called upon to do your sonic duty, one of the first things you'll have to figure out is "What tools do I need?" In real-world terms, the question is more likely to be "What can I do with the tools I have?"

In this chapter we will describe three hypothetical audio systems for three different levels of users. We will talk about using the hardware and software tools you already have and examine what additional tools you might want to acquire to get more mileage out of your system.

Three User Profiles

We make some broad assumptions about levels of audio experience in this section, but they are solidly based on years of technical support phone conversations with end users and meetings with clients in multimedia production suites. Let's be really imaginative and dub users as beginning, intermediate, or advanced.

❏ **Beginning** users have only a computer, a microphone, a CD-ROM player, and perhaps some speakers. Creating multimedia may not be your full-time job, but you're happy to dive in when the opportunity arises, because it sure beats writing reports. You're probably creating sound on a basic platform for one of two reasons:

- There is neither the need nor the budget to spend lots of time and money creating sounds, but you do need the capabilities for simple voiceover, background music, and a few button clicks for a presentation.

- You enjoy noodling around with multimedia and sounds, but you're still trying to convince your boss, spouse, or coworkers that you need some equipment.

❏ **Intermediate** users have some equipment to work with: a more powerful computer, more storage, and some audio- or video-digitizing hardware. You may be working primarily in graphics, video, programming, or any one of the many multimedia disciplines. All of us have become accustomed to wearing a number of different hats in this business—and you've just been handed a pair of headphones. You need a few more options than beginning users because

- you're responsible for delivering a range of multimedia services, and people expect you to produce high-quality audio.

- your business is large enough to have invested in some basic tools, and it's your job to use them to the best advantage.

❏ **Advanced** users are doing full-time multimedia production with lots of audio. Your work includes lots of voiceover, music, and sound effects. You're editing as well as recording audio on-site, using a dedicated studio space with standard audio recording equipment and digital audio hardware for the computer. You need to be "armed to the teeth" because

- you're processing audio for big projects on tight deadlines and must work as efficiently as possible.

- you need flexibility and lots of options. Today's job may be a corporate presentation with music and voiceover, but tomorrow you're doing a children's title with four tap-dancing monkeys singing at Carnegie Hall, and the day after that is a space opera, and after that is . . . Well, you can get the general idea by looking through an Educorp catalog.

In the Beginning

This section is devoted to beginning users. *Everyone* is a beginner at some point. But if you have a Macintosh, you have the tools you need to create digial audio from the moment you first take it out of the box and turn it on. Since the release of the LC and IIsi, Apple has included an audio input jack on every Macintosh model. (For a complete discussion of audio input hardware, see Chapter 2.) But don't despair if your ancient Macintosh doesn't have a built-in input jack; other options are available.

Input Devices for Older Macintoshes

If you have an older Macintosh model, you can use either Macromedia's MacRecorder or Articulate Systems' VoiceImpact. These are inexpensive audio digitizing devices that combine a microphone, a 3.5 mm mono input jack, and an analog-digital converter chip. The digitizer passes the digital sound information to the Macintosh through one of the serial ports (modem or printer). Stereo recording requires two digitizers, one for each port. These devices can create 8-bit sound at rates up to 22.254 kHz. The VoiceImpact uses an external power source, while the MacRecorder draws its power from the port. Both devices have knobs that allow you to adjust your input volume. (We'll discuss input volumes shortly.)

Hooking It Up

There's not much to configuring a basic audio system. Depending on the vintage of your Macintosh, you can use the newer PlainTalk microphone, the older Silver Dollar, or the even older serial port digitizer. Plug the microphone or line source into the microphone jack (remember to use an in-line attenuator when inputting line-level signals on older Macintosh models). Plug speakers or headphones into the speaker jack. *Voilá,* you're ready to go!

Look to the
CD-ROM

If you have third-party audio hardware, you can access it through the Sound Control Panel as long as you have a software driver (a System Extension) for the hardware and you're running Sound Manager version 3.0 or later. If you've read this far, perhaps you've already looked at the CD in the back of the book and installed Sound Manager version 3.1 from the CD. If not, be sure to install it the next time you fire up your Macintosh. If you're using System 7.5 or greater, Sound Manager 3.1 is already installed in the system.

Recording into the Macintosh Audio Input

The Macintosh's built-in audio input is a 3.5 mm stereo jack (denoted by the microphone icon) on the back of the CPU. Some models—the PowerMac 8500, for example—may also have RCA jacks for input. There are three ways to record a signal into a Mac with a standard configuration:

- Use the external microphone;
- Capture directly from an internal CD-ROM drive; and
- Run a line-level audio source into the input jack.

Look to the
CD-ROM

Here's the sequence of steps for recording with the built-in audio input. (Refer to the tutorials on the CD for a demonstration.)

1. Open the Sound Control Panel.

2. Click on the pop-up menu in the upper left corner and select Sound In. You should see a window similar to Figure 5.1. If other input drivers (such as Macromedia's MacRecorder, Articulate Systems Voice Impact, or the Digidesign sound driver) are installed, they will be displayed here. Clicking the Options... button displays the dialog box shown in Figure 5.2.

3. Click the Options... button. If the Macintosh's built-in input is selected, and you have an internal CD-ROM drive, you should see a dialog box similar to the one in Figure 5.2. Selecting an input option routes that audio source to the Sound Manager. The Playthrough option passes

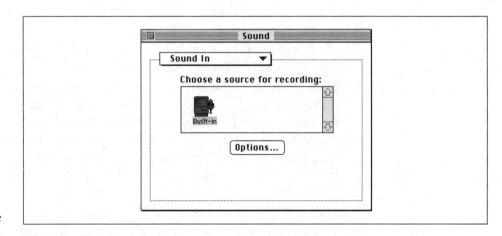

Figure 5.1

The Sound Control Panel showing that built-in sound input is available

Figure 5.2

A Macintosh with an internal CD-ROM drive shows these sound input options.

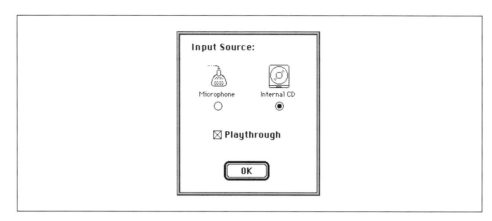

Figure 5.3

The standard Apple recording panel

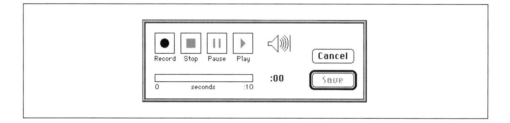

the signal directly to the Macintosh speaker so you can monitor your input while capturing or just listen to CDs through your Macintosh.

4. Now that you've selected an input source, you're ready to record. Click on the pop-up menu in the upper left corner of the Sound dialog box again and select Alert Sounds.

5. Click the Add... button to open the standard Apple recording panel. A dialog box similar to the one in Figure 5.3 appears. If you speak into the microphone or play your audio source material, you should see sound waves animating from the speaker icon. The sound waves correspond to input volume. The vertical line to the right of the waves indicates that the maximum input volume has been exceeded and clipping is taking place.

6. Click the Record button to record a sound.

7. When you've finished recording, you'll be prompted to name the new sound. Type a new name and click OK.

After recording, you should see your new sound listed along with the standard alert sounds. Sounds that are recorded using this method are saved as System 7 sounds within your System File. To access them, open the System Folder and double-click on the System File. Drag the sound out of the System onto the desktop, or any folder or drive. You can play the sound simply by double-clicking on it.

Recording with the Apple Microphone

When you record directly into the computer, you obviously have to be close to the CPU. In many cases, you may be in the middle of an office, with computer peripherals humming gaily, coworkers chatting busily, and HVAC systems droning. It's not exactly the ideal situation for a nice, quiet recording session. Here are several countermeasures you can take to achieve a better recording.

Being careful with your microphone technique will help a lot. If possible, put the microphone on a stable surface (the Plain Talk microphone is designed to rest atop your monitor) and keep the microphone about six inches away from your mouth. Try to keep your voice tone as even as possible. If you're recording in your office, take a moment to listen to the background noise and do what you can to minimize it. This could include closing doors, turning off fans or ventilators, and shutting down unneeded computer peripherals (mounted Syquest drives are particularly dangerous!). Think of creative ways to minimize the noise from your environment, even if it means crawling under your desk.

Even though all Power Macintoshes, AV models, and the Powerbook 500 series support 16-bit audio, you can only record 8/22 sound if you're using the Sound Manager's standard recording panel. To capture sounds at higher bit depths and sample rates, you need software that supports these rates.

When you record using the Sound Manager's standard recording panel, it's likely that you're recording to RAM rather than to disk, so you can't capture long passages. Although the Sound Control Panel shows a maximum recording length of ten seconds, the sample rates and recording lengths supported depend on the software program you're using. Simple Text, for example, can record 25 seconds at 8/22 with 6:1 MACE compression. This high a compression rate should be used only for speech, as the audio quality is poor.

Recording from CD

Recording directly from CD is a snap if your Macintosh has an internal CD-ROM drive. Just select the CD-ROM drive as your input source in the Sound Control Panel (see Figure 5.2) and record away. Direct CD recording isn't the best method, however, because the analog audio output of the CD is digitized during capture. You'll obtain better quality by copying digital audio directly from the disc using QuickTime and MoviePlayer. The first CD drive to support this function was the Apple CD300 (earlier-model Apple CD drives such as the venerable CDSC won't work). A number of sound-editing programs and dedicated CD-capture utilities also support copying of audio data (for a discussion of such programs, see Chapter 9). Let's look at how it's done in Apple's MoviePlayer.

Audio CD Capture from MoviePlayer

Look to the CD-ROM

Before continuing with this topic, please read the sidebar "About Copyright." End of sermon.

If you don't already have a copy, Apple's MoviePlayer utility can be found on the CD in the back of this book, along with a tutorial demonstrating this process. When QuickTime is installed, MoviePlayer lets you import audio from an audio CD (also called *RedBook audio,* after the color of the cover of the official audio CD specification). You can save audio from CDs as an audio-only QuickTime movie.

To capture an audio track, select Open from the File menu and navigate to your audio CD within the File dialog box, selecting the track you'd like to grab (Figure 5.4). You'll need to know the track number; the Macintosh can't determine actual song names from the disc. Once you've selected a track, click the Convert... button, which displays a second File dialog box that prompts you to save the track with a file name. If you name the track and select OK, you capture the entire track. To capture just a limited section of the track, click the Options... button, which displays the dialog box shown in Figure 5.5.

To define a region of data for capture in the Import Options dialog box, you can either drag the handles at either end of the track or type values into the Start and End time displays. Pressing the spacebar starts or stops

Figure 5.4

MoviePlayer's File dialog box for capturing audio directly from a standard RedBook audio CD

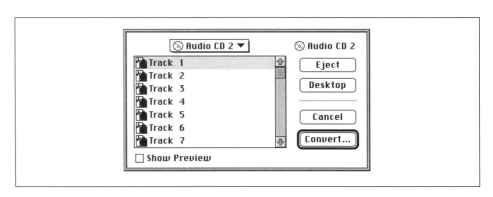

Figure 5.5

MoviePlayer's Import Options appear when you click the Options button of the Convert File dialog box.

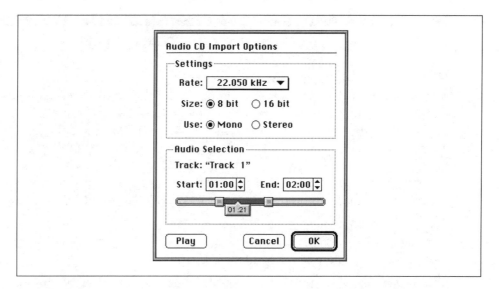

playback. The arrow keys move the current time marker (the moving box below the region) so that you can scan forward and backward through the selected region. Pressing Option and the forward arrow moves the current time marker to the end of the region; pressing Option and the back arrow moves it to the beginning of the region.

If you set the rates to anything other than 16/44 stereo, your sound data is automatically downsampled (and mixed to mono, unless you click the stereo button). Previews from the CD take place in mono, even if you have selected stereo for the final source.

ABOUT COPYRIGHT

Heads up! Unless you own a record company, have recorded your own material, or own a production music library, you're exposing yourself to copyright liability when you lift that Liberace tune off a CD. Many people assume they can get away with stepping over this boundary, but that's not always the case. Aside from the legalities, imagine how you'd feel if someone "borrowed" your multimedia presentation without permission. If you can write your own music, here's your big chance to show off. If not, look into buying some clip music; better yet, hire a musician to create a custom soundtrack. Your money will be well spent and will keep you out of court.

A REVIEW OF CD FORMATS

There are many different ways to format a CD, depending on the type of data you want to put on the disc. As a result, multiple formats have been defined by various standards organizations and manufacturing groups. Most of the standards are described by the name of a color, which is derived from the color of the cover on the final document that defined the specification. In the realm of audio for multimedia, you need to be concerned with only three varieties (*RedBook, YellowBook,* and the new *BlueBook)*, but we've listed the whole range here just to satisfy the curious. For more information, refer to "The Enhanced CD Fact Book" document on the CD that accompanies this book.

❏ *RedBook*, or CD-DA (Digital Audio) is the standard format for audio CDs, defined by Philips and Sony back in 1982.

❏ *YellowBook* is the format most often used in multimedia computing. It is a combination of computer data with audio data. There are three subsets of the Yellow Book specification:

■ *Mac HFS* uses the Macintosh Hierarchical File System for Mac CD-ROMs

■ *High Sierra* was designed to be read by any CD drive and eventually evolved into the ISO 9660 format, described next.

■ *ISO 9660*, named for the International Standards Organization, is common on DOS and Windows systems.

■ *CD-ROM XA (Extended Architecture)* is an extension of the YellowBook specification. It is derived mainly from the ISO 9660 format but has better audio and video capabilities for multimedia. CD-ROM XA also defines the physical format for Kodak Photo CD discs.

❏ *GreenBook* is the specification for *Compact Disc-Interactive (CD-I)* players like those available from Philips. This format insures compatible playback of audio CDs and Kodak PhotoCDs on CD-I players. CD-I discs, however, cannot be read on other types of CD-ROM drives.

❏ *OrangeBook* specification is for *CD-R (Recordable)* systems intended for archiving data on *magneto-optical (MO)* discs. It's proprietary to Philips and Sony and available only to their licensees. OrangeBook is a different recording technology from the one used by most CD recorders currently on the market, since the directory structure of the disc can be rewritten to reflect changes in the data structure (most of today's CD recorders can create only YellowBook or RedBook discs).

(continued)

❑ **WhiteBook** is a specification for video CDs and is rarely seen in the United States. This format will most likely be leapfrogged in the United States by the forthcoming *Digital Video Disc (DVD)* format announced by a consortium including Sony, Philips, and Matsushita and expected to be available by the end of 1996.

❑ **BlueBook** is the new standard for *stamped multisession enhanced CDs* (also commonly referred to as *CD Plus* or *CD+,* although the term is trademarked by Sony). The term "stamped multisession" reflects the fact that data is written to the disc in two sessions: the audio portion is similar to a RedBook partition, and the data portion is somewhat like a YellowBook partition. When a stamped multisession disc is mounted on a computer with the proper CD drivers, it appears as two separate volumes.

Sampling straight from CD can give you great audio, but you may be disappointed with the sound quality you achieve when you downsample directly from the Options dialog box. This has more to do with the sound volume of the content on the CD than with the nature of the downsampling algorithm. It's likely that captured data will be far below its maximum possible volume. Figure 5.6, for example, shows a 16/44 sample of a jazz trio captured directly from CD. When music is this quiet, it will sound bad

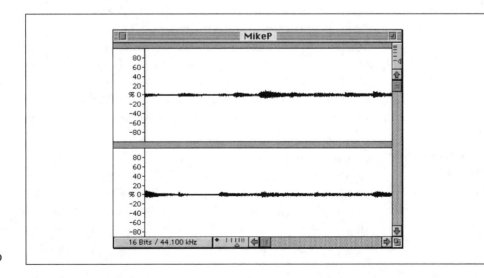

Figure 5.6

A 16/44 stereo sample of a jazz trio captured directly from CD

Figure 5.7

The music in this 16/44 stereo sample captured from CD is guaranteed to try the patience of even the most indulgent parents.

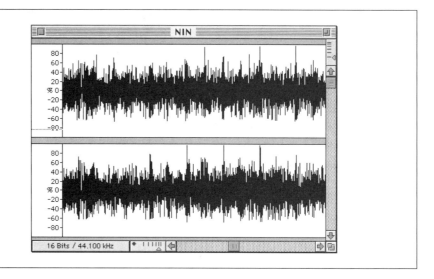

at lower bit depths and sample rates unless you increase the signal level before downsampling. The quality of music content with a broad dynamic range, such as jazz and symphonic styles, can suffer when downsampled, because background noise is more likely to be noticed by the listener.

Figure 5.7 shows yet another 16/44 stereo sample captured from CD. This example is about as loud as music on a CD will ever get. It has a high enough level to downsample well, but your boss may not find it appropriate for presentations.

The CD audio format of 16/44 has great dynamic range (96 dB), so it can reproduce quiet passages of music without discernible background noise. If you capture directly to an 8/22 file, on the other hand, the sound will be at the same volume, but it will be converted into a format that has much less dynamic range (48 dB), so background noise becomes a big problem. For best results, capture the data at 16/44 and then normalize and downsample it using a sound-editing program. More information on downsampling techniques will be provided in Chapter 6.

Line-level Capture

If you have source material on video or audio tape, you can capture straight from the line output on the video or tape deck (from here on, we'll use the device-neutral term "deck"). If your Macintosh was built after 1993 and is PlainTalk compatible, it has the newer line-level audio input jack. All you need to run a line-level signal is an adapter that converts two RCA inputs to a 3.5 mm stereo jack. If your Macintosh has the older microphone-level input, you'll need a specialized adapter that converts voltage levels as well as connectors (see "Sound and Macintosh Hardware" in Chapter 2 for a more in-depth discussion of this issue). From this point, line-level capture works the same as input using a microphone.

Controlling Input Volume

If you use a Macintosh with built-in audio, you can't control input volume through the Sound Control Panel. You must control input volume through software, and if your software doesn't give you that control, you need to take another route. Many presentation programs and even some word processors let you record audio using Apple's standard recording dialog box. This is the dialog box that appears when you click Add in the Alert Sounds section of the Sound Control Panel (see Figure 5.3). But there's no way to adjust input volume from that dialog box. In fact, SoundEdit 16 1.0, Audioshop 2.0,and Premiere 4.0 don't let you adjust input volume (thankfully, Macromedia fixed this oversight in SoundEdit 16 2.0).

You may be wondering, "Why is input volume control so important? I can amplify the signal using sound-editing software." Yes, you can, but the resulting signal will be much noisier, as Figure 5.8 illustrates. It's best to make the input volume as loud as possible without clipping. Remember the discussion of signal-to-noise ratios from Chapter 1? Every signal contains a certain amount of noise. To see a frightening example of this, try

Figure 5.8

Background noise is always present *(a)*. Signals recorded at low volume levels *(b)* contain a high proportion of background noise, even after amplification *(c)*. A good strategy is to record at a higher input volume so background noise makes up less of the signal *(d)*.

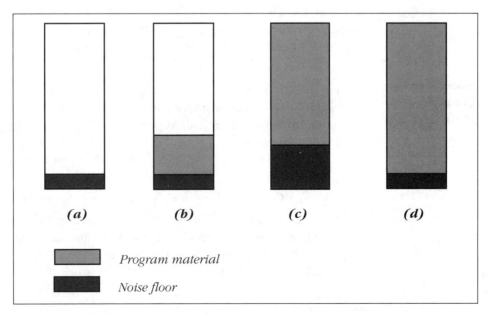

recording "silence" and just hold your microphone up in the air for a few seconds. If you open this recording in a sound-editing program, you'll see a thick black line representing audio sludge. To get the best sound, the noise must be the smallest possible portion of the overall signal. The greater your input volume, the lower the proportion of noise to the total signal.

If you use the external microphone, there's not much you can do to adjust the volume, aside from keeping an eye on the recording dialog box and monitoring the volume to ensure a level that's decent, but not so high that you begin to clip. When capturing from CD, you still can't set an input level, but at least you're capturing from a high-quality source. High-quality audio is much more forgiving when you amplify or normalize the signal in a sound-editing package. Again, ensure that your sample rate is set to 16-bit, 44.1 kHz, and capture from the disk directly to a file using MoviePlayer, Audioshop, or SoundEdit 16.

When you record from an external line-level source such as audio or video tape, the ideal solution is to use a small mixer to control the input volume. But you can improvise with a standard consumer audio cassette deck. Just put the cassette deck into record/pause mode, run your audio input into the deck, and run the deck's line out to the Macintosh (you'll need a stereo RCA-to-3.5 mm stereo plug adapter). Then you can adjust the level of the signal by changing the record level on the deck.

A few words about tape decks are in order. Most decks won't function in record/pause mode unless you have first inserted a tape. If possible, use a blank cassette so you don't accidentally wipe out a recording. If you're using a prerecorded tape, ensure that the plastic record-enable tab on the top hasn't been punched out.

Trouble-shooting Tips

❑ If you're having trouble trying to record sound from within an application, try recording from within the Sound Control Panel to ensure that the basic Macintosh audio system is functioning properly.

❑ If you're not getting sound input in the Control Panel, check whether your input device is set to Internal CD or microphone.

❑ Don't try recording with the older "Silver Dollar" microphone on Power Mac or Quadra AV models. They require the PlainTalk microphone.

❑ If you use a line input and have trouble regulating the signal, it may be that your "line level" isn't line-level after all. Taking a signal from a deck's headphone jack is *not* the same as taking the line out. You'll end up with much more noise if your levels aren't matched.

**Other Items
to Consider**

If you plan to extend your forays into audio, you may want to get a few more tools to boost the capabilities of the beginning-level system. These include:

❑ **Sound-editing software**—not only for the sake of the editing features, but also to enable you to capture sound at the highest bit depth and sample rate supported by your hardware. For less than $100, you can get into basic editing and recording with Opcode's Audioshop.

❑ **CD-ROM drive**—It's a great tool for accessing sound effects and music libraries. (You *weren't* going to use copyrighted material, were you?) You can't do multimedia without a CD-ROM.

❑ **External speakers**—to let you preview sound quality. You can't really achieve this through the built-in speaker on the Macintosh. A case in point: the PowerMac 6100 speaker is mounted facing *down,* and the sound comes out the bottom of the Mac. You shouldn't expect an accurate picture from this scheme any more than you should if you edit in Photoshop while looking at your monitor reflected in a funhouse mirror.

❑ **Good headphones**—to provide isolation for yourself and your co-workers. They *will* want to strangle you after hearing the voiceover fifty times. More important, though, headphones can isolate you from background noise in the environment. Listening through headphones is like having a microscope for your sound: you hear *everything,* including all the clicks, pops, and hissing. When it sounds clean in headphones, you know it's clean. Don't use the little foam headphones that came with your Walkman. Invest at least $50 in a good pair of closed-ear phones that completely cover your ears.

And if you're really trying to work your way up the food chain, you should consider the following accessories:

❑ **A decent microphone**—If you're planning to record voice only, you can get a good microphone for less than $100. This price range includes time-tested models like the Shure SM-57 and SM-58. Pick up a microphone stand while you're at it; sound quality will be more consistent if you're not holding the microphone while you record.

❑ **A small mixer**—You'll need this for the microphone, and it will also come in handy for controlling the volume of several sources at once. You can run the outputs of an external CD, tape deck, and microphone

Figure 5.9

The Mackie
1202 VLZ mixer

into the mixer simultaneously and then take the output into the CPU.
This configuration lets you switch easily between sources without
having to fumble around behind your computer every time you want
to record from a different source. A good mixer for this purpose is the
Mackie 1202 VLZ, shown in Figure 5.9; use it as the basis for comparison while shopping.

If you've already come this far, you're well on your way to fitting our
definition of an intermediate user. Let's see what that entails.

The Intermediate System

Many people have been swimming in the multimedia pond long enough to
have a good handle on manipulating audio. After all, this is the kind of
business where you're expected to do project management, writing, graphics, video, and programming. Once you've learned how do all that, it's not
too much of a stretch to add audio to your list of responsibilities. One of
the reasons people love (and hate) to work in multimedia is that the field
is interdisciplinary. You get to learn many different skills, but because of
the complexity and speed of change, it's difficult to achieve mastery in
more than one field. It certainly helps us to have picked up a few things
about video, graphics, and programming when creating audio for a project.

Similarly, you may bump into audio when you're editing video or coding a game. You're probably able to capture audio and get some work done in a sound-editing program. More importantly, you're likely to have a few more powerful tools at your disposal. They may not be on your desk all the time, but you can probably lay your hands on a microphone when you need one.

Another category of intermediate user includes musicians and audio professionals looking to break into the growing multimedia market. Thanks to the proliferation of relatively affordable digital audio and MIDI products, many of you have been able to cobble together sophisticated project studios. Now, your goal is to wrest some money back out of all the equipment stacked in your basement.

In addition to the basic Macintosh configuration described for beginning users, you probably have a more aggressive CPU (bigger drives, more memory, faster processor, and so forth) and some options for audio capture (see Figure 5.10). This could be an entry-level audio digitizing board such as the Audiomedia or Spectral Innovations' NuMedia. More likely, you can capture audio through a video capture card such as the Radius VideoVision or the TrueVision Targa 2000. You have access to a DAT (Digital Audio Tape) deck and a reasonably decent microphone (more than $75). Following are some of the configuration issues for hardware at this level.

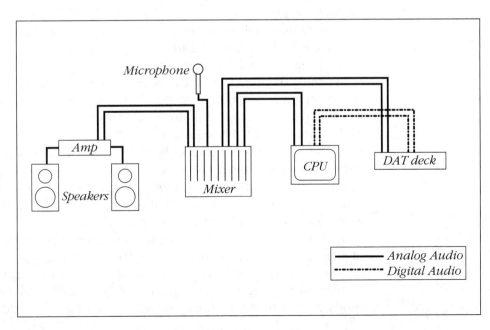

Figure 5.10

A typical intermediate-level digital audio system includes a mixer, a microphone, and a DAT deck as well as audio capture hardware.

Hooking It Up

Figure 5.10 shows that we've added a few more items than were mentioned in the previous paragraph. There are plenty of cables, certainly, but you can see that they're all connected in one place. The missing ingredient from the conglomeration of hardware that you probably have scattered around your studio is the piece that ties the whole mess together: a mixer.

You can get away without a mixer if you make two sacrifices. First, if you have a good microphone that hooks up directly to a video camera, you can use the camera rather than a mixer as your microphone *preamp*. (A preamp, short for *preamplifier,* is often used to amplify a low-level source, such as a microphone, to standard line level.) Second, if you're using your old home stereo receiver as an amplifier, you can hook the outputs of the DAT and CPU to separate inputs on the receiver and switch between them. In either of those cases, however, you're limited in the extent to which you can adjust volumes while recording and dubbing material. A mixer solves this problem and makes all the connections easily accessible at the same time. An intermediate-level digital audio installation is perfect for a small mixer like the Mackie 1202 shown in Figure 5.9.

You can see from the diagram in Figure 5.10 that our configuration requires at least a five-channel mixer. Mixers are usually built in multiples of four channels (4-channel, 8-channel, 12-channel, and so on), so look for at least an 8-channel mixer. If you have more equipment that you'd like to patch in (video decks, CD-ROM drives, and the like), and that equipment is enough to fill eight channels at the outset, leave yourself room to expand by getting at least a 12-channel mixer. When calculating the number of inputs you'll need, remember that stereo sources require two channels—one each for the left and right signals.

Most small to midsize mixers have only one main stereo output, which is fed to the amplifier. This is a limitation when you want to send the output of the microphone straight to the DAT deck instead of to the amp. There are two ways to solve this problem. The most obvious is to unplug the cables running into the amp and connect them to the analog inputs on the DAT. But there may be a better way if your mixer has *auxiliary* (sometimes also called *effect) sends.*

What are auxiliary sends, and how can they get you out of this dilemma? A brief explanation of mixer signal routing is in order here (see Figure 5.11 for a visual representation). A mixer, as we've already indicated, lets you control the volume of various inputs and sends the resulting mix to a pair of main outputs. Most mixers also let you insert signal processors like reverb or delay so that you can add effects to the signal. The effects are connected by means of a separate set of inputs and outputs (auxiliary sends and returns). Controls on each mixer channel let you vary how

Figure 5.11

A mixer's auxiliary send and return taps the signal, sends it to an effects processor, and then returns the processed signal to the mixer *(a)*. But you can also use auxiliary sends to pass signals to a recording device, or use the returns as additional input channels from other audio sources *(b)*.

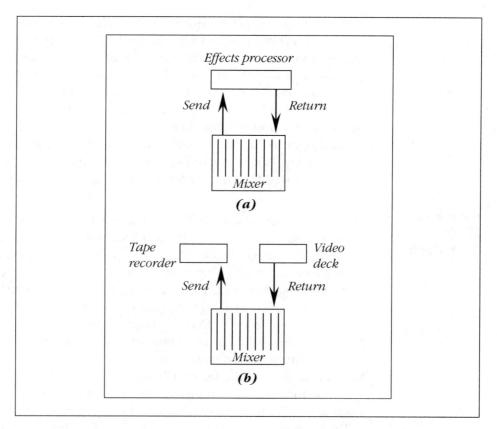

much of the unprocessed original signal is sent to the effects device, and there is a master control for setting the level of processed signal coming back from the device by way of the return. Instead of sending a channel's signal to an effect device, however, you can send it to any device you want—a DAT deck, for example, or the audio input on an audio or video capture card. One caveat: most mixers have mono auxiliary sends, so you need two sends for each stereo pair. For many multimedia applications, however, especially voiceover, stereo isn't needed.

Another issue you should be aware of when dealing with a full-featured mixer's auxiliary signal is the distinction between pre- and post-routing of the audio. For example, the signal sent out the auxiliary send may be pre-fader or post-fader. With a *post-fader* auxiliary send, the signal reaches the auxiliary control knob only after it passes the fader for that channel. If the fader's volume is zero, no signal will reach the auxiliary output, no matter how much you turn up the auxiliary send. A *pre-fader* auxiliary send, on the other hand, taps into the signal before it reaches the fader and sends signal to the auxiliary output regardless of the fader's position. Mixers may also differ as to whether the signal send to the auxiliary is *pre-* or *post-EQ:* the mixer equalization may also affect the auxiliary signal. More expensive mixers (usually over $1000) let you select pre- or post-settings, but most smaller mixers are hardwired. The common configuration of hardwired auxiliary sends is post-fader, post-EQ. But beware: some mixers wire half the channels one way and half another way, leaving you to choose the best signal routing options for your needs. When in doubt, read the documentation for the mixer. When in even deeper doubt, try hooking up a signal, twiddling the faders, EQ, and auxiliary sends, and watching the results.

Basic DAT Decks

Figure 5.10 shows two sets of connections between the DAT deck and the audio capture card in the CPU. One set is for analog audio, while the other is for digital audio. This configuration assumes that the capture card supports digital input and output (most likely the S/PDIF standard).

As we discussed in Chapter 2, DAT has become a standard format for transferring digital audio during production. It's common for voiceover and music to be recorded to DAT for later capture. With DAT, it's easy to make backup copies (if you can avoid SCMS copy protection). But this begs a frequently-asked question (sorry, for you netheads that's an *FAQ).* How do you transfer audio digitally from DAT to the computer? You need to be aware of the standard digital transfer formats (S/PDIF and AES/EBU), and you need to acquire the appropriate digital capture hardware for your computer.

Unfortunately, you can't make a digital transfer by putting an audio DAT tape into a SCSI DAT backup device (although the industry is working toward this obvious solution). Also, you lose quality if you take an analog line output from the DAT to the line input of the CPU or capture hardware. When you attempt to make digital transfers using analog inputs and outputs, you actually add an extra step of digital-to-analog conversion followed by analog-to-digital conversion. This adds noise and distortion to the signal. The answer, of course, is to buy more hardware!

Audio Digitizing Hardware

For many years, the sole contender in the audio digitizing hardware arena on the Macintosh has been Digidesign, which uses software and a card with a DSP to capture at rates up to 16/48. Digidesign's Audiomedia card was targeted to the "prosumer" and multimedia markets. The original Audiomedia had RCA line-in and line-out jacks and a 1/4-inch microphone jack. It was ideal for anyone wanting an easy way to record high quality analog audio directly to the Macintosh. In 1991, Digidesign released the Audiomedia II, replacing the microphone input with S/PDIF digital input and output. The Audiomedia II filled a void: it was the first relatively affordable solution for the digital transfer of audio from DAT to the computer. Let's take the Audiomedia II out for a quick spin.

Setting Up the Audiomedia II

I won't take time here to discuss the recommended hardware connections for the Audiomedia: these are well covered in the product documentation. Let's assume that you will be hooking the digital inputs and outputs to a DAT deck with RCA S/PDIF inputs and outputs. If your DAT has a different digital format (or has optical connectors), you can use a digital translator box like the Alesis A1 to convert between types. Here, we cover two of the more confusing issues you are likely to encounter using this hardware for the first time: 1) using the card in conjunction with the Sound Manager and 2) setting input options for analog and digital audio capture. The CD that accompanies this book also contains applicable tutorials.

Look to the
CD-ROM

Audiomedia and Sound Manager You can operate the Audiomedia II in one of two ways: as dedicated audio software that has no relation to the Sound Manager, or (when using the Digidesign sound driver) as a replacement for the Macintosh audio system, in conjunction with the Sound Manager (Figure 5.12).

The Audiomedia II can function as dedicated audio hardware if you plan to use it with software such as SoundDesigner II, Deck II, or a MIDI sequencer with digital audio support (Opcode's Studio Vision, for exam-

Figure 5.12

The Sound Control Panel with the Digidesign Sound Driver selected as the output device. The only available sampling rate is 44.1 kHz, but you can select between mono and stereo and between 8- and 16-bit resolution.

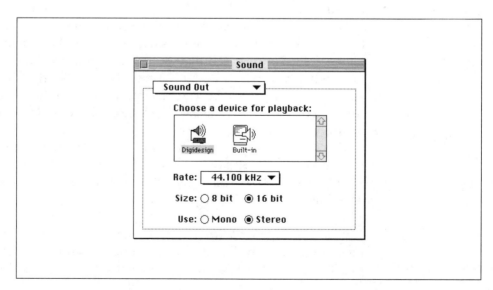

Figure 5.13

The Digidesign
Sound Input
Options are
accessed by
clicking the
Options... button
in the Sound In
dialog of
the Sound
Control Panel.

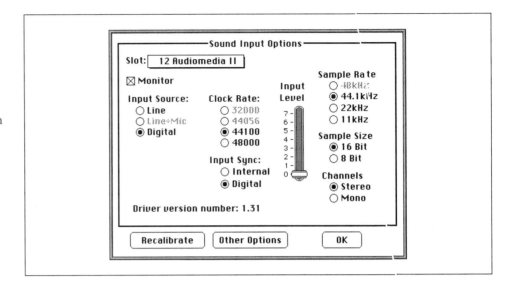

ple). In such cases, 16/44 audio is sent directly to the Audiomedia. Other audio—for example, System beeps or sound in Premiere, Audioshop, or SoundEdit 16—is handled by the Macintosh audio system.

If you choose to use the Audiomedia II as a replacement for the Macintosh audio system, you can tie it into the Sound Manager through the Digidesign Sound Driver. In this scenario, Audiomedia handles system beeps as well as any audio within software programs such as Audioshop, Premiere, or SoundEdit 16. This configuration is less efficient than sending the audio directly to the card.

Why? Well, recall that part of the Sound Manager's new improved functioning is its ability to convert sample rates and bit depths on the fly. In Figure 5.13, you can see that Audiomedia always sends its output at 44.1 kHz. When you play an 8-bit, 22.050 kHz file, Sound Manager has to convert it to 16-bit, 44.1 kHz. The Macintosh CPU handles this conversion, and Audiomedia's DSP isn't used. If you don't have a zippy Mac, your performance will suffer.

The solution is to match the card's output sample rate and bit depth as closely as possible. If you're playing lots of 8-bit, 22.050 kHz sound, set the sample size to 8-bit. You'll still pay a penalty for converting a 22.050 rate to 44.1, but every little bit helps.

Setting the input options As you may have surmised from Figure 5.13, there are two main options for capturing with Audiomedia: digital and analog. There is a key distinction between these two methods:

❏ During analog capture through the line input, the card converts incoming voltages to digital data, and the card determines the sample rate and bit depth of the file.

❏ In digital capture, the card is merely transferring existing data and therefore maintains the existing sample rate and bit depth of the file.

The two main options you need to change when switching back and forth between analog and digital capture are the Input Source and the Input Sync. Control of the Input Source option is obvious: select "line" for analog input and "digital" for digital input. The Sync option is a bit more subtle. Setting it to "Internal" lets Audiomedia's internal clock control time—for example, measuring 44,100 units every second for a sample rate of 44.1 kHz. When sample data is being transferred digitally, however, it's best to slave the Audiomedia's clock to the rate of the incoming digital data. This assures that samples coming from DAT are mapped to the exact same time when copied across to Audiomedia.

Are you thoroughly confused yet? Don't feel bad; most people are when they encounter this for the first time. Here's a summary of the preferred settings for each option when you perform audio capture with Automedia.

Source	Input Option	Input Sync	All other options
Analog	Line	Internal	As desired
Digital	Digital	Digital	Same as source

For an analog source, once you've selected line input and internal sync, you can set the clock rate, sample rate, sample size, and channels however you like. Actual settings, of course, depend on the level of quality you desire; we suggest a clock rate of 44.1, 16-bit size, 44.1 kHz rate, and mono or stereo as needed.

For a digital source, it's imperative that your clock rate and sample rate match the rates of the incoming material. If it doesn't, your data will play back at the wrong rate. This makes sense when you consider that when you have 48,000 samples per second and you transfer that at a rate of 44,100 samples per second, you leave 3,900 samples stranded (48,000 − 44,100 = 3,900). These extra samples don't just disappear; they slide over into the next second. Doing some math, you'll discover that a sound that used to play for 10 seconds now plays for almost 11 seconds. The effect you hear is similar to when a vinyl record (remember those?) plays at a slower speed: the pitch drops. If you're enough of an audio hacker to be dangerous, you may be thinking, "Heck, I've got a pitch shifting effect, I'll just shift it back!" This will get you out of the woods if you're really stuck, but it's best to do the job right the first time to minimize processing.

One other tip about digital sources: you can't adjust the input volume when transferring digitally. The "volume" is an integral part of the sample data—namely, the amplitude of the waveform. You can modify the amplitude using a sound editor, but you can't adjust it during a digital transfer (just as you can't tweak the hue of a graphic image while copying it over a SCSI connection).

Other Digital Audio Cards

Another option for digital input is the Spectral Innovations NuMedia card, which uses the same DSP found in the Macintosh AV series. The NuMedia card is about half the price of the Audiomedia II, but its optical digital connection are nonstandard, and it doesn't include editing software.

Aside from these two products, the only other audio-specific options for digital transfer are more expensive systems from Digidesign (SoundTools and ProTools) and Sonic Solutions. Meanwhile, rumors abound that several companies are working on an inexpensive S/PDIF digital interface card for release in 1996. Finally, high-end, full-scale video editing systems such as the Radius Telecast and Avid support digital audio capture. If support for digital audio transfer isn't one of your primary considerations, you might be able to get by with the audio features included on a video capture card.

Capturing from Video Cards

Just about every video capture card (save the humble VideoSpigot) supports simultaneous audio capture. These cards ship with drivers (System Extensions, actually) that link the hardware into Apple's Sound Manager so you can access them from the Sound Control Panel. Selecting the capture device's driver in the Sound In and Sound Out windows of the Sound Control Panel routes all sound (including system beeps) through your hardware. These drivers often display an Options... button that lets you set input volume, sample bit depth, and sample rate.

One drawback of the VideoVision hardware is that it supports capture at 8/22 only. If your Macintosh supports 16/44 audio, you might come out ahead by capturing the audio through the Macintosh's input instead. For instance, if all your output is destined to become 8-bit, 22 kHz, the fidelity saved in the digital transfer process will be totally lost in the downsampling conversion.

The fact that you're dealing with a video capture card doesn't mean that you *have* to capture video. Video capture cards work just as well capturing audio alone.

**Trouble-
shooting Tips**

❑ If you're getting screeching feedback trying to record with Audiomedia, uncheck the Monitor option. When checked, audio being recorded by way of the Audiomedia inputs is passed to the Audiomedia outputs. If the Audiomedia outputs are patched into the inputs on a device at the same time the output of the device is being sent to the Audiomedia inputs, you've just created a feedback loop.

❑ If you can't get enough level from a microphone connected to a mixer, be sure you're not plugged into a line-level input. There are many "line mixers" on the market that support only standard line voltage (–10 dBv). If your microphone is connected to a channel that's designed for a microphone-level signal, there may be an additional gain or trim adjustment (often near the input or at the top of the channel strip) to increase the gain.

**Other Items
to Consider**

❑ A *patch bay*—If you need to connect the audio inputs and outputs of many different pieces of hardware, use a patch bay for flexibility in making connections, especially if your mixer doesn't have enough input and output connectors to connect all your equipment at the same time.

❑ A *MIDI/SMPTE interface*—Use this if you want to create original music or if you need to sync digital audio to videotape.

❑ A *dynamics compressor*—If you're recording lots of voiceover or processing music prior to downsampling, a compressor is an invaluable aid. It minimizes variations in recording levels so that you can achieve a higher overall level.

Speaking of reaching a higher level, what might you be able to achieve with just a bit more gear?

The Advanced System

If you've reached the point where your primary responsibility is audio production, give yourself a pat on the back. You're among the fortunate few who have managed to acquire the tools and expertise to cram the equivalent of a full-blown recording studio onto your desktop. Let's qualify that: it's probably two or three desktops, but that still beats the heck out of needing an entire building.

Figure 5.14

An advanced
audio system

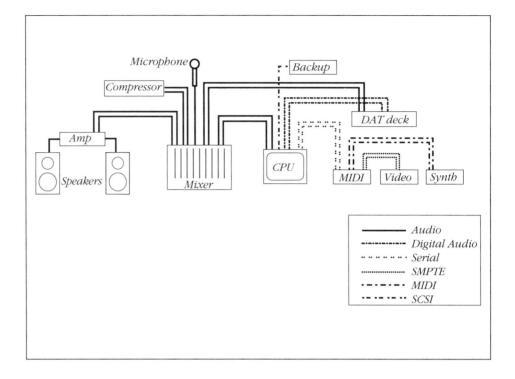

In addition to the tools collected as you worked your way up through the intermediate system, the advanced system (Figure 5.14) includes a digital transfer-capable card for the CPU (at least Audiomedia II); hardware or software (or both) to provide dynamic compression, equalization, and other effects; a professional-quality amplifier and monitors; computer peripherals for archiving and transferring sizeable chunks of data; and a MIDI/SMPTE interface. Let's get an overview of the system and then discuss the added hardware elements in more detail.

Hooking It Up

The configuration for an advanced-level digital audio system is similiar to that of the intermediate system, with a few alterations. Figure 5.14 shows a typical installation.

The main hardware addition is a MIDI interface with built-in SMPTE synchronization. This allows synchronization to audio and videotape decks while also adding music capabilities using MIDI. MIDI hardware is important not only for writing music, but also for the creation and playback of MIDI files that may eventually be distributed in General MIDI or QuickTime Music Track format. Almost all MIDI interfaces that include

SMPTE also function as MIDI patch bays. They include several MIDI inputs and outputs, each of which can contain a full 16 channels of MIDI data.

The dynamics compressor, equalizer, and other effects can be connected directly to the mixer, but at this level of complexity it may be wiser to route them through a patch bay. If these effects are implemented through software (for example, the Waves series of plug-ins for Sound Designer or the CyberSound FX plug-ins for Premiere), the need for a patch bay is consequently reduced. Some effects, however—particularly dynamics compression—should still be applied as the signal is being recorded.

Choosing an Audio Interface

Depending on the type of work you do, it's possible to get quite a bit of mileage from a basic audio interface card like Audiomedia II. However, many high-level professionals choose to step up to a more advanced system such as Sonic Solutions or ProTools. What are some of the deciding factors?

One advantage of the larger and more expensive systems is a higher number of discrete inputs and outputs. Audiomedia offers only two inputs and outputs. If you want to record three things at once onto separate tracks, you have to do it in separate passes. When mixing down, you may be able to play four or more separate audio tracks from the hard disk at one time, but their output is combined into the two outputs. You can't route them into separate channels in your mixer for individual processing (although you usually can control their relative volume and pan within the editing program).

Digidesign's ProTools and products made by Sonic Solutions, on the other hand, are expandable systems that can provide 4, 8, 16, or more discrete inputs and outputs. Expandability is most helpful when recording music, when it's important to maintain separate control over a number of instruments until final mixdown.

Another advantage of the high end systems is their ability to process audio during playback through their DSPs. Standard processing options usually include basic equalization and dynamics, but software plug-ins can add reverb, delay, or spatialization, or (like the Waves plug-ins) extremely sophisticated dynamics and equalization tools. The most popular example offering these sophisticated tools is Digidesign's TDM system, but Sonic Solutions also has these capabilities.

A final important advantage of the high-level systems is more robust support for SMPTE. If synchronizing to videotape is a key element in your work, it's probably worth looking at a more expensive option.

There are disadvantages to high-end systems, too. For most people, the chief one is cost. You can expect to spend at least $8,000 to $10,000 on a basic ProTools system, while Audiomedia II ($1200) can be had for a relative song. The entry-level cost of Sonic Solutions systems is about $3,000, but its total cost also can climb rapidly depending on the configuration you need.

> **Note:** *In my personal experience creating audio just for multimedia, I've found I can do almost everything I need with Audiomedia II. While I compose a lot of music, the performance and mixing is all controlled through MIDI and mixed directly to stereo DAT. Then I transfer the DAT using Audiomedia for more editing, processing, and final downsampling. SMPTE is rarely an issue because most video has already been digitized into QuickTime before I see it. The real-time effects potential of Digidesign's TDM is tempting, but as more audio editors support plug-in processors (and as faster CPUs continue to reduce the need for dedicated DSPs) these features will become more widely available at far lower cost.*

Effects Processing

To achieve a professional-quality voice recording, you need to use a dynamic compressor. As we discussed in Chapter 2, a compressor helps you get more consistent volume, avoids distortion associated with excessive levels, and silences background noise when the signal falls below a certain point. On low-budget multimedia projects, the person doing your voiceover is often not a trained professional voice talent, so the individual's voice level is far more likely to fluctuate during recording. This is all the more reason to use a compressor while recording to help even the score.

If you're creating titles with environmental spaces (rooms, caves, basements, and so on) you should also have a digital reverb/delay processor for adding ambience to these spaces. Sorry, but you won't be able to get away with Sound Edit's venerated "Outer Space" at this level (although "Empty Room" is great for cheesy 50's reverb in campy products like Spaceship Warlock).

Finally, it's good to have more flexible equalization at the advanced level. EQ can be tricky, especially when your material is destined to be downsampled. It's also invaluable for controlling low frequencies that turn to mud when your sound comes out of the Mac speaker. If you're on a budget, look for a multi-effects unit that combines reverb, delay and EQ effects. There are a number of products like this on the market in the $350 to $450 range.

A Professional Amp and Monitors

At this point, you shouldn't be relying on "computer speakers." You also shouldn't be relying on your old home stereo system. The main goal of a professional monitoring system is to present the sound without any added coloration. You almost certainly cannot expect this from either of the above. Most computer speakers are woefully inadequate at playing low frequencies; even with a subwoofer it's likely that low-frequency response is uneven. Home stereo systems are almost always built with a "smiley curve" EQ; that is, the low end and high end are boosted to give the music more presence.

It's time to invest in a good-quality power amp and speakers. Be prepared to spend at least $600 to $700 for components of decent quality. Unless you're in a professionally-designed acoustic space, you'll do best with smaller, near-field monitors than with big, booming wall-sized speaker cabinets. They're more accurate in acoustically adverse conditions, and they represent the performance of small computer speakers more accurately. Remember to keep a set of small, cheesy computer speakers set up side by side with your good speakers, and make sure that you can switch back and forth between the two sets of speakers instantaneously.

Using a Patch Bay

If your system suffers from too many inputs and not enough outputs (or vice versa), you may be ready for a patch bay. By connecting all of your equipment's input and output connectors to a patch bay rather than to each other, you can change your configuration by moving a few easily accessible patch cables. This saves you from having to fish around behind your equipment every time you want to change your setup.

Patch bays come in several varieties, so it pays to spend time up front thinking about your particular needs. The main differences relate to the internal wiring of the patch bay. The most basic patch bay (called *non-normalled*) routes a signal from an input to an output only when a patch cord makes the connection. Other patch bays (called *semi-normalled* and *normalled*) automatically send a signal from the top connector to the bottom connector when no patch cord is inserted. Inserting a patch cord into the upper jack either interrupts or splits the signal so that it can be sent two places at once.

Finally, some patch bays have RCA jacks on the back and 1/4-inch phone jacks on the front. Others have 1/4-inch jacks front and back or RCA jacks front and rear. Choose one that best matches the types of connectors on your equipment. If the patch bay is really central to your system, don't stint here. Choose a professional model with the wires soldered or punched onto the back and with high-quality jacks on the front. Just about any patch bay will survive for a year or two, but if you use a cheap model, you may end up spending too much time troubleshooting bad connections.

Backup Storage

By now you should know to be prepared for data overload. Digital audio applications practically sneeze at anything smaller than a 1 GB drive. If you haven't already invested in a system that lets you archive data quickly and easily, it's time to take the plunge. SCSI DAT has long been a medium of choice for this purpose, but with the prices of CD-ROM writers and blank media continuing to fall, it's becoming more and more feasible to consider CD as an option.

MIDI/SMPTE Interface

If you're not composing music, a MIDI/SMPTE interface may not be a requirement for you. If, on the other hand, you're ready to become the Jerry Goldsmith of CD-ROM, be sure you have enough MIDI firepower to create rich and diverse soundtracks. It helps to have a MIDI interface that supports at least 32 channels, if not more. While it's not likely that you'll have 32 separate tracks playing at the same time, you'll work more efficiently if you can easily access all the available channels in your synthesizers at once. Also, if you ever need to score music to videotape, you'll need the SMPTE sync capability.

Software Tools—the Great Leap Forward

Up through the Intermediate level, you could get by using a basic audio editor like SoundEdit 16 or Audioshop. Depending on your hardware, you could also use a product with more features and better performance, such as Macromedia's Deck II, Opcode's Digitrax, or Digidesign's Session. Once audio processing becomes your primary focus, however, you should have the right software tools for the job. The tools you may want to add include:

❏ A robust multitrack mixing/editing package such as Deck II, ProTools, or Sonic Solutions

❏ Dedicated CD-audio capture tools such as OMI's Disc-To-Disk and Gallery Software's CD Studio

❏ Effects processors, such as the plug-ins from AnTares Systems, InVision Interactive, and Waves, as well as stand-alone processors like Arboretum's Hyperprism

❏ Automation software such as CD Software's QuicKeys or the Precision Audio Tools package from Gallery Software

**Trouble-
shooting Tips**

At the advanced level, let's face it: you've created a monster! It's difficult to offer many tips when a system contains so many variables, but following are a few trouble spots that most people may encounter.

❏ We could probably write a whole chapter about synchronizing to SMPTE, but our experience dictates that most troubles revolve around three issues: 1) having good timecode striped on tape (adequate signal, no dropouts, and good alignment between the tape and heads); 2) matching frame rates exactly (be sure your MIDI sequencer isn't set to 30 frames per second (fps) when the real rate is 29.97); and 3) properly setting devices to be either the master or slave. For more information on SMPTE, refer to the "What's SMPTE?" sidebar.

❏ It's at this point that you're also most likely to have trouble tracking the path of a signal so that it gets all the way from the input to the proper output. To see where the signal is going, start at the source and track through each connection along the way. Let's say, for example, that you're having trouble hearing the signal from a video deck that runs through a patch bay into your mixer, out to an amp and speakers. Grab another cable (always suspect the cables!) and connect the deck directly to the mixer. If you have signal at that point, you've isolated the problem to the patch bay and its associated cables. If you still don't have signal, ensure that the other channels on the mixer are working and that you're getting signal out of the mixer's main outputs. If you don't hear anything through the speakers, the problem may be in the amp or speaker cables. As your system becomes more complex, you need to isolate components in order to determine the source of the problem. Always start at the front and work to the back, switching out only one component or cable at a time and then putting it back in its proper place before moving on to the next link in the chain. Avoid the temptation to turn your volume up really loud in order to hear what's going on. Many fine studio monitors have been reduced to smoking heaps of slag through this process.

**Other Items
to Consider**

At this point, the sky's the limit. You should have most of the tools you need to do great work. If you're not, don't blame your equipment! It will probably be enough to just keep up with growing requirements for RAM, disk drive space, and hardware and software upgrades.

WHAT'S SMPTE?

SMPTE (pronounced "simp-tee") *time code* derives its name from the Society of Motion Picture and Television Engineers. This specification was established to provide a common timing reference for synchronizing video devices.

Before we wade deeper into this discussion, here are my own insights on SMPTE. I rarely encounter it in multimedia and CD-ROM audio production; most video has already been digitized into QuickTime. Once video is in the digital realm, synchronization is handled by the computer and by the QuickTime architecture itself. Where SMPTE becomes useful or even indispensible is when your work is destined to be transferred back to videotape, or when you're creating soundtracks to hand over to a video editor using Adobe Premiere or a similar editing product. It's also useful for synchronizing MIDI sequencers to external tape decks. With that in mind, here are a few basic things you should know if SMPTE is in your future.

The SMPTE Signal

SMPTE time values are expressed in hours:minutes:seconds:frames. A typical value would be 00:02:36:20. There are six different flavors of SMPTE, each with its own frame rate. We can dispense with two of them pretty quickly:

- ❏ **24 frames per second** *(fps)* is used for film
- ❏ **25 fps** is used for *PAL/SECAM* (a video format common in Europe and Southeast Asia)

Now we get into murkier territory. In the early days of black-and-white TV, video was broadcast at 30 fps. When color TV was introduced, the standard video rate was changed to 29.97 fps to prevent color distortion. But frames were still numbered from 0 to 29. This numbering convention introduced a discrepancy between real time and the time reference on the video tape. If no adjustments are made for this imbalance, the video could gradually get farther and farther out of synchronization with the clock on the wall. So a compromise was made in which frame numbers are skipped at regular intervals (two frames per minute, except when the minutes are an even interval of ten). When frames are dropped, the video time jumps ahead to resume a closer relationship to real time. In the real world, then, we usually see two additional flavors of SMPTE: 29.97 fps drop frame and 30 fps.

- ❏ **29.97 fps drop frame** is the standard rate for broadcast video
- ❏ **30 fps** and **29.97 fps non-drop** are often used for music applications that include MIDI and audio, but no video.

(continued)

Finally, there is an additional rate that you might encounter: 30 fps drop frame.

The bottom line for any SMPTE frame rate is this: if you're responsible for adding audio to material that references time code, be positive that you're using the right format. Otherwise all your edits will be out of synchronization.

Masters and Slaves

Synchronizing with SMPTE requires that one device be the source of all timing information (the *master),* and all other devices (the *slaves)* defer to the master clock. When the master device reads a time code value, it transmits that value to all the other devices so that they can automatically advance to the same value. Usually it takes a few seconds for this to occur. The slave devices chase to the designated location and then take a moment to lock up in synchronization with the master. If you're editing with SMPTE, always leave yourself at least three seconds of pre-roll before you expect devices to be in mutual synchronization.

Recording and Synchronizing with SMPTE

SMPTE timing information is usually recorded onto tape in one of two ways. The simplest method is called *longitudinal time code (LTC,* pronounced "ell-tee-see"). SMPTE is recorded in one long, continuous stream (a process referred to as "striping the tape"), on either an audio channel of the videotape or an audio track of a tape deck. SMPTE can also be recorded as part of the video signal using a method called *vertical interval time code (VITC,* prnounced "vit-see"). With VITC, the SMPTE information is encoded in the vertical interval of the video signal.

A brief explanation is in order here. Video is drawn onto the screen from top to bottom. When the electron gun reaches the bottom of the screen, it must travel back to the top. This creates a very short blank period, called the *vertical blanking interval.* Other types of data, such as SMPTE or closed-captioning, can be written into this blank space. One advantage of VITC is that it preserves the audio tracks on a video, rather than using them for LTC.

The quality of a SMPTE signal is only as good as the source that generates it. Most professional video houses provide *house sync,* where one central source of timecode information synchronizes all the devices in the facility. Most of us working

(continued)

on our own, however, are likely to be reading SMPTE from tape. This can leave you at the mercy of tape dropouts and errors. Practically everyone has seen a car stereo devour a cassette, and we all know how fragile the medium can be. Luckily, there are ways to bail yourself out if your SMPTE signal begins to disintegrate. Many MIDI interfaces include the ability to read and write SMPTE, but they can also freewheel through sections of bad time code. Once the device synchronizes itself to timecode read from a good section of the tape, it can generate its own time code on the fly to maintain synchronization. These devices can also regenerate time code, writing fresh SMPTE while reading from a marginal SMPTE source so you can transfer SMPTE data to a more reliable tape.

If you're doing lots of synchronization between video, analog tape decks, and DAT tape decks (especially if you're originating the SMPTE time code), you may need an obscure device called a *black-burst generator* to serve as a stable time source. This device ensures that SMPTE is rock-steady, which is especially important when you're trying to re-synchronize the signal with video and DAT decks. Although the built-in SMPTE sync generator on a MIDI interface is sufficient to stripe an analog tape and re-lock to it, it's extremely unlikely that a video deck or SMPTE-equipped DAT machine would be able to lock onto this signal successfully. This could result in the video rolling frames as it tries to maintain synchronization with the SMPTE signal. A black-burst generator costs about $500, but it's much cheaper than having to redo a project because of unstable time code.

MIDI Time Code

MIDI Time Code (MTC) is used to pass a SMPTE-like signal down a MIDI cable. It's used extensively with MIDI sequencers and some digital audio software. The same times and formats as in normal SMPTE are used, but MTC replaces both LTC and VITC, at least in the sections of the system where it is used. Use a SMPTE-to-MTC converter for this conversion. You must still take all the same precautions that you do for normal SMPTE, but MTC is a digital signal traveling on a MIDI cable, not an analog signal travelling down an audio path. If you use MTC, you should dedicate the entire MIDI cable to it. Don't try to run other MIDI information down this cable, as it will degrade the timing of both the MTC and the other MIDI data. MTC converters are built into a number of higher-quality MIDI interfaces. Very few MIDI interfaces can handle VITC, but most can convert from LTC to MTC and back.

(continued)

Troubleshooting

Here are a few tips for recording and using SMPTE on audio tracks:

❏ First, be sure to record the signal at a good level (anywhere from –15 dB to –5 dB on the input meters), but don't record at a high enough level to introduce distortion.

❏ If you're recording through a mixer, don't use any equalization or processing on the signal.

❏ Defeat any noise reduction processing (Dolby or dbx) that may be engaged.

❏ If your master is multi-track tape, put the SMPTE on one of the "outside" tracks (tracks 1 or 8 on an 8-track, 1 or 16 on a 16-track deck) to reduce the amount of SMPTE signal which may bleed over onto an adjacent audio track.

❏ If possible, don't record any material on the track next to the timecode track. High-energy signals (a thumping bass drum, for instance) may bleed across to the timecode track and interfere with your sync, or you may hear the SMPTE signal bleed into your audio track.

❏ Always stripe the entire tape before recording and then start your actual program material at least one minute into the tape. The first minute of tape is the area where you're most likely to experience dropouts and errors.

❏ If you use a patch bay, DON'T run the SMPTE signal through it; you're just asking for trouble. Instead, run a completely separate cable from the tape input or output that you're working with to the computer or video deck that you're synchronizing to. It's best not to even run this cable next to other audio cables; separate it by a foot or so.

❏ If you're scoring for film or video, synchronize to a SMPTE track that the client provides. Always ask what format they're working in (24, 25, 29.97 dropframe, 29.97 drop, or 30 fps), and set your equipment likewise. *Always* take a short piece of audio or music that you've synchronized and send it back as a test. If the test doesn't work, you know you'll have to adjust things until they're right. Don't wait until a project is complete before testing the synchronization. In extreme cases, you could end up redoing everything in order to collect your paycheck. And if that's not bad enough, you should always act as though the SMPTE signal supplied to you is suspect. Even if the first videotape works well, that's no guarantee that the next one will.

Summary

In this chapter we covered basic system configurations for three levels of users: beginning, intermediate, and advanced. Hopefully it's helped you to make some decisions about which system best meets the needs of the kinds of work you need to get done. But now that we've configured a system, what do we do with it? In the next chapter, we'll finally dive into the nuts and bolts of hands-on audio-editing techniques.

Part Two

TECHNIQUES

6

Working with Audio,
Part One

Ready to roll up your sleeves? In this chapter, we discuss hands-on strategies and techniques for making your way through four of the seven stages of audio production—planning, recording, capture, and editing. Our focus is on the issues that you might encounter when working on a relatively large project. As the scale of a project increases, the potential for one wrong decision to wreak havoc increases tremendously. It's not a disaster when you have to fix ten files, but fixing a thousand files can set you back weeks.

First, an important disclaimer: there isn't a simple step-by-step recipe for audio production. The process changes every time you go through it. Sometimes the change is based on new experiences, but more often it's due to the speed with which tools and technology are changing.

Planning

There's not much glamour in planning. While it isn't nearly as much fun as hands-on creative work, most people agree that it's necessary. It's impossible to know what obstacles lie ahead when you consider producing an audio or multimedia product. On the other hand, many aspects of production remain similar from project to project, and a bit of planning can save you from taking the same painful detours time after time. Arrange the planning process so that it addresses three areas:

- ❏ **Creative**—sound design and the assets required to fulfill the design.
- ❏ **Technical**—the features and limitations of hardware and software.
- ❏ **Project management**—scheduling, budgeting, and structure of the production team.

In the initial planning phase, the sound designer should meet with the project producer, the graphic designer, and the programmer to sketch out a rough outline of the scope of the product. To develop a plan, you need information about each of the three planning areas.

Creative

Here's what you should know in order to plan the creative aspects of the project:

- ❏ The intended audience (children, adults, business customers, etcetera)
- ❏ The "look and feel" (hip and techno, futuristic, cartoonish, and so forth)
- ❏ The structure and pacing of the presentation
- ❏ Outside talent or assets (voiceover, music, etcetera) that will be needed

Technical

Consider these factors when planning for the technical side of the project:

- ❏ Playback platforms (Macintosh, PC, Enhanced CD, CD-I, video, and so on)
- ❏ Distribution medium (CD-ROM, floppy, online, and so forth)
- ❏ Minimum system requirements (RAM, disk space, CPU speed, etcetera)
- ❏ File formats, sample rate/resolution, and file naming conventions
- ❏ The authoring tool and its audio capabilities
- ❏ Additional hardware and/or software needed for audio production

Management

Observe these considerations when planning for project management:

- ❏ The production schedule (including dates of key milestones)
- ❏ Roles and responsibilities of members of the production team
- ❏ The budget for audio production

Let's look at each of these factors in greater depth.

**Creative
Planning**

Start your planning from the creative angle, to the fullest extent possible. Rather than wondering what you can afford to do or what the hardware will let you do, think about what you would *like* to do. Of course, the rational side of your brain knows that what you'd *really* like to do almost certainly isn't possible unless you're working on a kiosk for Cray. But this isn't the time to limit your horizons. Remember, there will be plenty of opportunities for paring back later on, when it's time to shoehorn your sounds into an authoring environment.

Pardon me while I climb up on the soapbox. The multimedia field is already getting a bad rap with "shovelware" (existing content that has been dumped onto a CD-ROM) and look-alike (even worse, sound-alike) products. If those of us responsible for producing content don't put forth our best creative effort, we won't have an audience for very long. Through audio, we have a tremendous ability to set or change a mood. Depending on the sounds we use, we can make a scene seem comedic, tragic, or frightening. Another area where sound can really shine is in maintaining continuity. It's one of the best ways to bridge the gaps of "click-and-wait" presentations, and it can lead you seamlessly from one scene to the next. Sound is also a powerful tool for creating environments. It's not uncommon for an artist to spend a few weeks modeling and rendering a three-dimensional environment. But you could create an equally effective auditory environment in a few hours and let the listener "visualize" the space through sound.

People often bemoan audio's status as the neglected stepchild of multimedia. Our job as audio producers is to raise awareness among production managers, graphic artists, and programmers so that they fully appreciate the benefits of good sound design. When you get involved in the planning stage of a production, you can present creative options for sound design that may not occur to other people on the team. At the same time, take care not to get caught in "creativity by committee." If the producer or client has definite ideas about the tone of the audio, get him or her to be as clear as possible and to provide examples of other works that demonstrate the desired style (look out for someone who wants music that's "classical, but kinda jazzy, and with a reggae feel and lots of synthesizers").

**Technical
Planning**

See? Here come the limitations already! Granted, the barriers are becoming a bit lower with every improvement in hardware and software, but we still have quite a way to go before we can compete with *Blade Runner.*

From the beginning, it's imperative that everyone on the team understand the capabilities and limitations of your final playback system. This will affect everything you do. This is also your best opportunity to do some research and development. Research new file formats, audio production tools, and compression schemes. Create test examples and play them back on different hardware configurations. Work with the programmer to experiment with memory management and system throughput when playing files in different formats. In short, make your mistakes early and try to determine which strategy will give you the most dependable, highest quality performance.

This is also the time to shop around for new tools that may help you work more effectively. As multimedia production becomes more of a practiced art than an improvised experiment, hardware and software developers are creating tools geared specifically to the needs of multimedia audio. Take advantage of this opportunity to improve your tools and methods before you wade neck-deep into the full-scale production process.

Management Planning

When you're about to embark on a long project, it's important to have a clear understanding of the roles and responsibilities of everyone on the team. Different groups may arrange their responsibilities in different ways. You may need to coordinate some things (scheduling, for example) with the production manager, and other things (such as file naming conventions) with the programmer. Alternatively, the production manager may want to be the point person for every decision. Either way, while your role is mostly creative, you also need to wear a management hat. Other people on the team will look to you to provide realistic estimates for schedules and budgets, and they will depend on you to manage the flow of audio assets. You will need a system for tracking and archiving files as they travel from recording to capture to editing to downsampling.

You also need to establish who has the final say on approval of your creative work. Striking a balance between your creative ideas and the needs of the client is the eternal struggle of creative work for hire. Because your work involves creative input, you need to know where the boundaries are, and you need good feedback from the producer about what is acceptable.

Recording

In this section, we'll browse through a range of recording-related topics, including microphone placement, location recording, and voiceover recording. During the recording process, you have the greatest exposure to one of the perils of analog audio signals: noise. Unwanted noise is *the* main enemy of audio production. It tries to creep in at every phase of the recording and production cycle. Your job is to be ever-vigilant in keeping noise to a minimum. That said, let's begin this section with some self-defense tips.

Noise—Your Constant Companion

At every turn, an analog audio signal can pick up unwanted noise. Noise is undesirable because it masks meaningful audio content and interferes with the listener's ability to hear what you're trying to present. We've all experienced trying to talk through a faulty telephone connection, or trying to hold a conversation in a loud setting. Noise distracts the listener, forcing him or her to concentrate on sifting the important audio information out of a sonic blizzard.

In audio production, noise is even more insidious because it is very difficult (or at least expensive) to remove noise once it is present in the signal. Moreover, noise multiplies at each step of the audio process, so a little bit of noise at the beginning of the signal chain becomes a lot of noise at the end.

You may recall our discussion of signal-to-noise ratios from Chapter 1. Simply put, the signal-to-noise ratio represents our acceptance of two facts:

- ❏ Regardless of how quiet the setting, we will *always* hear a bit of background noise; and
- ❏ Some devices are noisier than others.

Each element in the signal chain is slightly less than perfect in transmitting electrical signals. The strength and quality of an electrical signal decays over time as it moves through successive wires and devices, each of which is less than 100 percent efficient in transferring electrical energy. Because of these inefficiencies, some energy is radiated away as heat, and the signal that arrives at the end of the cable is therefore slightly weaker than the original signal. As energy is lost, the signal may be amplified to bring it back to the desired strength, but as it is amplified, some noise is added.

Determining which device is causing noise is straightforward but potentially dangerous to your speakers, headphones, or ears. Try the following steps in sequence to get an idea of how much noise is in your signal:

1. Stop any devices currently playing audio so that your system is "silent."
2. Turn the volume of every device down to zero.
3. Raise the master volume until you can hear background hiss in the signal. (Note the exact volume level so you can stay well below it from now on!)

4. Starting from the final output stage and working backwards, raise the volume of each device one by one until you hear noise. Note the level at which noise becomes apparent.

When checking the noise inherent in a particular device, you may hear a jump in the amount of noise as you go beyond a certain level (90 percent, for example). This is your clue to maintain the volume of the device just below that level. You may also find that one device is causing most of the noise in the signal chain. Check the grounding and cables for that device to see if you can reduce the noise level.

To paraphrase an old saying, the quality of your signal chain is only as good as its noisiest link. Let's explore the many paths by which noise can sneak into your recordings and the safety precautions you can take to avoid noise.

Environmental Noise

Noise can be introduced at the very beginning of the signal chain if you record with a microphone in a noisy space. Many people create multimedia productions with voiceover they have recorded while sitting in the middle of a noisy office, using the microphone that was included with their computer. If you need to record directly into your computer, try to make your surroundings as quiet as possible. Wait until evening, then listen carefully to the background sounds of your office, and try to identify as many sources of noise as you can. These may include the computer itself (especially fans and hard disks), computer peripherals (printers, SCSI devices, and so on), building ventilation systems, humming fluorescent lights, and outside traffic. Air flowing across a microphone can cause a substantial amount of noise. Even if the ventilation system is quiet, a microphone can pick up noise from the air flow itself. Try to turn off as many of these as you can, and find the quietest possible place to record.

Radio Frequency Interference

Audio signals are electrical voltages traveling through cables. Low-quality cable can be highly susceptible to strong magnetic fields and *radio frequency interference* (RFI). Strong electrical currents, as well as many electronic devices, emit electromagnetic fields. This electomagnetic energy can be transferred to a poorly shielded audio cable, in the same way that a radio signal is received by an antenna. You may have noticed this effect if you've ever talked to someone using a portable telephone located next to a computer. The RFI generated by the computer creates static in the radio telephone signal.

The most likely culprits for RFI are computers, electric motors, and power cables. The first step in reducing RFI is to use high-quality shielded cables. These cables have metallic shielding wrapped around the audio cable to absorb RFI. To minimize RFI from computers and electric motors, keep the cable as far away as possible. To reduce the effects of power cables, keep audio cables as far away as possible from power cables. Try not to run audio cables parallel to power cables, as this increases the audio cable's exposure to RFI. Instead, run the audio cables at right angles to power cables.

Ground Loops

A *ground loop* is an electrical phenomenon that creates a low hum in audio signals. They are caused when devices are plugged into a poorly grounded electrical circuit, or when several devices are plugged into different circuits. When these devices are connected by audio cables, unwanted electrical current flows through the audio cables in order to find the shortest path to ground. This unwanted current is running at 60 Hz (the standard electrical cycle in the United States), so it creates a low, steady 60 Hz hum. To avoid ground loops, be sure all your equipment is running from one well-grounded circuit. In a pinch, you can try to isolate the piece of equipment responsible for the noise and use a *ground lifter* (a three-prong adapter) to defeat the ground. When you defeat the ground, however, you increase your risk of receiving an electrical shock when you touch the equipment, because *you* may become the ground for the electricity. Use balanced cables whenever possible, as they are much less susceptible to ground loops.

Gain Staging

Every component in the audio signal chain has an ideal operating level at which it delivers its best performance. *Gain staging* is the process of optimizing input and output levels so that your equipment operates as quietly as possible. For an analogy, think about driving your car on the highway in first gear versus starting it from a standstill in fourth gear. Like a car, your equipment is most efficient (creating less noise) when it's working in its optimal range.

A good rule of thumb is to set each volume control to near 70 percent of its full scale. If you have to radically change the control to make everything work properly, that's a good indication that the equipment may need an attenuator or preamp to achieve the proper level.

Poor-Quality Equipment

Even if you record in a quiet space, you can create noise by recording with a poor quality microphone, a low-quality tape recorder, a noisy mixer, or bad cables. The quality of your signal can be only as good as the weakest link in the chain. When selecting your audio hardware, try to get the best you can afford, but make certain that all your devices are of relatively similar quality. There's no point in using a $2,000 DAT recorder with a $20 microphone. If your microphone, mixer, or recorder can't duplicate the full range of the frequency spectrum, your recording will suffer.

If there's any one place to invest in quality, it's the microphone. Current technology has brought most electronic equipment to a reasonable level of performance at moderate prices, but microphone technology has not changed significantly, and prices remain high.

Digital Noise

Once an audio signal has been digitized, it is much less susceptible to noise. But this doesn't mean you're home free. Many digital audio operations—sample rate conversion, for example—add some quantization noise (see Chapter 1 for a review of quantization noise). When you perform a processing operation on a 16-bit sample, the algorithms often convert the data to a 24-bit value. After the processing is complete, the data is downsampled back to 16 bits. Granted, this creates far less quantization noise than working in 8 bits, but the amount begins to add up if you do lots of processing.

Quantization noise can also become a problem if you record your signal at a very low level. Think of it from a mathematical standpoint. When your audio values are being represented by a 16-bit number, you'll need all 16 bits to represent the loudest possible signal. But if the peak of a signal is at 10 percent strength, you might have only 12 bits of real signal information; the other four bits would be zeroes. If you normalized this file, you'd be adding quantization noise, and you'd also be increasing the background noise. A better strategy would be to record the signal with a high level in the first place. But be sure you don't exceed the maximum input value and create distortion. Analog systems (such as tape) are relatively forgiving when the signal level is excessive; in fact, many audio engineers use this kind of distortion as a deliberate effect. Digital distortion, however, is a truly terrible thing to hear; avoid it at all costs.

Quantization noise is just one type of digital noise that you can introduce. You also can inadvertently increase the noise in a digital signal through excessive equalization, or through amplifying the signal to the point at which clipping occurs. Finally (as you'll see in the upcoming section on output), downsampling to lower sample rates and resolutions adds lots of noise to a file. This is a one-way street, unfortunately—if you later upsample the file from 8/11 back up to 16/44, you won't magically remove the noise or restore the file to its former pristine state.

Recording Voice

Many productions use recorded voice, yet it's one of the more difficult audio sources to handle in multimedia. The human voice presents three issues you'll need to manage.

First, human speech has a wide dynamic range. The differences in vocal volume between two different people, or between the whisper and the shout of a single person, can be extreme. But even when one person talks in a normal tone, there are abrupt changes in volume. Certain sounds (especially "p" and "b") can overload a microphone, while other sounds (particularly final consonants such as the "d" in -ed combinations like *wanted*) can be so subtle as to be implied rather than actually spoken.

Second, human speech alternates between lots of sound (during periods of talking) and blank spaces of silence (the pauses between phrases and sentences). These silences can pose a problem when lots of background noise is present during recording, as well as after downsampling occurs, since downsampling creates additional background noise.

Third, human speech also has a relatively wide frequency range. The warm, rich tone of a deep male voice can be less than 100 Hz, while the high frequencies contained in the pronunciation of the letter *s* can fall in the 7 kHz range. Frequency variation can be a real problem if your final sample rate is going to be 11 kHz (which, as mentioned in Chapter 1, gives you only 5.5 kHz of frequency response). This can make an *s* sound more like an *f* and add a lisping quality to speech.

Enough about the problems. What about solutions? First, let's assume that you're using a decent quality (at least $50) microphone rather than the one that came with your computer. If you use a compressor or limiter with a built-in noise gate, resolving the dynamic range and alternating speech-and-silence issues is relatively straightforward. Use the compressor to reduce the volume of loud spikes, and set the noise gate so that it shuts off the signal (and the background noise) during breaks in the speech.

Using a Dynamics Compressor

To save you from flipping back to Chapter 2 (where we first met compressors), here's a quick recap. Most compressors have two main functions: dynamic compression and noise gating. Compression settings include:

❏ *Threshold*—the point at which the compressor begins to affect the signal. Threshold typically ranges from -40 dB to + 20 dB. At -40 dB, the compressor is almost always active; at +20 dB, it only reduces the volume of extremely loud signals (use this setting to save a band from blowing up its public address system).

❏ ***Ratio***—the degree to which volume is reduced once the threshold has been exceeded (see Figure 6.1). Common compression ratios are 1:1, 1.3:1, 2:1, 4:1, 8:1 and ∞:1 (infinity-to-one). At 2:1, for example, 1 dB of gain is added to the signal for every 2 dB of gain over the threshold. At settings above 10:1, a compressor becomes a limiter. At a setting of ∞:1, the output volume never goes above the threshold, regardless of how much you increase the input volume. This is another great feature for saving your speakers or your PA system.

❏ ***Attack***—the speed at which the compressor becomes active. Sometimes it's desirable to apply compression gradually so as to maintain some dynamic diversity. In many music recording applications, for example, the initial signal contains much of the complex frequency information. A guitar note initially has a very complex waveform, containing both the sound of the pick striking the string and a jumble of scattered waves as the string begins to vibrate. But over time, as the string resonates, the vibrations settle into a more uniform pattern. With a slower attack, some of the character of the note can be maintained so that the recording doesn't sound squashed and lifeless. Attack times are often shown in milliseconds and may range from less than 1 ms to 500 ms.

Figure 6.1

Compression ratios affect output volume by reducing additional gain as the signal level passes the threshold. At a ratio of ∞:1 (infinity to one), the signal never exceeds the threshold.

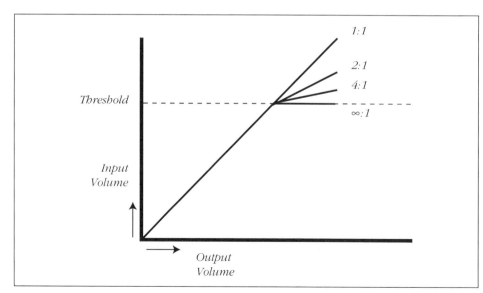

❏ ***Release***—the speed with which the compressor returns to an inactive state once the signal has dropped below the threshold. By twiddling with the attack and release, you can adjust the compressor so that its effect is gradual rather than abrupt. If the release time is too short, you might hear noticeable changes in gain after sharp spikes of volume. This phenomenon is known as *pumping* or *breathing,* and it sounds like someone rapidly twisting a volume knob up and down. If the release time is too long, on the other hand, the compressor may not react quickly enough after a volume spike and so reduces the volume of signals that you may not want to compress. Release times range from 50 ms to several seconds.

❏ ***Output gain***—for setting the output volume of the signal after it has been compressed. By its nature, compression reduces the peak volume of a signal. You can adjust the output gain to bring the overall level back up to where you want it.

The series of voice waveforms in Figure 6.2 demonstrates why compression is such a great tool for multimedia production. The original signal *(a)* evidences substantial variability in volume levels. When the signal is compressed at a 4:1 ratio *(b)*, higher-volume peaks are reduced. The overall volume of the file is somewhat lower, but it's much more consistent. After the file has been normalized *(c)*, the total volume of the file is greater.

This series of steps—recording with compression and then normalizing—yields a much better signal-to-noise ratio before downsampling, assuming that the original recording was relatively quiet. When you normalize, both the noise level and the voice volume increase, so you really *do* need to make an effort to reduce background noise before recording. For a hint of how noise can creep up, compare noise levels in parts *(a)* and *(c)* of Figure 6.2.

You can also see how the threshold setting affects the compressor. While the larger peaks are greatly reduced after compression *(b)* , the final *consonant* (the last small spike in the file) is the same size in the uncompressed and compressed versions. Be judicious when using compression. If you set your threshold too low and the ratio too high, you'll begin to squeeze the life out of your audio. We're used to hearing a lot of dynamic variation in speech; the goal should be to reduce that variability rather than eliminate it altogether.

What settings should you use on a compressor? It depends on the type of signal you're compressing. With voice recording, the main variable is the consistency of the reader's delivery. If you're working with professional voice talent this is less of a problem; seasoned pros know to keep their

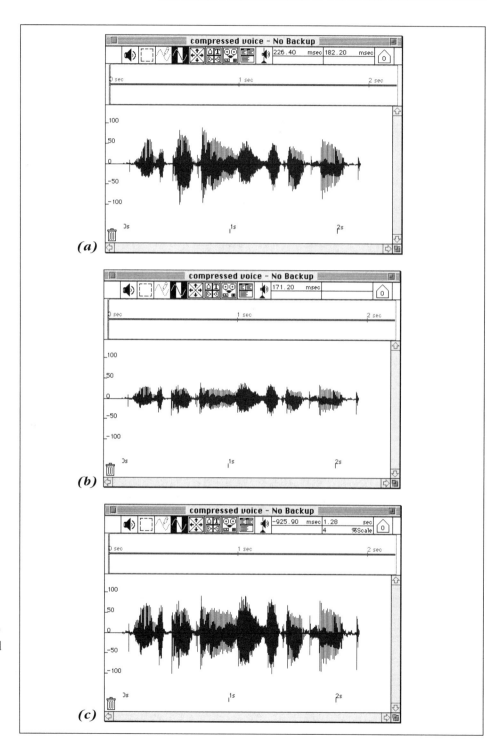

Figure 6.2

Three stages of processing a signal using compression: *(a)* an uncompressed signal; *(b)* 4:1 compression ratio; *(c)* signal normalized after compression.

tone under control, and to maintain both a consistent volume and a constant distance from the microphone. As a result, you can usually get away with using less compression. "Less" in compression translates into a slightly higher threshold (around -10 to -15 dB) and a slightly lower compression ratio (2:1).

If you're doing the voiceover yourself or have asked a friend to help out, it's likely you'll need to compress the voice more heavily to control changes in volume. Amateurs tend to have wider variations in speaking tone and are less attentive to microphone technique. A good starting point is a threshold of –15 to –20 dB and a ratio between 2:1 and 4:1.

Noise Gates

Many compressors include a noise gate function, first discussed in Chapter 2. Similar to compressors, noise gates have controls for threshold and release (some manufacturers have proprietary names for some of these functions). Once the signal falls below the threshold, the gate "closes" after the release time. One common application of a noise gate is to turn the volume all the way off and so eliminate unwanted background noise.

Noise gates work by *attenuating* (lowering the strength) of the signal by a certain amount whenever it falls below the gate's threshold. If you set the amount of attenuation too high, you may end up removing the noise but eliminating all the transient information from the signal. *Downward expanders* are similar to noise gates, but their effect is opposite to that of a compressor. The further the signal is below the threshold, the more it is attenuated. Ratios of 1:2 and 1:3 are usable, but anything more usually degrades the signal.

Voiceover Recording Tips

Maintain a constant distance from the microphone. When your mouth moves farther away from the microphone, three things happen: the volume decreases, the frequency content can change, and the ratio of room noise and ambience to vocal content varies. If you have to pause recording and walk away from the microphone, put a strip of masking tape on the floor to mark your position relative to the microphone so that you can return to the same spot when you're ready to resume recording. Otherwise, there may be a noticeable difference in vocal quality between sessions.

Use a foam windscreen or *pop filter* to reduce popping "p" and "b" sounds. Pop filters are screens of nylon mesh that you place in front of the microphone to disperse the strong bursts of air pressure that accompany those dreaded plosive consonants. Although many diferent pop filters are commercially available, in a pinch you can stretch a nylon stocking across a 6-inch diameter embroidery hoop and get good results. Most commercial-grade pop filters are simply refinements of this principle.

Use a microphone stand to maintain good microphone placement and to reduce any rubbing or squeaking noises that may occur as you handle the microphone. If you're reading from a large script, take care to avoid paper rustling and page turning noise. Use a reading stand or sheet music stand to hold the script.

If you're striving for that smooth radio voice, try to record when your voice is well-rested. If you've talking on the phone all day, your vocal chords will be tighter and your voice will have less resonance. If possible, take a minute to stretch your vocal chords with a short warm-up. Start with your normal voice, then repeat a phrase several times, making your voice lower with every repetition. Try to make your voice as low, warm, and resonant as possible.

Another way to warm up your vocal tone is to keep your mouth close to the microphone. This "proximity effect" enhances bass frequencies. But you need to be extra careful with your vocal volume, because it's easy to overload a microphone at close range. You also have to be careful to avoid mouth noises such as lip smacking.

Try to record with as little ambience as possible. When listening to voiceover on TV and radio, notice that it doesn't have reverb or other ambient effects (unless, of course, you're listening to an ad for a Monster Truck show). If you're aiming for a specific effect—say, a ghost in a cave—do whatever sounds good. But if your voice is for standard presentation purposes, keep ambience to a minimum. To find a good location within a room for recording, walk around while clapping your hands until you find a spot where reflected sound is least prevalent. Spaces with rugs, drapes, or other hanging fabric help to reduce reflected sound.

Wearing headphones while recording has the advantage of letting you hear the proximity effect (as well as any unwanted noises) clearly. You won't perceive the proximity effect using an omnidirectional microphone.

Note: *Once I recorded Bud Colligan, the CEO of Macromedia, in his bedroom closet. I'm sure he thought I was being a bit silly, but acoustically speaking, it was the best location in the house. We got a good recording!*

If you're recording to tape and plan to transfer and edit the material later, give yourself a short cue before every session (this practice is called *slating,* after the Hollywood slate tradition). Start the recording with a summary, like "This is voiceover for Big Al's CyberDonuts Web site, December 31, 1999." Also slate each take—for example, "Line 3, Take 2."

Speaking of scripts, if your script is long and complex, be sure it's well organized. Either number every line or assign a number to each discreet section of dialog. Create a document that cross-references line numbers to filenames so that you can name the voice files properly after they have been edited. It's amazing how easily you can get lost when listening to multiple tapes of the same material.

Recording Music

This is a vast topic beyond the scope of our book, so we can't cover it in detail. Here, we'll focus on issues that apply specifically to recording for multimedia. We'll also add a few tips for those who may be noodling in a small home project studio. For more information, refer to the Suggested Reading section in the back of the book; many books on studio music recording are already available.

Recording and mixing original music for multimedia present two special challenges, both of which result primarily from the computer's limited processing power when playing back a presentation. You must decide whether to use mono or stereo. You must also be sensitive to issues of equalization and frequency response when music is destined for lower sample rates and sample resolutions.

Stereo Versus Mono

It's very important to resolve the stereo versus mono issue before you mix. There's no question that stereo sounds better than mono. But stereo files are twice the size of mono files. Stereo uses twice as much disk space, twice as much memory, and twice as much processing power. The majority of CD-ROM title developers currently deliver their products in mono. This doesn't mean that mono is the ideal; it's simply a reality for titles intended for playback on older, slower systems. The emergence of 4:1, 16-bit compression schemes will soon change this situation for the better.

When you're mixing music that you know will end up as a mono file, it's best to actually mix in mono; don't pan instruments across the stereo field, and don't get hooked on ping-pong delays or stereo chorus effects. Most sound-editing programs let you mix two stereo tracks to a single mono file, but you may not be pleased with the results. This is due to *phase cancellation,* a phenomenon that occurs when two waves with different values combine in such a way that frequency content is lost or masked. The resulting file often sounds lifeless and flat. Figure 6.3 shows a worst-case scenario of phase cancellation—waves that are 180° out of phase with one another. Even when the phase differential is less extreme,

Figure 6.3

When waves are 180° out of phase as in this extreme example, they cancel each other completely, resulting in silence.

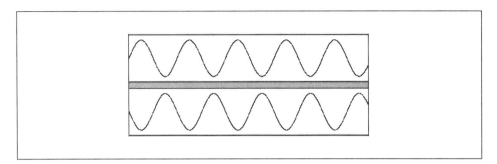

the two waves can combine to create frequencies that weren't previously present in the signal.

Equalization and Frequency Response

For composers and musicians, recording audio for multimedia can be heartbreaking. There are some things you just can't get away with when your audio is going to end up as a mono 8/22 file. If you downsample cymbals or wind chimes to 8/11, you'll end up with metallic hash. High-frequency information is lost, and lower midrange frequencies may be accentuated when you downsample. Take some time to experiment with the effects of downsampling to see how it alters your audio content. Then, take the colorization into consideration when recording and adjust your EQ to reduce its effect. Better yet, record your source material so that it sounds its best at 16/44, and then use EQ processing software to tweak it to taste. That way, you're not printing the EQ to tape, so you'll have a clean master for future work in higher-resolution formats.

Another technique is to make a test recording at the final sample rate and bit resolution and then listen to how it affects the music. This procedure will give you a better understanding of what will work in the final product.

Music and Dynamic Range

Whether you're recording music or voice, use a compressor to reduce the dynamic range of a mix. Most commercially-produced mixes are compressed pretty heavily during mastering so that they will hold up well when broadcast. You may want to do your own "mastering" pass on finished mixes to tweak equalization and compression.

Sound Effects

Recorded sound effects usually fall into two categories: real-world location sounds that suggest environmental ambience, and effects recorded in a studio setting.

Recording in the Environment

You need four things in order to capture sound in the real world: a portable DAT, a microphone, closed-ear headphones, and lots of patience. If you're buying a DAT primarily for location recording, get one with XLR inputs and meters that can be seen clearly if the unit is strapped over your shoulder. If your microphone requires *phantom power* (the small amount of power needed to maintain a magnetic field in a condenser microphone), you may need a separate phantom power supply, usually a small box that holds a battery. Your headphones should provide as much isolation as possible so that you can hear what's actually going onto tape.

Finally, you need lots of patience and ingenuity. Out in the real world, you can't always control who or what may be passing through your auditory field. Be prepared to wait it out as cars drive by, planes fly over, people stop yelling, and the wind stops blowing. When you try to record a sound in the environment, you are certain to hear at least ten other sounds that you never noticed before. Unfortunately, you won't be able to make them go away.

If your goal is to achieve a balance of several sounds but you find that one sound is too prevalent, you don't have the option of turning that one sound down with a mixer. But you *can* experiment with microphone placement to get the effect you want. For example, if you're recording a crowd noise and a person in front of you is too loud, find a wall and then point the microphone at the wall. This technique helps you pick up more reflected sounds to balance the levels.

Studio Effects

Some people refer to studio-recorded effects as *Foley effects.* The term commemorates one of the first practitioners of this craft for film, who recorded sound effects such as footsteps and doorslams while watching the picture. Applying this term to multimedia is somewhat of a misnomer, since one seldom records while watching animation on the computer screen.

You can create all sorts of effects in the confines of a recording space. All it requires is a microphone, a mixer, a recorder, and access to a large and diverse amount of junk that you can stick in front of a microphone. Your home is a Foley studio just waiting to happen! As with voice recording, good sound effect recording requires a quiet space, a microphone with a stand, headphones, and a compressor. In a controlled studio environment, you can experiment with microphone placement and effects processing to create truly unique audio textures.

Capture

Now that you have some great material on tape, it's time to transfer it to the computer. If you never even wanted to bother with tape and were more interested in recording straight into the computer, this section is for you also. There are three main pathways for capturing audio:

❏ **Analog capture**—digitizing source material as it enters the computer

❏ **Digital capture**—transferring digitally from DAT using special hardware

❏ **CD capture**—copying data from a standard audio CD

Lots of programs support capture from CD, including MoviePlayer, Audioshop, and SoundEdit 16 version 2.0. There are also dedicated CD capture programs like OMI's Disc to Disk and Gallery Software's CDStudio. If you're using a large CD library, Disc-to-Disk and Audioshop can make your life simpler with their support for CD track names. The track names can't be automatically read from disk, but if you take the time to input them once, you can call tracks by name for all your future editing. CDStudio has another nice feature—support for *track indices*. A track index is a subcode written on the CD, which serves as a marker within a CD track. Since the RedBook format supports only 99 tracks, track indices are often used to subdivide different samples within a single track.

In the previous chapter, we discussed a few issues dealing with capture, including how to capture from an analog source using the Macintosh's input, how to grab audio from a CD using MoviePlayer, and how to transfer digitally to an Audiomedia card.

Aside from the specifics that we've already covered, there are several general guidelines to follow when capturing audio. Here's a sampling of the most important ones.

Capture at High Fidelity

Even if your end product will be 8/22 audio, you should capture at 16/44 whenever possible. Time to recap a basic rule: work at the highest sample rate and resolution for as long as possible, and then downsample in the final step.

This rule applies mainly to the capturing and editing stages of production. Downsampling should occur when you're ready to output the files. Why is it important to capture at 16/44 when your samples will end up at 8/22? Background noise is much greater at lower resolutions. If you mix two 8/22 files, the final file will contain more noise than if you had mixed the files at 16/44 and then downsampled the result.

Working at higher resolutions does exact a toll on your productivity. Files are larger, so processing time, RAM requirements, and disk storage space increase. But the gains in quality and flexibility are well worth the trouble.

Capture at High Volume

If you always transfer digitally, you can skip this advice because you can't change the volume of a signal during a digital transfer (and you *did* record a good, hot level, right?). But if you're digitizing as you capture, use the highest volume level possible without allowing the signal to clip or distort.

Capture en Masse

Try to capture as much as you can into one large file, rather than capturing each segment into its own file. This allows you to do all your processing on one large document, then snip it up into little pieces just prior to output. Your audio will be much more consistent if you make all the volume and processing adjustments to one large document.

When making a large bulk capture, be sure to leave enough blank space on the disk for your processed files. At most, your original capture file should not use more than one-half of the available disk space. We're assuming that any temporary or scratch files needed by the editing package are stored on another disk; if that's not the case, don't use more than one-fourth of your disk space for the bulk capture.

In a typical session in which the target format is 8/22, you might proceed like this:

1. Start with a mono 16/44 file that consumes 100 MB of disk space.
2. Downsample the file to 16/22 (add 50 MB, for a total of 150 MB).
3. Perform two processing operations (EQ and compression, for example), saving a copy of each. These processes add 50 MB twice, bringing the total to 250 MB.
4. Finally, downsample to 8/22, adding 25 MB to the file for a grand total of 275 MB.

In this case, your original file should not take up more than one-third of your available space, since you'll need almost twice as much space for processing.

**Optimize
Before
Capturing**

If you're about to shovel several hundred megabytes of data onto your disk, be sure it's up to the task. If data on your disk is fragmented, recording and playback performance will suffer as the disk tries to find places to read and write data. Use a hard disk utility program to optimize the disk before big sessions. If possible, dedicate a complete disk to audio work and keep your system and applications on a separate disk. If you have only one hard disk, you might want to partition it and put the digital audio in its own partition. Some programs don't perform well when recording audio to an internal startup drive.

Editing

At last we come to the heart of the matter. For our purposes, let's consider editing to include mixing and signal processing as well as basic cutting and pasting. We'll review four types of editing processes:

❑ General editing techniques
❑ Editing techniques for voice
❑ Editing techniques for music
❑ Editing techniques for sound effects

Of course, these categories aren't hard and fast; you might be thrilled with the results of a voice-editing technique on a sound effect.

Since this book is about multimedia, the focus is on dealing with sounds that began as 16/44 and are on their way to a multimedia audio format such as 8/22, 8/11, or IMA 4:1 compressed. To put the process in perspective, here's an overview of the steps we usually perform after capturing sounds:

1. **Normalize**, just to be sure the sound is at the highest possible level before processing.
2. **Edit and mix**—Take care of tasks such as mixing music beds behind voice or blending multiple sounds into a background before you scale down the sample rate or sample resolution.
3. **Convert the sample rate** from 44.1 kHz to 22.050 kHz.
4. **Process with final mastering effects**—Perform final dynamic compression and equalization on the 16/22 file.
5. **Convert the sample resolution** from 16 bits to 8 bits.

At this point, the file is ready for final output (no, of course it's not that simple). Let's examine some of the finer points pertaining to each step, starting with some general techniques that apply equally to voice, music, and sound effects. We'll also take a quick look at equalization for multimedia.

General Editing Techniques

Most of the techniques covered in this section deal with noise reduction and good editing practices. While you may often need to process music differently from voice or sound effects, in the end *all* of your sounds will benefit when you keep noise to a minimum.

Normalizing

Normalizing a file makes it as loud as possible without distortion. The process finds the loudest peak in the file and then amplifies the entire file by whatever amount is required to make that peak value 100 percent. It's a quick, easy way to ensure that you're working with the loudest possible signal. Since a 16-bit file has a better signal-to-noise ratio than an 8-bit file, it has less noise that's inherently associated with the sampling process (assuming your source material is relatively quiet).

Balancing Volume Levels

When you're working on a large project, it's important to maintain a consistent level of volume among all files. If some voiceover files are considerably louder (or softer) than others, the listener may be forced to dive for his or her volume knob in the middle of the presentation. There goes your continuity! Normalizing helps bring files to relatively similar levels, but it can also be misleading (see Figure 6.4). If one file is a rhythmic piece of

Figure 6.4

Two files after normalization. File *(b)*, without a large peak of volume, normalizes to a higher overall volume than file *(a)*.

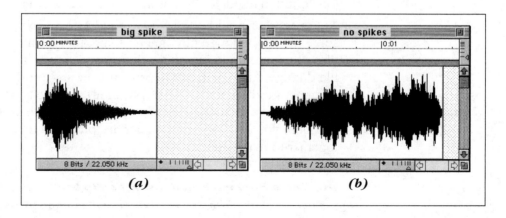

(a) *(b)*

music with loud peaks on a downbeat and a relatively quiet midsection, its overall volume will be determined by the largest peak. A file consisting of a background ambience of nature sounds, on the other hand, probably won't have a large peak. Its overall volume will therefore be much higher after normalization, leading to a volume mismatch when files are played one after another.

There are several measures you can take to control the potential dangers of normalization.

❑ For voice and music, keep levels as consistent as possible while recording. Use a dynamics compressor to help give you a more consistent level.

❑ Capturing large sections at once helps you maintain better control of levels, since you can audition the entire file and make volume adjustments while you're still at high resolution. Practically every sound-editing program has an "amplify" or "gain change" effect to increase or reduce volume for a section of the file. If you're lucky, the adjustment units will be in decibels. If not, remember the logarithmic nature of sound. Amplifying by 200 percent increases the gain by 6 dB; a 50 percent decrease reduces the gain by 6 dB; and a 75 percent decrease reduces gain by 12 dB.

❑ Create a finished "test level" sound file of voice or music and save it as a System 7 sound. Leave it on your desktop so you can easily click on it and play it for comparison purposes.

❑ There are also differences between the *perceived* loudness of a sound and the amount of gain that a signal registers on metering devices or in waveform displays. If two files *look* as though they have similar levels but sound markedly different in volume, let your ears be the judge.

❑ Not every file should be played as loud as possible. You will want some files to be inherently quieter than others. Unfortunately, quiet files often end up being noisy. Before you reduce the volume of the file during editing, talk to the programmer and producer. The programmer (and the authoring application) may be able to control the overall system volume to set levels. Whatever path you take, be sure that both you and the programmer are prepared to work closely together to make adjustments.

Note: *There is an important distinction to keep in mind if you take the approach of controlling the overall system volume to set levels. The level of the Macintosh's total output volume, as it is controlled in the Sound*

Control Panel, is an analog signal and changes as such. Levels within the Macintosh's individual sound channels, on the other hand, change in the digital realm. By now you should know what happens when volumes are reduced in the digital realm, particularly with 8-bit sample resolution: noise and distortion become much more noticeable. The level of the analog signal present at the main output, however, can be reduced without adding too much noise (otherwise, any System alert sounds would sound like hash at low levels). If the circumstances of your presentation are such that the programmer can change the overall system volume to adjust volume levels, good-quality audio should result. If you're using multiple audio channels and know in advance that the level of a sound must change at a particular point (for example, fading music down to a lower level at the start of a voiceover), it's probably best to do the fade yourself while editing. Otherwise, your signal level will be changed digitally. If you're in a fully interactive situation in which relative channel volume levels could change at any time based on a user action, you'll have to rely on the digital-level control and put up with the extra noise.

Silencing the Start and End

It's a good idea to have just a little bit of silence (actual digital zeroes, not just a quiet spot) at the beginning and ending of a file. Silence helps you avoid clicks and pops that may occur if the sound starts at a point other than the zero axis. Also leave at least 50 ms of silence before the audio begins. Some PC sound cards (and their drivers) are slow to react to sound playback and may clip off the beginning of the sound.

Remove Excess Silence

Yes, you should *add* some silence, but within reason. If there are several seconds of silence at the start or end of a file, remove them when you're editing. Silence takes up just as much file space as sound data; it's just that you're storing a bunch of zeroes instead of different sample values.

Note: *Actually, silence is one of the few types of sound data for which data compression programs actually buy you some storage savings. Silence compresses more compactly than other types of sound.*

The presence of excess silence in a file has another disadvantage: it can throw off synchronization during authoring. Many programs let you check whether sound is currently playing, but they can't identify whether it's silence data or audible data. If there are three seconds of silence before a voiceover starts, you can forget about lip sync. And if there are three seconds of silence at the end of the file, the user may have to sit and wait for it to finish playing the silence before the presentation can continue.

Choose Fades Carefully

Many editing programs let you select a region of data and apply a fade-in or fade-out. But be sensitive to how the slope of the fade may affect sound quality (see Figure 6.5). When you perform a straight-line linear fade, the data at the end of the fade is reduced in volume. When your files are destined for low-resolution delivery, however, the reduced dynamic range of straight-line linear fades makes background noise a problem. You may hear decent sound for the first half of the fade, but the last half will become increasingly dominated by the "frying bacon" noise found mainly in the 8-bit realm.

If your editing program supports logarithmic fades, use one that approximates the curve shown in the lower part of Figure 6.5. As the sound begins to fade, it's likely that the listener is already mentally preparing for it to fade completely. Fading the sound more quickly at the tail end reduces its exposure to background noise. This technique also applies to fade-ins (but in reverse, of course). Logarithmic fade-ins are less susceptible to background noise.

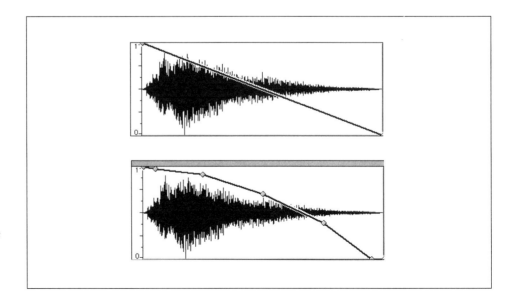

Figure 6.5

A linear fade **(top)** and a logarithmic fade **(bottom)** as shown in SoundEdit 16.

Panning Effects

If you have the luxury of working in stereo, you can take advantage of stereo effects like *panning*—the placement of the sound within a stereo field. Deck II, Digitrax, Session, and other programs have good interfaces for panning control; you can draw the panning information right on top of the data using the classic "rubber band" controllers familiar to Premiere users. Used creatively, panning adds lots of depth to a mix. Figure 6.6 shows how Deck II uses panning to "stereoize" a mono file and give it some character.

Here is a suggested sequence of steps for panning a file:

1. After importing the file, place a copy in the second track.

2. Offset the time of the copied track 50 to 75 milliseconds by dragging it to the right. In Deck, this may require changing the Grid Interval and Time Mode settings under the Options menu. Any offset value is fine if you like the results. Small values (in the 50 to 75 range, for example) create a very short delay, often called a slapback—a signature sound of the ghost of Elvis. Short delays also can create interesting phasing effects.

3. Set the view in the Track window to Pan.

4. Draw the pan so that each track is a mirror image of the other. Feel free to experiment here; create a tremolo effect by allowing both tracks to ping-pong rapidly, or pan slowly from left to right to create a motion effect.

5. Play the tracks. *Voilá,* the previously one-dimensional mono file has become much more interesting! You can do similar tricks with stereo files, too, but you need to be careful if you want to maintain the

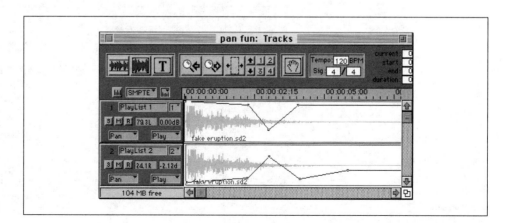

Figure 6.6

Panning information drawn onto tracks in Deck II

stereo imaging of the original file. Offsetting one channel from the other could cause phase cancellation.

Equalization for Multimedia

Equalization (EQ) can be a powerful tool for emphasizing a certain sound or for eliminating frequencies that cause one sound to interfere with another. In multimedia, where frequency response and dynamic range are limited and the sound playback hardware is marginal, equalization becomes even more important. Let's take a closer look at the basics of equalization.

Types of EQ

You'll hear many new terms bandied about when you begin to work with EQ. First, there are three main types of EQ that you're likely to run into: *graphic, parametric,* and *shelving.*

❑ ***Graphic EQ*** (Figure 6.7) is the type you've probably seen in stereo systems. The frequency spectrum is divided into sections called bands. Each band has a slider for adjusting the volume level of that band. Look closely at a graphic EQ and you'll usually see a pattern in the frequency divisions: 62 Hz, 125 Hz, 250 Hz, 500 Hz, and so on. The frequencies double with each successive band. Graphic EQs are most often used to shape sound across the entire frequency spectrum, usually to compensate for frequency characteristics within a room. You might use them, for example, to brighten the high end in a car-

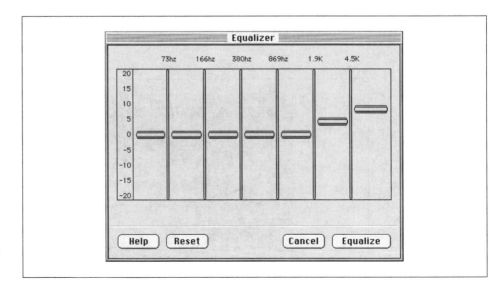

Figure 6.7

A standard graphic EQ interface. In this example, the high frequencies are boosted.

peted room that soaks up high-frequency sounds, or to reduce the high end in a room full of reflective surfaces such as glass or concrete. That's why you find them in PA systems at clubs and concerts, as well as in car and home stereos.

❏ ***Parametric EQ*** (Figure 6.8) has much more precision than graphic EQ. It lets you hone in on a particular frequency with surgical precision. Parametric EQs usually focus on the middle of the frequency spectrum, between 250 Hz and 8 kHz. There are three main control knobs on a parametric EQ: Center frequency, Bandwidth (often called Q), and Level. The center frequency is adjustable, and the range it covers depends on the device. The bandwidth determines the range over which the EQ will have an effect, and the level controls how much the EQ will increase or reduce the gain of the frequencies within that bandwidth. Ideally, bandwidths should be listed in octaves rather than in Hertz (an octave is a doubling of frequency, much as we just saw with the controls for graphic EQ); a 500 Hz bandwidth at a 500 Hz center frequency is approximately two octaves wide, whereas a 500 Hz bandwidth at 10 kHz is only about 1/20th of an octave wide.

Let's look at it another way. A bandwidth of 500 Hz is barely significant when the center frequency is 10,000 Hz (this would control the

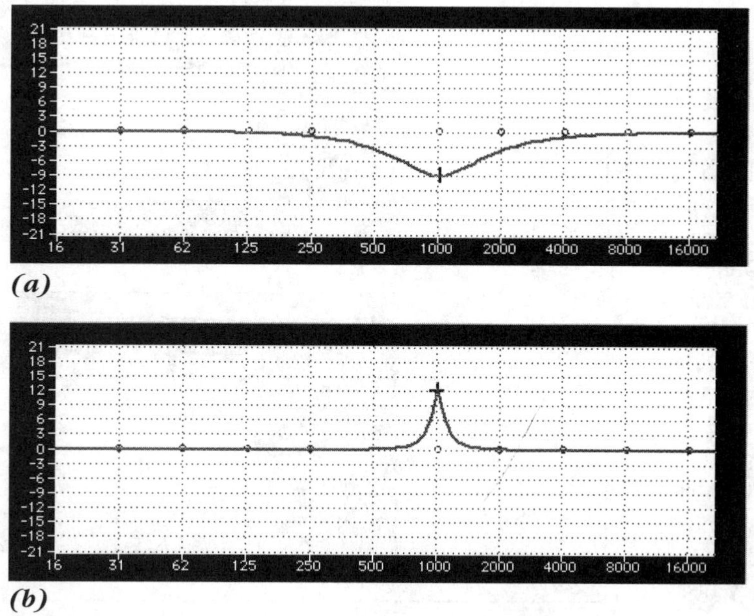

Figure 6.8

Two examples of a Parametric EQ curve (from Waves' Q10). In example **(a)**, gain is reduced on a wide range of frequencies around 1 kHz. In example **(b)**, the gain of a narrow range of frequecies around 1 kHz is increased.

range from 9,750Hz to 10,250 Hz). But 500 Hz is a significant amount when the center frequency is 500 Hz (controlling from 250 Hz to 750 Hz). The ear hears octaves, not Hertz. Unfortunately, many sound editing packages ignore this phenomenon and use numerical units that are more convenient for programmers to work in, rather than units that have meaning for the user. Professional analog parametric EQs use octaves exclusively to specify bandwidth settings.

❑ **Shelving EQ** (Figure 6.9) is common on many mixers. Probably the most familiar examples are the bass (low shelving) and treble (high shelving) controls found on home stereos. The EQ is preset to a certain frequency (called the cutoff frequency). Whereas the cutoff in software EQs is often adjustable, it's rarely adjustable on any but the most expensive hardware EQs. For a low-shelving EQ, the cutoff may be around 100 Hz, and for a high-shelving EQ it may be 10 kHz. On a high-shelving EQ, you can adjust the gain of all high frequencies above the cutoff; on a low-shelving EQ, you can adjust the gain of all low frequencies below the cutoff.

There's one other class of EQ you may encounter, although it's most often described as a filter, because it removes all frequencies *except* for the

Figure 6.9

A low-shelving EQ *(a)* and a high-shelving EQ *(b)* in Digitrax. The low-shelf setting could be used to eliminate hum from a ground loop (60 Hz). The high-shelf setting would reduce high-frequency hiss.

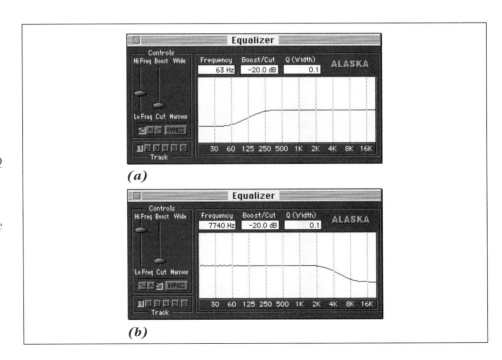

ones you specify. Such filters are called *bandpass, high pass,* and *low pass* filters. Bandpass filters are similar to a parametric EQ, except that instead of increasing or decreasing the gain of a frequency range, they eliminate other frequencies except those within the specified band. High pass filters, true to their names, let high-frequency information pass through and remove low frequencies from the signal. Low pass filters do the opposite.

> **Note:** *A bandpass filter behaves like a crop tool for frequencies. It's simply a combination of a high-pass filter and a low-pass filter, lopping off the ends of the frequency response while leaving the center frequencies unaltered.*

General Guidelines for Using EQ

Now that you know a bit more about the types of EQ, you might well wonder, "How do I use it?" Glad you asked! To start, here are two cardinal rules for EQ in most recording situations:

- ❏ Apply EQ only *when all else fails.* Ideally, careful microphone placement and choice of recording space should yield exactly the sound you want. Use EQ for subtle tweaks and to recover from mistakes, but don't rely on it as a matter of course.

- ❏ It's usually better to reduce frequencies you don't want than to boost the ones you do want. Boosting EQ in a specific band basically raises the volume of that band, including background noise. It's also more likely to create unwanted distortion and phase shifts.

Look to the
CD-ROM

That said, here's a disclaimer for those of us doing multimedia on our way down to sample rates of 22 kHz and 11 kHz. When you're doing your final processing before downsampling, go ahead and tweak the high frequencies up a bit—but only in the final processing phase! You should still keep EQ tweaks to a minimum while you're working at 16/44. For a demonstration of EQ in action, check the CD tutorial on non-destructive editing.

Using EQ to Reduce Noise

Let's look at a typical scenario in which EQ can rescue a session. A friend records some voiceover using a portable DAT and microphone and asks you to turn it into AIFF files for a presentation. You pop the DAT into your deck and take a listen. Hmm, what's that buzzing noise? Your pal didn't *say* he was going to record it inside an apiary. The buzz could have come from fluorescent lights, from a vibration in the ventilation system, or from a noisy piece of hardware. No problem if you have EQ at your disposal. If you have a dedicated hardware EQ, you might want to run your signal through that processor as you transfer it to the Macintosh (you'll pay a a price for taking an extra trip through analog to digital conversion, but it may be required to save the track). If you have good EQ software, you can fix it in the computer.

The first task is to pinpoint the frequency you want to change. This process is easiest if your processing software is interactive, giving you a real-time preview of the EQ's effect. If you have an external EQ processor, you're home free. Unfortunately, not all software has real-time preview (SoundEdit 16, for example, lacks a preview option), so you'll have to process the file to hear the results and then undo the effect if necessary after every test.

If your program has a graphic EQ display (as in Sound Designer II and SoundEdit 16), raise each band, one at a time, to the maximum until you find the band that contains the greatest amount of the frequency you're trying to eliminate. If a particular band doesn't seem to affect the offending frequency very much, lower it back to the center position and try the next band. Once you find the band that *adds* the most noise, you'll know you've also found the band that will remove the most noise. Both Sound Designer II and SoundEdit 16 let you adjust the graphic EQ a bit; use this flexibility to pinpoint the sound as closely as possible before processing.

With parametric controls (as found in Sound Designer II, Digitrax, or Q10), the process of making equalization adjustments is much easier. Set the bandwidth (Q) to about one-third of an octave and increase the level to the maximum volume. Then use the center frequency control to sweep the EQ curve back and forth through the spectrum until you find the spot that contains the most noise. Once you're in the neighborhood, set the level to its minimum value and fine-tune the bandwidth so it's as narrow as possible. Of course, sometimes the noise is not in a single band, so you'll have to use multiple bands of EQ or make multiple passes through a single band of EQ. The accompanying CD includes a tutorial showing the effects of an EQ changing in real time. This may help you get a better idea of the way EQ can affect a signal.

Notice in this example that one of the goals in applying EQ is to affect the smallest possible range of the frequency spectrum. It's important to leave the majority of your audio as unaffected as possible. If you remove too many frequencies from a voice track, it will sound unnatural. Removing too much low frequency makes a file sound as though it's coming through a telephone. To the creative ear, of course, such an effect *can* be useful; you can hear examples in Paul McCartney ditties such as "Honey Pie" and "Uncle Albert."

Using EQ to Add "Oomph"

The small speakers used to present your finely-honed creations to the world is a shortcoming of many multimedia delivery systems. These systems typically have very poor bass response, since their small size makes it difficult for them to reproduce the slower, low-frequency vibrations. If your presentation contains bass-heavy material such as rap or house music, or lots of rumbling spaceships or earthquakes, it may sound downright wimpy coming out of a small speaker. You can use EQ to compensate for this. No, boosting the low, low end probably won't help. But you can boost the midrange slightly (around 250 Hz) to give the sound more punch. It's better to use discretion so that your mix doesn't sound out of balance for those fortunate enough to be listening on a good system. If you choose to boost the midrange, listen using both big and small speakers to find a happy medium.

EQ and Anti-aliasing Filters

If your sounds are destined for delivery at 8/22 or 8/11, take note. Most sound-editing applications apply a low pass filter to incoming signals. But as you'll recall from Chapter 1, the highest frequency you can represent in a sound is just one half of the sample rate (for example, the highest frequency you can hear in a 22 kHz sample is 11 kHz). To avoid *aliasing* (in which frequencies above the sample rate are erroneously represented as lower frequencies), sound programs run the data through an *anti-aliasing filter* that automatically removes all frequencies greater than half the sample rate. In the case of a sound sampled at 22 kHz, an anti-aliasing filter would remove all frequencies above 11 kHz.

Anti-aliasing filters are a fail-safe measure designed to keep garbage out of your sound. You can take a pre-emptive approach during editing and recording to anticipate how your sound will fare after the high-frequency content has been stripped away. One trick is to place an external equalizer between the main output of your mixer and the amplifier (with most decent mixers, you can use the main insert bus). Once your sound has been captured into the computer, you can also use EQ processing in software. Waves Q10, a 10-band parametric EQ, ships with sample setups for previewing audio destined for 22 kHz or 11 kHz.

Voice Editing

Most voice production falls into one of two categories: announcer-style and character voices. Character voices sometimes provide an opportunity for creative tweaking, but most announcer-style VO has a straightforward delivery. More than music or effects, voice editing can seem like grunt work after you've done it a few times. I often liken it to the audio equivalent of scanning graphics: dump in the content and crop it down. Since voice is relatively consistent (assuming a good recording), voice editing is ideally suited to automated processing.

Automated Voice Editing

We've developed a system to speed up the voice-editing process considerably using Sound Designer II and CE Software's QuicKeys. It uses Sound Designer's Regions and Save Playlist as Soundfile features to generate individual files from one master file automatically (see the Sound Designer discussion in Chapter 7 for a fuller description of how this works). One new product that helps make voice editing more efficient is the Precision Audio Tools package from Gallery Software. It contains modules for auto-generating file names from a written script. It also senses gaps of silence in a file and automatically generates Sound Designer regions based on the gaps. PC-based users can find an auto-regionalizing function in SoundForge.

Noise Gating for Voice

Voice can benefit tremendously from carefully applied noise gating—even more than music or sound effects can. When you pause between phrases and sentences, background noise quickly rears its ugly head. Gating needs to be used judiciously. When all the background noise is removed from very short pauses within a sentence, a voice can sound unnatural and stilted. Adjust the release time of the noise gate so that it's applied only where at least two seconds of silence occur. Also be careful with the threshold control; setting it too high may clip the last consonant off a word.

Tweaks for Character Voices

If you're creating a "special-effect" voice, you can have lots of fun with a sound-editing package. Pitch shifting a voice up a few steps gives you chipmunks and munchkins. Shift the pitch down or reverse the sample for demonic monster characters. To create robotic voices, use EQ to remove frequencies below 250 Hz, and then use the slapback echo effect as shown in the steps that follow Figure 6.6 on page 155. If your sound editor supports time expansion or compression (SoundEdit 16, Sound Designer II, and Steinberg's Time Bandit do), try pitch shifting a copy of the voice (this changes its length), and then restore it to its original length and mix it back into the original. You'll have a voice that speaks in chords!

Music Editing

Music editing falls neatly into two categories: linear files that play once, and looped files that repeat over and over. Looped files tend to be relatively short, since they usually must be loaded completely into RAM in order to loop smoothly. Linear files may be longer, since they can stream from disk, but many linear files are short *stings*—introductory or transitional pieces that last only a few seconds. Looped files and linear files each have their own particular idiosyncrasies.

Looping Music

The most difficult task in creating a loop is finding a good splice. The best spot for a loop splice is the point at which both ends of the loop are on the zero axis (such splices are often called *zero crossings*). Some programs (Sound Designer II, SoundEdit 16 2.0, and Alchemy, for example) have special Loop Windows for nudging the start and end points of the loop until they create a seamless splice. When a loop is inserted into an AIFF file in any of these programs, it will be recognized as a loop when imported into another program.

Another trick to creating a good sounding loop—especially if you're using a MIDI sequencer to compose your own—is to record several iterations of the loop and then loop the second iteration. If you capture the first iteration of a loop (the one at the beginning of the recording), there won't be any resonating frequencies. For example, imagine that your loop section ends with a cymbal crash. The first time you play the loop, you won't hear the decay of the cymbal at the beginning because it won't have happened yet. But by capturing the second loop, you'll hear the decay of the cymbal mixed into the "beginning" of the piece. If you had captured the first loop, the cymbal's decay would have cut off abruptly. Looping the second section assures that sustaining sounds will carry smoothly across the loop point.

Figure 6.10 shows this principle at work. In the example shown here, the second segment creates a better loop because the cymbal hit at the end of the second segment splices seamlessly into the decay from the cymbal in the first loop. Since the first loop has no decaying frequencies at the beginning, the cymbal would cut off abruptly if the first segment were looped.

There is an additional concern if you are creating music destined for playback under Windows. This is because Windows allows loops only at the beginning and end of the buffers being passed to the wave playback device. You'll have to work carefully with the programmer to ensure that

Figure 6.10

Capturing multiple iterations and looping the second one in the series gives looped music better continuity because sounds carry across the loop point.

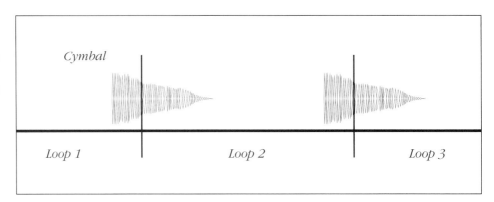

the buffers are of a size that both supports your loop points and doesn't create other problems in the wave playback.

Fading Linear Music

If you're using a piece of linear music that fades in or out, you may get better results creating the fades during editing than simply relying on the fade as it's recorded. Long, slow fades created in a recording studio may expose your music to undue amounts of background noise. You'll often come out ahead by drawing your own logarithmic fades (as shown in Figure 6.5 on page 154).

Making Music From Noise

When you're using a sound-editing package, you actually have a digital sampling synthesizer at your disposal! You can create interesting rhythms and industrial backbeats by manipulating samples of voice or music. Try this exercise:

1. Copy one second from a voiceover into a new file.
2. Pitch shift the new file down one octave.
3. Reverse the sample, loop it, and play. Instant insanity! You have a two second loop.
4. Now take a syllable and turn it into a snare drum. Copy a 1/4 second syllable into a new track.
5. Offset it so that it plays at the one-second mark.
6. Pitch shift the track up two octaves.
7. Loop both tracks and play.

You get the idea. You have a tremendous musical instrument at your disposal, one that lets you create a variety of unique audio textures. Put it to good use!

**Effects
Editing**

You can divide effects into three main categories:

❏ **Foreground effects**—door slams, horn honks, comedic effects, and so on

❏ **Background effects**—nature, city sounds, or crowd ambience

❏ **Interface effects**—button clicks

Each type of effect has a different role in a presentation, and there are editing tricks that come in handy for each.

Foreground Effects

More so than any other sound category we've discussed so far, foreground effects are usually tied to an animation or other action on the screen. Synchronization is therefore a high priority. In most situations, good sync in an interactive environment requires the sound to be available instantly. To achieve this level of performance, the sound should be in RAM, since seeking to sound data on a CD-ROM may take too long. Since the sound must fit into RAM, it should be as small as possible.

If your animation requires several effects in sequence, edit them into separate files whenever possible. In most authoring environments, triggering several small sounds at the proper point in an animated sequence yields better sync than playing one long file that combines multiple effects.

There's another benefit to making foreground effects as short as possible. Since sound effects are usually relatively high in volume, background noise is much less noticeable than it might be within music or voice files.

Background Effects

Adding a background ambient track can really bring a scene to life. In many cases these tracks are looped, especially in interactive games where the user might decide to stay at a spot for an indeterminate length of time.

Background ambient effects are usually lower in volume than foreground effects, voice, or music. The lower volume leaves them more susceptible to unwanted noise. On the other hand, background ambience actually serves to *mask* noise, especially when you mix a voiceover track into an ambient bed.

Crossfading Background Loops Creating a good ambient loop can be difficult when the character of the sound changes radically over time. For example, it's hard to loop a section of howling wind when the frequency content of the wind sound is always changing. One strategy for getting around this is to create a crossfade between the end and the start of the loop. Here's how to create a crossfade loop (see Figure 6.11).

1. Select one second of sound data from the beginning of the file.
2. Cut the first second and paste it into a new track.
3. Offset the second track so that the end of the second track matches the end of the first track.
4. Draw a crossfade: fade out the last second of the first track while fading in the data in the second track (logarithmic fades are often better than linear fades at maintaining a consistent volume).
5. Mix to a new file.
6. Loop the entire file and play.

By merging the splice point into the middle of a crossfade, the loop point becomes much less noticeable. Depending on your material, you may want to crossfade over a period longer than one second. But keep in mind that every second of crossfading is a second that's subtracted from the total length of the loop. If you start with a ten-second loop and create a two-second crossfade, you end up with an eight-second loop.

Interface Effects

Multimedia titles can really outshine other software applications in their ability to add audio feedback to buttons. Buttons that animate, buttons that respond to the mouse rolling over them, button sliders that change in pitch as you move them—there's plenty of interesting work to be done.

Button sounds are usually pretty short. Like foreground effects, they need to respond rapidly to user actions. In most situations, it's also helpful for button sounds to be relatively unobtrusive. Typically, the main job of a button sound is to let the viewer know that a mouseclick has been received properly.

That doesn't mean the sound has to be boring, though! Granted, it's probably not a good idea to use four wildly different sounds for a page forward button (unless you're going for novelty value in a kid's title). But with a few sound-editing tricks, you can subtly alter one button sound to create several versions with different characteristics. Then you can either randomly cycle through the variations or use them for groups of buttons with similar functions.

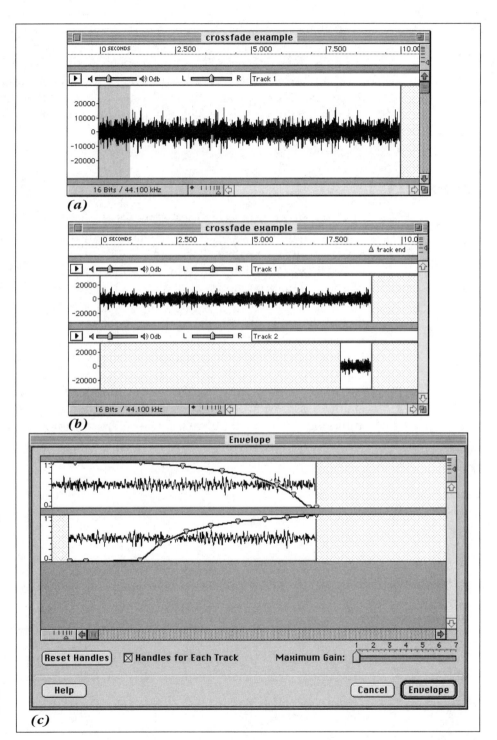

Figure 6.11

Three of the four steps in creating a crossfade loop. *(a)* Select the beginning of the section to be looped. *(b)* Cut it and paste into a new track and align the ends of the tracks. *(c)* Draw a logarithmic crossfade and apply the envelope effect. Mix the result to a new file and set loop points at the start and end.

To make one button sound into five different button sounds, shift the pitch of each one just slightly (two to three half-steps at the most). Then apply slightly different EQ settings to each one (SoundEdit 16's Smooth and Emphasize effects are good for this . . . in fact, it's about the only thing they're good for!). The result is a group of sounds that have some individual personality yet are related, like colors drawn from a unified palette.

Summary

In this chapter, you've learned some of the gory details of audio production for multimedia. We've seen that a good team effort in planning can save you time and pain during production. Recording is a crucial stage in creating raw material, and reducing noise during recording and processing will yield better sound in your finished files. We also discussed how different types of equalization can help you fine-tune audio tracks or rescue them from oblivion. Finally, you learned some new editing tricks for voice, music, and sound effects tracks.

Once you've made it through the editing stage, you have amassed a veritable cornucopia of data. Now you're ready to slice and dice, then serve it up. In the next chapter, we'll cover techniques for outputting finished files at lower sample rates and resolutions and for integrating those files into authoring environments. We'll also see some sample delivery systems and discuss their ramifications for sound playback.

7

Working with Audio, Part Two

In the previous chapter, we covered audio production techniques up through the editing process. Now we're ready to look at the steps involved in implementing finished sounds in a production. These include:

❏ **Output**—final processing, downsampling, and extraction of individual files from larger master files

❏ **Integration**—implementing sound in an authoring application

❏ **Delivery**—considerations for audio playback in specific environments, such as speaker support, kiosks, CD-ROM, or the Internet

These phases of the production can be less glamorous than the creative processes of recording and editing. But they're no less important in determining both the overall quality of your production and the way it is perceived in the market.

Output

In previous chapters, we've discussed the benefits of working with sound at the highest sample rate and resolution for as long as possible. This approach reduces the amount of noise inherent in files at lower sample resolutions. But once you have finished editing and mixing, it's time to downsample your audio from high-bandwidth CD-quality to lower band-width for multimedia playback.

The techniques we cover in this section apply equally to an individual voice, to a music or sound effect file, or to a whole series of takes contained within one file. To the best of your ability, keep takes together in one file. It's much easier to process a single 20-minute file that contains 100 15-second clips than to process 100 files individually. But you probably shouldn't mix audio types within a file. You may want to process voice differently from music and music differently from sound effects. It often works best to save each type of sound in a separate file. With that approach in mind, here's an overview of the typical processing steps involved in output:

❏ Balance levels and normalize the final master file.

❏ Convert the sample rate to the desired final level.

❏ Do a final pass of dynamic compression and EQ.

❏ Perform bit-depth conversion.

❏ Extract finished files from the master file.

Let's look at some techniques for each of these steps.

Balance Levels

This is your last chance to be sure you're achieving optimal volumes before you begin your journey on the long road down to 8/22 or 8/11. Avoid changing the volume level of files once they've been downsampled, because every edit you make at lower 8-bit resolution creates more noise than if you had performed it at 16-bit resolution.

> **Note:** *The above caveat applies only to edits that scale or recalculate sample data—amplifying, filtering, or normalizing, for example. It doesn't apply to cutting and pasting operations, which are edits that simply rearrange data.*

When a file contains many takes, it's imperative that you balance levels within the file. Use your sound editor's amplify effect to increase or reduce the volume of sections that have a marked difference in volume from the bulk of the material. As in all things audio, let your ear be the judge. Just looking at the height of the wave data isn't accurate enough, since the perceived volume of the signal may be different from the level you observe in the file. You should also give yourself some leeway for maintaining dynamic variation. If your voiceover ranges from whispering to shouting, you don't really need to have all the takes at the same level. Instead, balance them with respect to each other and with respect to the rest of the file.

Normalize

If you've been following the steps discussed in the previous chapter, your files should have been normalized during editing and may not need to be normalized at this point. But if levels have been reduced during mixing, normalizing is in order.

Ensure that your file hasn't been normalized with reference to an aberration in volume. For example, if you're working on a voiceover file that contains a loudly popping "p" or "b," the entire file could be normalized to one very sharp transient. If that transient hadn't occurred, the file might have been quite a bit louder after normalization. There are two ways to deal with this problem, depending on the location of the transient. In many cases—for example, in voiceover sessions in which the reader laughs, coughs, or calls out during the course of the recording—the transient occurs as an isolated event. If the offending spike isn't embedded in the program material you need to keep, simply cut it out or silence the transient, and then renormalize the entire file.

If the transient *is* embedded into sound data that you need to keep, you can use your sound editor's amplify or change gain effect to lower the volume for that portion of the wave. Zoom in as close as you can so that you're changing only the volume of the spike, not the volume of surrounding data. If the offending sound is only a single spike, you may be able to use the Pencil tool available in many waveform editors to redraw that portion of the sound. Don't just lop off the transient at the top; try to keep its shape rounded. Then play the sound to be sure that the transient is gone and that there's no noticeable dip in volume.

When you're satisfied with the overall balance of the various sections contained in your master file, you're ready to take the first step in the downsampling process.

Convert Sample Rate

Sample rate conversion changes the sample rate of the file from 44.1 kHz to 22.050 kHz or 11.025 kHz. This process reduces the size of the file by 50 percent or 75 percent so that it occupies less space on disk and in RAM, thus leaving more of the computer's processor free for handling graphics and animation. It's the first point in the production process where you hear high-frequency information removed from the signal—the 22.050 sample rate can't reproduce frequencies higher than 11 kHz, and the 11.025 sample rate can't reproduce frequencies above 5.5 kHz. To hear a more accurate representation of the final sound quality, perform sample rate conversion before final EQ processing.

You may be able to stay at 44.1 kHz if you're compressing 16/44 audio using the IMA compressor. At a 4:1 compression ratio, this results in the same size as an 8/22 file. For even more file economy with the IMA compressor, you can convert your sample rate to 22.050 and then compress the 16/22 file. This results in a file with the same size as an 8/11 document. (You can also deliver your material at 16/44 if it is destined for MPEG compression with video.)

Throughout this book, we encourage everyone to use 44.1 kHz as the standard working rate instead of the DAT standard of 48 kHz. At the sample rate conversion stage, Sound Designer users will reap the benefit of that strategy. Sound Designer lets you reduce sample rates by only 50 percent in a single operation. To get from 48 kHz to 22.050 kHz, you first convert from 48 to 24, and then from 24 to 22.050. This extra step is time consuming and also adds more noisy artifacts to the file.

You should not use the old standard Macintosh sample rates of 22.254 or 11.127 unless you're certain that your presentation will always be played on a particular Macintosh model that uses those rates (a kiosk, for example). Macintoshes that use these sample rates are capable of only 8-bit output.

Final Compression and EQ

In the recording industry, finished mixes are subjected to a final round of processing during *mastering,* when the actual master disk is pressed prior to duplication. This is the point at which final tweaks of compression and EQ serve to balance or emphasize certain aspects of the mix. It's a subtle process of final polishing.

You should consider doing the same for your multimedia mixes. In the multimedia field, though, the goal isn't so much polishing as it is basic survival. Those sounds that you so lovingly caressed and layered at 16/44 are about to be dragged into the sonic mud. Final processing is like putting hip waders on your audio so that it doesn't sink too far into the muck.

A final pass through a dynamics compressor helps raise the overall level of your signal after it has been normalized. You may be wondering why we recommend compressing the signal several times rather than just smashing it down once and getting it over with. The answer is that compression is much less noticeable to the listener if you compress the signal slightly in several stages rather than all at once.

As you perform final compression, notice that it may change the balance of your mixes. You can better anticipate this effect as you gain experience with it, but being aware of it ahead of time can be helpful as you're setting levels. Compression, as you may recall, reduces the peaks in a file so that the overall level can be increased. It also has the corollary effect of making background tracks more prominent in the mix. For example, if a sound file contains voice mixed over a background of city noise, the background will be louder in the mix after compression has occurred, especially in the gaps between voice segments. Beware, though—sounds are clearer and more distinct at 16/44 than at 8/22. Before downsampling, having the background track a bit louder in the mix can sound ear-pleasing because it's not interfering with the voice—yet. But what sounds well balanced at 16/44 may not sound as good at 8/22. When in doubt, err on the side of caution; put the background effects a bit lower in the mix if you know you'll be using compression later.

At this stage, use compression only if you have it available in software. Don't take another pass through an outboard analog compressor. Digi-design's Sound Designer II has a compressor feature that takes advantage of the hardware's DSP. Plug-ins to Sound Designer, Deck II, and SoundEdit 16 from Waves and InVision Interactive also offer this functionality. These tools let you perform the equivalent of analog compression on a digital audio file.

As for equalization, base the level of EQ processing you use on the frequency content of the material and your own personal tastes. It's not uncommon, though, to boost the high end slightly to compensate for high frequencies that have been lost in downsampling. If a 22.050 kHz sample rate is your final destination, boost the frequencies from 10 kHz to 11 kHz by 4 to 6 dB. If 11.025 kHz is your goal, boost the 4.5 to 5.5 kHz range. See the "Downsampling" tutorial on the CD for an example.

Bit-Depth Conversion

The final step in output is to convert the 16-bit, 22.050 kHz file to an 8-bit, 22.050 kHz file. Here we enter the world of bit-depth conversion strategies. There are many different approaches one can take when trying to derive an 8-bit sample value from a 16-bit sample value.

To understand this process a bit better, let's first review the structure of the data itself. Computers are just using bits, ones, and zeroes, usually in groups of eight. A 16-bit value is made up of two 8-bit words and has a structure like this:

```
XXXXXXXX XXXXXXXX
```

In the case of a sample, that might be represented as

```
10011010 11010011
```

Sorry, but it's time to retreat to math class. We all know that in our base 10 system a number like 4,620 has a zero in the "ones place," a 2 in the "tens place," a 6 in the "hundreds place," and a 4 in the "thousands place." In the computer we're in a base 2 system, so the last number to the right in our 16-bit value is in the "ones" (either 0 or 1), the next value to the left is in the "twos" (either 0 or 2), to the left of that is the "fours" (either 0 or 4), and so on.

When deriving an 8-bit value from the 16-bit value, the most important information is in the leftmost set of 8 bits. Considering that a 16-bit value can represent a number up to 65,535 and that the first 8 bits (often called the "upper" 8 bits) can represent values between 0 and 255, we can see that the upper eight bits of a 16-bit sample coarsely determine the sample's value in 256 discrete steps.

The fastest and easiest way to convert from 16 bits to 8 bits is to lop off the lower eight bits. This strategy is usually called *truncation*. But with truncation, we lose valuable information. If the lower 8 bits have a value greater than 128 (in other words, greater than half of 256), it makes more sense to round the upper 8-bit number up by one when converting from 16 bits to 8. This approach is called *rounding*.

Another feature included in some conversion algorithms is *dithering*, the audio equivalent of Photoshop's anti-aliasing (which helps smooth the stair-stepped edges of images known as *jaggies)*. Conversion can create low-level distortion and quantization noise (that "frying bacon" sound you're hearing), so some programs add a small amount of *white noise* (like the steady hiss you hear while tuning a radio) to smooth the signal. If you're wondering why you'd ever add noise to a signal after going through all that trouble to eliminate it, keep in mind that in some situations, hearing a low hiss can be preferable to listening to a sputtering crackle. In other situations, dithering can be noticeably bothersome, so you may want to disable it if it's creating more problems than it's solving.

Far and away, the best solution for sample rate conversion currently on the market is the Waves L1 Ultramaximizer, a plug-in for Sound Designer II, Deck II, Premiere, and SoundEdit 16. While its capabilities as a limiter are also useful in getting one more boost in output volume, it's the bit-depth conversion that sets this utility apart. The Waves staff recommends that Sound Designer users perform all processing operations prior to applying the L1 and that Sound Designer's dithering option be disabled. When the L1 processes a file, it rearranges the data so that all the information is in the upper 8 bits, leaving the lower 8 bits empty. After the file has been processed, you can use their Wavestrip freeware utility to remove the unused bits, leaving you with an 8-bit finished product. See the "My Personal Recipe" sidebar for a step-by-step example of the downsampling process.

Extract Finished Files

Once you've completed output processing, you may be left with one file that contains numerous takes that must be extracted into separate documents. Now is the time to turn to automated solutions like CE Software's QuicKeys. Using Sound Designer's Regions and Playlist features, we create regions for each section, using the desired filename for the region name. Opening the playlist window, the regions we've defined are listed at the top. Then we launch a QuicKeys sequence that performs the following steps (a bit nutty, but it works):

1. Click on the region at the top of the region list in the playlist window and drag it down into the playlist.
2. Select Rename Region... from the Playlist menu (not to rename the region, but to get the name).
3. Copy the region name to the clipboard.
4. Close the Rename Region dialog box.
5. Select the Save Playlist as Soundfile option from the Playlist menu.
6. Paste the region name into the File Save dialog box.
7. Save the file.
8. Close the file when it's displayed in a new window.
9. Delete the region from the top of the region list in the playlist (automatically removing the region from the playlist area as well).

A single QuicKeys keystroke thus extracts the file. Even better, the QuicKeys Sequencing function lets you set how many times you'd like a particular sequence to repeat. You can set this sequence to play 100 times in a row, automatically creating 100 files from within Sound Designer.

As multimedia audio production becomes a recognized discipline in its own right, companies have begun to develop software tools to speed the process. One noteworthy solution is Precision Audio Tools from Gallery Software. It includes modules for automatically creating regions in Sound Designer files, extracting files from Sound Designer regions, auto-naming and batch conversion of files, and more. The folks at Waves are also filling this need with their WaveConvert application, and version 2 of SoundEdit 16 includes a batch conversion utility. These products are welcome additions to the toolset of multimedia audio producers.

MY PERSONAL RECIPE

If you've been searching through the book saying to yourself, "I just want to find out how to downsample files," look no further. Here are the steps I usually go through on my way from 16/44 heaven to 8/11 heartache. My tools include Sound Designer II, the C1, Q10, and L1 plug-ins from Waves, Waves freeware utility, Wavestrip, and (for downsampling to 11 kHz), SoundEdit 16. In this example, we'll work with a file called "Sound."

1. Normalize at 16/44 and save the file as **Sound.master**.

2. Convert the sample rate to 22.050 and save the file as **Sound.22**. If you're planning to add lots of regions to create separate sound files, do so after sample rate conversion, since the regions won't be copied to the new file. Better yet, use Gallery Software's Region Reader product to save the regions from the 44.1 file, and then reapply them to the 22.050 file. If you create regions, save the file as **Sound.regions** and back it up as soon as possible.

3. Do dynamic compression using C1. This plug-in is great for reducing background noise in voiceover, especially when the final product will be at 8/11. I've found the C1 Speech Compress/Expand 1 preset to be particularly effective.

4. Save a copy of the file as **Sound.22.C** and then undo the C1 process. This procedure yields a clean copy of the file without processing in case we need to back up to this step at some future point.

5. Equalize using Q10. This plug-in has presets that increase high-frequency information as you approach the sample rate ceiling frequency. The 22.05 post comp and 11.025 post comp presets are very useful.

6. Save a copy of the file as **Sound.22.C.Q** and then undo the Q10 process.

7. Perform final limiting and bit-depth conversion using L1. Depending on the signal level of the file, you may be able to apply the L1's limiter in any range from –3 dB to –12 dB. Applying the limiter beyond –12 dB yields a result that sounds overprocessed to my ears. I also reduce the total output by –1 dB to reduce the potential of distortion from PC sound cards. The generally agreed settings for processing seem to be 8-bit resolution, non-IDR, and "non" noise shaping, but feel free to experiment. In one situation, settings of Type 2 IDR and no noise shaping gave the best results because the file content was filled with resonant synthesizer sounds and buzzing insects.

8. Save a copy of the file as **Sound.22.C.Q.L** and then undo the L1 process.

MY PERSONAL RECIPE *(continued)*

If your end goal is an 8/11 file, you're not home free yet. First, you should EQ the file differently since its highest frequencies will be in the 5 kHz range. Second, it's not necessary to do sample rate conversion to 11.025 kHz in Sound Designer, because you can take advantage of a little trick I discovered in SoundEdit 16. Use this one cautiously, though; depending on the frequency content of the source material, it doesn't always yield the best results. Try this method and then compare it to file that's been downsampled "normally" (using a straight conversion from 22 to 11) and see if it improves the clarity and high frequency content of your sound.

10. Open the 8/22 file in SoundEdit 16. If you're working with a lot of files, you may want to set SoundEdit 16's default sample rate to 11.025 kHz so that all new files are automatically created at that rate.

11. Select All, choose Shift Pitch from the Effects menu, and shift the pitch down one octave. This step reduces all the frequencies by one-half, bringing more high-frequency information under an anti-aliasing filter designed to remove frequencies greater than 5.5 kHz.

12. Copy and paste the data into a new 8/11 document. Sample rate conversion takes place as the data is pasted into the new file.

13. Shift pitch up one octave and then save the finished file. Restore the file to its original pitch.

Although purists might have reservations about using the foregoing strategy because of the potentials for aliased data and other artifacts, the overall result often sounds better than straight downsampling. To verify that you've actually gained something through this process, do an A-B comparison between an 8/11 file created with straight downsampling and one created by pitch-shifted downsampling from 22 kHz.

One final note: this technique doesn't work well at all for going from 44 kHz to 22 kHz, as the unwanted artifacts are far more noticeable.

Integration

So now you have several hundred sound files on your hard drive, ready and waiting to drop into your multimedia masterpiece. Welcome to the next bottleneck! Your audio will be jostling with graphics and digital video in the battle for precious system resources. This is where your foresight in selecting file formats and sample rates should pay off. We'll examine some of the major issues you'll need to address as you integrate audio into a presentation. We'll also look at audio integration in Macromedia Director, one of the leading multimedia development tools. First, let's briefly review how file formats affect performance during authoring and playback.

Formats in Review

As discussed in Chapter 4, the three main considerations in determining the proper file format to select are:

❏ Whether you want the file to play from disk or RAM

❏ What size requirements you have to meet

❏ Whether the data needs to be cross-platform

Although you can expect to see a number of file formats when editing sound, only a few standard formats are supported by most authoring applications. On the Macintosh these include AIFF, snd resource, and QuickTime audio. On the PC the standard is WAV. For cross-platform work, AIFF and QuickTime audio are the formats of choice. Table 8-1 compares the main file formats and the degree to which they are supported.

RAM-based Versus Disk-Based Playback

There are two main ways to play back sound files: load them into RAM prior to playback, or stream the audio data from the disk as it plays. Each strategy has advantages and disadvantages. Sounds played from RAM are often more responsive. This is especially true for CD-ROM, unless great care is taken to minimize head seek time by writing the sound files close to the document that calls the sound. Playing sounds from RAM also reduces the chance that sound playback might be interrupted when the

File Type	Play from Disk	Play from RAM	Cross Platform
AIFF	yes	yes	yes
snd Resource	no	yes	no
QuickTime audio	yes	on Mac only	yes
WAV	yes	yes	yes*

* Although many Macintosh sound editors support the PC-based WAV format, Macintosh-specific authoring tools don't.

Table 8-1

Common file formats and their capabilities

new graphics are loaded from the disk while sound is playing. Finally, looped sounds must be played from RAM in order to loop smoothly. The main drawback of playing sound from RAM is obvious. Sound can take up lots of room. Thirty seconds of 8/22 mono use over 650 KB. The memory needed for an authoring or playback application and a screenful of graphics is often at least 2 MB. If animation is occuring, additional graphics will be waiting in RAM. This leaves precious little room for audio. Formats that play from RAM include snd resources, AIFF files, and WAV files.

Sounds played from disk, on the other hand, require very little RAM because the sound is played continuously through a small buffer. When you need to play several minutes of continuous audio, this is the best approach to take. As mentioned above, the main drawback is that sound playback may stutter if the disk needs to access other information while the audio is playing. Formats that play from disk include AIFF, WAV, and QuickTime audio.

Size Requirements

In the context of multimedia audio, "size" refers to both size on disk and size in RAM. In most cases, available RAM is the more pressing concern. The size requirement is a function of sample resolution, sample rate, and, for compressed audio, the compression ratio. Knowing the sample resolution and rate of a file, one can quickly determine how much space a file will require on disk or in memory. An 8/11 file requires 11 KB per second, while an 8/22 file uses 22 KB per second.

Another important consideration is *disk throughput*—the length of time required to access and read a sound. Let's assume that the CD is a double-speed drive capable of 150 KB per second of sustained data transfer. In cases where the sound is spooling from disk, a stereo 8/22 file will claim almost one third of the bandwidth. Similarly, loading a 600 KB sound into memory takes four seconds. Some developers choose to reduce sound file sample rates just to speed the load times of a presentation.

Primary Issues of Integration

As you begin to integrate audio into an authoring application, be prepared to deal with a variety of issues. Some are related to audio, while others apply to the overall authoring process. The important issues include:

❏ Performance

❏ Synchronization

❏ Volume control

❏ File management

Performance

Performance issues include whether to play sounds from RAM or disc (discussed previously) and how to achieve the best perceived audio quality while other demands are being made on the system.

The RAM versus disc issue need not be an either/or decision. You might choose to play longer sections of music or voice from disk and have other elements, such as music loops and button clicks, play from RAM. To achieve the best audio quality, consider saving your available audio bandwidth for those sections where you'll get the most payoff. If your maximum available RAM for audio is 500 KB, you can use that for 45 seconds of 8/11 mono voiceover at some points in the presentation, and use it for 10 seconds of 8/22 stereo at other points.

Synchronization

Synchronization can be one of the most difficult issues to handle. When synchronization between sound and graphics falls apart, the weaknesses of multimedia are laid bare for all to see. People are accustomed to sounds accompanying motion. It's what they see in the real world, on film, and on video. If they *don't* see it on their computer screen, even the best graphics and audio seem hokey and amateurish.

One key to synchronization is being sure that all the required media for a scene are loaded into RAM. If images and sounds are being read from CD-ROM, it's practically inevitable that sync won't be maintained. Even if everything is in RAM, you can place excessive demands on the processor. Large bitmaps may not move quickly enough to keep up, and a sound may play at the wrong time while the graphics struggle across the screen.

Another obvious solution to synchronization woes is to use QuickTime. QuickTime is designed to drop video frames to keep up with a soundtrack. Not that you should count on frame-dropping to fix your problems—when QuickTime has to calculate which frames to drop, performance suffers. To get the best QuickTime playback from CD, use a utility like MovieShop to adjust the movie's data rate so that QuickTime doesn't have to step in and drop frames in order to keep up. Still, it's comforting to know that even if the video gets choppy, the timing can be maintained.

Volume Control

If you've been careful up to this point, your files should be relatively consistent in volume levels, allowing for some dynamic variation between loud scenes and quiet scenes. But as files are integrated into the presentation, volume control will probably pass from your hands and into the hands of the programmer—unless, of course, you *are* the programmer. If not, you'll need to work with the programmer to assure that volumes set within the authoring application are appropriate.

In many productions, there are two aspects of volume to keep track of: general system volume (as you would set it from the Sound Control Panel or mixer software on the PC) and relative channel volume within the authoring application. If your authoring tool supports multiple sound channels, be sure that volumes are tracked and changed appropriately when jumping randomly between different modules of the presentation. If you set a high volume for voice in the first channel and a low volume for music in a second channel, then switch to another module that plays voice in the second channel, the volume will need to change also. The best way to manage this situation is to keep foreground audio in the first channel and background audio in the second channel.

If the authoring tool provides volume control for separate audio channels, you have a clear indication that the authoring tool is mixing the audio in software. Turning down a software-based volume control can undo all the noise reduction and normalization that you've worked so hard to achieve. In such cases, keep the volumes close to maximum to preserve what fidelity still remains. If everything sounds buzzier after you've installed the sound in the authoring environment, software mixing in the authoring tool is almost certainly the culprit.

File Management

Some authoring tools give you the option of storing files either internally (as part of the media document) or externally (the media document keeps a pointer referencing the sound file). External files may be more appropriate if you need to play the same sound from several different files, but it's likely to increase disk access time. You also have to be careful to include the external sound files with the authoring document when transporting the files, and you may have trouble if pathnames (drive or directory information) change.

With these issues in mind, let's look at how sound is handled in one of today's most popular authoring tools, Macromedia Director.

Using Sound in Director

This section is of interest to those of you who are already up to your necks in Director. (Users of other authoring tools should refer to the sidebars pertaining to those applications.) We can't cover the general structure of the program or the basics of handling sound (for example, importing files and making sounds play in the score). There are a number of good Director books on the market that provide information on these tasks; we list a few of them in the Suggested Reading section. Here, we'll limit our discussion to audio-oriented topics not fully explained in Director's extensive documentation.

Recording and Editing Sound

Starting with version 4.0, Director added some nifty new features for editing sounds from within a movie file. One of these is the ability to record audio directly into a castmember using a standard recording dialog box. If you've been following the story thus far, we hope you've learned to avoid recording from the desktop in this fashion. It's okay for quick and dirty work, but in most cases you'll get much better sound quality if you use an audio-editing program. If you do use this feature, be aware that you're recording directly into RAM, so you may not be able to record for a long period.

With version 4.0.4 and later, Director supports copying and pasting of sound data between Director and Sound Edit 16. This can be a real time saver when you need to tweak a sound. But for some reason, sounds pasted back into Director's cast have the "Loop" checkbox automatically selected. This is not usually the behavior one would prefer for voiceover or a buttonclick. In most cases, you'll want to deselect the Loop option after pasting sound into the cast. In version 4.0.4, the Lingo command l*oop of cast* applies only to digital video castmembers, not to looped sounds, so you can't automate the process with a Lingo script. The *loop of cast* command *does* work with sounds in version 5.0.

Synchronization

For many Director users, getting animation to sync to audio is like the search for the Holy Grail: a noble goal which seems straightforward at first, yet which becomes more elusive and intangible as the journey progresses. For starters, you should refer to Director's "Tips and Tricks" documentation for some ideas on maintaining synchronization.

When discussing synchronization within Director, we find it useful to distinguish between three basic types:

❑ *Starting sync*—launching a sound and animation at the start of a sequence

❑ *Ending sync*—having audio finish before the end of a sequence

❑ *Continuous sync*—hitting multiple sync points within a sequence

Starting synchronization can be pretty simple: start the sound and the animation at the same frame. For optimal sync, it's best to have the sound and graphics already loaded into RAM. Otherwise there may be a slight lag as elements are loaded from disk.

Ending sync is easily achieved by setting a Wait for Sound to Finish event in the Tempo Channel. You may want to avoid using the Tempo Channel, however, if you have created interactive buttons on the screen. The Wait for Sound events in the Tempo Channel draw from the same routines as Wait for Mouseclick, and mouseclicks on a button could be misinterpreted. Another drawback of Wait states in the Tempo channel is that they force the cursor to be displayed. This drawback is also related to the Wait For Mouseclick function, which changes the cursor to a mouse with a blinking button during the Wait state. If your presentation is in a slideshow mode and you want the cursor to be hidden, you should use Lingo's soundBusy command to test the activity of the sound channel.

Trying to sync animation to hit points in the middle of a sound file can become far more complicated. Herein lies one of the key differences between Director's frame-based playback strategy and time-based strategies like those of QuickTime and Kaleida's Script X.

Time-based products like QuickTime use an internal clock to drive events. If the events don't keep up with the clock, information is dumped until sync is re-established. Director, on the other hand, *wants* to do everything within a given frame before it moves on to the next frame. As a result, the playback speed may vary depending on how many things have to occur within a particular frame. Just because you set a tempo of 15 frames per second, don't expect Director to maintain that tempo. Director's frame rate can vary dramatically depending on the speed of the CPU, the amount of memory available, and the size and number of media elements (bitmaps, digital video or sounds) that are playing at the time.

As Director's playback head moves through the score, it checks all the things that might happen within a given frame: transitions, palette changes, sounds, Lingo commands, and, of course, moving graphics. Depending on how many things have to occur, your actual playback rate may be slower than the frame rate you've set, and the animation can slow down.

That's not true of sound, however. No, by golly, our plucky little audio heroes are always chugging right along at the proper speed. If sound were to slow down, the pitch would drop as the speed is reduced, like a record slowing to a stop. Slowing down the sound would be unacceptable. You can see the conflict coming at this point. If the animation playback rate falls behind the audio playback rate, sync is lost.

Director isn't built to skip frames to keep up with real time. But you can use Lingo to force Director to jump ahead if the playback rate lags behind the desired frame rate. An example script can be found in Director's "Tips

AUDIO AND THE APPLE MEDIA TOOL

Rich Shupe is a New York-based multimedia developer specializing in CD-ROM and Enhanced CD titles, with an emphasis on digital video, audio, and QuickTimeVR technologies. He shares his experiences in handling audio within the Apple Media Tool.

The Software

The Apple Media Tool (AMT) is an easy-to-use, yet feature-rich, multimedia authoring tool that differs from others on the market. Both novice and experienced developers appreciate the ability it gives you to create multimedia titles for both Macintosh and PC platforms—without ever having to write a single line of code.

The AMT accomplishes this by using object-based authoring— you can manipulate your media elements directly using a pre-configured set of actions, effects, and commands arranged in an icon system. Simply drag an icon from one area to another, and you've quickly finished what might, in other authoring tools, have required a few lines of code (or more) and a programmer's knowledge.

Audio

The AMT handles audio much as it handles other media in its icon-based system. Simply add an audio element to the master list of available media, drag it to one or more screens you're created, and you're on your way.

File Formats

Before we discuss AMT's audio features, let's talk about acceptable file formats. AMT supports a variety of audio formats, including AIFF (.AIF); 8-bit-only WAVE (.WAV); QuickTime MooVs (.MOV), which can be audio-only, MIDI, and/or video; System 7 Finder sounds (sfil—Macintosh only); and K_W, a file format created by AMT's Media Converter application. This diversity of importable files, together with the attention paid to PC formats as well as those common on the Macintosh, make cross-platform development that much easier.

Features

In addition to the features found in popular authoring tools, AMT also offers several new features and unique ways of dealing with sound files. The main actions that

APPLE MEDIA TOOL *(continued)*

you can apply to audio are start and stop, go to beginning and end, set volume, and the new GoToTime and RunToTime. The latter two allow you to jump to, or play up to, a particular time in a movie or audio file (measured in *ticks,* the multimedia standard unit of measurement, which equal 1/60th of a second). RunToTime also lets you specify a start time, and GoToTime is available as an action for AMT's new built-in Audio CD object, allowing you to manipulate an audio CD in your CD-ROM drive.

You can trigger audio files using the mouse up and down, mouse enter and leave (also known as *rollover)*, and key down events. Other events that can trigger audio include entering or leaving a screen or displaying an object. Audio also can play as the result of a timer such as an elapsed duration or the completion of a sound, video, or graphic display.

Looping and preloading options are available in AMT. You can also define audio files as interlude sounds to be played during transitions, or as *ambient sounds*—a new AMT feature that plays audio across multiple screens until it finishes or until another event halts it.

As with most QuickTime 2.x-savvy applications, AMT supports general MIDI files and the IMA compression standard. Both allow longer, better-quality audio passages than the 8-bit looping methods of the past. MIDI files trigger a CPU-generated sound source that can reproduce long passages of music using remarkably small file sizes. (A four-minute MIDI composition, for example, might take up less than 40 KB.) MIDI, however, is not digital audio. The IMA compression standard allows high-quality, 16-bit digital audio to be compressed at a rate of 4:1. (A one-minute, 16-bit stereo track sampled at 22.050 kHz would consume approximately 1.4 MB— the same file size as a 22.050 kHz, 8-bit mono sample).

Another QuickTime feature that AMT integrates into its own feature set is the ability to search a QuickTime text track and to jump to that segment of the movie if the text is found. Text searches can thus trigger audio.

Flexibility and Ease of Use

The Apple Media Tool is a versatile authoring package that combines the flexibility of audio formats and features with the simplicity of an icon-based authoring system. Even the most basic developer can control sophisticated audio needs easily. For instance, a double-click on any icon displays its relevant parameters. If you want to get the tick value for the GoToTime or RunToTime functions just described, there's no need to do the math. Simply double-click on the icon, select the Movie option,

(continued)

and play the movie (both video and audio-only movies have this feature). When you get to the part you want to jump to or play up to, simply click OK and AMT will place the tick value in the parameter setting.

Limitations

Because the AMT has no native programming language, its inherent ease of use can also prove to be a limitation. (The separately packaged AMT Programmer's Environment can introduce programmed enhancements to AMT titles.) Functions common to other authoring packages, such as code-controlled fades, synchronization, and tempo setting, are not present in the Apple Media Tool package.

The Right Tool for the Job?

Unfortunately, no brief outline of a software package can fully document its features and limitations. Only by assessing the needs of each project individually and evaluating the pros and cons of the software can each prospective developer decide whether AMT is the right tool for the job. It's clear, however, that AMT warrants a close look from any creator interested in manipulating audio (and other media) without an in-depth knowledge of programming languages.

and Tricks" booklet. If you use this approach, you need to be sure that you don't accidentally skip a frame that contains information you need—a palette change or a critical Lingo statement, for example.

Granted, it's difficult enough to deal with playback rates that may vary. But there's another issue to contend with. When Director launches a sound file, it doesn't automatically keep track of time once the file is playing. You have to build this functionality with Lingo. Two standard ways of dealing with this are to use Lingo's *timer* function, or to use the *movieTime* property with an audio-only QuickTime movie. But even these approaches may not always be manageable. What happens when you have hundreds of animations that need to have continuous sync?

Multiple Sync Points

We've faced this issue on several projects that had short animated sequences with multiple sync points. In each case, the programmers used a similar strategy: loading graphics into RAM and playing sounds from the disk using Lingo's *sound playFile* command. Each animation had a named marker, and the associated sound file used the marker name with the file extension .AIF for cross-platform compatibility. Here's a boiled-down version of the basic script, with the example animation named "balloon":

```
on mouseDown
    go to "balloon"
    put the frameLabel & ".AIF" into theSound
    sound playFile 1, the pathname & theSound
end
```

> **Note:** *Here's a disclaimer for you hardcore hackers: we won't pretend that the foregoing script is elegant Lingo. In actual practice, this could be done with objects or lists—at least with an argument—but we don't really want to get into that here, do we?*

When the user clicks a button to select a particular animation, Lingo jumps the playback head to the appropriate marker. The marker name is retrieved using the *frameLabel* property, and the .AIF extension is added to the end of the name. The result is passed to a *sound playFile* command, and the sound associated with the animation is played. Notice the inclusion of Lingo's *pathname* function. This helps assure that the sound is properly located on the disk. Sounds called using sound playFile are very particular about getting exactly the right pathname. If you're off by one character, or if the sound is in another location, the file won't play and no Lingo error message will be generated. You'll just be rewarded with silence.

Seem pretty straightforward? Sure it does—if you're the programmer! When you're the sound designer responsible for creating effects that sync to the animation, it's a bit more daunting. After some experimentation, I devised a method using SoundEdit 16 which is described step by step in the following section.

**Synchro-
nizing with
Director and
SoundEdit 16**

For the task of integrating sound using multiple sync points, SoundEdit 16 is an essential tool for one reason: it's the only sound-editing package that lets you set any frame rate you desire for rulers and editing dialog boxes. Most editors support SMPTE, PAL, and film frame rates such as 30, 29.97, 25, and 24 frames per second. SoundEdit 16, however, lets you set a rate of 8 frames per second so that all audio edits can be calculated from Director frames.

SOUND ADVICE FOR AUTHORWARE AUDIO

Tom King of Solis, Inc., is a top-notch Authorware developer. He was kind enough to share his knowledge about the details of using audio within Macromedia's Authorware Professional, one of the leading tools for creating interactive training presentations.

The bulk of this chapter deals with audio production and integration using Director. But for those working in training, Authorware is the predominant tool. What issues should you be aware of regarding sound production and integration with Authorware? Here are some tips and techniques for making the most out of audio from within Authorware.

1. Keep it lean. When loading sounds, Authorware incorporates the entire sound into your Authorware file. Smaller files will play back more reliably on a broad range of hardware devices without bogging down the rest of your application. Use the lowest reasonable bit depth (8-bit mono) and sample rate (11 kHz). If the sound is too critical to skimp on resolution or sample rate, then edit judiciously. You often can save significant amounts of space by trimming leading and trailing silences.

2. Loop sounds when you can. Like Director, Authorware can loop a smaller sound many times to create the illusion of a longer audio track. Edit your sound files so the beginning and end dovetail nicely, and then use the Repeat option.

3. Be aware of the stray erase. The easiest way to stop a sound in Authorware is to erase it with an Erase icon or even with an automatic erase. Watch for gotcha's like this one, shown in Figure 7.1—an automatic erase will prevent the sound from ever being played.

4. Want to stop any sound that may be playing? That's hard to do with erase icons, but easy to do with a short snippet of silence. Authorware doesn't mix sounds; instead, it plays them one at a time. Playing a fraction of a second of silence will therefore cancel out or "erase" any sounds already playing.

5. Avoid compression on cross-platform projects. If you'll be converting files between Macintosh and Windows, don't use the Macintosh compression options. Since there are no reliable equivalents under Windows, Authorware won't be able to convert Macintosh-compressed sounds into its internal Windows format.

6. Likewise, avoid using artificial playback speeds on cross-platform projects. Macintosh hardware handles playing most sounds at up to half or twice their

AUTHORWARE AUDIO *(continued)*

Figure 7.1

A sound icon
with an automatic
erase may never
actually play
the sound.

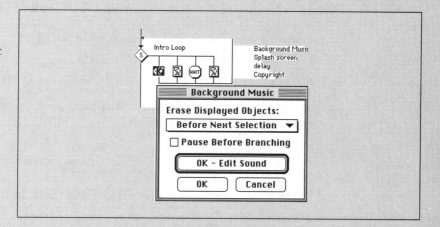

normal playback speed. Avoid the temptation to make your narrator sound like a helium addict by using a 250 percent playback speed, because he or she will be back down to earth when you convert the file to Windows. However, if your project is Macintosh-only, you can play the same sound back at different speeds to simulate everything from a buzzing insect to a warning buzzer.

7. Watch the sample rate closely on cross-platform projects. Some Macintosh editors default to a 22 kHz (22.255) sample rate that differs slightly from the 22 kHz (22.050) rate that Windows uses. This can result in clipping of audio; in some cases, it can make brief sound effects virtually inaudible. If I use 22 kHz-sampled sounds, I use the 22.050 kHz sample rate on both platforms, just to be sure.

8. When working on larger projects, keep sound icons in their own library. This practice will greatly simplify your life if you need to do localization or translation—you won't have to dig to find all the audio scattered throughout your Authorware file. This practice also makes it easy to use your own placeholder audio until the professional narration is recorded and edited. In a few minutes' time, you can swap out your tinny voice with the soothing sounds of a sophisticated sound professional.

9. Have you lost a sound file? Are you unsure of the name of the source file, its location, sample rate, or bit-depth? Use the Info… button to track it down.

10. Have fun. Make sure your media is truly multi-media by including sound wherever it adds value. Even a simple sound effect can spice up a short Motion icon animation.

Look to the
CD-ROM

The animation in this example starts with a picture of a mirror. When the mirror is clicked, a ghost appears, leans out of the mirror, and drinks from a water glass located in front of the mirror (to see the example, check the tutorial files on the accompanying CD). The three sync points to hit are:

❏ The appearance of the ghost, with howling

❏ Slurping through a straw in the glass

❏ The ghost saying "ahhh!" after finishing the drink

Setting multiple sync points involves these steps, each of which is described in the sections that follow:

1. Determine a base platform.
2. Determine sync points in the Director file.
3. Create a multi-track document in SoundEdit 16 by importing files.
4. Set the ruler to 8 frames per second.
5. Position the tracks at the sync points.
6. Mix the sounds to a sound file.
7. Use a sound playFile command to audition the sound.

Determining a Base Platform

The first goal is to set an achievable frame rate for the slowest machine in the potential audience. We refer to this as the "slowest common denominator." If your animations are small and relatively simple, you can expect to achieve at least 8 frames per second on a modest platform like a Macintosh LC III (25 MHz 68040) or a 25 MHz 486 Windows PC.

Armed with this knowledge, animators should create their artwork to look as good as possible at the slow frame rate. Once animation has been created in Director, you can begin creating sound effects to match.

Determining Sync Points in the Director File

Working from the Director movie, count the number of frames between sync points, as shown in Figure 7.2.

If you're really ambitious, you can generate a little Lingo tool to help. First, create new markers in the file at each sync point (this assumes that you're working with a copy of the movie file and that the extra markers won't confuse the programmer's job). Call this handler from the frame of the first marker needing a sync point. When calling the handler, you can pass an argument for the total number of sync markers for that sequence, including the starting marker. For example:

Figure 7.2

Markers placed in
Director's Score
Window indicate
points for
synchronizing
sounds.

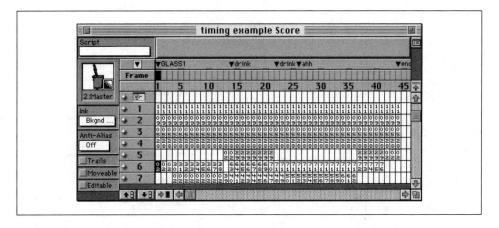

```
on exitFrame
    showSyncPoints (5)
end
```

This statement calls a handler that generates a listing of the marker frames
and displays it in the Message window:

```
on showSyncPoints howMany
    put 1 into counter
    put "Start Frame is marker" && the frameLabel && ":    frame"
        && the frame
    put the frame into startSyncFrame
    repeat with i = 1 to howMany

        if counter = howMany then exit
        go to marker (1)
        put the frame-startSyncFrame && the frameLabel
        set counter = counter + 1
    end repeat
end
```

Once you know the different frame values you need for sync points,
you're ready to lay out the audio in SoundEdit 16. In this case, we see that
our sync points are at frames 1, 14, 22, 26 and 44.

Creating a Multi-Track Document in SoundEdit 16

You create a multi-track document in SoundEdit 16 by importing files. As a
file is imported, it's automatically placed on a new track. In this example,
we'll import three sounds into a new file as shown in Figure 7.3.

Figure 7.3

The track name display in SoundEdit 16 automatically recognizes the filename for each imported file. Three files are being imported in this example.

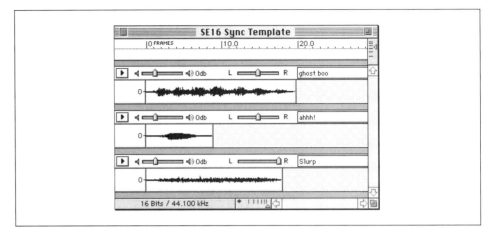

Setting the Ruler to 8 Frames per Second

Select Display Preferences to set the ruler to 8 frames per second, the speed of our Director movie (see Figure 7.4).

Now every frame in the SoundEdit 16 ruler is the equivalent of a frame in Director.

Positioning Tracks at the Sync Points

We're ready to position the tracks at the sync points. In SoundEdit 16, you can hold down the Option key to click and drag tracks so as to move them into position. For absolute precision (or using QuicKeys automation if you're *really* clever), you can use SoundEdit 16's Track Offset function.

Figure 7.4

The SoundEdit 16 preferences dialog box lets you select ruler settings that snap to various frame rates, in this case 8 frames per second.

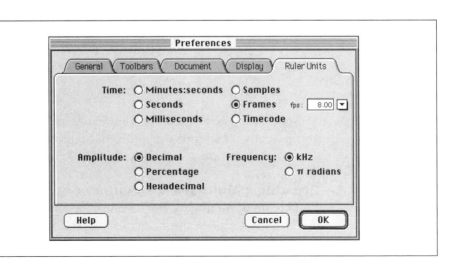

Figure 7.5

SoundEdit 16's Mix dialog box lets you select a destination for the file you're mixing.

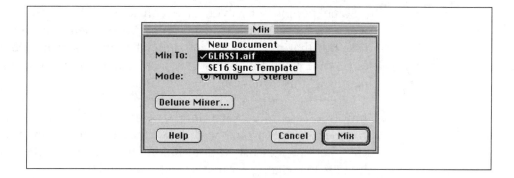

After choosing Track Offset from the Modify menu, just enter the starting frame number for that track. Keep an eye on the end points of the tracks as you move them. If you need a sound to end by a certain point (especially the last frame of the animation), you'll need to trim the end of a track.

Mixing the Sounds

After the sounds are positioned, mix them to a sound file as shown in Figure 7.5. Save the file as an AIFF document. To make the next step as painless as possible, save into the same folder as your Director movie.

Auditioning the Sound

Switching back to Director, use a sound playFile command to audition the sound. If the file is in a different folder, you'll need to add the full path-name to the sound file. If you need to make additional changes after hearing the file in context, switch back to SoundEdit 16 and tweak away. Then, when you're ready to remix, take advantage of the pop-up in the Mix dialog box that lets you mix to an existing file. Be sure to save the file after mixing so that the changes are actually written to the disk. That way, when you switch back to Director for auditioning, your sound playFile call should still work, and you won't have to worry about updating the script.

Looping Sound

Loops are a commonly used device for playing a continuous bed of background audio. Director lets you loop audio that's directly imported into the cast. Linked AIFF sounds or sounds called using sound playFile cannot be looped. There are exceptions, depending on your definition of the term "loop." In this book, we're referring to a seamlessly looping file playing from RAM. One example is a looping piece of music that maintains its rhythm across the loop point.

Some people, however, also consider a file that's triggered over and over as a loop. You can make an audio segment play repeatedly from the disk, but that may not be an optimal loop. You'll hear a brief gap at the loop point when the disk seeks back to the beginning of the file. For looping music, this hesitation is usually unacceptable.

Director's looped sounds must play from RAM. AIFF files that are imported as linked castmembers or called using sound playFile are streamed directly from the disk, so they can't be looped. If you import an AIFF file into the cast without linking it, you can set the Loop checkbox in the Cast Info dialog for that sound castmember.

No AIFF Loop Markers

Be careful if you've set loop points in the file using an audio-editing program like SoundEdit 16 or Audioshop. In AIFF files, the loop points are ignored and the entire file is looped. That's not the case for files saved in the old SoundEdit format, however. This brings us to a stratagem that you can use to get more mileage out a loop: using internal loops and sounds in the Score.

Internal SoundEdit Loops

By reproducing the steps in this section, you can create a sound file which, when played in Director, will play through an introductory segment of audio, then drop into a looping segment, and finally play out through the loop point to the end of the file. This is a great way to create a piece of music that has an introduction, main theme section, and conclusion.

Note: *There's one potential hazard in this trick: it works only with standard SoundEdit files, which support nothing but the old standard Macintosh sample rates of 22.254 kHz and 11.127 kHz. If you know your application will run only on Macintoshes, this is relatively safe, but you sacrifice some sound quality when the sound is played back on newer Macintosh models that support only 22.050 kHz. If your project is cross-platform, there could be trouble with older PC sound cards that can't handle rates other than 22.050 kHz and its mathematical cousins. Be sure to test your work on a few PCs before distributing it.*

Here's how the trick works:

1. Create an internal loop in a sound file as shown in Figure 7.6.
2. Save the file in the original SoundEdit format (not SoundEdit Pro or SoundEdit 16).

Figure 7.6

A sound file
with an
internal loopback

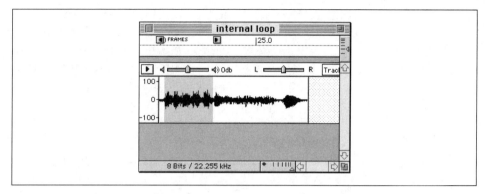

3. Import the file into Director and place it in the Score Window. Copy the sound channel data to the point where you want the sound to play out through the loop point.

Now play the file and hear the results. Once the playback head passes the last frame containing the sound, the sound will continue to play out through the loop point to the end of the file.

Sound and Lingo

Most Director users eventually reach a point where they turn to Lingo to achieve the level of control and continuity required for an effective presentation. There are a number of sound-oriented commands in Lingo, some of which have unintended consequences. Here are some of the bright spots—and some of the black holes—of which you should be aware the next time you feel the urge to hack some code.

Puppetsounds

People run into two common problems when they use puppetsounds. The first is that sounds placed in the first Sound Channel in the score don't play properly anymore. That's because once the sound channel is puppeted, it obeys only Lingo commands, not Score data. To restore control of a puppeted sound channel to the Score, use the command *puppetsound 0.*

The second common problem is that puppetsounds don't play when they're supposed to. This can usually be solved by issuing an *updatestage* command right after the puppetsound command. Otherwise, the sound might not play until a frame boundary is crossed. The sound might never be heard if you're cycling around in a repeat loop. Think of the updatestage command as an "updateSpeaker" command when it comes to *puppetsounds.*

There's also a third problem most people run into with puppetsounds. Invariably, experienced users become frustrated with the *puppetsound* command being limited to playing sounds from sound channel 1. Those days are over for you! Director does have the ability to play puppetsounds from *any available sound channel!* That's right, puppets for sound channels 2 through 8 have been there all along; this feature is simply undocumented. To play a puppet from another channel, use the syntax

```
puppetsound (channel number), castNumber
```

Not Fade Away

Pardon the allusion; we're not really Deadheads (even though we did do some work on the Dead-heavy "Haight Ashbury in the Sixties" title). But this title seemed particularly appropriate considering some of the peculiarities of Lingo's *sound fadeIn* and *sound fadeOut* commands. For the sake of simplicity, let's call them the "fade commands" from this point onward. If you've done any sound hacking in Lingo, you've probably found these two commands to be quite helpful.

One tip for sound fadeIn: place the command in the frame *before* the sound starts. Otherwise, you'll hear a blip of the sound at full volume before the fade-in begins.

The fade commands can cause problems with volume levels. If you've used the volume of sound property to set a level for a particular sound channel, you probably know that its value can range from 0 (silence) to 255 (full volume). This is useful for interactive control when you're balancing the levels between two different tracks. But the fade commands automatically set channel volumes to 255 after the fade is completed. That is, when using sound fadeIn, volume is automatically faded up from 0 to 255. When using sound fadeOut, volume is first faded from the current channel volume down to 0 and then automatically reset to 255 after the sound stops. If your channel volume is important, save it in a global variable before performing a fadeout. Then you can reset the channel to the previous volume once the fade is complete.

An alternative approach is to build a custom handler that uses the volume of sound property to increase or decrease the volume incrementally. This lets you fade up or down between any two volume levels you desire. A good example script for this function can be found on The MediaBook CD from gray matter design, shown next.

```
on soundFadeDownTo endVol, chan, fadeTime
        -- note: fadeTime is optional!
        -- default fadeTime is same as sound fadeOut command
           (15 * current tempo)
```

```
    if NOT param(3) then put the frameTempo*15 into fadeTime
    put the volume of sound chan into startVol
    put (startVol - endVol)/fadeTime into fadesPerTick
    put the timer into startTime
    put startTime + fadeTime into endTime
    repeat while the timer < endTime
        put startVol - ((the timer - startTime) * fadesPerTick)
            into newVol
        set the volume of sound chan = newVol
    end repeat
        — just in case the repeat loop isn't fast enough set the
volume to its final value
    set the volume of sound chan = endVol
end soundFadeDownTo
```

Another potential "gotcha:" fading a sound doesn't necessarily stop it from playing. Sounds streaming from disk or playing as a loop continue to play at zero volume after a sound fadeout command. Issue a sound stop command after the completion of the fadeout time to ensure that the sound channel is properly released.

Finally, we should re-emphasize that volume control using Lingo's fade commands and volume of sound command affect the bit resolution of your file as volume changes occur. In many cases, you will find it better to set fades and volume levels within a sound editing program rather than letting Director manipulate the sound data. In interactive situations, however, this isn't always an option.

A Few Notes on QuickTime

One obvious advantage of using QuickTime audio in Director is its ability to return timing data about the current position of the playback head within the audio stream. Another advantage is its ability to start and stop playback from any point in the file using one of the following three functions:

❑ movieTime of sprite

❑ startTime of cast

❑ stopTime of cast

You can figure out how these work using the manuals. But did you know that if you set the stopTime to be less than the startTime, the file will play backwards? And that you can use the movieRate of sprite command to play QuickTime audio at different speeds? We used this technique in *Stradiwackius: The Counting Concert,* a children's music title from

T/Maker, to make a slider that changed pitch as it was dragged back and forth. Playing audio-only QuickTime in reverse or at different speeds can create other interesting audio effects, such as *Doppler shift* (the change in pitch as a sound source moves away from the listener) or haunted, spacious, or industrial noise beds.

Gotta Do Windows

When you're authoring for cross-platform distribution, Director 4.0 or later provides a breakthrough for audio playback under Windows 3.1: support for multiple sound channels through a custom external, the MacroMix DLL. MacroMix takes the output of multiple sound channels and mixes to one channel on the fly. Early versions of this DLL had a limitation, though: all sounds had to be at the same sample rate in order to be mixed.

Starting with Director 4.0.4 for Windows, this limitation is removed. MacroMix now performs sample rate conversion on the fly so that files are automatically resampled to 22.050 kHz—a great bonus for people who distribute presentations using 11.025 kHz audio. The DLL performs interpolation as the material is upsampled, and the resulting file sounds substantially better than a standard 11.025 file played back through the Windows Media Control Interface (MCI).

Of course, there's an even better alternative for playing 8-bit, 11.025 kHz sound. Compressing a 16-bit 22.050 kHz sound at a 4:1 ratio with a IMA compression results in greatly improved sound quality, yet the file size remains nearly identical. The IMA format works on both the Macintosh and Windows platforms. As noted elsewhere, Macintosh playback requires either QuickTime 2.0 or Sound Manager 3.1 (or later versions). On the PC, decompression of IMA audio is handled by the Microsoft IMA Audio Compression Manager (ACM). This software is automatically installed by Windows 3.1 and Windows 95, but if your product depends on Microsoft's system of handling IMA playback, you should consider licensing the latest versions from Microsoft and installing them when the user first installs your application. Also keep in mind that IMA decompression requires additional processing power from the CPU. Playback of graphics or animation may be affected during playback of IMA compressed audio.

There's another option for 4:1 compression under Windows: using Microsoft's proprietary 4:1 ADPCM to compress WAV files. Director doesn't directly support the playback of these files from within the cast, but you can trigger them through the MCI that's built into Windows. Using Director's *mci* Lingo command, you can send command strings to Windows MCI devices. Managing playback through MCI, however, is somewhat more difficult and cumbersome than using Director's built-in sound playback capabilities.

Using External Commands

Many high-end authoring programs provide extended functionality through external code resources. These resources function similarly to plug-ins for a graphics program. They add features to an existing program, yet they aren't stand-alone products that can be used independently of the program for which they were created. In version 4.x and earlier, Director used its own XObject format and could also use XCMDs (X-Commands) and XFCNs (X-Functions) created for Hypercard. Director 5.0 adds a new external code type, the Xtra, which is intended to replace and enhance the functionality of the earlier Xobject standard. From this point, we'll refer to the whole genre as *externals*. These externals let you stretch the boundaries of what's possible with Director. To write your own externals, you need to know the popular C programming language and whatever particulars about the Macintosh or Windows operating system that apply to the functions of your external.

We've worked on several projects that used custom XObjects to add features to Director. One, the aforementioned *Stradiwackius,* used an XObject to mix multiple sound files so that kids could create their own wacky instruments by stringing several objects (and their related sounds) together. In another project, a SoundFont demonstration disk for E-mu Systems, an XObject was created to let Director communicate with a Windows Dynamic Link Library (DLL). This XObject provided real-time control of the wavetable synthesizer on a Creative Labs Sound Blaster AWE32 so that users could tweak synthesizer settings such as envelopes, filters, and effects.

Look to the
CD-ROM

Another important use for sound-oriented externals is to handle recording and playback of sound during a presentation. The Sound XObject from Red Eye Software is one good example (see the demo included on the CD). Yet another common use is to control volume levels on multiple audio tracks embedded into a single QuickTime movie. Well-known examples include popular titles like David Bowie's *Jump Interactive* and Peter Gabriel's *Xplora.*

It's a good thing that Director provides a functional backdoor through externals. You may be wondering about one popular audio playback method that Director doesn't seem to notice: MIDI. This lack of support is particularly curious, since MIDI is well-supported on Windows platforms and is an ideal solution for maintaining interactive control over a soundtrack while also reducing demand on the CPU. Like any good QuickTime-compatible application, Director can play back QuickTime Music Tracks. But QuickTime Music Tracks aren't *quite* MIDI. You can't send MIDI data—MIDI volume changes or program changes, for example—to a QuickTime Music Track and expect real-time response.

Fortunately, you can add MIDI functionality to Director through XCMDs. The most powerful product currently available is HyperMIDI Tools from EarLevel Engineering (for more specifics, see Chapter 10).

To implement MIDI under Windows, you'll have to use Director's mci command to access the Windows MCI. You can use Lingo to send MCI strings to a MIDI device. Here's a sample of code we created for the afore-mentioned demo of E-mu Systems' SoundFont technology in the Creative Labs Sound Blaster AWE32:

```
mci "open" && the pathname & "midi\hallway.mid\type ¬
    sequencer alias hallway"
mci "play hallway"
```

Then, a few frames later, this string tells the demo to wait for the sequence to finish:

```
mci "wait hallway"
mci "close hallway"
```

Although MIDI isn't impossible with Director, it's more labor-intensive than simply playing a sound file. One can only hope that the advent of Director 5.0 will inspire someone to write an Xtra for MIDI functions. As MIDI support becomes more prevalent, it will provide a huge advantage because you won't need to create large sampled music files. Of course, you will still need to record voiceover and sound effects.

Audio in Authoring Tools

Although Director is one of the most widely-used authoring products, many other powerful tools are also available. Several multimedia producers were kind enough to contribute some of their tips on handling audio in Macromedia's Authorware Professional, the Apple Media Tool, mFactory's mTropolis, and Allegiant's SuperCard. (Information on using audio in Apple's HyperCard appears in Chapter 11.) We also added some tips for integrating audio into QuickTime movies and for using PCs for audio development.

mTROPOLIS: SUPPORT FOR INTERACTIVE COMPOSING

contributed by Hal Steger, mFactory

mTropolis provides multimedia applications with unprecedented capabilities to perform real-time dynamic mixing and control of audio. mTropolis sound elements consist of an audio file and modifiers. The modifiers affect the audio file's playback and are activated by messages.

mTropolis supports standard audio and sound file formats. Once a sound element has been defined, you can easily reuse it in one or more projects. Sound elements have built-in capabilities— looping, pausing, volume control, and balance (left/right channel)—that you can set statically and dynamically using no coding or only minimal coding. For interactive composing, you can dynamically and transparently change an audio file at run time if it is associated with a sound object.

mTropolis also supports real-time, dynamic MIDI performance and mixing. This includes support for all MIDI controllers, such as changes to tempo, volume, notes, mode, and so on. Real-time MIDI support is regaining importance, partially because of its applicability for bandwidth-constrained applications and titles such as Internet applets.

By default, mTropolis dynamically mixes audio files on both Macintosh and Windows platforms. You can resample audio files dynamically during development or at runtime for optimal playback, ease-of-authoring, and ease-of-composition. You can define ranges for audio files that enable playback of portions of those audio files. mTropolis authoring refers to ranges rather than to the physical attributes of the audio file, making it possible to separate the authoring from the audio. This allows you to reuse authoring without changes for different audio files; it also allows you to change audio files without affecting the authoring.

A sound-effect modifier lets you associate sounds with other mTropolis elements for easy authoring. Without coding, a sound panning modifier lets you mix audio files dynamically across a left and right channel, according to an element's position on the screen, or you can mix them to a specific different balance over a specified timeframe. A sound fade modifier, which also requires no coding, provides a time-based relative or absolute fade capability for sound and audio files.

SOUND AND QUICKTIME VIDEO

Audio is a very important element in QuickTime documents. We have discussed creating audio-only QuickTime movies and bringing MIDI tracks into QuickTime. But you may also be working with audio that relates to a video track. Our preference has always been to edit audio in a dedicated audio-editing package that integrates the playback of QuickTime movies, and then add the audio back into the movie as a final step. This lets us take advantage of all the features of an audio editor while still referencing the QuickTime video. But you may find yourself handling audio within a QuickTime editor such as Adobe Premiere. Here are some considerations to keep in mind.

Premiere Audio Capture Tips

Premiere is a great tool for editing video, and it has many good features for handling audio as well. Version 4.0 allows an unlimited number of audio tracks. While many video digitizing boards let you simlutaneously digitize audio and video into Premiere, it's usually best to capture each of these elements in a separate pass. That way the computer can devote more processing power to the video.

There are two ways to capture audio into Premiere:

❏ Select Movie Capture from the File/Capture menu to capture as QuickTime audio, or

❏ Select Audio Capture from the File/Capture menu to capture as AIFF.

One advantage of the Movie Capture method is that Premiere retains your capture settings for sample rate and sample resolution. If you choose the Audio Capture route, watch to ensure that Premiere doesn't automatically reset your sample rate for you! When you choose this method, Premiere presents a new item in the menu, Audio Capture. Selecting Sound Input from this menu opens the Sound Settings dialog box. Here you can select sample rate and resolution for your audio capture. As we've suggested many times, this should be set to a 44.1 kHz sample rate and 16-bit resolution to capture at the highest quality. But if you click the Options button to select an audio input source (the Macintosh built-in input or internal CD), you'll notice that your sample rate and resolution options have been reset to 8-bit, 22 kHz. Always double-check your settings before exiting the Sound Settings dialog box!

SOUND AND QUICKTIME VIDEO *(continued)*

Premiere Editing and Processing

Premiere's audio display is limited compared to most audio-editing packages, but this is understandable considering its focus on video editing. The best place to see audio data is in the Clip Window. If the waveform display is too small, select the Boosted option in the Clip Window Options dialog box. Premiere lets you use "rubber bands" to adjust the volume of tracks over time. Be wary of dragging this control too far up, however, as it may cause clipping and distortion of the audio signal. While you're editing, be sure to set the Preview options to the same sample rate and resolution as the audio in your project. Otherwise, Premiere will have to resample on the fly, resulting in reduced playback speed and poor audio quality. Also ensure that the main Audio Preferences match your Output Options settings so that rates are maintained when you make movies.

Watch That Rate!

Premiere is downright cavalier in its depiction of audio sampling rates. Throughout the program and its documentation, reference is made to "22 kHz" and "11 kHz."

What is rarely made explicit is that Premiere's default rates are actually the outmoded Macintosh rates of 22.254 kHz and 11.127 kHz. For today's audiences, you shouldn't use these rates; instead, choose 22.050 and 11.025. Most Premiere dialog boxes that let you define a sample rate have an Other... button at the bottom of the pop-up menu that lets you select the newer rates. Be sure to check these values every time you see a reference to 22 or 11.

Going Separate Ways

As previously mentioned, we believe that you achieve the best results when you edit audio in a dedicated audio program. In the course of many projects we've worked on, the capture, editing, and processing of video have been handled by video specialists. They'll often digitize audio at 16/44 and then turn the files over to us for processing and downsampling. Once the video and audio data have been processed separately, you can recombine them using Apple's MoviePlayer utility. Here's how:

1. Open the QuickTime movie that contains the video.
2. Import the final processed AIFF audio file into an audio-only QuickTime movie.

SOUND AND QUICKTIME VIDEO *(continued)*

3. Select the entire audio track (Command-A) and copy it to the clipboard.

4. Select the file that contains the video to bring it to the foreground.

5. While pressing and holding the Option key, select Add from the Edit menu to add the sound.

6. Save the movie.

Pressing the Option key changes MoviePlayer's Paste function to an Add function, which adds the audio as a separate track rather than just pasting the audio data onto the end of the video track. Once you have created a file using this method, be sure to select the options Save as Self-Contained and Playable on non-Apple computers. These ensure that the audio data is interleaved (interspersed with the video data) and will play on PCs. Otherwise, all the audio data may be stored in the beginning of the movie, which can negatively impact movie playback performance. The Self-Contained option ensures that all the data required to play the file is contained within the file itself (normally, QuickTime uses pointers that reference the data in an external file). Using pointers could cause problems if you move the file to another computer or hard drive.

OPTIONS FOR THE PC

If you're one of the intrepid souls slugging it out with Windows and Intel, you may have been wondering when we would get around to discussing your particular options. As mentioned elsewhere in the book, it has been our experience that the vast majority of multimedia developers create the bulk of their content on the Macintosh platform, and audio is no exception. But if you're committed to the PC platform, there are several options to consider for capturing, editing, and delivering audio for multimedia.

Audio Capture/Digitizing

By definition, every multimedia PC has a sound card, and most of the cards on the market support analog audio capture. This may be enough to get you through a crunch, like recording a scratch voiceover or putting music behind a presentation. But for serious production work, you should consider a card with digital audio input and output. At this point, there are three main alternatives: CardD from Digital Audio Labs and Audiomedia III and Session 8 PC, both from Digidesign.

Software Options

For many years, most audio-editing packages on the PC were extremely limited in their features. But within the past two years, several powerful tools have appeared on the market. Sonic Foundry's Sound Forge is one of the best, offering a wide-ranging suite of powerful tools for single-track editing. The recent addition of plug-ins for noise filtering (as well as third-party support from companies like Waves) makes this package a solid contender with many Macintosh applications. Sound Forge also supports a multitude of Macintosh and Windows file formats, has good looping tools, and can perform both non-destructive and destructive editing.

For multi-track mixing, Studio Audio Workshop (SAW) has earned a good reputation and compares favorably with programs like Deck II and Session. Digidesign products like Session 8 and Audiomedia III for the PC provide features that are similar to those of their Macintosh counterparts.

In the MIDI arena, Opcode's Vision, Mark of the Unicorn's Performer and Freestyle, and E-Magic's Logic Audio are available on the PC. Another popular PC sequencing product worth investigating is Cakewalk Professional from Cakewalk Software. The most recent version of Cakewalk integrates digital audio playback.

OPTIONS FOR THE PC *(continued)*

File Format Issues

If your presentation is intended exclusively for the Windows audience, you have several options for delivering good-quality compressed audio. You can use files compressed with Adaptive Differential Pulse Code Modulation (ADPCM), which compresses 16-bit data at a 4:1 ratio, resulting in a 4-bit sample resolution. The Microsoft ADPCM Audio Compression Manager (ACM) delivers the same quality as the IMA 4:1 compressor that is available on the Macintosh. There's also an IMA ADPCM ACM available from within Windows. If your product uses either the Microsoft or the IMA ADPCM format, you should ensure that the proper ACM file is installed in the user's system; it's part of the Windows 95 setup, although you have to specify it in some cases. Also keep in mind that once you take this path, end users are exposed to driver conflicts or errors and may experience playback problems within Windows 3.1.

In October 1995, Microsoft introduced Direct Sound, a new way for game developers and interactive multimedia authors to play sound. It allows several channels of sound to be mixed together and played simultaneously. Although this technology is still in its infancy, it is the direction that Microsoft has chosen for future development. Currently, it adds at least 20 milliseconds of latency in order to mix sounds together in software, and it mutes all but the foreground application. If the user switches your application to the background, even for a moment, your audio goes away. These problems will be addressed by Direct Sound 2.0, which is due in late 1996 or early 1997. At that time, the audio model for Microsoft will switch from the current MMSYSTEM driver model entirely to Direct Sound. In the meantime, sound card manufacturers will be required to supply both an MMSYSTEM driver and a Direct Sound driver, which will create confusion until the dust settles. Because of this, most content providers probably will not support Direct Sound unless they absolutely need the features it provides.

Another new feature that is part of Windows 95 is *streaming MIDI.* Streaming MIDI lets an application send a large chunk of MIDI data all at once (perhaps even an entire MIDI file) to the MIDI driver. Instead of using an external sequencer, the driver will be able to decode and play the music, offloading this functionality from the program. This should reduce the need for custom programming in each piece of software that uses this feature, and should give composers a more direct pipeline for the music.

(continued on page 208)

SUPERCARD 2.5 AND SOUND

SuperCard first gained a popular following as an alternative to HyperCard, with faster processing speed, more scripting functions, and support for color. Aldus Corporation eventually purchased the product, and for a time its future was uncertain. But following the merger of Aldus and Adobe, SuperCard was released back to its original developer, Allegiant Technologies, and they've really put a shine on the updated version. Rick Harper, the Director of Content Development & Training at Allegiant, discusses the uses of audio in SuperCard.

Allegiant Technology's SuperCard supports four distinct sound protocols: AIFF, internal sound resources, QuickTime sound movies, and MOD files. External AIFF sound files play asynchronously (allowing other events, like screen changes or button clicks, to occur), triggered and controlled by simple SuperCard scripts. For example, to play an AIFF file, the scripter starts the sound with the command play sound file *"BigBeat."* In order to trigger events at specific times during *sound play,* scripters use the *filePlayBack()* command. This function monitors the current time of the playback, permitting simultaneous execution of other actions, such as card-to-card transitions, processing user input, and so forth.

SuperCard utilizes a second sound type, the internal star (or data fork) sound resource. These sound resources load quicker than external files, and since they are internal to the project, they are always assured of being available. Data fork sounds are protected from copying because they exist as internal resources, unique to SuperCard. Again, the scripter simply issues the command *play sound "MySound"* to start playback. Of course, users can export, edit, and reimport star sound resources to their projects. Developers can selectively initiate or terminate sound playback of external AIFF and internal star sound resources, providing powerful sound control in multimedia and computer-based training.

The third type of sound media used by SuperCard are headless, or "sound-only," QuickTime movies. With the *movie* function in SuperCard, programmers can specify "in" and "out" points and adjust sound volume over 255 levels. With the *movieCallBack* function, the programmer can again trigger events based on the current playback time in the sound. Because these sounds are also asynchronous, animation, user input, and number crunching can take place simultaneously.

SuperCard is extensible through the use of XCMDs and XFCNs. Using the *playMOD* XFCN, scripters can control pattern-based MOD files, whose footprint, or

(continued on page 208)

OPTIONS FOR THE PC *(continued)*

Microsoft has also defined a new Multimedia PC (MPC) specification, MPC III. This is a platform containing a minimum of a 90 MHz Pentium, stereo 16-bit audio output, a quad-speed CD player, and a wavetable synthesizer in either hardware or software). This new specification represents a significant step up from the earlier (and considerably less rigorous) MPC I and MPC II standards. The new MPC standard should prove a boon to audio content developers who were limited by the earlier standards.

SUPERCARD 2.5 AND SOUND *(continued)*

memory requirements, are quite modest—a four-minute polyphonic symphony might require 100 KB! This fourth type of sound is also asynchronous, which is ideal for kiosks, presentations and edutainment titles.

SuperCard's flexible sound capabilities, coupled with a highly versatile scripting language, helped it win the 1995 MacUser magazine Editors' Choice award for Best New Multimedia Authoring Application. The ability to work with these multiple sound formats also make SuperCard a natural choice for many types of applications that rely on complete sound control—from computer-based training to multimedia CD-ROM titles to information kiosks.

SHOCKWAVE: MORE THAN JUST SITES AND SOUNDS

One of the software options available to multimedia developers who need to play sounds over the Internet is Macromedia's Shockwave. We asked DXM Productions of San Francisco, an early user of Shockwave whose clients include other Web developers like Internet Shopping Network, Organic Online, and Macromedia, to tell us about Shockwave. The principals of DXM, Cathy Clarke and Lee Swearingen, have a strong track record in multimedia production, and are now applying their skills to the World Wide Web. To experience their work, investigate their site at http: //www.dxm.com. Their latest book/CD-ROM, Shocking the Web *(Peachpit Press), provides tips, tricks, and case studies.*

Shockwave is a software plug-in for Web browsers that allows you to play files created using Macromedia Director within Web pages. The Shockwave for Director Kit is available for both Macintosh and Windows. Director users can download the software free of charge through Macromedia's Web site (http://www.macromedia.com).

Using Shockwave technology, Director developers can instantly publish their multimedia content to a global audience on the World Wide Web. Audio can enhance Web pages by providing an alternative or supplement to screen text, reinforcing animation, adding ambience and background music loops, and providing feedback to user input. It's even possible to create a Director movie that contains only sound, without any visuals, so that the movie is invisible to the viewer.

Although a handful of applications for playing back and/or recording audio by way of the Internet currently exists—SoundMachine, SoundApp, and Sound Player, for example—Shockwave provides added capabilities for combining graphics and animation with interactivity and synchronized sound.

The trick to creating Shockwave movies is to create something meaningful in a very small file. On a typical 14.4 Kbps connection, a 30KB file takes about 20 seconds to download. Keep in mind that 30KB of monaural 8-bit audio at 11.025 kHz has a duration of only 3 seconds! Figure 7.7 provides a handy reference for calculating download times of specific types of multimedia content.

For this reason, it's important to use small sounds and small sound loops downsampled to at least 11.025 kHz. It's possible to reduce file size by further downsampling the audio, but this mandates a trade-off with audio quality and compatibility with the widest range of audio cards. The Director authoring environment supports imported AIFF, AIFC, SoundEdit and SND resources on the Macintosh, and .AIF and .WAV file formats on Windows PCs.

SHOCKWAVE *(continued)*

Figure 7.7

This comparison shows how file size and modem speed affect the time required to download and view a Shockwave movie.

Content	Size	Download time at			
		14.4 kbs	**28.8 kbs**	**64 kbs**	**1.5 mbps**
small graphics & animation	30 k	30 secs	10 secs	6 secs.	1 sec.
small complete title	100-200 k	90-180 secs.	30-60 secs.	20-40 secs.	1 sec.
short video clip	500 k	N.A.	120-240 secs.	90 secs.	3 secs.
full size title	1 m	N.A.	N.A.	180 secs.	6 secs.
title with full video & sound	2 m	N.A.	N.A.	N.A.	N.A.
MPEG video stream	--	N.A.	N.A.	N.A.	continuous

For the introduction of Shockwave at Macromedia's International User Conference, DXM took existing graphics from the Macromedia Web site and enhanced them using Shockwave. We added rollover and highlight sounds to buttons in order to provide feedback to users. In some cases, the Shockwave movies that we created were as small as the original GIF files they replaced.

We also "shocked" Macromedia's home page, or spotlight page, by adding a small sound of fire burning that we synchronized to animated flickering flames around the button labeled "Hot Contents." The fire sound and animation repeat at random intervals of one to four seconds. Varying the length of time between repeats adds realism and prevents the audio from becoming monotonous.

Creating small, downloadable Shockwave movies that contain compelling audio requires planning and design to maximize efficiency. Compression options continue to improve as bandwidth increases. Looking beyond today's bandwidth constraints to the promise of cable modems (and 1.5 Mbps transfer speeds available on a large scale) the same 30 KB sound file that was mentioned earlier would download in a fraction of a second!

The Shockwave Tools

The software tools required to make and distribute Shockwave movies include:

❑ Director version 4.0 or later (for Macintosh or Windows)

❑ Afterburner (Macromedia's compression software)

❑ Netscape version 2.0 or later Web browser

❑ Shockwave plug-in for Netscape browser

SHOCKWAVE *(continued)*

Developers will also find it necessary to define a new MIME type, or data type, for your browser and http server. This allows both to recognize the Director file format.

The Shockwave Process

The Shockwave process is straightforward:

1. Build a Director movie.
2. Compress it using Afterburner. Compressing a Director movie changes the file extension from .DIR. to .DCR.
3. Embed the movie within your Web page using the <EMBED> HTML tag. This tag designates the height and width of a rectangle for your movie to play within, and specifies the location of the source Director file. Here's an example:

```
< EMBED height=120 width=320 SRC="http://www.dxm.com/game01.dcr">
```

4. Serve Shockwave files.

Delivery

At last, your work is done. Now it's time to sit back, listen, and try not to cringe at the compromises you may have had to make along the way. How well does your audio production hold up when it's delivered? Much depends on the sound playback system.

If you're working on a specific installation, you can create and mix your audio to sound best on that particular playback hardware. But this strategy can come back to haunt you. One of the watchwords of multimedia is *repurposing*—taking existing content and reusing it in different situations. With the potential for future uses of your audio in mind, it makes sense to strike a balance so that it will sound decent when played back on a range of systems. Here are some of the issues you should consider when your sound actually plays back from a speaker.

Mass Market

When creating audio for mass distribution on CD-ROM, floppy disk, the Internet, or whatever interactive delivery method may be coming down the pike, you need to mix for the average user's audio system. This begs the question: who is the average user? Some people may hear your audio through a small speaker like the one on a Macintosh, a TV, or a computer monitor. Others may be listening through a home entertainment system with subwoofers.

The best defense is to know your enemy. Do the bulk of your mixing on good-quality, near-field monitors, but test your mixes on both cheap computer speakers (to see how it sounds without low frequencies) as well as on your home stereo (where the lows are likely to be accentuated). Try to strike a balance between all three.

The Internet

The phenomenal growth of the World Wide Web is fueling the online distribution of multimedia. Technologies like RealAudio, IWave, and VoxWare can play continuous sound over an Internet connection, while Sun's Java and Macromedia's Shockwave are capable of playing interactive media and sounds as part of a Web page. But given the current speed of modems (28.8 Kbps is the standard as of this writing), the data throughput capabilities of the Web are far more limiting than CD-ROM. Since most Internet players are designed to spool continuous audio, their bandwidth is limited by the amount of data that can be tranmitted through a phone line. As a result, fidelity at the end-user level is much lower than that of the original audio. Speech is just barely acceptable and music is grainy and distorted. Products like Shockwave, on the other hand, send the data to the viewer's computer for playback, so the content creator can select the most appropriate audio format. But to minimize download time, it's safe to assume that most Shockwave producers will opt for low quality, 8-bit 11 kHz audio.

All the tricks one learns creating low-fidelity audio for CD-ROM distribution become doubly valuable when creating sounds for online distribution.

Kiosks

Kiosks have one advantage over CD distribution: in most cases, you know the specific playback platform. Kiosks usually have to balance three demands:

- ❏ Achieving adequate volume when playing in loud or busy settings
- ❏ Being subtle enough not to drive users, bystanders, or staff crazy
- ❏ Using audio to attract users from a distance

The simplest approach for kiosks is to use small loudspeakers. Most shielded computer loudspeakers are fine for this purpose. Avoid speakers that aren't shielded, since if placed next to the monitor they can interfere with the video, causing a discoloration of the video signal. If the speakers are to be mounted within a secure cabinet and space is a problem, consider using small satellite speakers on top, and place a subwoofer in the bottom of the podium. If part of your goal is to attract people from a distance, remember that lower bass frequencies are audible at a greater distance than high frequencies. You might also want to program your application so that the volume drops slightly when there's user activity and rises when the system has been inactive for a certain length of time.

For those who have a larger budget for the audio playback system, another interesting technology is available. Brown Innovations in Boston has developed a speaker system that uses overhead parabolic reflectors to form a "cone of sound" that surrounds listeners as they stand beneath the parabolic speaker. This technology localizes the sound around the user's head. It also helps immerse the listener in the presentation, since background noise is significantly reduced.

Speaker Support

With speaker support as with kiosks, you're likely to know the playback platform. But in this case, the audio will be heard in large rooms or in reverberant halls playing through a large PA system. Depending on the specifics of the room and the sound system, bass frequencies are likely to be accentuated. You should therefore avoid using lots of reverb or delay effects processing. When you add in natural room reverb, you'll end up with sonic mud.

If you're the person in charge of setting up a speaker support sound system, be sure you have enough audio horsepower to do the job. Equipment could include a microphone for the speaker. A clip-on lavalier microphone relieves speakers of having to worry about standing too close or too far away from a microphone. If your speakers like to wander around a lot, consider getting a wireless microphone. These microphones send the audio signal through a small radio transmitter to a receiver. The audio output from the receiver can be patched in to a mixer for amplification through a PA system. Speaking of mixers, they're a necessity for combining signals from a microphone, the audio output from a computer, and audio outputs from a CD player.

If you're really ambitious, or if your presentation is given in a wide variety of spaces, consider investing in a graphic equalizer. This can help you adjust the audio signal to fit the specific frequency characteristics of different rooms. For example, rooms with lots of carpet, drapes, and soft furniture absorb high frequency sounds. Rooms containing predominantly glass, tile, hardwood, or metal, on the other hand, cause high-frequency sounds to bounce around the room. A graphic equalizer lets you tweak specific frequencies to compensate for the effect that different spaces may have on your audio. It also allows you to isolate and eliminate frequencies that may cause feedback if the signal from the PA speaker leaks back into the microphone.

In many speaker support situations, the presentation space is always changing. This puts a premium on portability, durability, and ease of setup and disassembly. Rack-mounting your equipment can be a real time saver. Powered PA monitors may be easier to use than a separate amplifier and speakers. Buy cables that are twice as long as you think you'll need; sooner or later you'll find yourself in a spot where the cable won't reach. And always have your "roadie" tools—a flashlight and duct tape—handy.

Summary

In this chapter, we completed our review of the major stages of the audio production cycle. After audio has been recorded, captured, and edited, the raw sound files are processed, downsampled, and output in the appropriate format. Automating with software utilities can save lots of time on projects using hundreds of sounds. As sounds are integrated into an authoring environment, it's important to work closely with the programmer to achieve synchronization and continuity. The more you know about the authoring environment, the better you'll be able to devise creative strategies for squeezing the best possible performance out of a presentation. Also keep the final delivery system in mind as you work; the sound playback hardware may place restraints on the types of sound you can use. On the other hand, the delivery system can create opportunities for certain types of projects.

Throughout the past two chapters, we've covered a range of techniques for moving audio through the production pipeline. But our craft involves more than just production. It requires artistic vision, the desire to tell a story, to evoke emotion and create an atmosphere. In the next chapter we'll discuss some approaches to sound design and look at the very important role audio can play in bringing multimedia to life.

8

Techniques and Elements of Sound Design

As multimedia designers, we aspire to many of the same creative goals as filmmakers, videographers, and recording artists: rich, beautiful imagery and sound combined to command the viewer's attention and draw him or her into a world of our own creation. In fact, we intend to go one step further than other media, adding interactivity, random access, and intelligent branching so that the viewer can explore, alter, and reinvent the experience.

It seems that multimedia is still searching for its own voice. Our own "Great Train Robbery," a product that points the way to new forms of expression, has yet to be made (or if it has been made, it has yet to be generally recognized as such by the creative community). In the meantime, multimedia continues to draw heavily from existing styles: film, cartoons, documentaries, and of course, gaming. Our challenge is to recreate rich environments that can include any or all of these elements—and to do it in spite of memory and performance constraints. There's no single "right" way to approach sound design; what *is* important is that you give some thought to overall strategy before you dive into the actual production process.

In this chapter we'll discuss basic conceptual approaches to sound design and look at specific strategies for integrating voice, music and sound effects. We'll also explore ways to design around some of the problem areas you may encounter with voice, music, and sound effects in multimedia.

Setting the Tone

Regardless of how you visualize your array of sound elements, your design goal is to support the story, using audio to create moods and environments and to communicate a message. One of the first questions you should ask clients is, "How do you want the user to feel?" The interplay between sound and graphics can take several directions. While the visuals are communicating information to the viewer, we can use sound to support their message. Alternatively, we can contradict the message of the visuals using sound that's inappropriate to them. And there's a third possibility: we can change the message so that different sounds lead the same viewer to respond in different ways to the same graphics. Such is the power we wield!

What's the overall tone for your presentation? How do you want people to feel when they've finished watching? If it's a sales presentation or a speaker support situation, you probably want users to have confidence in your company, its people, and its products and services. The tone is likely to be serious, direct, and upbeat rather than quirky and humorous. On the other hand, if you're doing a children's title, you may want sounds that are wacky and unpredictable. Allow a lion's roar to come forth from a kitten's mouth, and you may have the kids rolling on the floor.

How you derive the design for your sound isn't the most important part of this exercise. What *is* important is that you use some type of creative model to serve as a framework for making design decisions. Use the model to balance the mix of audio types so that your soundtrack has variety, depth, and dimensionality. Graphic designers know that the blank or "white" space around an image can be as important as the image itself. The same is true for the relationship between audio and silence. You probably don't want a continuous wall of sound unless you're working on a "drive/shoot/kill" game. Users will feel browbeaten if sound is constantly playing at full volume throughout a presentation.

Another good analogy from graphic design is the strategic use of colors and typefaces. An image is unified when it contains just a few mutually complementary colors and fonts. When too many of either are present, the visual result is a cluttered hodgepodge that obscures the message. The same holds true for audio. Skipping through several musical styles or sound effect treatments just for the sake of variety is distracting and may leave listeners feeling disjointed. Then again, if you're going for a hi-tech, MTV-style quick cuts approach, the use of multiple styles and effects may be effective. There are no definitive right or wrong directions. Base your strategy on the effect you want to have on the listener.

Approaches to Design

Let's mentally retreat from the world of bandwidth and bytes for a moment. Close your eyes and really *listen* to your surroundings. Notice that as you continue to listen, you hear an increasing amount of detail. You're tunneling back through layers of sound—from foreground sounds such as voices, to background sounds such as the low, constant rumble of a city, a distant highway, or a passing airplane. Thinking about the three different layers of sound—foreground, midground, and background—is one way to approach sound design.

Here are some common examples of sounds in various layers:

- ❏ *Background:* city noises, wind, crickets, music loops
- ❏ *Midground:* moving, visible, or off-screen objects (passing cars, ticking clocks, dripping water)
- ❏ *Foreground:* voice, interface effects, musical themes or stings, click animation effects, crashes

Let's look more closely at each layer of sound and its ramifications for sound design.

Background Sound

Look to the
CD-ROM

We're constantly immersed in sound. No wonder, then, that we're also astoundingly good at filtering the information that streams in through our ears. The more familiar something becomes, the more likely we are to tune it out. City dwellers become accustomed to a constant din. Office workers don't notice the hum of the lights and ventilators. But while you may not be consciously aware of background noise, you would definitely notice its absence. The same is true for multimedia. Background sounds can make your imaginary world seem more like the real one. They also have the added benefit of laying a blanket of sound behind other elements in your mix, masking background noise that might otherwise be audible in voice files. See the "Bad Day on the Midway" demo on the CD for an example.

Midground Sound

Moving up a notch from the background are (for want of a better term) *midground* sounds associated with specific activities taking place within the environment. In a city environment, for example, midground sounds occurring closer than and in addition to general background noise might include a passing bus, a street vendor, or construction site activities. In a multimedia presentation, mid-ground sounds are usually associated with a specific action on screen. Rather than looping, they are often played linearly, and are triggered at the appropriate point to synchronize with animation.

Midground sounds are the "color commentators" of your audio landscape. They fill in the environmental details that lend realism, familiarity, and immediacy to the scene.

Foreground Sounds

Foreground sounds should command the listener's attention. These are primary audio communicators. Rather than creating an environment, they usually convey information, which may take the form of voiceover or interface sounds like button clicks and alerts. Music can also be a foreground element, most often in introductory themes, transitional pieces that bridge different scenes, or stings that add emphasis to an event in the presentation. See the "HeadCandy" demo on the CD for an example of a musical interface.

Look to the
CD-ROM

Slicing Audio Layers

The three-layer scheme is by no means a definitive theoretical approach. You could also define four layers—background effects, foreground effects, voice and music—or three audio types—effects, voice, and music. In fact, the traditional approach in the film industry is to produce effects, music, and voice independently, and then create a final mix from those three sources.

Visualize the Environment

One way to generate ideas for an audio environment is simply to imagine yourself in that place. If your setting is a room, what are the sounds made by objects in the room? What sounds would you hear from outside the room? This exercise can lead to great off-screen effects—sounds that describe the environment or advance the story without any associated graphics.

Here's another visualization that may be useful. Think of your audio assets as different sections of a symphony orchestra. You can combine the sections in various ways so that each section has a moment in the spotlight at some point. At other times, a section's sound may be in the background supporting another section. Finally, a given section could be completely silent at another point, so that it sounds new and different when it re-enters the mix.

Object-Oriented Audio

As tools like Apple's ScriptX, mFactory's mTropolis, the Apple Media Tool, and newer versions of Macromedia Director make object-oriented programming more popular, you may want to think of object-oriented sounds as well. Any object can have graphic or sound elements associated with it. Using such an approach, it's possible to create objects that play sounds when certain events or interactions with other objects occur.

For the near future, it's likely that an object-oriented approach would be limited by the number of available sound channels. But as other playback technology (for example, MIDI synthesis in software) becomes more powerful, interesting possibilities could arise. One of these new approaches is Thomas Dolby's AVRe (pronounced "aviary"), an object-oriented music playback system that changes the musical score based on the actions of the user or of an object in software (see the interview with Thomas Dolby for more information).

Designing by Audio Type

Another way to approach sound design is to categorize audio elements according to their basic types: voice, effects, and music. You can use each of these elements in ways that lend additional meaning or color to the presentation. Let's examine some considerations for each type of sound.

Voice

In most cases, voice is recorded dry (i.e. without ambient or reflected sound), ideally with as little background noise as possible. Unless you or someone you know has a background in radio or recording, it's a good idea to hire professional voice talent whenever possible. The average viewer is going to expect voice material to sound at least as good as on TV. If you need character voices, such as cartoon characters, contact a talent agency and request demo recordings from affiliated voice artists. In a pinch (or if you really prefer the sound), use an effects processor or pitch-shifting functions in a sound editor to tweak a normal voice into a character voice. Another software option is available from VoxWare; their voice data compression technology lets you alter tonal characteristics of a voice to change the pitch without altering the length of the file.

If time and budget permit, have the voice artist record several takes of the material using different levels of energy and pacing. What may seem appropriate in the studio may not always work well when you integrate the audio into the presentation. By having a few different tracks to choose from, you'll leave your options open.

In most cases, voice is used to directly transmit information to the user. Take a tip from presentation software packages and standard presentation techniques: use voice to deliver the message, and save text for emphasizing short phrases in the message. A viewer gets more from a presentation when the information is received in the most natural way. Listening to another human voice is usually more compelling than reading text from the screen. This is doubly true if you're creating a title for children who are still learning to read. Voice is your best asset for describing how a product works.

INTERVIEW: THOMAS DOLBY

Thomas Dolby achieved tremendous fame as a popular musician, with hit songs like "Blinded by Science." Among keyboard players, he has long been admired for his innovative use of synthesizer and computer technology. But in recent years he has been less visible as a recording artist. Instead, he's been forging ahead into sound design for multimedia. He formed a company, Headspace, to create music and sound for CD games, including "Cyberia" from Interplay and "The Dark Eye" from Inscape. He's also developing AVRe, the Audio Virtual Reality engine, an object-oriented method of playing music in interactive situations.

What got you involved in multimedia technology?

The thrill of breaking new ground, experimenting in an area that's unexplored. That's why I'm enjoying some of these new areas, rather than going into a studio to record a song that will be played on the radio. That's gotten a bit old for me.

I get that old buzz back by working in new areas. No one really knows the answers, and though I may not either, I'd like to take a stab at it and maybe raise a few eyebrows.

How did you become involved in interactive composition?

My company has been doing audio for high-tech entertainment for the last two-and-a-half years. We've been supplying content and technological know-how to help developers use audio in novel and effective ways that will enhance their experiences. But it's been frustrating because there are no nuts-and-bolts tools available. So I've set about trying to build them.

The questions that have come up for me are: "Would this be something that would work for me?" or "Would this be something that should work for everyone else as well?" A lot of factors have fed into that. But I hit on the notion that instead of creating a personal tool for myself, I would ultimately develop a tool that I could release to the public. It would work for different kinds of composers, and I could build a business around it.

The first thing I did was to talk to the programmers, who have the ability to code software from scratch and brainstorm and try to match my aesthetic ideas to what was actually workable in code. Right about that time I met Hamish (Hamish Forsythe, the CEO of mFactory), and he showed me mTropolis, in which a multimedia author could fire messages around to specific targets, make variable states of games, could create characters that had their own sets of designs and metabolisms and so on.

I was very intrigued, both by what he showed me and by the philosophy behind it. And I asked him how sound would work as well. He said, "Just pick a sound file

THOMAS DOLBY *(continued)*

that plays for as long as the scene goes." I said that it seems to me that your approach to sound should be similar to your approach to graphics or QuickTime, where you actually build something that is the sum of the parts.

There are certain applications of audio in new media where there is a correct way to do it. Take a simulation, for example. If you're trying to create it in virtual reality and navigable 3-D space, then there is a correct way to represent the geometry of the world. In the same way, there is a correct way to represent sound within that space, because we know what it feels like, what it sounds like to move around in space. There's no question that having the sound disappear off into reverb just because you turn your head to the left is the correct way of doing things. We know that is not the correct way. We also know that a big space with solid walls is probably going to call for reverb. We know that from life.

Music and scoring, on the other hand, are fiction. Like so many of the tricks of fiction being the novelist's craft and the filmaker's craft, there isn't a right or wrong way of doing it; there's only style—a style that works and styles that evolve over a period of time. So when we talk about music as an underscore to entertainment, we're talking about style. If we were to draw a line here and say that the linear age is over and we're going to start with a clean sheet, it might be possible to evolve a brand new style. But what I'd like to see instead is that there would be a smoother transition so that all of the composers like myself who are intrigued by this new area don't feel completely disarmed.

There's kind of an assumption that linear and nonlinear entertainment will just magically be married, but that's not the case. What I'd like to see happen is that the suite of skills that Hollywood composers and performers have developed over the course of the century not disappear as we move into the nonlinear age of entertainment. I don't think there's any magical formula that will make that happen. Unfortunately, although a lot of composers that I know are intrigued by the possibilities of interactive media, they don't see any sets of tools or techniques available to them that would allow them to use the skills they've honed in linear media and carry those over into the nonlinear arena.

How would you describe AVRe? Is it like an AIFF file, or a MOD file, or a MIDI file?

The closest to those would be a MOD file. An AVRe file goes beyond a MIDI or sound file because AVRe files are relational; they need knowledge of each other and the context in which they can be played.

THOMAS DOLBY *(continued)*

Let's say that you triggered chunks of music the way you trigger sound effects, synchronized to events in an environment. You would get some level of cacophony. And if you wanted to observe tempo and key signatures, you would have to manage that traffic, that cacophony, in some way. You have to avoid conflict; you have to know the tolerance level for playing back a given chunk of music in a given context.

There are two parts to AVRe. There's the engine, which does the management of those files; and there are the AVRe files themselves, which are relational and contain enough additional information on how they can and can't be used that when they are brought into a given context they know how to behave.

The hard part of AVRe is the compositional technique. The code is something that any engineer can take a crack at, but the compositional technique is something that I'd like to add to it: "Here are some techniques that I have adopted that work." As other composers start to work with the tool, they will have their own techniques that they will bring to it, and they will request that these techniques be incorporated into future versions. I would like to see composers adopt AVRe as an approach to scoring.

You have a history of recording and live performance. How do you think your audience has changed? What's their response to your new direction?

I probably get about 12 pieces of e-mail a day asking when I will make a straightforward album. At this point, I think it would be very relaxing to make a straightforward album, and I certainly will sooner or later, but when I'm good and ready.

Having an e-mail address in the public domain has gotten me a lot closer to the real core of people that listen to my music. My fan mail in the past consisted of autographing pictures. My typical e-mail today is made up of very personal and articulate reminiscences of my music and people's life events. These fans go into my file, called Fan Base, and these are the people I could only imagine before. Even when playing live, you never get to talk face to face with them. I had to remain the star. I sometimes get into correspondence with them. The next time I go to the piano to write, those people in the Fan Base folder aren't faceless anymore; they are actual individuals who have shared what they get from my music. And that is fantastic. Trying to imagine them based on chart positions, record sales, and so on (like in the old days) was a very abstract process. You don't actually get a sense of how you are affecting people.

THOMAS DOLBY *(continued)*

But now you can sit down at the piano, upload the song instantaneously, and get feedback from those people by morning. If I could make a living doing business over the Internet that way, that would be wonderful.

I'm hearing from other musicians who would like to do business over the Internet also. I did an event with Apple at the House of Blues in Los Angeles for musicians only, and it was an interesting cross section. We knocked the idea around that we could cut out the record companies. Most of these people have a back room with recording equipment and no disadvantage technically over what the studios have. They just don't have the manufacturing facilities to make the actual piece of plastic. Except for the retail end, we have everything we need. These are exciting possibilities.

Sound Effects

Sound effects, even more than voice or music, are usually driven by events on the screen. The whole purpose of sound effects is to add realism and color. When we see a door slam and at the same time *hear* the door slam, we're more inclined to accept the illusion as reality. In the best of all possible worlds, graphics should be completed before you create the sound effects to accompany them. In practice, it's likely you'll be called on to create sounds before some of the graphics are done. In such cases, find out as much as you can about the scene: where it takes place, what's moving, how long the motion occurs, and so on.

Once you've determined an overall goal for the mood you're trying to create (realistic, surreal, threatening, or comic), use effects that support and reinforce that goal. Low, groaning, thumping industrial textures are great for a science fiction thriller. Lots of zips, boings, and other cartoon sounds are good for animated children's stories.

When you're aiming for realistic effects, think about how sound works in the real world. Take the setting into account. Is it interior or exterior? Exterior settings don't usually have reflected ambiance like reverb or echo; the sound simply travels away into the atmosphere. You may want to add some reverb if the environment is a subway tunnel, a basement, or a warehouse. Very short reverbs are great for tiled spaces such as kitchens, bathrooms, or hospitals. Carpeted spaces, on the other hand, soak up reflected sound.

You can also use differences in volume and equalization to make objects seem closer or further away. High frequencies tend to drop off faster than low frequencies. When you hear music booming in the distance, for instance, you're really hearing just the bass and drums, not the high frequencies in cymbals, voices, or other instruments. Most authoring programs let you change volume on the fly. You can take advantage of this feature to fade sounds up or down interactively as the user navigates through an environment.

Of course, sound effects can also be tweaked to create bizarre atmospheres. Shifting or bending the pitch of a sound often lends an otherworldly quality to a scene. Some audio programs, like Sound Designer and Deck, let you "scrub" through audio data on the hard disk, changing the playback speed depending on how fast you move your mouse. Use this technique to generate dense textures that are loaded with subtly shifting frequencies.

Look to the
CD-ROM

Music

Music helps reinforce the emotional content of a presentation. We're convinced that it is *the* most compelling data type in multimedia. But people aren't always cognizant of the effect it can have. If a dull presentation contains no music, it's unlikely that viewers would point specifically to the lack of music as the factor at fault, even though they might walk away uninspired by the graphics alone.

Most people can quickly describe their feelings about a piece of music, but they don't always know the reason for them. Here, in broad generalizations, are some common responses to different styles of music:

- ❏ **Sad, reflective:** slow music in minor keys
- ❏ **Suspenseful, driving:** fast music in minor keys
- ❏ **Dignified, confident:** slow music in major keys
- ❏ **Happy, busy:** fast music in major keys
- ❏ **Mysterious, scary:** slow music in unusual or altered keys

It can be helpful to think of music in two categories: linear and looped. Linear pieces are one-shot segments that play from beginning to end. One of the most common types of linear music in multimedia is often referred to as a *sting*. Stings are very short pieces (5 to 30 seconds long) used for introductions, closings, and transitions. An opening sting can help set the mood for a scene. Closing stings serve the same function as punctuation at the end of a sentence. A closing sting can be a period ("OK folks, show's over"), a question mark ("What will become of our hero?"), or an exclamation point ("We're absolutely fabulous!"). Transitional stings are useful for covering file load times between scenes.

Looped pieces, often referred to as *beds,* should be constructed to play continuously (see the "Looping the Loop" section following this one for some thoughts on composing music loops). If the music is destined to play behind voiceover, strive to keep it simple. Too much activity in the music track (prominent melodies, instrumental solos, or dense, busy orchestration) can draw too much attention away from the voice, making it difficult for the listener to focus on the real message. If you're a composer, you may find these admonitions frustrating to your creative urges. But keep in mind that the main goals of music behind voiceover are to support the message of the speech and to create a consistent emotional tone that helps the listener become more involved in the presentation.

If your loop is playing during a scene without voiceover, you may still want to be unobtrusive, so that the listener isn't driven to distraction. If the scene has lots of action, the music should have more energy so that it helps sustain the momentum. In this case, a driving beat often does the trick. Another good place for looped beds is during navigational sequences in which the user is traveling from one scene or environment to another. In an interactive presentation, you can never be sure how long it might take a person to get from one point to another. Use a loop to maintain a mood of tension, suspense, wonder, or anticipation during these sections.

While we're on the subject of loops, let's examine some creative looping strategies. A carefully crafted loop can be a great ally when you're trying to provide continuous audio for a presentation.

Looping the Loop

Most sound editing packages (including SoundEdit 16, Audioshop, Sound Designer, and Alchemy) let you create looped sounds. Looping is a great way to turn 15 seconds of audio into 60 seconds. But as with all things multimedia, loops must be used carefully for the best effect. Loops are most often created for sections of music or sound-effect background ambiances. Here are some tips to help you get the best loops.

Background Ambiance

A looping ambiance helps maintain the feeling of an environment (birds in the country, chatter and clatter in a cafe, and so forth). But be careful to choose the right segment; otherwise, one element—for example, one car horn honking in a city scene, one bird call in a nature ambiance, or one spoon clanking in the cafe—may jump out of the background and become too noticeable. Once the listener identifies a repeating element, the loop becomes obvious—and maddening. The best solution is to get rid of the offending sound. First, try just cutting it from the file. If the cut is too noticeable, crossfade the splice point. A complete description of crossfading techniques appears in Chapter 6, but here's a brief recap of the basic steps:

1. Copy and paste the section after the cut into a second track.
2. Slide the second track back so that it starts about one second before the end of the first track.
3. Fade the first track out while fading the second track in.
4. Mix both tracks to a new file.

A loop can also become noticeable when volume or frequency content changes drastically. In some cases, such as surf, the rhythmic nature of the sound can work to your advantage; just create a loop that maintains the rhythm. But whistling wind can be very difficult to loop well, since volume and frequency are constantly changing. You may need to process the sound with *volume envelopes* (available in most sound editors) to smooth out changes in volume.

Looping Music

This section is for all the composers among you. Here are several basic rules for loop composition and capture we've found that may be useful to you.

❏ **Keep it simple.** As with background sound effect loops described previously, you should focus on a steady rhythm or pulse, avoiding strong melodic hooks that stand out in the mix.

❏ **Use repetitive styles.** Some music styles are built around looping patterns or repetitive ostinato. These include rap, techno, reggae, Afro-Cuban, blues, and certain types of rock. When someone hears one of these styles, they *expect* it to have a loop, so they're less likely to be dismayed after the fourth or fifth cycle.

❏ **Start with a turnaround.** A *turnaround* is a common device for bringing a segment of music back to the beginning. The one most musicians are familiar with is the last V (five) chord in a blues progression. (Perhaps you can devise something a bit more creative!) Use a turnaround to start the segment, but then follow the next rule.

❏ **Make the listener work to figure it out.** Throw little curves at the listeners so that you'll hold their attention longer before they realize that what they're hearing is a loop. To throw them off your trail, use a turnaround to start the listener in midstream, and then quickly run through some type of musical transition before settling back into the main pattern. Another effective device is to use unusual time signatures (5/4 or 7/4) or to divide a time signature in different ways at different points in the loop. A piece in 6/4 could be counted as 4 & 2 in some places, and 3 & 3 in others. Finally, if the loop doesn't resolve harmonically, you'll keep the listener on edge. Once the loop becomes predictable, you're more likely to be tuned out.

❑ **Use the second loop, not the first.** We touched on this subject in Chapter 6, but it bears repeating here. This is a two-part rule. The first part applies to using a sequencer when composing. If you're using a loop-based sequencer such as Vision, Performer, or MasterTracks, you've probably already found that it's ideal for composing loops. But if your music contains accents that fall slightly ahead of or behind the beat, the "feel" may suffer if you're looping only one iteration of the music. If, for example, you're creating an eight-bar loop, record the sequence as a 24-bar loop. That way you'll capture notes that are slightly ahead of the first beat. When capturing the loop for editing, be sure to loop the second iteration so that sustaining frequencies (which won't exist at the start of the first iteration) don't cut off abruptly.

More Tips for Composers

I don't pretend to be a latter-day Stravinsky (even though he's a great inspiration) or even a classically trained composer. But it's astounding how many lessons one learns while making the transition from writing music for personal enjoyment (i.e., "I don't care if anyone else likes it so long as *I* like it") to writing for clients and commercial projects. If you want to make the leap into scoring for multimedia, you may find a few of these nuggets helpful. And keep in mind that one of the primary rules of any creative endeavor is knowing when to break the rules. We'll start with some general stylistic thoughts and then move into more specific ideas for multimedia music.

Let Go

The first difficult task is putting your ego in the back seat. When you're composing for a client, you have to do the equivalent of a Vulcan mind meld: imagine that the producer or the client has taken over part of your brain, and then let them take advantage of your musical expertise to create the right piece. Of course, you also have to know where to draw the line. The client is also counting on you to use your best judgment about how an audience might react to a particular style or approach. Just because they have a passion for klezmer doesn't mean it's always the way to go.

Keep Moving

When I first started really *listening* to commercial and advertising music, I noticed that it constantly changes, never staying in the same place for more than a few seconds. I, on the other hand, was accustomed to standard structures with verses, choruses, and a bridge. I knew I had finally crossed over to the commercial mindset when one of my former bandmates listened to my demo reel and asked, "Why do your songs have so many changes?" The answer, of course, is that we rarely have the time or the luxury for long song forms on a multimedia CD. Also, quick changes in music help to keep the listener's attention, so long as they're not gratuitous, distracting, or in conflict with the visuals.

Share the Spotlight

This rule ties back into the potential dangers of creativity for the sake of ego gratification. In most situations, your role is that of an accompanist, not a soloist. Your music is there to support graphics, video, or voiceover. Don't get too attached to that ripping part you just played until you determine that it helps your effort to support the presentation.

Write for the Mood

When music is an integral part of a visual presentation, the goal is usually to create a mood, not to write a song. Feel free to jettison your preconceived notions about what constitutes a piece of music. You might not need a standard drum/bass/chords/melody arrangement. One or two different instruments may be all you need. Thanks to the power of today's synthesizers and samplers, you can have a broad tonal palette at your disposal.

Resolve Not to Resolve

One way to maintain tension, suspense, or mystery is to abandon all thoughts of a tonal center. You may notice this approach in soundtracks, in which dense, altered chords shift back and forth. If the music never lands in one place, the listener is likely to be captivated. It's as though you're performing a musical high-wire act.

Stay in the Pocket

You don't always need a melodic figure. A good rhythmic bed can help drive the piece forward, with or without a melody. In fact, if your piece is designed to work behind voiceover or as a loop, a strong melody can be distracting.

What Would Your Heroes Do?

When you find yourself struggling for an idea or an approach, think of how another person might handle it. Unless you're a well-practiced arranger or a good multi-instrumentalist, it can be hard to create compelling parts for certain instruments. For example, when writing bass parts, I often think about some of the great people I've been fortunate enough to play with and how they might play a particular line.

In the same vein, I often think of classical composers and their command of the nuances of orchestration. Now that we have digital orchestras at our fingertips, we can draw from some of their techniques for using texture, timbre, and dynamics to add character to musical scores.

Abandon Ship

When all else fails, know when to cut your losses and try another approach. Few things are more frustrating than spending several hours working on a piece and then finding that it's moving farther and farther in the wrong direction. Writing music for multimedia is a lot like building a house. If you're not happy with the shape of the foundation, everything you build from that point on is a compromise.

Save for a Rainy Day

If, on the other hand, you've created something you really like, but you or the client doesn't think it's appropriate, stash it away. It may come in handy for another scene or project.

Do the Rough Thing

Before you spend too much time fine-tuning a piece of music, create a demo for the client to approve. Be sure the client understands that this is just the musical equivalent of a sketch on a napkin. Once you've received the go-ahead, you'll feel much more comfortable going through the time-consuming process of recording, capturing, processing and downsampling.

Be a Chameleon

It helps to be familiar with a broad range of styles. On one particular job, I had to write surf music, polkas, funk, Chinese and Italian restaurant muzak, a "Leave It To Beaver"-style theme, and an imitation of bad video game music. All in a day's work! Try to identify thematic or stylistic elements that give the listener a cue about the setting. In the surf piece, for example, I included tremolo guitar with whammy bar (pitch bend, actually),

INTERVIEW: KENT CARMICHAEL

Pop Rocket's Total Distortion was one of the most widely anticipated titles of 1993 (and '94, and '95). When it was finally released, the extra time and effort showed in every scene. One of the most striking aspects of Total Distortion (hereafter called TD). is the barrage of audio that accompanies every button, motion, and scene. Kent Carmichael was the lead sound designer; here, he describes some of his techniques.

There's hardly a moment in TD when you don't hear sound. Is that your design work or a team effort?

I just started making sounds and got a lot of different sounds for things. We put them in a folder—say, 60 different sounds for a button. I don't want to say that there wasn't a lot of design, but it was more individual and less formal, like Joe (Sparks) making and filling rooms with as much of everything as possible. For the first year and a half, there were just three people. Then Kevin (Krecji) came on, and everyone has done a little of everything.

In many multimedia productions, a producer says, "I need sounds A, B, C, and D." Once you create the sounds and give them back to the programmer, that's it. But there's much more integration going on in TD.

In many ways, there was really no one to stop us but ourselves. For the sake of business orientation, it's probably good to have someone who has to have a product by a certain date. The bad side was that we'd be going off on some tangent—we'd put a lot of work into an area and then not follow through with it. It's cool to have the freedom to do it, because you don't usually have a lot of time to goof around and make up a lot of tweaky sound designs and get into it. In many of the areas in TD, there was a lot of cleaning up of the video, so I had more time to come up with some good stuff. But you need to know when to stop. You need a good balance.

It's frustrating being at the mercy of a production schedule. Did you have many chances to go back and tweak the sounds after implementing them?

If something didn't work, Joe sometimes would say, "I need a new sound." And I'd go back to my studio and do it. There was a lot of doing "stuff", like making a library. Our audio library is almost two CD-ROMs in itself. I'd see something that needs a sound, so I'd either just do it at the office or take the file back to my studio. One of the problems was that we had so little equipment and the equipment

KENT CARMICHAEL *(continued)*

was so slow, so that being in two different locations and working together a lot was difficult. Sometimes I could put in a graveyard and work out the ambiance and fit it in there, and other times I'd do more funky loops, and then after demoing it for six months I'd hate that and change it.

Any advice for people who compose loops?

That is where the real art is, the fun stuff. A lot of the tunes in TD are "heavy metal Archies," tongue in cheek. It's silly and an obscure inside joke. I'd say that 80 to 90 percent of the loops in TD are four bars or fewer. To do stuff that you can listen to over and over and that doesn't make you sick—that's a feat. I have a lot of anxiety over it sometimes. My advice, especially on the loops, is do it to please yourself, or to try to catch a mood. If you are pleased about it yourself, other people will be pleased with it too. I like to do more acoustic stuff. I have a Korg 01/W synthesizer, but about 75 percent of the time I use it like a drum machine with keys.

What sound file formats are you actually using in Total Distortion?

They're 8-bit, 11 kHz.

How do you downsample to 11 kHz?

I don't have ProTools or anything like that yet. Believe it or not, the best stuff was done through a cassette deck and then digitized at 11 kHz or 22 kHz using a MacRecorder, to sound good coming out of a Mac speaker. It's hard to tell quality on reference monitors or Macintosh speakers. Sometimes it sounds good on Mac speakers—then you go to a trade show with a super sub woofer and you crank the bass. I've tried all kinds of different things, (Waves) L1 and such things, which are great. But for me, the simplest things work the best. Everything else is really inconsistent and would sound good on some tools only. One of the hard things in Total Distortion is the amount of distorted guitar, because it's so harmonically complex. If you tweak too much with the processing, it just sounds like bad radio tuning.

Did you plan on doing Macintosh and Windows versions from the start? What cross-platform issues did you encounter?

A couple of different versions of Director came and went while we were doing TD. At the end, it converted well. It hardly took a month and a half with the installer and that sort of thing. Fate worked out for us, and we were able to do Macintosh and Windows simultaneously. We didn't sit on it for very long.

KENT CARMICHAEL *(continued)*

The sound problems we had involved Director and PC sound cards. That seemed to work itself out. We didn't have to redo a lot of stuff. Actually, our biggest problem was that a lot of work had been done, and then we realized that we had to do 8-character filenames for DOS. That was the biggest hassle, to rename 4 million bleeps and chords so that they would work in Windows. That was the major conversion for sound.

I know you used SoundEdit 16 a bit. What were some of your favorite likes and dislikes about it compared to some of the other editing products?

Maybe because I'm a Pisces, I think I see both sides of things. But I like SoundEdit because of its simplicity. It's so easy to get lost in a 900-band graphic EQ, and every adjustment you make just makes the sound worse and worse. Usually at the very best it isn't better; it's just different.

If it's sounding bad in the beginning, I always get in more trouble by isolating this or that frequency, and it always comes out sounding worse. From a technical standpoint of how SoundEdit processes the data when compared with Sound Designer, I just know that sometimes it sounds better and sometimes it doesn't. For me, the more processing I do internally, the more clouded and bad the sound gets. So I digitize it, maybe pitch-shift it, and then downsample, and that's it. Usually I try to do most of the manipulations when I'm recording.

glissando pick bass, cheesy organ, and lots of ride cymbal. (*Ride cymbals* are long-sustaining cymbals that form the main rhythm in musical styles like swing jazz. Their tone is very different from the sounds produced by the "crash" cymbals used to accent a particular point in music.)

Orchestrate to Mask Noise

If your music is destined for 8/22 or 8/11, you should know by now that noise likely to be a problem. One way to mitigate the noise is to compose using sounds that hide the hiss and crackle. Breathy synthesizer pads, shakers, and some cymbal sounds can be particularly effective.

At the opposite end of the spectrum, beware of sparse orchestrations with large gaps of "silence" that may allow background noise to become overly noticeable. The problem becomes worse if you add lots of reverb, because background noise is liable to overwhelm the reverb decay.

Watch the Highs

Look out for instrument tones that might self-destruct as they are down-sampled. Among the worst offenders are bells and other high, ringing metal tones. As high-frequency information is lost and quantization noise sets in through the downsampling process, the sound may lose its purity. Instead of a clear bell, you'll hear a grainy metallic crackle.

Cymbals can suffer dramatically at 8/11. Even a great jazz drummer like Tony Williams can end up sounding like a kid beating on a trash can lid. If your arrangement calls for a ride cymbal, try to use the sound that the cymbal makes when it's struck near the center (the bell) rather than at the edge.

Designing for Multimedia

You may recall a basic tenet from our earlier discussion of sound design as an aspect of planning (Chapter 6). Think about your *ideal* sound design—what you'd really like to achieve—before limiting yourself to the *real* sound design—what you can get away with considering the technical limitations.

Someday (soon, we hope!), the ideal multimedia audio experience will be a lot like film: a constant mix of foreground, midground, and background effects, shifting seamlessly between scenes. Going a step beyond film, we could add new audio elements on the fly and alter the musical score as the user directs the action. What would it really take to make this ideal become a reality?

The Ideal Scenario

For starters, we'd need at least four independent sound tracks: one each for music, background sound effects, midground or foreground sound effects, and voice. Actually, all the tracks should be stereo, with three-dimensional spatialization processing, so we'd need eight discrete channels to permit left/right separation in each of the four tracks. The music could be streamed as MIDI, using an onboard synthesizer, but the three remaining tracks should be 16/44. Using 4:1 compression of the audio tracks, we'd be playing 132 KB of data per second. But two tracks, voice and foreground effects, would need to play from RAM to maintain the interactive element of the presentation. That means 88 KB of memory for every second the two tracks are playing, or almost 1 MB of RAM for every 10 seconds of sound. Background audio could stream from disk. But we'd have to load new elements into RAM at various points, so the disk would need to have extremely fast access, with a large buffer to continue playing background sound while the disk searches for other data.

Meanwhile, Back in the Real World

A substantial number of today's end users have "multimedia PCs" with a mere 4 MB of RAM. Hmmm . . . seems we'll be waiting a while before our dream configuration is the predominant home platform. As the PowerPC and Pentium platforms gain in market share, perhaps multimedia developers will be able to worry less about the installed base of older, "legacy" machines. And as CD-ROM drive speeds increase from 2x (double-speed) to 4x (quad-speed) and higher, we'll be better able to load large sound files into memory. But there's a major bottleneck that we have yet to face: the inability of a CD-ROM drive's read mechanism to be in two places at the same time.

Pundits and soothsayers may continue to shift back and forth trying to figure out which distribution medium will dominate the market (CD-ROM, interactive TV, or the World Wide Web), but CD-ROM already has gained enough of a toehold to be a viable medium. Meanwhile, interactive TV trials stumble. And while access to the Internet and World Wide Web is getting faster all the time, the time it takes to access data from a CD-ROM is blindingly fast in comparison, and people are already impatient with double-speed CD throughput of 160 KB per second.

When the goal is broad distribution of multimedia content, therefore, we're still in a CD-ROM world. The access time of double-speed drives still leaves multimedia audio producers with difficult choices when selecting a playback strategy. The choice you make will have a major impact on your sound design.

Two Heads Are Better Than One

We've established that there are two primary approaches to audio playback:

❏ **Load sound into memory and play it from RAM**—great for quick response, looped sounds and short sounds

❏ **Stream sound directly from the disk**—good for playing long segments that can't fit entirely into memory

Either of these approaches works great until you add interactivity, limited RAM, and other types of media, such as graphics and digital video, to the equation. What happens when you want to play a three-minute animation with continuous audio? You have only two real choices: (1) load the sound into RAM and get graphics from the disk as they're needed, or (2) play the sound from disk, and be sure the graphics are all loaded into RAM.

If you stream the audio from disk, you run the risk of playback being interrupted if the disk has to load other data. The streaming technique actually *does* use a bit of RAM, because the sound is loaded into a small buffer prior to playback. If you could increase that buffer to hold 10 seconds of audio, it's possible you could access other data off the CD during the 10 seconds of buffered playback, then hope the CD read head gets back to the audio data before the buffer runs out. (In fact, Macromedia Director for Windows lets you set this buffer size in an .INI file.) But you would lose some interactive control with this scheme. What if a user clicks a button while you're playing from the buffer? You wouldn't hear the button click at the right time, and audio from the previous screen would still be playing when the new screen appears, wreaking havoc with scene changes. Well, maybe it would be better to play the audio from memory . . .

Or would it? If you try to load the audio into memory, you might not have enough. Three minutes of mono 8/22 consume just over 3.5 MB of RAM. Even if your minimum platform is an 8 MB machine, the operating system may require 3 MB of RAM, and your playback software—even if it's only a *runtime* version (a stripped-down version of the authoring tool designed for distributed playback)—may require almost 1 MB of RAM. That's 7.5 MB so far, leaving about 500 KB for graphics. One full screen background (640 x 480, 8-bit color) uses 300 KB. This doesn't leave much latitude for a graphics-rich presentation.

It looks as though another tradeoff is in order. If you can juggle memory-management chores and implement a streamed audio strategy, you can also reap the benefits of higher-fidelity audio. The 4:1 IMA compression scheme implemented in Sound Manager 3.1 permits excellent fidelity while streaming audio. In fact, many authoring tools require that IMA sounds be played directly from disk. If you can't stream from disk (that is, if all the graphics *can't* be loaded into memory before audio playback starts) you'll need to play sounds from memory. In limited-memory environments, your knowledge of good downsampling techniques will pay off yet again. This tradeoff, we believe, is the main consideration keeping 8/11 audio alive.

Looking back to our original ideal of a four-track design integrating voice, music, background and foreground effects, we need to solve the dilemma squeezing all of our audio into a two-track (or one-track) playback solution, while also keeping a close eye on memory-management and disk access requirements. This calls for some audio sleight-of-hand—perhaps a better term would be sleight-of-ear. Here are some of the tricks you can try to keep the whole thing moving.

Channel Surfing

If your authoring tool supports at least two sound channels, one solution is to switch channels to accommodate the different types of audio data. Juggling may be a better description than surfing! We need to keep three or four audio types active using only two audio channels. In some cases, you can premix elements together. Be as sparing as possible with premixing, however, since you can lose flexibility. If, for example, you premix a background ambiance with a foreground effect tied to an animation, you'll have to remix the file if the animation is changed later during production.

Premix Tracks

If you're doing a linear presentation that contains no interactive audio elements, you're in luck. You can premix all the audio into one track. You may end up with a sizable file if it's a long segment, so you'll have to decide whether to load graphics into RAM so that audio can stream uninterrupted, or load the sound into RAM so that graphics can be loaded from the disk as the sequence plays. You might also have to work harder to synchronize graphics and audio, especially if the end product will be distributed to a broad audience on CD-ROM.

Borrow From a Hard Drive

Although CD-ROM is a great medium for distribution, its relatively slow access time can cause problems. Streaming audio from the disk is risky unless you're absolutely certain that all the other elements of your presentation are in RAM. But if you ask nicely and don't take up too much room, you *might* be able to borrow some hard drive space from the user. This approach lets audio stream from the hard disk while other elements are accessed on the CD. Be extremely conservative in your estimate of what users may be willing to sacrifice for the sake of your sound. But just 5 MB of hard disk real estate buys you almost five minutes of 4:1 compressed 16/44 mono.

Optimize for Access

This rule should be obvious enough that you've already taken it into account. If you're playing from CD-ROM, place the sound files near the presentation file. If the sound file you need is on the other end of the disk from the presentation document, you'll hold up the entire show as the playback head travels back and forth.

Use Stepping Stones

If you've chosen to load graphics into RAM and stream audio from disk, you run the risk of hitting a dead spot when audio playback ends and the disk's read head goes in search of the next file. One way to bridge this gap is with a *stepping stone,* a small file loaded into RAM that can play while the disk is accessing more data.

Embrace Randomness

If you're playing a looping background ambiance from RAM, it may become repetitive after a minute. If you have a second sound channel available, try creating eight to 10 small effects that you can add randomly to the mix. If, for example, you start with an outdoor ambiance, you could add dog barks and bird calls. You'll have to work closely with the programmer to implement this approach, but it can help you get much more mileage out of a background loop.

Good News & Not-So-Good News

The good news is that, when it's used effectively, audio can have the greatest impact of any media type on a user's perception of your presentation. Compared to digital video and 3D graphics or animation, audio offers the most "bang for the buck" in creating perceived value for a multimedia product. Audio can provide information (voice), create an environment (effects), and elicit a powerful emotional response (music). Audio is also the best tool for creating and maintaining one of the most elusive goals for multimedia producers: continuity.

The not-so-good news is that, in the real world of production schedules, it's difficult to find the time required to achieve this level of integration. Anticipate this situation—it helps you better prepare to deal with it.

Squeezing In Under the Deadline

To be effective, audio must succeed simultaneously on a number of levels: tone or mood; audio quality; continuity; and synchronization. One of the most difficult aspects of sound design for multimedia is that you're rarely able to see the presentation in a state that is close enough to a finished product before you're required to start production to meet a deadline. For most types of CD-ROM titles, audio production requires only a fraction of the time necessary for tasks like graphic production and programming. It's a good thing, too, because you can count on not having nearly enough time to do your job!

In an ideal world, sound design for multimedia would begin at the earliest design stages for the entire product, but actual sound production wouldn't start until the graphics were nearing completion. Also, enough of the programming structure would be in place so that you could get a good idea of the pacing and flow of the product; you'd know the lengths of scenes, the length of pauses between scenes, and the timing of "hits" or synchronization points for every animation. Then you could create sounds that are appropriate for the visuals and timing. This is the model used in the film world, and it works quite well.

It seldom happens this way for multimedia products. As the schedule slips and tightens (a hanging analogy might be appropriate here), the deadline begins to loom. You often need to start creating sounds based on a hodgepodge of small animations, still graphics, storyboards, and written scripts. In other words, use your imagination, do the best you can, and be prepared for lots of last-minute changes and additions.

The best strategies we've found to cope with this situation are to keep sounds as modular as possible, and to keep *everything* accessible for as long as possible: the source audio, the multi-track mixing documents, the various stages of processing and downsampling, and of course, the finished downsampled files. You'll invariably find yourself dipping back into this material when last-minute changes come through. Plenty of storage and a hefty back-up medium will pay off.

Continuity— Smoothing the Surface

One of multimedia's most vexing problems has been continuity—the ability to deliver a constant stream of graphics and sounds to reproduce the user's experience with film and video. The bottleneck is obvious: at any given point, the user may choose to go in any one of several directions. There's usually not enough memory to keep all these options loaded in RAM at the same time, so there's a lag as new material is accessed and loaded. Interactivity—it's as easy as click and wait!

Playing audio is often the best way to keep the user's attention during the lull. You can also use this opportunity to play music or effects that help to set up the next scene. But in order to do the fine-tuning, you need to know how much time and system resources are available to work with. As we've just seen, it's difficult to determine this until the project is close to completion. But you *do* have a window of opportunity.

The ABCs of Alpha and Beta

In software development parlance, a project should pass several milestones on its way to a finished box on the shelf. One important milestone is *alpha,* the point at which a product should be "feature complete." That is, all the structure, functions, and interface conventions should be locked in place. It's often the case that content is not yet finished in an alpha version, but placeholder graphics and sounds might be used to test functionality.

A second milestone is *beta*. Once a product reaches beta, all content should be integrated, and the program should be free of *crash bugs*—glitches that lock up your computer. Ideally, once a product reaches beta you should be tweaking only content or programming that already exists.

The third and final milestone is the revered *golden master,* the final bug-free version (as close to bug-free as you can get, anyway) which is shipped off for duplication. The approach of this milestone is the period in a project when all hell breaks loose. Changes are made hourly, tension is high, and patience runs low. But if you're brave enough to run into this flaming structure, you'll find it's your best opportunity to enhance continuity. You'll see how long it actually takes to move from one file to another when the presentation plays back from CD on a slow machine, and how much RAM is available for sounds to play between files.

You'll also see the programmer and project manager become extremely nervous at the thought of making changes at this stage of the game. It's important that you work very closely with them to address their concerns, and that you pick your additions and changes carefully. But by adding just a few sounds at the right points, you can help tie the entire product into a cohesive, seamless experience for the viewer.

Summary

Audio plays a substantial role in the way end users perceive an entire presentation. It's important to consider sound from a design perspective before you launch into production. In this chapter, we've considered a number of methods, including a layered approach (design by the location of the sound in physical and cognitive space) or a functional approach (design by the type of sound). The most popular models for sound design draw from film. But multimedia has both more demands and more limitations than film, providing interactive options while also struggling with limited bandwidth. If you're crafty and creative, you can work around these limitations to maintain continuity.

We've also seen that digital audio-editing and audio-processing tools can help you achieve specific effects with voice, sound effects, and music. In the next section, we'll review the features of specific products to help you determine which tools you need to create a tonal masterpiece.

Part Three

PRODUCT REVIEWS

9

Audio Editors

We enjoy an embarrassment of riches in terms of the range of audio editing and processing software on the market today. Much of this technology barely existed ten years ago! Obviously, there's plenty of room for improvement. But even if one tool doesn't have all the features you need to do a given job, you can probably find another product that does. In this chapter, we'll survey many of the popular audio editing packages on the market, at prices ranging from under $100 to more than $10,000.

These reviews are no substitute for a thorough evaluation of your own, based on your particular process and needs. But we will point out some of our most (and least) favorite features so you can get a jump on the learning curve. And we'll pass on whatever shortcuts, workarounds, or hacks we've gleaned from working with some of these products.

First, let's revisit a few basic concepts about editing software and the way it mimics traditional audio mixers and tape recorders.

Look to the
CD-ROM

❑ ***Destructive editors*** actually change the file data on the disk as you cut, copy, and paste. ***Nondestructive editors,*** on the other hand, don't change the data; they change the length of the region that plays back and the order in which segments of the file are played. The nondestructive approach is often faster for editing because you spend less time waiting for the disk to move large files.

❑ Many editors use a *session* metaphor. A session is a global container (usually a folder) that includes all the information specific to the working document. The actual audio files may be an exception, since they can be referenced from various locations. Once you import files into the session, most of the editing is nondestructive.

❑ The control buttons for stop, play, rewind, record, and so on, usually appear together in an area of the interface called the *transport,* which in the days of analog-only audio editing had the function of transporting tape. Other controls often found conveniently located in the transport section are *autolocators* and *punch-in/punch-out.* An autolocator lets you enter a location and automatically advance playback to that point (handy for jumping to a particular line of dialog or note of music). Punch-in and punch-out controls (sometimes displayed as *in* and *out)* let you set points at which recording will automatically start and stop on a specific track. These types of controls can be useful for inserting new dialog or fixing a section of an instrumental performance.

This chapter is divided into two main sections. The "Standard Editors" section covers discussions of Macromedia's SoundEdit 16 version 2.0, Opcode's Audioshop version 2.1, and Digidesign's SoundDesigner II version 2.0. The "Session Editors" section takes you on a whirlwind tour of Opcode's DigiTrax version 1.2, Macromedia's Deck II version 2.5, Digidesign's Session version 2.0, ProTools-TDM, and Sonic Solutions. Prepare for information overload!

Standard Editors

For each product reviewed in this section, we summarize its strongest points ("Especially Nifty Features"), its potential drawbacks ("Potentially Heartbreaking Features"), and useful tips and tricks ("Special Tricks"). We also provide contact and pricing information.

SoundEdit 16 Version 2.0

Look to the CD-ROM

Macromedia's SoundEdit 16 version 2.0 is the latest generation of the venerable SoundEdit, one of the first sound editing programs for the Mac. It's a good workhorse for multimedia audio, especially when you're dealing with files at lower sampling rates (8/22, for example). It's also a good choice for people who need to work with 16/44 files but don't have a sound card, a 16-bit-capable Macintosh, or other requisite hardware. Figure 9.1 shows the Track, Controls, Selection, and Levels dialog boxes for SoundEdit 16.

Especially Nifty Features

❑ The interface is clean and intuitive, in part because, unlike its competitors (Deck II, Session, and Digitrax), it doesn't mimic a recording studio

Figure 9.1

The main windows of the SoundEdit 16 2.0 interface include the Track, Controls, Selection, and Levels controls.

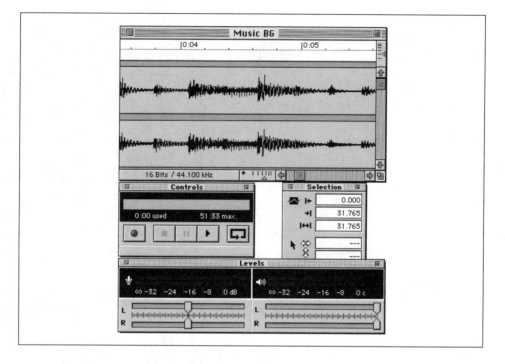

or multi-track mixer. This non-traditional interface may be easier for and best suited to people who need to edit sound only occasionally during the course of a project, such as animators and video editors.

❏ This is the only popular editing package that supports variable frame rate settings. You can adjust rulers, markers, and pointer positions by any frame rate you specify. If your QuickTime or Director movie is running at non-SMPTE rates like 15 fps, this feature can be very helpful.

❏ Speaking of QuickTime, SoundEdit 16 2.0 lets you edit soundtracks within QuickTime movies and then save those edits right back into the movie. In a similar vein, you can copy and paste audio in and out of the cast in Macromedia Director for last-minute tweaks to Director sounds.

❏ Starting with version 2.0, SoundEdit 16 includes the Automator, a utility for batch processing (Figure 9.2). The Automator is a godsend for converting sample rates and file formats.

❏ Also new with version 2.0 is an open architecture, which allows you to access plug-in effects (called Xtras) from within the program. Third-party developers, including Waves and InVision Interactive, are supporting the new architecture.

Figure 9.2

SoundEdit 16's new Automator utility uses Apple Events to drive the program. You can even process several different file formats in the same session.

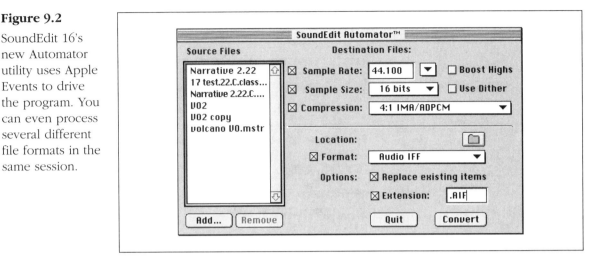

❏ Speaking of formats, SoundEdit 16 2.0 supports *lots* of them. In addition to the standard AIFF, snd, SoundEdit, SoundDesigner, and WAV formats, you'll also find support for .au (used by Sun Microsystems computers and the Internet) and Apple's IMA 4:1.

❏ SoundEdit 16 can capture CD audio using dialog boxes similar to those found in MoviePlayer. Even better, it supports pasting from the clipboard in Disc-to-Disk, a great CD audio capture utility that we cover later in this chapter. Pasting from Disc-To-Disk isn't supported in programs like Sound Designer or Deck II.

Potentially Heartbreaking Features

❏ The biggest gripe many users have with SoundEdit 16 concerns its playback of complex files—and rightfully so. Even on a PowerMac 9500, the sound jerks and stutters when you play four tracks of 16/44 audio. Compare this performance to that of products like Deck II, which can easily achieve simultaneous playback of over 10 tracks. As a partial solution, SoundEdit 16 lets you select a "Premix" option that premixes large files before playback. Premixing helps reduce the stuttering, but you also spend more time waiting for premixing to finish before playback can begin.

❏ One reason for this performance hit, according to Macromedia engineers, is that SoundEdit 16 is optimized for fast editing. As a destructive editor, it cuts and pastes sound data as you work. So think twice before you wipe out that "Undo" buffer after cutting something.

Compare this with non-destructive editors like Deck II or Sound Designer II, which change the section of audio they're referencing but don't actually alter the audio data. Because SoundEdit 16 is constantly moving file data around as you edit, playback of complex files can suffer as the hard disk searches from one chunk to the next. SoundEdit 16's approach also has its advantages, though: you avoid the whole session metaphor imposed by Deck, Digitrax, and Session, requires you to create a session, import files into the session, and then finally place the files into a track. In SoundEdit 16, you just open the file and start working—another reason why it's so intuitive. Rumor has it that some folks spend 20 minutes just trying to figure out how to open a file in Deck. (One can only assume they didn't read the manual, as Deck is very well-documented and easy to use once you're familiar with it.)

❏ It's a good thing SoundEdit 16 2.0 supports plug-in Xtras, because the built-in effects are pretty limited. The reverb is only good for a cheesy 1950s sci-fi sound, and the flanger settings can't be adjusted at all. In our opinion, a good dialog box design for effects like Noise Gating would show numerical values for threshold and attack. Instead, we're presented with "Quiet" and "Loud" for the threshold and "Fast" or "Slow" for the attack. Some dialog boxes, as well as the Levels Window, sport what appear to be very precise rulers—until you look closer and discover that there are no values on the rulers (Figure 9.3). As a result, once you select a setting, you have to count it yourself, as in "Five big marks and three little marks . . . oh, it's 18!"

❏ SoundEdit 16 lets you quickly shift tracks back and forth by Option-clicking and dragging them. But you can't select and shift multiple

Figure 9.3

The Noise Gate Effect dialog box is pretty to look at, but it would be nice to have some real numbers, especially if you plan to keep track of the settings you use.

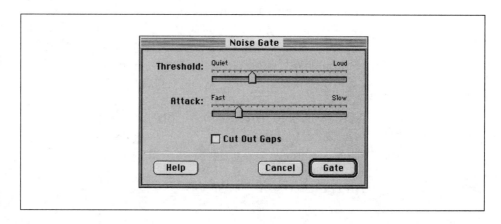

tracks at once. If you have a group of related effects in separate tracks and you want to shift all of them, you either need to carefully reposition them one at a time or mix the section to a separate file and then paste it back into your main document.

❏ Be careful when using SoundEdit 16 to edit audio in QuickTime movies. If the audio extends beyond the end of a movie, SoundEdit 16 creates blank frames for the duration of the audio. The best way to avoid this is to immediately place a cue point at the last frame of the movie and then take care not to go beyond the cue point.

❏ What a segue! Speaking of cue points, SoundEdit 16 has Cues and Labels. These are roughly similar to Sound Designer's Markers and Regions. But while SoundEdit 16 version 2.0 sports improved Cue and Label windows, you can't actually edit the data from within the window—it's not possible to rename cues or labels or to change their time values. The only way to edit Cue and Label information from within a comprehensive window is to use an Xtra.

Special Tricks

❏ You can copy and paste values between the Selection Window and the editing dialog boxes for more accurate (or more automated) editing.

❏ Use the logarithmic fade presets rather than the linear fades. Specifically, use the "Fast" setting for Fade-In and the "Slow" setting for Fade-Out. As discussed in Chapter 7, logarithmic fades help reduce apparent background noise during fades.

❏ Once you've selected a particular effect, you can Option-click to bypass the settings dialog box and reapply the previous effect settings automatically.

❏ Importing a file into a track places the filename in the Track Name box as long as you have the "Show Track Information" display option selected. If you're processing to a new, untitled file, you can copy the filename from the Track Name field and paste it into the File Save dialog box to retain the filename information.

Who, Where, and How Much
SoundEdit 16 2.0
Macromedia
600 Townsend, Suite 310 W
San Francisco, CA 94103

415-252-2000

http://www.macromedia.com

Suggested Retail: $399

Audioshop Version 2.1

Look to the
CD-ROM

Distributed by Opcode Systems, Audioshop is one of the most affordable audio editors available, but it still manages to pack in a ton of functions. It's a great product to have in your toolkit, because it has features that you just won't find anywhere else. Figures 9.4 and 9.5 show representative CD and playlist-editing screens from Audioshop.

Especially Nifty Features

❏ Far and away, a favorite window in Audioshop is the Playlist Window (shown in Figure 9.5). By clicking the Add button in the lower left

Figure 9.4

The CD interface in Audioshop's main window is non-standard, to say the least.

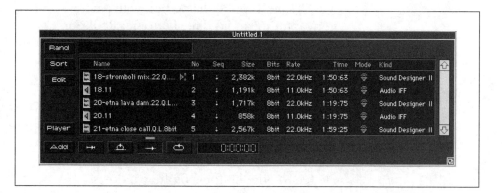

Figure 9.5

Audioshop's Playlist window is a great tool for auditioning, tracking, and converting files.

corner of the window, you can add to the playlist all the files in a folder or on a volume. (The Add function also searches through folders nested within folders.) Clicking the column headings lets you sort the list by any attribute (Name, Size, Bits, etcetera)—a fabulous audio database tool!

❏ From the Playlist window, you can play every file in sequence just by tapping the spacebar. It's a great way to audition files and check relative volume levels.

❏ Audioshop's Playlist Window lends itself well to batch processing. To convert formats, for example, you simply highlight a range of tracks and then select "Save Selected Tracks..." from the File menu.

❏ Audioshop can find hidden and invisible files. This isn't a license for thievery, but it does allow you to check out audio files on your favorite CD-ROM title. Audio tracks from QuickTime movies, snd Resources embedded into HyperCard stacks, sound castmembers from Director 3.x movies . . . they all magically appear in the Playlist window.

❏ You can use Audioshop's playlists to create names for audio CD tracks, in the same way that you create track names using the AppleCD Audio Player usually found under the Apple menu. This feature can really come in handy if you're dealing with sound-effect libraries on CDs. Better yet, the track names can be read by Disc-To-Disk, so they'll appear in that program's pop-up menu (yes, it's the second mention of Disc-to-Disk and we *still* haven't explained it, but it's coming, so please be patient).

❏ Audioshop supports a good range of file formats, including Sound Designer II, QuickTime, and WAV, as well as good old AIFF and snd.

❏ You can capture audio straight from CD using the standard QuickTime capture dialog box used in MoviePlayer. The combination of the QuickTime capture dialog box with Audioshop's CD control is great for capturing audio directly from a RedBook CD (although it's still no substitute for—you guessed it!—the aforementioned Disc-To-Disk).

Potentially Heartbreaking Features

❏ Most of our complaints about Audioshop fall into the interface category. Many people are completely satisfied with the current look and feel of the program, but there are things about Audioshop that just make us wonder. Why the CD-player metaphor, right down to the little feet on the bottoms of the windows? Why not follow the Apple

Interface guidelines for displaying windows? In addition, some menu items seem to be misplaced. The "Edit Track" function, for example, is under the Control menu rather than the Edit menu.

❏ Audioshop's Edit window (Figure 9.6) will do the job, but we'd like to see other conventions used here—such as displaying waveforms as lines instead of dots, editing on a white background, and having a choice of waveform color. Most other Macintosh sound-editing applications support these options.

❏ Audioshop isn't completely clear on sample rates. When you see a program using sample rates of 22 and 11, stop and ask yourself, "Is that 22.050 and 11.025 or 22.254 and 11.127?" When you change sample rates in the Player window, it changes only the playback rate of the file, not the actual sample rate. For example, if you're playing a 22.050 file and click the 11 button, the file will play at half speed. Finally, you can change sample rates from with the Track editor, but all the rates below 22.050 are for older Macintosh models (11.127, 7.418, etcetera). If you want to create 11.025 files, you'll need another program.

❏ Audioshop's multitrack mixing is limited. You can mix the contents of the clipboard with another track and set relative volumes for each one. This is a bit of a hit-or-miss proposition if you're creating complex effect backgrounds with multiple layers.

Figure 9.6

Audioshop's Edit window has all the functions you need for basic work.

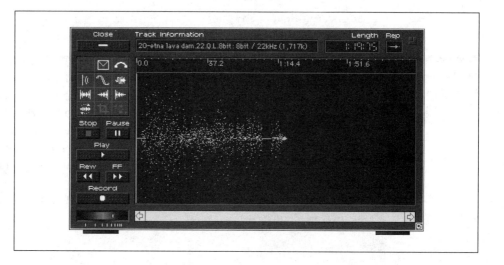

Special Tricks

❏ Audioshop is a great environment for automation! When a track is highlighted in the Playlist window, pressing the Tab key selects the track name in the name display at the top left of the window. With a little help from QuicKeys, you can use this feature to rename a bunch of files. You can also open files in the Track Edit window to convert sample rates, as mentioned previously. After changing the track, though, you must use the Save Track As... menu option to save the new version of the file with the new name and attributes.

❏ When you're creating files for clients, tell them to pick up a copy of Audioshop. Then, when you send them a batch of sounds, include a playlist so they can audition your work easily.

❏ Use Audioshop Playlists to be *doubly* sure that all your files are at correct sample rates. If your project is cross-platform, it's essential that all files be at standard PC rates. The sorting features of the Playlist window greatly simplify this task.

Who, Where, and How Much

Audioshop 2.1

Opcode Systems

3950 Fabian Way, Suite 100

Palo Alto, CA 94303

415-856-3333

http://www.opcode.com

Suggested Retail: $88

Sound Designer II Version 2.8

The venerable Sound Designer II from Digidesign set the original standard for high-quality audio editing. In some ways, it doesn't feel *quite* right to put Sound Designer II in the standard editors category, since it's mainly a nondestructive editor. But it doesn't have session-oriented multi-track mixing features either, so this seems as good a place as any to check it out.

Sound Designer is bundled with Digidesign's DSP hardware. In fact, it won't even run unless it sees a Digidesign audio card with a DSP, such as an Audiomedia II. But the hardware assist gives this program enough muscle to handle lots of serious production work. The main editing window is shown in Figure 9.7.

Figure 9.7

The main edit window in Sound Designer II. The overview at the top shows the entire soundfile and is useful for auditioning or navigating to different parts of the file.

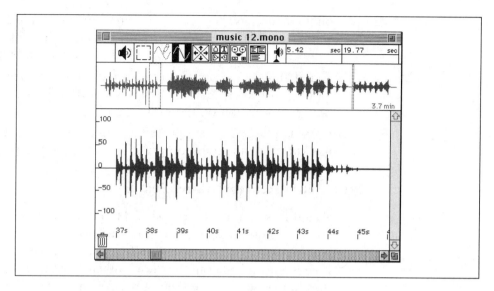

Especially Nifty Features

❏ Sound Designer lets you specify regions within a file and then arrange those regions into a playlist. This is an efficient approach for working with large files, because you're only changing reference pointers to sections within the file, not rewriting the file data itself. Regions and playlists are also useful for bulk processing, because you can process a single large file instead of many small files. You'll get more consistent results and spend less time opening and closing files. Finally, Sound Designer's regions and playlists are supported by many popular audio editing tools, including Deck II, Session, Studio Vision, and Digital Performer. When importing an audio file into one of the programs, you have the option of importing the entire file, a playlist within the file, or just a specific region.

❏ Sound Designer has a nice, simple interface for capturing audio, whether you're digitizing from an analog source or capturing from DAT. An especially useful interface convention is the display that shows time used and time remaining on the hard disk.

❏ The overview display at the top of the file offers a handy guideline for viewing your current position within a file and for previewing audio throughout the file (see Figure 9.7). Click and hold the mouse button on the overview, and the file begins playing from that location. If the Scroll After Play option is currently selected, the view automatically jumps to the point where you released the mouse button.

❏ Sound Designer supports lots of useful plug-ins, including most of the tools from Waves, AnTares Systems, and Digidesign's own DINR (more information on these in Chapter 10).

❏ Looping playback is supported in Sound Designer. The Loop window lets you fine-tune the loop point so that the splice point is seamless.

Potentially Heartbreaking Features

❏ Sound Designer uses a preset RAM buffer, which determines the amount of audio data that can be auditioned in previews (from the compressor or from a plug-in effect, for example). It also determines how far you can zoom the view outward, limiting the amount of data that can be seen in the editing window at any one time. You have to increase the size of the buffer to see more than a few seconds' worth of audio. Unfortunately, the RAM buffer always defaults to four seconds, and there's no way to set a higher default value. Set yourself a QuicKey work-around, because it's to your advantage to increase this value when you create a new file—once you set a higher buffer size, that information is saved with the document.

❏ Among the most common operations to perform when editing are highlighting and playing a selected area. The only way to do this in Sound Designer is to click and hold the mouse button over the speaker icon. If you press the spacebar to play the area, it starts playback at the start of the selection but then continues to play past the end of the selection. Having a lock button on a trackball can thus be a real wrist saver.

❏ Sound Designer's markers are a mixed blessing. On the plus side, you can insert markers on the fly by pressing the Enter key during playback or even while recording. Each marker is automatically numbered, and you can jump to the marker location by typing its number. But you can't name the markers as you're placing them, and unless you keep track of how many times you've pressed the Enter key, you don't know which number corresponds to which point in the file. It would also be nice if there were a key command to advance to the next and previous markers.

❏ The mixer in Sound Designer seems to be part of Digidesign's strategy to drive people toward their mixing products, Session and ProTools. The mixer is useful only for mixing stereo files to mono. To reposition the start time of a file, you have to know the number of milliseconds of offset—not exactly user friendly.

❏ Sound Designer's downsampling function only lets you downsample by a maximum of one-half the sample rate. For example, if you start with a 48 kHz file, you can downsample only to 24 kHz, not to 22.050 kHz. This is why we recommend always working at 44.1 kHz if you know you'll be passing through Sound Designer. That way you only have to downsample once on your way to 22.050 kHz.

❏ When you process data to a new file, you lose all the regions associated with the file. This can be a real shock if you create regions at 44.1 kHz and then downsample to 22.050 kHz. One great workaround for this is Precision Audio Tools' Region Reader utility. It saves the region data as a separate file and then can reapply the regions after downsampling.

❏ Sound Designer's orientation toward nondestructive editing becomes painfully clear when you try to cut one second of audio from the middle of a ten-minute file. Destructive cut-and-paste operations can take a really long time. If you find yourself needing to do this, a quicker procedure is to define regions, then arrange the regions in a playlist and save the playlist as a new file. As an alternative, you could use SoundEdit 16 or Audioshop for massive cut-and-paste sessions.

❏ A word of warning is in order. If you create a playlist and set crossfades between regions, *don't* set any fades for the last region in the list; you'll crash. We hope that a future release will fix this problem.

Special Tricks

❏ Sound Designer's Scrubbing feature is great for creating tweaked-out sounds. Just run the audio output from the card to a recorder (ideally, go digitally to DAT), then load a file, press and hold the Option key, and drag back and forth. You'll get really rich textures that are great for industrial and sci-fi noise.

❏ You can use Sound Designer's playlists in conjunction with QuicKeys to batch process voiceover as described in Chapter 7.

Who, Where, and How Much

Sound Designer II Version 2.8
Digidesign, Inc.
1360 Willow Road, Suite 101
Menlo Park, CA 94025

415-688-0600

Suggested Retail: $1,299 with Audiomedia II (bundled with hardware)

Session Editors

Among the current crop of session editors, the most notable are Alaska Software's DigiTrax, Macromedia's Deck II, Digidesign's Session and ProTools, and products from Sonic Solutions.

**DigiTrax
Version 1.2**

DigiTrax, created by Alaska Software, is another offering published by Opcode Systems. It was one of the first programs released to take advantage of the DSP in the Macintosh Quadra 840AV and 660AV models. As such, it also works with the Spectral Innovations NuMedia card (the same DSP as in the AV Quadras) and now runs without additional hardware on Power Macs. It's a straightforward, inexpensive editor and mixer. Figure 9.8 shows an example of this ease of use.

Figure 9.8

The DigiTrax Mixer window has separate controls to set different levels for actual input volume and monitoring the input volume.

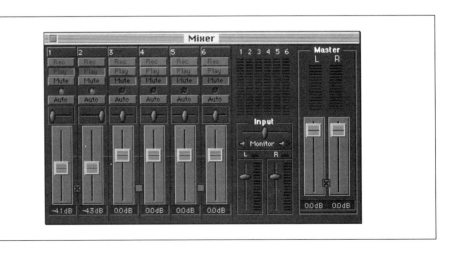

Especially Nifty Features

❏ DigiTrax has a simple interface that's easy to navigate. It has more than enough power if the bulk of your audio work involves basic cutting, pasting, and volume control within a limited number of tracks.

❏ It's also the most affordable package to offer "pro" features like volume and pan automation, a mixer-style interface with volume faders and mute buttons, and a recording controller that mimics the functions of a multitrack tape recorder. For example, the two icons at the lower left corner of the Transport window (Figure 9.9) are commonly used in audio-editing programs to indicate looping playback and punch-in/punch-out. DigiTrax also offers 20 customizable autolocation settings.

❏ The input section of the Mixer window lets you set one level for the strength of the input signal being recorded, and another level for the amount of input level that is sent to your monitor speakers while you record. This option is handy if, for example, you want to record a file at a high signal level (you *do* want to record a hot signal, don't you?), but you don't want your speakers blasting while you're recording.

❏ DigiTrax has a basic Equalization function. It includes high and low shelving and single-band parametric (see Figure 9.10). The EQ can either be used nondestructively (so that it's only applied to tracks during playback) or destructively, to actually change the file data. Use EQ sparingly; it's easy to create distortion if you boost frequencies. (For more information on EQ, see Chapter 6.)

❏ DigiTrax also has a QuickTime window for editing audio to picture. Although this window doesn't actually let you alter the soundtrack data within the movie (as you can with Audioshop or SoundEdit 16), it does let you play a multitrack file and watch smooth QuickTime

Figure 9.9

The DigiTrax Transport window

Figure 9.10

The EQ function in Digitrax. This setting could be used to remove low hum (the result of ground loop problems) from a track.

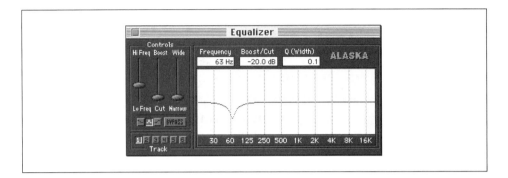

playback at the same time (something you *can't* do from Audioshop or SoundEdit 16).

❏ The Mixer window sports groupable faders (see the check box between channels 1 and 2 in Figure 9.8). These are handy for controlling the volume of stereo files that play back on separate tracks.

❏ The Timeline window (Figure 9.11) has a useful cursor tracking feature. It displays crosshairs out to the vertical and horizontal rulers (representing signal level and time, respectively) every time you press the mouse button. This is a useful visual aid for aligning files at precise points, or for changing volume or pan levels at specific times.

Figure 9.11

The Timeline window is the main audio-editing area in DigiTrax. The crosshair cursor appears when you click in a track.

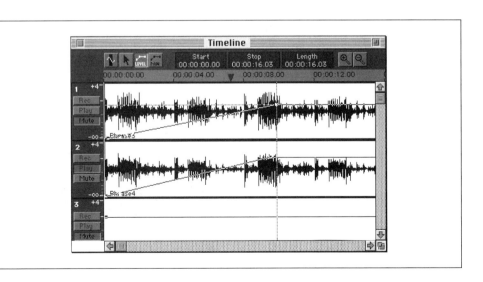

Potentially Heartbreaking Features

❏ One weakness of the otherwise useful cursor tracking feature is the resolution of the ruler scaling. It's bad enough that ruler marks are spaced four seconds apart, but there's no text display of the current cursor location. Without one, there's no way to determine the precise placement of the cursor.

❏ DigiTrax lets you draw fade-in and fade-out information over a track, but there's no easy command for applying a fade over a period of time; you always have to draw the fade manually. If you prefer to use logarithmic fades, you'll have to draw your own.

❏ You can scale the view of the Timeline window horizontally, but not vertically. Vertical scaling can be really helpful when you're editing quieter files that have less amplitude, because you can zoom in for better accuracy. Zooming magnification is limited, which makes it difficult to perform precise edits such as removing clicks and pops.

❏ The EQ effect is useful, and there *are* basic helpful effects like Normalize, Invert, and Reverse. However, it would be nice to have access to more types of effects. DigiTrax sports its own plug-in architecture, but at this point there are no third-party plug-ins available (compare this to plug-in support for Deck II, Premiere, and SoundEdit 16 version 2.0).

❏ The mixer has Record Enable, Play, and Mute buttons, but no Solo buttons. Most mixer interfaces have a solo function that plays a particular track all by itself. Solo functions help you hear exactly how one track sounds without interference from other tracks. But to audition a single track in DigiTrax, you must turn all the other tracks off manually—a cumbersome procedure that requires lots of unnecessary button clicking.

❏ DigiTrax has a six-track limit. In comparison, Deck II supports only four tracks on certain hardware (using an Audiomedia card), but it allows extra "work tracks" that can be used for editing and mixing even though they don't play in real time. Deck II scales up with faster hardware, so that Power Macs can play 10 or more tracks at once. With DigiTrax, six tracks is the limit. If you need more tracks, you'll have to "bounce" tracks (for example, mix four tracks to one, freeing up three tracks for new material). Granted, you can do *lots* of work with six tracks (The Beatle's Sergeant Pepper was produced with just two four-track decks). But for complex projects, the six-track limit may prove cumbersome.

❏ DigiTrax supports only the AIFF format. Admittedly, this is the one format you can use practically anywhere, so it may not pose a problem for you. But if you do lots of work with other formats, you may need to do frequent conversions.

Who, Where, and How Much

Opcode Systems
3950 Fabian Way, Suite 100
Palo Alto, CA 94303

415-856-3333

http:/www.opcode.com

Suggested Retail: $199

Deck II 2.5

Look to the
CD-ROM

Created by OSC and now owned and marketed by Macromedia, Deck II enjoys a legion of diehard fans. The original Deck was the first four-track recording product created for Digidesign hardware, at a time when Digidesign software could play only two tracks! Whereas early versions of Deck had a decidedly home-grown feel, the current version is a solid tool for multitrack work. Deck II is pretty deep; it has lots of features to speed the editing process. Luckily, the documentation and support are excellent.

We at our studio weren't avid Deck II users until relatively recently. But after subjecting it to heavy use while mixing tracks of music, voice, and effects, we came away quite impressed. Deck II always seems to be one step ahead of you, anticipating the features you'll want as you delve deeper. When you get into a particular situation and suddenly find you need feature X, there it is, waiting for you. This isn't too surprising when you consider that the developers of Deck II are also accomplished audio engineers and sound designers, known for their "Poke in the Ear with a Sharp Stick" sound-effect CDs.

Especially Nifty Features

❏ Deck II is spunky and well-behaved when handling multiple audio tracks. It gives audio data the highest priority, so don't be surprised if the screen redraw slows down during playback. On Power Macs, Deck II is capable of playing back more than 10 tracks at once. Actual performance depends on your CPU and hard drive.

❏ Deck II has great tools for fading and crossfading (see Figure 9.12). You can select from seven different preset fade curves and set your preferred curve to be applied automatically each time you apply a

Figure 9.12

The Tracks Window in Deck II. Although only four tracks are shown here, the program automatically scales to provide the maximum number of tracks of which your hardware is capable. Power Mac users can access 10 tracks or more.

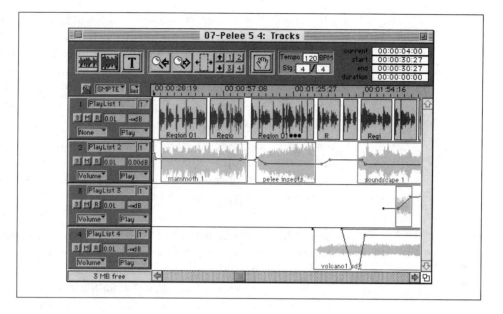

fade. To create a fade-out, you simply highlight the length of the desired fade (being sure to drag across the end of the region boundary) and press Command-F. No more "draw-your-own" manual fading (although you *can* draw manual fades if you want).

❏ The number of playback tracks you can use in Deck II is scalable, depending on the capabilities of your hardware. With Digidesign's Audiomedia II card on an older Macintosh, for example, you get four playback tracks. With a Power Mac 9500 and no additional DSP hardware, you get more than 12. But even if you run out of playback tracks, Deck lets you use *work tracks*—virtual tracks that you can swap in and out among the playback tracks. On a PowerMac capable of running 10 tracks, for example, you could create a 20-track document and make the top 10 tracks active (that is, audible) while you edit. Then you could move the bottom 10 tracks up to the top to make them active. Regardless of whether tracks are active or not, you can always bounce them (mix multiple tracks into one, then add more). You can also combine work tracks and active tracks in your final mix.

❏ There are two features that help you adjust your work area quickly. You can capture the current configuration of the mixer and store it as a Mixer State, and there's no limit to the number of Mixer States you can create. You can store up to 200 Location Times to jump to points within a file. Mixer states and location times can easily be recalled from the Transport window shown in Figure 9.13. You can also store four different "view memories" of the current view in the waveform display. Use view memories to jump quickly between sections of a large file, or to make radical changes in viewing magnifications.

❏ Deck II features a ton of key commands for commonly needed functions and has modifiers that change the behavior of the mouse. There are so many of these that they should be listed on a separate card. For example, in addition to the arrow keys, Deck uses Shift-arrow, Command-arrow, Command-Option-arrow, and Command-Control-arrow.

❏ Beginning with version 2.5, Deck II supports third-party effects that conform to the same plug-in architecture used in Adobe Premiere. As a result, all the CyberSound FX plug-ins from InVision Interactive (and the Waves processors) are now available from within Deck II. Version 2.5 also includes real-time, nondestructive processing, including EQ and delay effects.

❏ Deck II lets you import Sound Designer regions and playlists as well as entire files. This is really helpful for accessing just the sections you need within larger files. For example, on one of our recent jobs (*Volcanoes: Life on the Edge,* from Corbis Productions), we recorded over 20 short pieces of music to DAT tape and captured the audio into Sound Designer. Then we created a region for each piece and named it for a particular scene. When the time came to create finished mixes for each scene within Deck II, it was easy to locate and import the clips for that scene.

Figure 9.13

Deck II's Transport window lets you store an unlimited number of autolocation points. Also shown are controls for pitch adjustment, punch-in/punch-out, and looping.

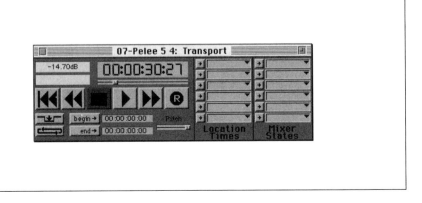

❏ Deck II is well integrated with MIDI and SMPTE. It includes a basic MIDI file player so that you can import a MIDI file and synchronize it with digital audio tracks (a nice option for those of you who aren't able to step up to Studio Vision, Digital Performer, or other combination MIDI/digital audio applications). Deck also supports OMS and SMPTE so you can lock your digital audio playback to an external MIDI sequencer or time code generated from videotape.

❏ You can select from several different methods for bit-depth conversion. In addition to standard truncation, Deck II offers dithering and two types of rounding.

Potentially Heartbreaking Features

❏ Deck II's method for importing files might be described as "byzantine." Once you figure it out it's not difficult, but first-time users may be perplexed if they don't have a manual handy. The confusion probably stems from the manufacturer's description of the process as "Add Audio to Clipboard." Wait a minute (you think to yourself)—how will they fit 10 minutes of 16/44 audio into the *clipboard?* There's no need for concern—what actually gets placed into the clipboard is a reference to the file or region name, not the file itself, so memory and time are economized.

❏ Although Deck II sports an ample number of key commands and modifiers (perhaps the company owns stock in a wrist brace manufacturing outfit?), there are a few holes. For example, there's no key command to switch the track view between normal, pan, and volume modes. This is one of the most commonly performed switches, yet you can't achieve this except by clicking the pop-up at the left of the window. It also would be helpful if you could switch between the four customizable views by typing a number from 1 to 4.

❏ The only rates Deck II supports are 44.1 kHz and 48 kHz. Files at other rates will be converted when you import them. Considering the core of Deck's market—people who know the importance of editing at the highest possible fidelity—this lack of support is understandable. But if you do lots of multimedia-oriented work at lower rates like 8/22, you'll either need to convert your files or have an additional editor on hand.

❏ You can't easily edit region names in the Library Window, although this seems the natural place to do so. Instead of being able to click on a name and start typing, you have to select the name, choose "Rename..." from the Edit menu, and then enter the new name into a dialog box. Being able to use this window as a filename management system would be much more efficient.

❏ The only way to group faders (for the left and right channels of a stereo track, for example) is through external MIDI control. The approach used by DigiTrax would be welcome here. Deck II does let you copy volume envelopes from one track to another, but this work-around could be difficult to manage in an editing session.

Special Tricks

Frankly, there aren't many tricks that you won't find in the manual. But here are two helpful hints for us multimedia types:

❏ When mixing a file to disk to create a final mix, you can choose to output the file at half of the session sample rate. This saves you a step in another program if your final destination is 16/22 or 8/22.

❏ Be sure the playback head is at the start of the file before mixing to disk. If it's midway through, or if you have an area selected, only a portion of the file will be processed.

Who, Where, and How Much

Deck II 2.5
Macromedia
600 Townsend, Suite 310W
San Francisco, CA 94103

415-252-2000

http://www.macromedia.com

Suggested Retail: $399

Session 2.0

The rumors had been circulating for months that Digidesign was working on a killer multimedia audio application. It would be an editor, of course, but it would also include great downsampling, plenty of file conversion utilities, and a powerful batch processor. Finally, Digidesign unveiled Session, which was not quite what we were expecting. The batch processing and conversion functions were nowhere to be seen. But Session does offer some features that should make the competition sit up and take notice. Session is Digidesign's first entry into the inexpensive, hardware-independent editing arena. As such, it goes head-to-head with Deck II. It will be interesting to see how these two products fare in the feature wars to come. Here are some of the features that already set Session apart.

Especially Nifty Features

❏ Session (see the main editing window in Figure 9.14) has some nice architectural approaches borrowed from Sound Designer. Whereas you can use only four tracks on an Audiomedia card, you can get more than 12 on a Power Mac, depending on the amount of memory allocated to the Digidesign Audio Engine (*DAE*), their background application for managing tasks between audio applications and the playback hardware. Like Sound Designer II, Session lets you create playlists (groups of regions in a track); then you can assign a playlist to a particular track. You can create up to 30 or 40 playlists as you edit. This feature is similar to Deck II's use of work tracks—the virtual tracks that you can edit but that you may not always be able to play back.

❏ Session's pan and volume envelopes are continuously available once you make envelope automation active. It's convenient not having to switch between volume, pan, or regular viewing modes. You can also save pan and volume automation envelopes into their own playlists so that they can be recalled later or applied to other audio files.

❏ There are useful options for viewing scrolling waveform data during playback. Most programs move the cursor across the screen as audio plays. Session's Power Scroll mode, on the other hand, keeps the cursor in one place and scrolls the data. This is somewhat disconcerting when you're not used to it, but there are many situations where it might be

Figure 9.14

The main editing window in Session lists regions on the right. The pop-up menu shows the current playlists available for Audio Track 2.

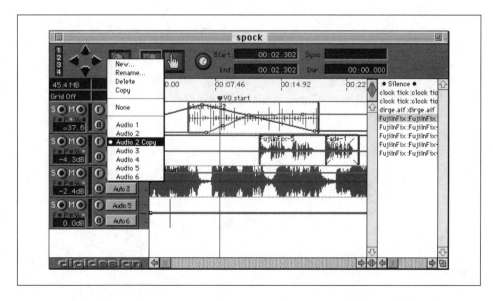

helpful—stopping to remove a pop or click, for example. Another well-thought out scrolling option is Page scroll, which scrolls the waveform view to the next page as the cursor moves across the screen.

❏ Session implements markers well. Although it lacks a dedicated Marker editing window, it lets you enter a default name for markers to be assigned as they're entered. You can also add an incremental numerical value to each marker. Markers also function as autolocation points from a pop-up window next to the transport.

Potentially Heartbreaking Features

❏ The first shipping version of a product usually has a few potholes, and Session is no exception. (Although the version number is 2.0, it's the first to become commercially available.) For example, if you click them just right, the buttons for changing viewing magnification flash briefly, but the view itself doesn't change. There are also circumstances in which stretching a region to its furthest extent renders it impossible to readjust the region boundary—the region is no longer selected, even though it *should* be, and even though the cursor also indicates that adjustment is possible.

❏ Playlists can be used by only one track at a time. If you set a track to show a playlist that is already displayed in another track, the playlist in the other track gets "stolen" so that it can be made available to the track you've just specified. If you accidentally make the wrong selection and steal a playlist, you can't undo the operation. You have to go back to the original track and reassign the desired playlist.

❏ There seems to be no way to set default fade curves. Instead, fade curves have to be dragged every time you want to use them.

Who, Where, and How Much
Digidesign, Inc.
1360 Willow Road, Suite 101
Menlo Park, CA 94025

415-688-0600

Suggested Retail: $299

Digidesign Hardware/ Software Products

When I started writing this book, Digidesign had a relatively straightforward array of offerings. Audiomedia II was known as the affordable, entry-level product, priced at about $1,200. Session 8 was the eight-track hard disk multi-track recorder, seemingly aimed toward musicians, for about $3,000. At the top of the line was ProTools, Digidesign's flagship product, starting at $8,000. ProTools incorporates a real-time effects processing system called Time Distributed Multiplexing (*TDM*) that harnesses added power through Digidesign's DSP Farms—cards holding four DSPs each, chained together with ribbon connectors. One DSP might be dedicated to providing real-time digital reverb, another might handle equalization or dynamics processing, and another might provide 3D spatialization. This is literally the equivalent of putting an entire recording studio inside a Macintosh.

Recently, Digidesign revamped its entire product line, with lots of offerings to arrive in 1996. It's hoped that the product line changes will make it easier to move work between different Digidesign platforms—a task which, in the past, was cumbersome, if not impossible.

Digidesign's new strategy aims are to make ProTools the editing environment for all their hardware, and to take advantage of today's more powerful CPUs to make the company's technology work with or without a dedicated DSP. The new AudioSuite products will provide similar functionality to TDM without the hardware requirements.

Does this mean that Digidesign stands to become a software-only company? Hardly. The advantage of DSPs is still too great to be overcome completely (although this could change in the future). Furthermore, until Macintoshes and PCs start featuring multichannel digital audio inputs and outputs, there will continue to be a market for hardware that moves sound in and out of the computer. Digidesign has four products in this category. The Audiomedia II has stereo RCA analog inputs and outputs, with S/PDIF digital input and output. The other three products are rack-mountable interfaces. The 442 includes four analog inputs and outputs, with both AES/EBU and S/PDIF digital input and output. The 882 is similar, but with eight analog inputs and outputs. Finally, the 888 provides eight analog inputs and outputs as well as eight digital inputs and outputs. This product offers the greatest flexibility when you're using one of the increasing number of modular digital multitrack recorders, like the Alesis ADAT and the Tascam DA88 (neither of these units has eight discrete AES/EBU digital inputs or outputs—yet).

Another rationale behind the changes in hardware strategy is to provide greater support for PCI products. These are also scheduled to be released in 1996. An Audiomedia III for PCI should become available for both Macintosh and Windows PCs.

Against this changing background, it still makes sense to consider the features of ProTools III. The basic structure of the application is likely to remain largely unchanged by the corporate transition. And if Digidesign makes this product available on a wider range of platforms (with a corresponding range of price/performance choices), ProTools may gain a substantial chunk of the market in the coming year.

Especially Nifty Features

❏ The processing power packed into ProTools far exceeds any of the tools we've discussed so far (although Deck II compares well in terms of editing features). The routing structure is very flexible. The autolocation includes view settings as well as the location itself. The waveform views are continuously scalable; you can choose to view routings in either the mixer or the editor. ProTools has features on top of features. Figure 9.15 shows the ProTools Edit window.

❏ Without doubt, what puts ProTools far ahead of the offerings already covered is real-time processing through TDM. While most of the fun kicks in with plug-ins (covered in Chapter 10), the built-in control over

Figure 9.15

The Edit window in ProTools 3.1 has many of the same controls found in Deck II, but the library window is integrated into the upper-right corner. You can scale the view in any direction using the arrow buttons.

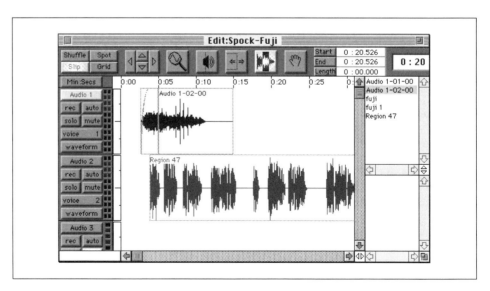

Figure 9.16

ProTools'
Equalization
window offers
two shelving and
two parametric
EQs. Notice the
flexibility you
have when
previewing. You
can bypass each
band indepen-
dently, or bypass
the entire effect
to do before-and-
after comparisons
of the signal.

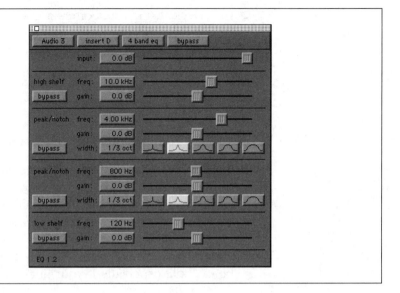

EQ and dynamics is very useful, rivalling the features you would find
on a $4,000 mixing board (Figure 9.16).

❏ ProTools also shines if most of your work involves synchronization
with SMPTE. Snapping, nudge, and shuffle features help keep regions
locked into the appropriate points. You can also group regions so that
moving one region moves the entire group.

❏ The Trimmer is a great tool; it would be nice to see this in other programs. Dragging across an area and automatically deleting the data
(nondestructively, of course) is quick and easy.

❏ ProTools uses the volume and pan envelopes we've seen in DigiTrax
and Deck II, but the implementation is more well thought out. Using
the Trimmer on a volume envelope, for example, you can easily drop
the volume of an entire region. If you reposition the region, the volume envelope automatically follows, and volume settings remain with
their regions.

❏ You can do punch-in/punch-out recording as with other programs,
but ProTools automatically punches in and out over a region you've
highlighted. You can also set up the program so that the existing track
will be heard right up to the punch-in point, where monitoring
switches to the incoming signal being recorded. At the punch-out
point, monitoring switches back to the incoming signal again. This
switching helps you hear your punched-in material in context.

❏ Like Deck II, ProTools offers a good selection of automatic fades. Unlike Deck II, however, ProTools always presents you with a dialog box for choosing a fade curve. There's no way to set a default and automatically apply it each time. However, you *can* select a whole bunch of regions and automatically apply the same crossfade to all of them in a single operation.

Potentially Heartbreaking Features

❏ Speaking of heartbreaking, this system is *not* for the faint of heart. It's designed like a complex mixing board with inserts, sends, and pre- and post-fader selection (see Figure 9.17). These are great features to have for a complex recording session, but if most of your work is simple track mixing, a program like Deck II or Session may better suit your needs. For many multimedia producers, ProTools' features may be overkill, especially if your final audio will be stripped of its sub-

Figure 9.17

The ProTools Mixer. Here, any similarities to other programs come to a screeching halt. Signals can be routed in a variety of ways. Inserts appear at the top of the window, and a few TDM plug-ins are currently active in this example.

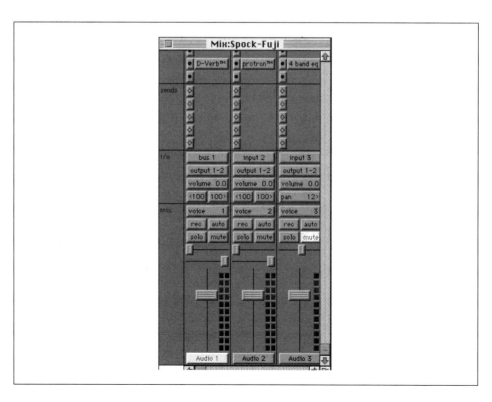

tleties on the way down to 8-bit 11 kHz. At the same time, keep in mind that audio quality is improving thanks to compression schemes like 4:1 ADPCM, so inconsistencies in audio quality are more likely to be noticed in higher-quality formats.

❏ In nondestructive editing mode, you can't undo a recording over an existing track. You can delete the track and then use the Trimmer to stretch the original track back across the newly deleted area, but this procedure seems more complex than it needs to be.

❏ Don't even *think* about bringing your low-class 22 kHz files into this environment. Be prepared to upsample.

❏ ProTools' method of "exporting" files is bouncing them to disk, creating a Sound Designer file at the session rate (either 16/44.1 or 16/48). Unfortunately, the AIFF file format is not an option when bouncing. Apparently, the Bounce feature is intended for mixing groups of tracks into one or two channels so that they can be imported back into ProTools, thereby freeing up additional tracks.

❏ In keeping with ProTools' nondestructive philosophy, TDM effects are applied only during playback. If you want the effects to actually be "printed" onto the track, you have to record the track (with effects) to a new track. There should be an option for simply applying the process to the file (while retaining the original, of course).

Special Tricks

❏ If you create a crossfade and want to get rid of it, there's only one way: use the Hand tool in combination with the Delete key.

❏ Press and hold the Option key when using the Zoomer so that only your horizontal scaling changes. Otherwise, you'll zoom both vertically and horizontally. In most situations, keeping one of the axes constant prevents disorientation.

Who, Where, and How Much

ProTools 3.1
Digidesign, Inc.
1360 Willow Road, Suite 101
Menlo Park, CA 94025

415-688-0600

Suggested Retail: $8,000 (plus 442, 882, or 888 interface)

Sonic Solutions

Sonic Solutions comes to the multimedia market from the lofty heights of CD mastering. Their systems are an industry standard for the exacting task of making final adjustments to a recording before a finished disc is pressed. Their editing environment therefore takes a slightly different approach than some of the tools we've already seen. The Sonic Solutions editing metaphor is based on *edit decision lists* (EDLs), most often associated with video. EDLs make sense when you consider that their primary task in the real world involves the editing of finished music tracks.

But Sonic Solutions also has a lot to offer those of us on the lower end of the spectrum. They provide a broad array of hardware and software tools so that you can configure a system that best meets your needs. There are two flavors of internal processing hardware—the SSP-3 and USP—each of which is a two-card NuBus pair. The SSP-3 is more affordable, with basic packages starting at $3,000 for eight playback tracks and two digital input and output channels. The USP systems start at $9,000, with 16 playback tracks and eight digital inpt and output channels. For most multimedia production, the SSP-3 provides plenty of horsepower.

The Sonic Nubus cards connect to interfaces with fiber optic cable. Several different interfaces are available. In most production situations, you need the ability to transfer digital audio (AES/EBU or S/PDIF) as well as convert analog signals to digital. Using the Sonic system, you need two separate boxes to accomplish these tasks and must outlay a total of about $1,600 for two channels of digital and analog input and output (not including the internal processor card). That's not cheap compared to the features of Digidesign's interfaces, but Sonic is fanatical about using high-performance, high-quality components. When your core business is CD mastering, cutting corners isn't a good strategy.

Especially Nifty Features

❏ The Sonic system has great tools for capturing audio. First, you can capture in the background while editing existing material in the foreground. If you capture lots of voiceover from DAT, this option can save you plenty of time. Second, you can specify start and stop times for capture. If you're capturing 30 minutes of audio, you don't have to worry about being at the computer to stop the process 30 minutes after pressing the Record button. Third, if you know the start and stop times of various tracks, you can enter those values and have the Sonic system automatically create a new file for each segment.

❏ The approach to waveform displays is really intelligent. In most programs, you draw volume lines over the wave data to change the output level. The Sonic system, in contrast, redraws the waveform to show how it would really look as the volume changes. For example, a fade drawn over a waveform would look the same as if you had done a destructive fade on the data. Also, Sonic automatically scales waveforms to fill the viewing window, so if you had one loud track and one quiet track, they would be of equal height. Although this display strategy doesn't convey the relative volumes, it does present the largest possible view of the data at all times so that it's easier to see edits. You can override this feature if you find the autoscaling confusing.

❏ The Sonic system contains four high-speed DSPs, so it has *tons* of horsepower; so much horsepower, in fact, that it can perform all of its processes—EQ, mixing, and even normalization—in real time. Sonic is especially admirable in its real-time handling of fades. Every other session-oriented system described in this chapter creates fades by actually calculating, mixing, and writing out a new file for the faded region, and then switching playback to the fade document automatically when you reach the fade. This process is invisible when you're editing and listening, but it does mean that you're stacking up lots of little files every time you create a fade-in, fade-out, or crossfade. Since the Sonic system relies on its DSP to generate fades on the fly, you can change them whenever you like, without worrying about leaving a multitude of files in your wake.

❏ The Sonic system has 100 levels of undo. If you never make mistakes, you might not care about this feature, but I, for one, certainly would have appreciated this during a few memorable encounters with Sound Designer.

❏ You can view data in either list form or wave form in an EDL. It's helpful to be able to see your data in different ways, or to edit start and stop times numerically (see Figure 9.18).

❏ Sonic has great built-in tools for managing massive quantities of data. When you first capture audio, you're led through a series of prompts that the system uses to tag all the audio relating to that particular project so that you can keep track of it while you work. As you can see by the icons at the top of the window in Figure 9.19, Sonic Manager helps you handle all the different data types associated with a project, as well as projects themselves. You can track *cues* (discrete regions

Figure 9.18

In Sonic Solutions' Edit Decision List window, sound data can be viewed either as waveforms or in a list. In this example, files on tracks 1, 2, 5, and 6 are being bounced to the selected area in tracks 15 and 16.

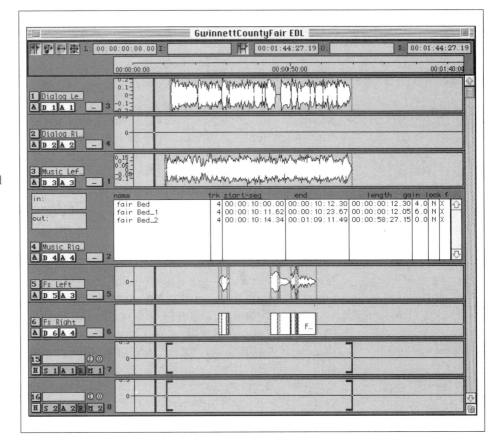

selected within a track of an EDL), sounds (complete sound files), EDLs, and sessions (settings of the mixer and transport functions). The Sonic system helps you manage the processes and edits applied to the files as well as the files themselves; it's great for reconstructing a piece of work five months after the fact.

❑ Sonic's MediaNet is a high-speed fiber optic network for sharing large amounts of data—such as high-resolution audio files—across a network. If you need to connect digital audio workstations to digital video and graphics workstations for high-throughput production work, MediaNet can really improve your throughput, since you don't have to wait for file transfers.

Figure 9.19

The Sonic Manager, a central repository for tracking files, could be a great tool for organizing large groups of sound effects for use across multiple projects.

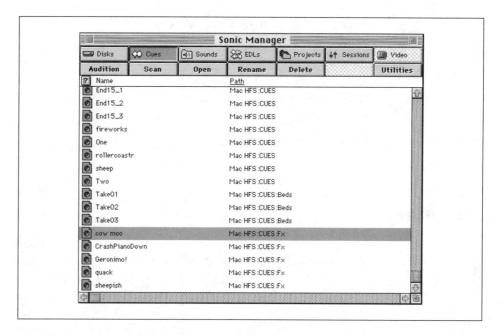

Potentially Heartbreaking Features

❏ Although the entry-level system is relatively affordable, by the time you assemble a full-scale system, you're approaching the price of Digidesign's ProTools. While the Sonic's quality is unsurpassed in this market, it may be more than you need unless you produce audio for Enhanced CD or formats at higher resolutions than 8/22.

❏ The Sonic system supports only AIFF files. If you want to take advantage of regions or playlists in Sound Designer files, you're out of luck. On the plus side, they're using a standard format rather than creating a proprietary one.

❏ The lowest sample rate available is 22.050. If you need 11.025, you'll need additional tools.

❏ Compared to the Digidesign products, Sonic is just beginning to look at using third-party processing add-ons (they do offer their own excellent packages for noise removal, pitch shifting, and filtering). If you also want tight integration with a MIDI sequencing application, you'll need to use Studio Vision from Opcode.

Who, Where, and How Much

Sonic Solutions
101 Rowland Way
Novato, CA 94945

415-893-8000

http://www.sonic.com

Suggested retail: systems starting at $2,995

Summary

This chapter has given you a glimpse of several of the major audio editors available today. There's quite a spread in price and capabilities. Fortunately for multimedia audio producers, there's a package for every budget and production task—well, almost. Even if you buy the most powerful editing software on the market, you'll invariably find yourself in a situation in which you need one very targeted feature to get through a particular job. In the next chapter, we'll look at some additional utilities and processing programs that may help to fill whatever gaps may remain in your toolkit.

10

Processors and Utilities

Audio-editing software is great for cutting, pasting, and mixing sound files. But when it comes time to *really* tweak a sound, reach for an audio processor. There are two standard approaches to audio processing. The classic method is to use an external processor connected to your mixer, print the processed signal to tape, and then capture and edit the previously processed sound. But as software and hardware become more powerful, it has now become possible to transfer this function to the computer.

Speaking of transferring functions to the computer, remember the myth that computers were supposed to make our lives simpler? (Yes, that certainly was a knee-slapper.) There are, however, several utilities that can boost productivity, and in this chapter we'll also review some of the software-based tools that can help reduce the amount of tedium in your work.

Did someone say TDM? Okay, then, we'll start with the processors. But first, here's an overview of the products we'll cover:

Plug-in Processors:

Waves	L1 Ultramaximizer
	C1 Compressor/Gate
	Q10 and Q2 Paragraphic Equalizers
	S1 Stereo Imager
Crystal River Engineering	Protron
Digidesign	D-Verb (reverb)
	DPP1 (pitch processor)
	DINR (noise reduction)

AnTares Systems   MDT (Multiband Dynamic Tool)
                                   Voice Processor

InVision Interactive   CyberSound FX

Stand-alone Processors

Time Bandit
Alchemy 3.0
Hyperprism

Utilities and Specialized Tools

Disc-To-Disk
Precision Audio Tools
WaveConvert
QuicKeys

Processing

Software-based processing has several advantages:

❑ **Flexibility**—You can keep a clean digital copy of a file and process another copy several different ways to see how the variations work.

❑ **Repeatability**—You can save settings for specific effects and instantly recall them the next time you have to process another file for the same project.

❑ **Reduced susceptibility to noise**—With digital processing, your files are much less susceptible to the added noise that can stack up when you run an analog signal through multiple outboard processors.

❑ **Power**—Best of all, there are things software-based processors can do that you just won't find in traditional outboard signal processors.

The products in this section fall into two broad categories: plug-ins and stand-alone applications. There are several different plug-in formats. Both Digidesign's TDM and Sound Designer have proprietary plug-in architectures and are the most widely supported. Another format is supported by Premiere and Deck II, with third-party offerings from InVision Interactive and Waves. Yet another format is Macromedia's new Xtras for Sound Edit 16. As if that weren't enough, DigiTrax has its own plug-in scheme. Confused yet? If a more standard "standard" were to emerge, it would surely be welcome.

Plug-In Processors

Plug-in processors add processing functions to existing audio software. They can't perform as stand-alone applications. As you read about these products, keep in mind that you will need the appropriate editing software in order to use them.

Waves

Look to the
CD-ROM

Plug-ins for TDM, Sound Designer, Premiere, Deck II, SoundEdit 16, and SoundForge

At least one company—Waves—is going the extra mile to make their plug-ins usable from within all the major audio-editing applications. The Waves L1 Ultramaximizer is *the* indispensable tool for downsampling to 8 bits. Before we examine each of the company's products in detail, let's look at the attributes that characterize their entire product line.

Waves plug-ins work from within a shell—WaveShell—which passes information between the plug-ins and the audio-editing application. The advantage of the shell approach is that, in order to support additional audio editors, Waves has to customize only one piece of software—the shell—rather than rewrite all the plug-ins from scratch. At this point, there are three shells: TDM, RT (for Sound Designer and Real Time processing), and Premiere. Since Deck II 2.5 can use Premiere-compatible plug-ins, it's automatically included in this camp. The WaveShell approach has made it possible for Waves currently to support a higher number of editing tools than any of its competitors.

Another shared technology in Waves plug-ins is *increased digital resolution (IDR)*. Waves is one of the few plug-ins to deal straightforwardly with one of the limitations of 16-bit technology. In case you have the notion that 8-bit technology is what we really have to worry about, you should know that there are shortcomings at the 16-bit level, too. When you're doing lots of 16-bit processing, values are converted to either 24 bits or floating point numbers. When a final result is achieved, the value is converted back to 16 bits. At that point, it can suffer degradation, in the same way that we lose quality going from 16 to 8 bits. Granted, 16 to 8 is *much* worse than 24 to 16, but if you're doing heavy processing or are mastering CDs, this type of distortion can start to add up. Waves IDR is a dithering process applied to samples as they are dithered back down to 16 bits. All of the Waves plug-ins let you select IDR processing. The L1 Ultramaximizer, originally designed for final CD mastering, has two types of IDR, which we'll explore later in this chapter.

The Waves plug-ins share other standard features. For example, they let you set input and output volumes, and they have attractive graphic meters with *peak hold,* a function that shows the highest volume level registered. During previewing, or after processing, you can easily tell whether or not your signal has clipped.

For tweaking purposes, Waves' use of two editing buffers is a nice touch. You can store current settings in a buffer, continue tweaking to obtain a slightly different sound, and then compare the changes to the settings stored in the buffer (this is similar to the Edit/Compare function in synthesizer editors). As with most plug-ins, you can bypass the effect to compare the processed and unprocessed signal, and you can save settings to a file and recall them later.

With the level of control that Waves plug-ins provide, all these editing possibilities can be overwhelming. Fortunately, the plug-ins ship with excellent libraries of preset effects so that you can get great results without having to learn every aspect of the controls. Presets are especially helpful for complex plug-ins such as the C1 compressor and Q10 Paragraphic EQ. Use the presets in the libraries as a jumping-off point for your own creations.

The audio-editing program you use with Waves plug-ins determines whether editing is destructive or nondestructive. To maintain a clean copy of the original file when applying Waves effects destructively (using Sound Designer or Deck, for example), be sure to save a copy of the processed file, and then undo the processing.

Next, let's take a look at the individual Waves plug-ins, starting with the L1 Ultramaximizer—the patron saint of downsamplers.

L1 Ultramaximizer

The L1 Ultramaximizer (which we'll abbreviate as *L1* from this point forward) is *the* tool that makes 8-bit audio acceptable. Its status is ironic when you consider that it was originally designed to be used in the final stages of audio CD mastering. The L1 assists 8-bit audio in two ways: it has a superior conversion algorithm, and it's a highly precise limiter. It doesn't let signals go higher than the output level you specify. This means that you can make an 8-bit signal much louder without having to worry about clipping, and as a result, files contain less background noise. Clipping simply never occurs (see Figure 10.1). But you *can* distort your signal if you push the L1 too far, so don't get too carried away. Also keep in mind that if you push all the audio content up to the level where it's affected by the limiter, you're left with audio roadkill: it sounds flat, with all the life squeezed out of it.

Of all the Waves tools, L1 is the only one to offer multiple types of dithering for IDR. The choices include Type 1 and Type 2. Type 1 is a typical

Figure 10.1

The L1 Ultramaximizer from Waves is an excellent limiter when the final goal is 8-bit audio. In this example, the sound would have been about 5 dB over clipping had the L1 not intervened and limited the signal.

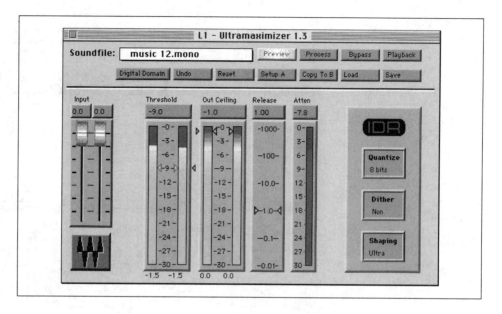

dither, where random numbers (resulting in white noise, like static) are added to the signal to smooth over quantization noise as the signal is converted from 16 to 8 bits. Type 2 is more subtle and may let some low-level distortion sneak through in exchange for less added hiss.

You can also select from multiple settings for noise shaping. For the best results when the final destination is 8-bit audio, the Waves staff recommends that you disable IDR (a setting of Non) and set noise shaping to None (no shaping). There's already enough hiss at 8-bit. Activating the dither just makes it worse at low sample resolutions.

Waves suggests that the L1 should be the last step in your downsampling process. If your final goal is 8/22, it's best to convert the sample rate of your 16/44 files to 16/22 before processing with the L1. Then, after L1 has done its work, use Waves' freeware utility, Wavestrip (included in the L1 package) to truncate 8 bits from the 16-bit file, resulting in an 8-bit final product.

Q10 ParaGraphic Equalizer

The Waves Q10 Paragraphic Equalizer may be simply the most flexible EQ you will ever lay your eyes on. The Q10 looks like a 10-band graphic EQ, but each band can be configured as parametric, high pass, low pass, high-shelf, or low-shelf. Does that seem like overkill? Perhaps, until you really need this level of flexibility. The Q10 lets you build EQ curves that would be next to impossible using standard outboard processing gear. Being able to see the EQ curve on your screen really helps when you're fine tuning sound.

Figure 10.2

In this example, only three parametric EQs (8 through 10) are active on the Q10 ParaGraphic EQ. The high-frequency information is spiked at 11 kHz to produce a brighter 22 kHz file.

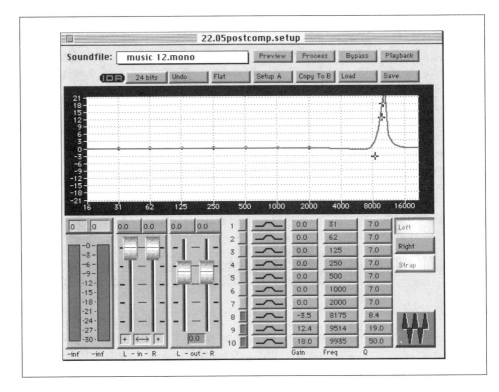

The Q10 is a great interactive tool for learning about EQ. You can change the center frequency by dragging the handles back and forth, or change the amount of boost or cut by dragging the handles up or down. By pressing and holding the Option key, you can change the bandwidth (Q) of the EQ. You can quickly sweep through the entire audio frequency spectrum until you locate the band that needs to be processed.

If your final destination is a 22 kHz or 11 kHz sample rate, you can use the Q10 to boost the upper frequency ranges just a bit (see Figure 10.2). Keep in mind that you lose high-frequency information when it's above half the sample rate. But if you boost high frequencies just below that Nyquist cutoff point (described in Chapter 1), it can compensate for the lost signal energy that would have existed in higher frequency ranges. The Q10 ships with presets you can use to spike the signal so that it seems to have more high-frequency energy than is actually present.

The Q2 is a little brother of the Q10, for use only from within Premiere or Deck II 2.5. It's a subset of the Q10, with two bands of fully configurable EQ.

Figure 10.3

The C1 Compressor is set in this example as a compressor/expander. The EQ window in the lower left has controls similar to those in the Q10 and lets you process multiple frequency ranges.

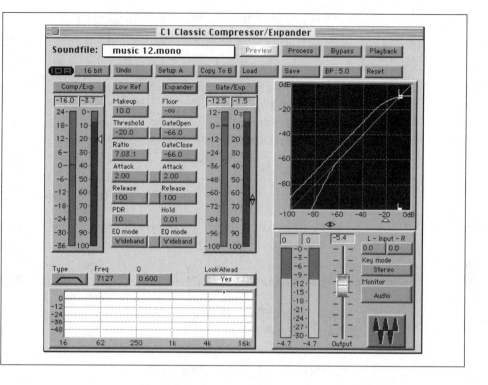

C1 Compressor/Gate

Waves' C1 is a compressor on steroids. One look at its wildly dancing screen (Figure 10.3) will have you shaking your head in wonder. Of all the Waves plug-ins, this one is most likely to leave you feeling overwhelmed. But given the right circumstances, it can raise the quality of your audio substantially. The C1 is particularly helpful on straight voiceover. It combines a compressor (which reduces big spikes in volume) with an expander (which increases the dynamic range of low-level signals) and a noise gate (which silences audio below a certain volume). As a result, the volume of voiceover is much more consistent, and background noise is removed in gaps between phrases or sentences. On one particular project, *Get Ready for School, Charlie Brown!* from Virgin Sound and Vision, we were asked to deliver all the audio (primarily voice for a 1,000 word dictionary), at 8/11. There's no way we could have achieved usable results without the C1 compressor.

As with all compressors, you must pay particular attention to levels in your mix if you know that heavy compression will be applied. Signals that had been quiet in the background will increase in relative volume and could obscure voice tracks. Compressors also tend to accentuate sustain effects (making them a favorite with guitar players), so sounds with a long decay (bells, for example) will sustain longer after compression is applied.

S1 Stereo Imager

The S1 Sereo Imager (Figure 10.4) broadens the image of a stereo field. For multimedia applications, where mono is often the rule due to bandwidth and storage limitations, you may not be in a position to use this tool as often as the other Waves products. But if you're fortunate enough to enjoy stereo playback, investigate the S1. It differs from other spatialization products (Protron or QSound, for example) in that it doesn't attempt to place a signal within a three-dimensional space. Instead, the S1 widens an existing stereo file, making music tracks seem more spacious and adding extra depth to stereo reverb or echo effects that might be used when sound effects are placed within a large, cavernous space.

Who, Where, and How Much

Waves
4302 Papermill Road
Knoxville, TN 37909
615-588-9307

http://www.waves.com/waves

Suggested retail: Waves plug-ins are priced differently depending on system configuration. Bundles are available.

Figure 10.4

The S1 Stereo Imager. Adjusting the Width control broadens the stereo field and widens the triangle in the display. You can also skew the stereo field in various directions by adjusting the rotation and asymmetry.

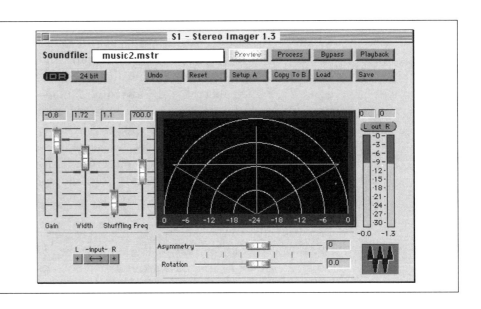

Protron

3-D spatialization plug-in for ProTools TDM systems

Protron (Figure 10.5) has the coolest graphic interface of any audio processor we've ever seen. It presents you with an overview of a head inside a box, and an icon representing the sound source pointing toward the head. At first glance you might think, "Great, I can drag this sound source to different places around the head." But that's not all. You also can change the size of the box, the reflective nature of the material itself (glass, marble, or carpet, for example), and the height of the sound source.

The effect is subtle but convincing. Human ears use a variety of clues to determine the direction of a sound source, including timing differences (sound reaching one ear before another), frequency differences (different frequency effects occur depending on whether the sound arrives at the ear from the front, the side, or the rear), and, of course, volume differences (closer sound sources are usually louder). The creators of Protron, Crystal River Engineering, built computer simulations to model these effects and then used those simulations to develop Protron. Now all we have to do is find the bandwidth for stereo sound in multimedia!

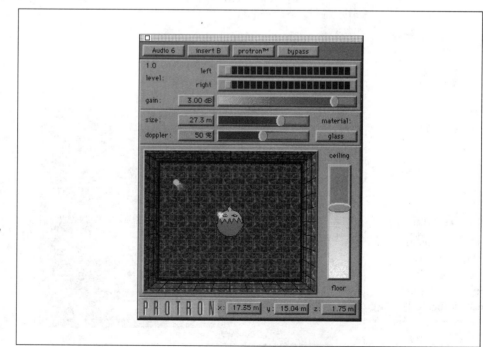

Figure 10.5

The Protron for TDM lets you specify room size, wall materials and speaker placements for the positioning of a sound in three-dimensional space.

Who, Where, and How Much

Protron

Crystal River Engineering

490 California Avenue, Suite 200

Palo Alto, CA 94306

415-323-8155

http://www.cre.com

Suggested retail: $995

Digidesign D-Verb

Reverb effects plug-in for ProTools TDM systems

Achieving good quality reverb from within an audio editing package has always been an exercise in frustration. Until recently, the only way to get decent reverb was to use an outboard effects processor. This required passing your digital audio signal back out through an analog device and then redigitizing the signal, thereby losing a generation of clarity. With Digidesign's D-Verb (Figure 10.6), we can finally dispose of this work-around.

D-Verb sounds good enough for just about any application. For musicians with TDM-compatible MIDI and digital audio software, it's an easy way to add reverb to vocals, percussion, or musical instruments. For multimedia sound designers, it's a great tool for simulating ambience in rooms, halls, or other spaces.

Figure 10.6

D-Verb has all the controls you would expect to find on dedicated outboard reverb units.

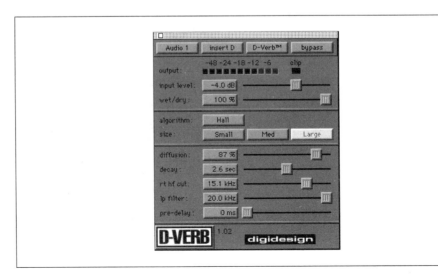

DPP-1

Pitch processing plug-in for ProTools TDM systems

There are two basic reasons why you might want to shift the pitch of a signal: to achieve a blatant comical touch, or to fix a musical note or alter the pitch of a speaking voice for a particular character effect. In the second instance, it's likely that you'll want to maintain the best possible quality in the shifted audio. But avoiding noise and artifacts in shifted sound is difficult. Just visualize metal fatigue: if you stretch a piece of metal, it begins to crack. Stretch it further, and the cracks become more pronounced. The same is true for sound. When you stretch a digital sound, an algorithm must fill in the gaps through interpolation, creating sample data that wasn't present in the original and possibly adding noise or unnatural sounding artifacts to the file.

Steinberg's Time Bandit, reviewed later in this chapter, is good for pitch shifting data, but it performs its work off-line. Processing a few minutes of audio can take an hour. Mark of the Unicorn's Digital Performer version 1.7 has superb pitch shifting, but you must buy a full-blown MIDI sequencer to get it. DPP-1, on the other hand, works in real time and does a more-than-respectable job in the process. Besides the pitch shifting function, DPP-1 (shown in Figure 10.7) also includes a delay algorithm and mix control so that you can vary the amount of original signal with the shifted signal. By

Figure 10.7

The DPP-1 Pitch Processor lets you combine pitch-shifted material with the unprocessed source to create dense textures. It also lets you fix wrong notes in recorded performances.

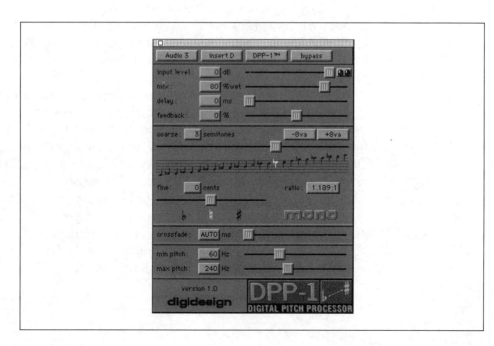

mixing the two signals and adding a short delay with a healthy amount of feedback, you can turn one person's voice into a small crowd speaking in unison. It's also great for pseudo "Darth Vader" voices, as well as for the traditional Alvin-the-chipmunk effect.

DINR (Dynamic Intelligent Noise Reduction)
Noise reduction plug-in for Sound Designer and TDM
Regardless of how careful you are to reduce added noise in your own recording and processing, you will inevitably be presented with a worst-case scenario: someone will bring you *their* noisy sounds and ask you to clean them up. There are some tricks you can attempt, such as equalization and noise gating, to reduce the overall noise. But it doesn't take much for a sound to seem over-processed using these methods. For example, you can get rid of low ground loop hum with a parametric EQ at 60 Hz, and as long as there's no other material in that frequency range, listeners may not notice anything missing. If your source material is music with a thumping bass drum, on the other hand, the results may sound weak. If noise permeates the entire frequency band (particularly white noise sources like air conditioning systems), you might try a noise gate to strip silence into gaps between sentences. But if the background noise magically appears and disappears, this too can sound very unnatural. At times like these, your best option is to turn to noise reduction software.

Four noise reduction software options are available: DINR from Digidesign, NoNoise from Sonic Solutions, the noise reduction function in Deck II 2.5, and a noise reduction plug-in for Sound Forge. To understand better how these products work, we'll look at DINR, the first and still one of the best.

DINR works best when you can isolate a section of background noise. The software analyzes the frequency content of this noise sample and "learns" the frequency characteristics that must be extracted (Figure 10.8). If you don't have a pure sample of noise, DINR still attempts to find noisy elements within the file; you just need to make more adjustments, and the results are less predictable. As with other noise reduction techniques, it's easy to overdo it with DINR. Low-level distortion and artifacts start creeping in when you over-process (this can be a great effect on its own merits—if you're trying to create a crowd of muttering trolls, that is). But if your back is against the wall and you absolutely *have* to work with a noisy sound file, DINR is a handy tool to have around.

Figure 10.8

DINR creates a
frequency curve
based on the
original signal
material and
determines
which "noisy"
frequencies
to extract.

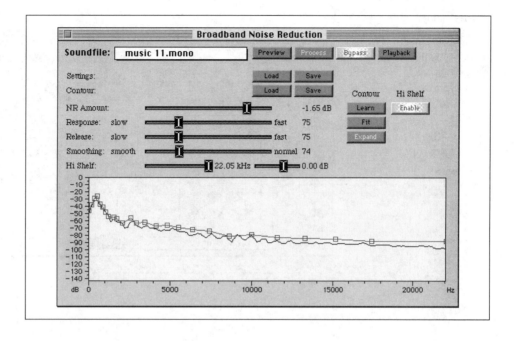

Who, Where, and How Much

Digidesign Inc.
1360 Willow Rd., Suite 10
Menlo Park, CA 94025

415-688-0600

Suggested retail: DPP-1: $495
                            D-Verb: $495
                            DINR: $995

AnTares Systems

Plug-ins for Sound Designer and TDM

AnTares Systems (formerly Jupiter Systems) offers two versatile products
that combine numerous functions. This Swiss Army knife approach results
in more features for less money. Depending on the job you're doing, these
plug-ins may have everything you need in one easy package.

AnTares Voice Processor

As the name suggests, the AVP (formerly the Jupiter Voice Processor) packs
in all the features you might want when processing voice. This one-stop

Figure 10.9

The Compressor display in the AVP. Clicking the Display button under each effect displays the controllers for that particular effect.

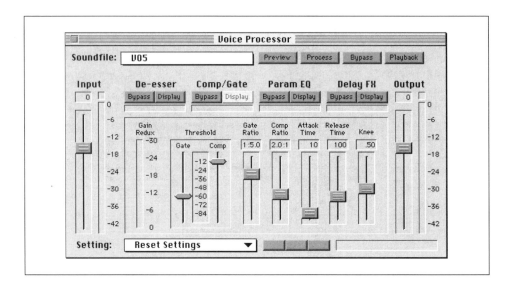

shop includes a *de-esser*, a compressor, EQ, and delay. De-essers help control the level of sibilance (hissing) in vocal tones like "s", "sh," and "th." They combine an EQ (to isolate the high frequencies) and a compressor, to reduce the gain of sounds within that specific frequency range.

Once those nasty little sibilants are under control, the signal passes through a compressor/gate (Figure 10.9). The compressor has an adjustable *knee*—the point at which the compressor kicks in—something you won't always find in outboard hardware compressors. A soft knee is often desirable because the compressor activates gradually rather than abruptly, making the compression a bit less obvious. The result is a more natural sound.

After compression, the signal passes through an EQ (Figure 10.10). Finally, you can use a delay effect to add fullness to the signal. All in all, the AVP is an impressive package for processing voices.

MDT (Multiband Dynamic Tool)

MDT is a versatile compressor that works selectively on different frequency bands (Figure 10.11). For example, you could compress a range of bass frequencies to tighten up the bottom and apply a different compression level to higher frequencies. MDT lets you select up to five discrete EQ bands for compression. This is the kind of power and precision that is affordable only when using digital audio plug-ins.

Figure 10.10

The Parametric EQ in the AVP has three bands. The first and last bands can be configured as shelving, bandpass, or parametric EQ.

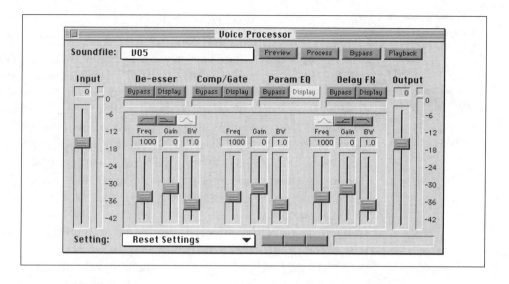

Figure 10.11

The MDT showing three bands of frequency-specific compression applied

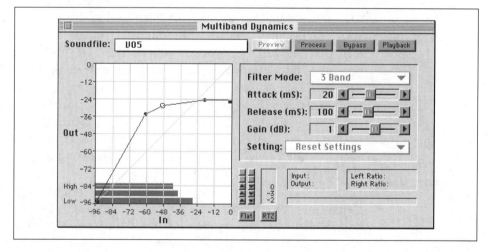

Who, Where, and How Much

AnTares Systems
RiCharde and Company, distributors
444 Airport Blvd., Suite 207
Watsonville, CA 95076

408-688-8593

http://www.richarde.com/web

Suggested retail: AnTares Voice Processor: $399
                       MDT: $499

CyberSound FX

Look to the
CD-ROM

Multi-effects for Adobe Premiere and Deck II

Unless you're a musician, you may not have heard of them before. But even though they seem like newcomers, the folks at InVision Interactive are no slouches when it comes to audio tools. They've been creating samples for E-mu and Korg synthesizers and developing and marketing sampling CDs for several years. Last year they released CyberSound FX, the first set of third-party audio plug-ins for Adobe Premiere. These plug-ins also work with Deck II (version 2.5 and above) and SoundEdit 16 version 2.0. CyberSound is hardware-independent and, unlike most of the other offerings described in this chapter, doesn't rely on DSP processing. The range of effects is impressive, covering reverbs, delay/echo, compression, and equalization.

The quality of the effects is not quite as high as what you can achieve with some of the other products we've discussed, but considering the range of effects and the price, it's an excellent value, especially for those who work at the lower resolutions of multimedia audio. Purists may squirm at this suggestion, but no one can dispute that the gains achieved by working with high-quality tools in high-quality formats are greatly reduced when you drop down to lower-resolution files. The difference that the listener perceives between high-quality and medium-quality tools for low-end destinations is less than it would be for high-end destinations. Granted, the high-end tools always produce superior sound (this isn't an excuse for folks to get stingy with quality), but the gains aren't as noticeable when the final product is 8/22 or 8/11. Here's where tools like CyberSound find their niche. Think of CyberSound as a blue-collar version of Digidesign's TDM.

CyberSound ships with a multitude of preset effects, which you can customize. All effect parameters are accessible through the same interface convention: slider controls for up to nine parameters (Figure 10.12). The labels assigned to the sliders change based on the effect type. Changing effect settings while previewing can be a bit sluggish (remember, CyberSound isn't drawing on DSP power), but you can vary the length of the preview by changing Premiere's clip preview preferences.

There's a good help function to assist you as you navigate through the settings. Clicking on Help from within each filter brings up a concise text document, which reviews the basic theory behind the effect and the functions of the parameters for that effect.

Who, Where, and How Much

CyberSoundFX
InVision Interactive

Figure 10.12

The faders in the main window of CyberSound FX are labeled differently for different types of effects. While the interface is somewhat limited, the excellent help windows provide good information for adjusting the settings.

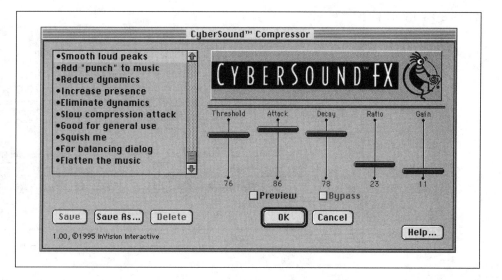

2445 Faber Place, Suite 102
Palo Alto, CA 94303
415-812-7380
Suggested retail: $129

Stand-Alone Processors

Stand-alone processors are full-fledged applications for altering or editing sounds. Unlike plug-ins, they aren't accessed from within a separate editing application; they *are* the application. If you need one particular processing function, it may make more sense to buy one stand-alone processor rather than to buy a plug-in that requires the purchase of a separate editing program. Here are a few options to consider.

**Steinberg's
Time Bandit**

Time expansion/compression and pitch shifting

Time Bandit may be a one-trick pony, but expanding or shrinking the length of a file without altering the pitch (or adding lots of bizarre artifacts or distortion) is a pretty tough trick and computationally intensive. Time Bandit goes beyond most time-based processors in this regard, using an approach similar to Digidesign's DINR. The software analyzes the file and builds a profile, and then performs the processing based on the profile (Figure 10.13).

Figure 10.13

Time Bandit's main screen

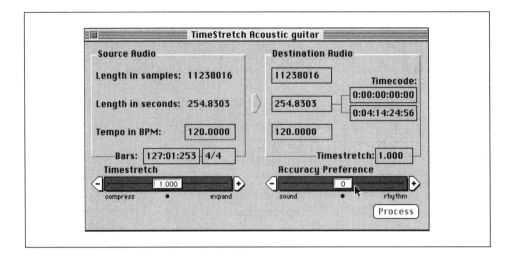

The most popular application for programs like Time Bandit is to adjust recorded notes that are slightly off pitch. In cases where you're altering a file to create a bizarre or colorful effect, slight artifacts may be more acceptable, since it's likely that you'll process the entire file so that the artifact will be consistent throughout. When fixing recorded notes, however, it's important that the processed note doesn't sound too different from surrounding unprocessed notes. Otherwise, listeners are likely to notice the change.

Who, Where, and How Much

Time Bandit
Steinberg
9312 Deering Ave.
Chatsworth, CA 91311

818-993-4091

Suggested retail: $399

Passport Designs Alchemy 3.0

Sample-editing software

Alchemy is a sound wave editor aimed primarily at users of digital sampling keyboards. It's the only Macintosh product of its kind (PC users should investigate Sound Forge). For awhile, it seemed as though the future of the product was in doubt, and many diehard fans were distraught at the prospect of losing their best tool for sample editing. With version 3.0, however, Alchemy is back and as healthy as ever.

Alchemy 3.0 helps solve a big potential headache for musicians who do plenty of sampling with synthesizers. As you may recall from the chapter on MIDI, a driving force in the musical instrument market (as with most markets) is the struggle to shoehorn the greatest number of features into a product while also striving to reduce the cost of the product. This trend is most apparent in synthesizer interface design. Programming a synthesizer can be pretty complicated. Parameters are linked to other parameters, and menus are buried within menus. One approach most manufacturers take to save money is to "simplify" the interface, using a small LCD panel, a 10-key pad, and a few sliders or buttons. If you think it's rough editing synthesizer functions in this environment, try editing sample waveforms! Granted, some synthesizers are friendlier than others in this regard, but none of them can compete with the ease of editing on a Macintosh.

Letting you edit sample waveforms on the Macintosh, though, is just part of the fun that Alchemy provides. You can import a range of file formats, including AIFF, Sound Designer II, and snd resources. Suddenly, any sound you can create on the Macintosh can be transferred to a sampler and played from the keyboard. Pitch shifting thus becomes a breeze, since it's handled by the sampler. In addition, you can use MIDI sequencing applications to spot sound effects. Depending on the number of effects and the power of your sampler, this approach can be speedier and more flexible than placing sound data in a sound editing application.

The new version of Alchemy takes advantage of SMDI, an addition to the MIDI specification which deals with transfering sample data across the SCSI bus. The older alternative, Sample Dump Standard, sent sample data through the MIDI cable itself. This was *much* slower, since MIDI is a serial protocol (SCSI uses a parallel interface, so more data can be sent at the same time). MIDI is limited to roughly 4,000 bytes per second, while SCSI typically transfers as much as three million bytes of data per second—a huge difference.

Alchemy's interface is easy to grasp (Figure 10.14) and gives you quick access to the most commonly used functions. As the mouse passes over items in the Tools Window, their functions are displayed at the bottom of the window. You can also set up to eight custom views to jump easily from a magnified view of the beginning of the file to a different magnification at the end of the file.

An especially handy feature of Alchemy's interface is its Open Special dialog box for opening files (Figure 10.15). Every program should have such features in their Open dialog boxes! You can see file information, play a preview, delete files, or rename files from within the window.

Figure 10.14

The main windows in Alchemy 3.0

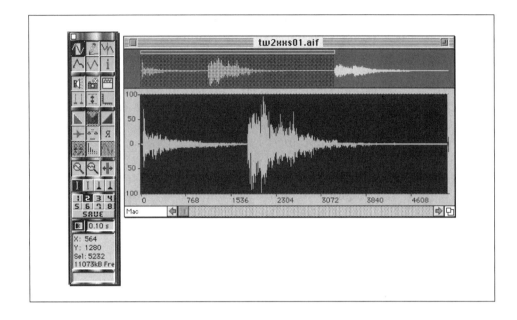

Figure 10.15

Alchemy's Open Special dialog box has features that should be standard in every sound-editing application.

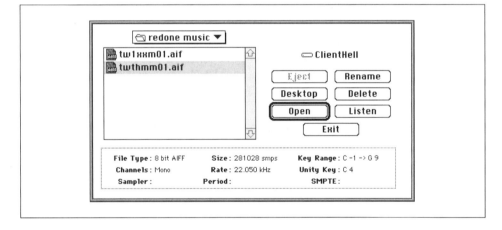

Who, Where, and How Much

Alchemy 3.0

Passport Designs

100 Stone Pine Road

Half Moon Bay, CA 94019

415-726-0280

http://www.mw3.com/passport

Suggested retail: $695

Arboretum Systems' Hyperprism

Real-time audio processing for Digidesign DSP hardware

If we had to choose the *one* tool that is guaranteed to blow the mind of even the most jaded multimedia producer, it would be Hyperprism. Here, the strangest tweaks you've ever imagined are right at your fingertips. Hyperprism uses Digidesign's DSPs to change pitch, filtering, and stereo placement in real time. You can wildly bend the pitch of a music file back and forth, simulating scratching on a turntable; change the EQ of a filter in real time to create "wah-wah" effects; or change the speed and depth of panning so that the sound bounces back and forth faster and faster between the speakers. Well, you have to really *hear* it to appreciate it, but Figure 10.16 should give you a good idea of how it looks.

When you first open a new processing window, the cursor (the crosshair circle at the end of the line in Figure 10.16) is often in the center, at coordinates 0,0. The top and left edge of the window form two axes for changing the nature of the effect. In the case of the effect shown in the figure (Pitch Time Changer, one of the most radical), the cursor's position relative to the top axis determines the playback speed of the file, ranging from zero (practically stopped) to 200 percent (double speed). The left axis controls pitch from a value of zero (more than two octaves below the original) to 200 (more than two octaves above the original). As soon as you press and hold the mouse button, Hyperprism begins recording your movements on the Blue screen, changing the playback of the file according to those movements. You can create wildly varying effects by dragging from one corner to another. Alternatively, you can achieve tighter control by entering numerical values into the range fields of the two axes. Settings of 95 to 105

Figure 10.16

The "Blue Window" in Hyperprism is where all the action takes place. The cursor follows the line you've drawn when you replay the file.

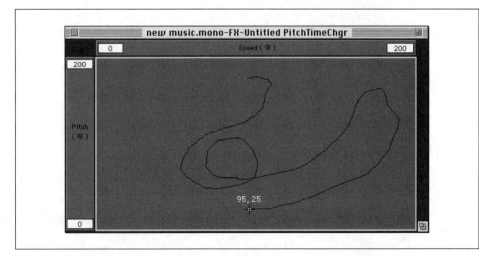

instead of 0 to 200 in each box will reduce the range of the effect for more subtle results.

Hyperprism is perfect for any space sound you could ask for: spaceships, closing doors, death rays, supernovas, robot voices . . . it's unending fun. But Hyperprism can also be useful for approximating real-world sounds that change over time (it includes a *Doppler effect*, the pitch change effect you hear when a train, for example, passes by quickly). It was exactly what we needed once to create the changing sound of wind as you step from full exposure to the relative shelter afforded by turning a corner and stepping into a doorway. We used Hyperprism's Low Pass Filter effect to slowly reduce the wind from a whistling sound to a low rumble.

> **Note:** *There are a few "gotchas" with Hyperprism version 1.5.2; we hope that they'll be fixed soon. It's a bit unstable, so be sure to save work in other applications before jumping in. It can also disable all menus (the "gray-out" effect), at which point the only way to exit the program is to force quit (Command-Option-Escape). Finally, when you process an effect to a soundfile, Hyperprism automatically tries to append the effect name onto the sound file name. The result is often more than 32 characters (the maximum allowed on the Mac), and attempting to save will generate disk error messages. Just shorten the name of the file before saving, and you should have no trouble.*

Who, Where, and How Much

Hyperprism
Arboretum Systems
P.O. Box 47050
San Francisco, CA 94147

415-931-7720

Suggested retail: $495

Utilities and Specialized Tools

Aside from audio editing and processing, a significant part of audio production involves transferring data and managing large numbers of files. Here are some tools to consider for these more mundane tasks.

Optical Media International's Disc-To-Disk

CD audio capture

Since the advent of QuickTime version 1.6, Macintosh users are able to capture audio directly from Redbook audio CDs. So why would anyone need a dedicated program for CD audio capture? Well, it depends on how much CD capturing you need to do. If you do a lot, it's hard to imagine life without Disc-To-Disk.

Disc-To-Disk has a great interface for navigating through audio files so that you can select just the region you need (Figure 10.17). It includes several other helpful functions, too. To put it in perspective, recall how audio is captured through QuickTime using the standard interface in MoviePlayer. First, you select the file you want to capture from a File dialog box; then, to preview or select a segment of the audio, you click an Options button. After previewing and setting a selection range, you double-click OK to generate an AIFF file on the disk. With Disc-To-Disk, on the other hand, you select the track from a pop-up menu, click Preview to preview it, set a desired region, and then either save the region to a file (several formats are available), add the region to a list for batch capturing, or copy the data to the clipboard, from where it can be pasted into compatible applications like Audioshop or SoundEdit 16.

That's not all, though. Disc-To-Disk can draw a waveform preview of the data so that you can select audio regions based on specific hits in the file (this isn't an instantaneous process, however; it can draw the wave only as

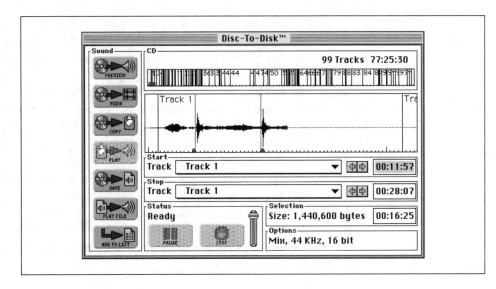

Figure 10.17

Disc-To-Disk has a comprehensive interface for capturing CD audio onto your hard disk.

fast as it can read from the disk). If you're really industrious, you can use Audioshop or the AppleCD Audio Player to create named track lists for all the files on a CD and import the names into Disc-To-Disk. Then, you can select tracks by name. Finally, like MoviePlayer, Disc-To-Disk lets you set output options so that stereo 16/44 data is automatically converted to a different format, such as mono 8/22. In most cases, leaving output options set to 16/44 mono lets you capture material at the highest possible quality.

Who, Where and How Much

Disc-To-Disk
Optical Media International
180 Knowles Drive
Los Gatos, CA 95030

800-347-2664

http://www.omi@netcom.com

Suggested retail: $99

Gallery Software's Precision Audio Tools 1.0

Complete solution for audio batch processing

Precision Audio Tools is really a suite of products. What they can accomplish together is nothing short of remarkable. The set includes Voice Pro (for voice-over automation), Sample Search (file management and batch processing), CDStudio (CD audio capture), Region Reader (storing, modifying, and reapplying Sound Designer regions), and Audition (a sound file player).

The entire toolset is designed to automate most of the functions of voice recording and processing. Processing starts with VoicePro and the voiceover script. The script should be prepared so that *voice lines* (takes that are meant to be stored as individual files) are separated by carriage returns. Before each line, you insert the desired filename in parentheses. The script text file is imported into VoicePro, which has two main components: a recording controller and a Prompt window. The Prompt window, meant to be displayed on a second monitor, shows the text to be recorded, and voice talent can read their lines straight from the monitor! Meanwhile, in the recording controller, the engineer can stop and start recording. Each time a new line is recorded, the new file data is named automatically according to the filename included with the script text file. Pretty slick! By the end of the session you've created a Sound Designer II file, with each voice segment stored as a region and with the filename for each segment saved as the region name.

Now it's time to process the file in Sound Designer. But many processes (sample rate conversion, for example) force you to process to a new file, and you lose the region information in the conversion. Precision Audio Tools' Region Reader comes to the rescue. This utility extracts the region data from the file and stores it as a separate document. After processing, you can reapply the regions to the file. Region Reader also lets you import text and apply a list of new names to the existing region names. If filenames change during the course of a project, you can quickly update the name list.

Once processing is complete, it's time to save each region as an individual file. Here's where SampleSearch comes into play. This is by far the most powerful and flexible utility in the Precision Audio Tools suite. It can perform batch conversion of bit-depths, sample rates and file types, change text within a group of filenames, and, most important, automatically create regions from existing files based on the length of silence between segments of audio (Figure 10.18). If most of your voiceover is captured from DAT, you might not get lots of mileage from VoicePro, but the Auto-Regionalizing feature by itself is definitely worth the price of admission.

A few caveats are in order. The Precision Audio Tools interface isn't the most straightforward. Some aspects of the windows are non-standard, and the pull-down menus are packed with options that may be unclear when

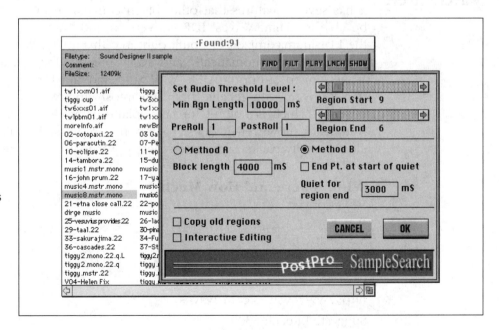

Figure 10.18

The Auto-Region window in SampleSearch lets you specify minimum region length, silence between regions, and the audio level that indicates silence.

you're first learning to use the product. The auto-regionalizing function also takes some practice. But if you're constantly churning through audio production chores, you'll definitely find the Precision Audio Tools to be a helpful addition.

Who, Where, and How Much

Precision Audio Tools
Gallery Software
Wodethorpe House
Great Saxham
Bury St. Edmunds
Suffolk IP29 5JN
England
44(0)1714316260

http://www/demon.co.uk/gallery

Suggested retail: $1,495

**Waves
WaveConvert**

Batch processing and conversion

This product recently became available from Waves. As you might imagine, it has several features that other batch conversion products would love to be able to claim. Waves' IDR conversion and limiting functions (found in the L1 Ultramaximizer) are built right into this utility. WaveConvert also can normalize files automatically and apply preset effects to add "brightness." WaveConvert supports AIFF, WAV, and snd file formats. When you buy WaveConvert, you receive both Macintosh and Windows versions of the product, which is helpful for cross-platform work. Unlike SoundEdit 16's Automator, however, it doesn't support compressed audio formats. All in all, this utility packs a lot of automated processing into one product.

Who, Where and How Much

WaveConvert
Waves
4302 Papermill Road
Knoxville, TN 37909

615-588-9307

http://www.waves.com/waves

Suggested Retail: $300

**CE Software's
QuicKeys 3.0**

Keystroke automation utility

If you're not inclined to invest in one of the batch processing solutions just described, consider building your own with CE Software's QuicKeys. Even if you *do* use an automated processor, think about adding QuicKeys to your toolbelt. QuicKeys records sequences of keystrokes, mouse clicks, and menu choices so that you can automate complex jobs. With its branching logic and support for Apple Events, it's on the way to becoming a programming language of its own, but it's still pretty simple to use for most tasks.

A substantial amount of work at the computer keyboard involves invoking the same functions over and over. How many times a day do you open your Sound Control Panel? Copy a portion of a sound file and paste it into a new document? Type ".aif" or ".wav" after a filename? QuicKeys alleviates this tedium, playing back the keystrokes faster than humanly possible, saving you time and wrist strain. You can make your Mac work for you all night long on big processing jobs so you can get more done in the daytime.

For example, we once used QuicKeys in conjunction with a pre-release version of a sound-editing package. Unfortunately, the program had a known bug (a memory leak) that caused it to crash after about fifty file operations. With some tinkering, we had QuicKeys processing fifty sound files, quitting the application, restarting the Mac, reopening the application, and processing the next fifty files. This got around the memory leak, and our files were finished in the morning. There's no better feeling than taking a break, secure in the knowledge that several Macintoshes are working on your behalf.

Who, Where, and How Much

QuicKeys 3.0
CE Software
1801 Industrial Circle
West Des Moines, IA 50265
800-523-7638
http:/www.cesoft.com
Suggested retail: $99

Summary

At its best, the computer frees us to create sounds that have never before been imagined. At its best, the computer relieves us from much of the repetitive worked involved in audio production. At its best, the computer is a stable, reliable apprentice that facilitates the creative process.

Well, two out of three isn't bad. It can be difficult to be creative when you also have to focus on engineering- and computer-related issues. Perhaps someday soon, audio and other media-editing products will have the power, flexibility, and stability to keep up with (and stay out of the way of) our creativity.

There is an ever-increasing number of audio-processing tools appearing on the market. Each year, progressively more interesting offerings make their debuts, and each year we get a bit closer to the ideal of the computer as creative partner. In the next chapter, we'll continue to explore this theme as we review several of the most popular MIDI applications.

11
MIDI Sequencers and Tools

MIDI may turn out to be the great savior of interactive audio. MIDI files are small and demands on the processor are low. Better yet, since MIDI is a data stream that plays at run time, the door is open for musical sequences that can turn on a proverbial dime based on user input. As programming and media presentations become more object-oriented and more frequently destined for playback on a variety of platforms—from CD-ROM to the Net—MIDI becomes an increasingly attractive solution.

At this point in time, however, many productions rely on downsampled digital audio, so MIDI's current main benefit is as a tool for music composition. With the rise of integrated digital audio in many MIDI applications, the line between MIDI sequencers and digital audio editors like Deck II and ProTools is beginning to blur. In this chapter, you'll see several products with audio-editing features that are far more powerful than those found in many of the dedicated audio editors reviewed in Chapter 9. Here's an overview of the packages covered in this chapter:

MIDI Sequencers

Opcode Studio Vision/Galaxy Plus Editors
Mark of the Unicorn Digital Performer/Unisyn
Steinberg Cubase Audio
EMagic Logic Audio
Passport MasterTracks Pro

MIDI Utilities

EarLevel Engineering HyperMIDI Tools
InVision Interactive CyberSound VS
Imaja BlissPaint

Before we examine the merits of individual products, let's look at the larger context: common features and design strategies that have arisen among MIDI software developers.

Sequencing Basics

Look to the
CD-ROM

Let's establish some basic definitions of features that are common to several MIDI products. Our assumption is that you have some knowledge of music fundamentals. You need to understand many basic concepts in order to deal with a music program on its own terms. If you don't know what bars, beats, tempos, and key signatures are, pick up a music fundamentals book at the library and keep it handy while you read. And if you're not completely comfortable with MIDI terminology and concepts, review Chapter 3.

Sequencers are often grouped into two categories: *linear* and *pattern-based*. Most of the products reviewed here are pattern-based. Linear sequencers function much like tape recorders. You start at one point and play or record in a linear fashion, going from point A to point B. Pattern-based sequencers are based on smaller segments that can be stitched together in any fashion. The advantage of a pattern-based approach is clear when you think about how many musical styles work. Mainstream popular songs are built from (A) verses and (B) choruses and, for added interest, often have a third section called a (C) *bridge*. Using a pattern-based sequencer, it's easy to create a song form by playing patterns A B A B C A. (You didn't think popular music was complicated, did you?).

Not only are musical forms often repeated, but the notes played by various instruments in a piece of music also tend to follow repetitive patterns. Many standard drum beats, for example, are built around 4- or 8-bar patterns. This should *not* be taken as an excuse to fire up a four-bar drumbeat and play it through your entire song (unless you're one of those techno types trying to emulate ancient Roland technology). However, being familiar with this convention makes it much easier to create a foundation for layering fills and variations on top of a basic beat.

Pattern-based sequencers have one potential drawback. Users tend to create music in little blocks, working on one pattern after another rather than focusing on the overall flow and pacing of the music. If you should notice yourself dropping into this mode, try creating an entire song within one "pattern." In other words, make your pattern-based sequencer function like a linear sequencer.

A final benefit of pattern-based sequencers is that they're ideal for creating looping music. That's what they're built to do. But remember our advice from Chapter 6: always capture the second playback iteration of the loop to avoid the cutoff of sustaining harmonics that might carry across the loop point.

Common Features

Many sequencers use similar conventions for handling the same types of data or functions. Rather than describing these for each product, we've grouped them here so that you'll have to go through this only once (or close to twice, if Chapter 3 is still fresh in your mind).

Stacking and Mapping

Unlike most computer applications, MIDI sequencers usually have to deal with a network of musical devices that are physically attached to the computer. You need to be able to reconfigure this MIDI setup quickly and easily. To assist in this task, most high-end programs let you create new "instruments" by sending the same data to different synthesizers (or different synthesizer channels) at the same time. Using this stacking approach, I can combine one sound from my K2000 synthesizer with another from my Morpheus to create a unique layered texture, and then save this as a custom instrument. Although you can often achieve the same results by copying data to a new sequencer track and then reassigning it to another synthesizer, it's logically much easier to deal with one combined "virtual" instrument than with two different ones.

Sequencers also let you route and re-route controller data, such as the real time control generated by keyboard aftertouch, footpedals, pitch benders, or modulation wheels. In MIDI parlance, this is called *mapping*. For example, I could map the data from my keyboard's pitch bender so that it alters the amount of reverb coming from a MIDI-controllable effects unit like the Lexicon LXP-1. That way I can automate changes in the reverb level throughout a mix instead of having to adjust knobs on the mixing board. A more common use of mapping for MIDI automation is to use a MIDI fader controller, like JL Cooper's FaderMaster, to control MIDI volume over time.

Program Name Management

When you have multiple synthesizers, each of which is capable of accessing 127 or more programs, you can quickly lose track of which sound is which. That's why practically every sequencer lets you enter and store program name lists. Most sequencers display program names from a pop-up list so that you can quickly find the sound you want and assign it to the appropriate track. It's a lot easier to find "ZootFlute" by name rather than having to remember that it's program number 22. With General MIDI (GM) synthesizers, this is less of a concern, because GM patches are named consistently according to the GM specification.

If your sequencer supports OMS or FreeMIDI and you're using an editor/librarian (Galaxy Plus or Unisyn, respectively), program names can easily be transferred from the synthesizer directly into the computer. This is much more efficient than having to type the data in yourself.

Viewing Data

As discussed in Chapter 3, most programs offer several ways to view data:

❏ *Piano roll*—Musical data appears as dots on a lined background. The length of the dot indicates the duration of each sound and the vertical position of the dot indicates pitch.

❏ *List*—Data associated with each note or event is displayed as text.

❏ *Notation*—Notes are shown as they would appear in standard printed music notation.

❏ *Graphic*—Controller data or other note attributes are shown plotted on a horizontal graph.

We'll see more examples of these display types as we survey individual sequencing applications.

Quantization

First and foremost, don't get quantization in MIDI confused with the quantization noise that we discussed in earlier chapters. MIDI-related quantization basically means "snap to grid." You define a quantization value (for example, quarter, eighth, or sixteenth notes), and then apply quantization to a selected area. Magically, any timing mistakes you make while recording a performance are adjusted to align with the timing grid. Be careful with this effect, however. If you quantize every note in the piece, it will sound boring and mechanical (what do you expect from a computer, anyway?). Most quantization algorithms let you specify a percentage for strength (for example, you can elect to move the note 90 percent of the way to a grid point) so that you can tighten up a performance while still maintaining a "human" feel.

Another approach, sometimes called *groove quantization,* uses the timing in existing MIDI files as a template for adjusting the timing of notes. Groove quantization is especially effective for certain types of musical feels in which certain notes need to fall just a bit ahead of or behind the beat.

Step Input Versus Real-time Recording

Along the lines of quantization, most programs let you enter notes in real time (as if you were recording onto tape) or in *step record* mode (somewhat like stop-action photography). In step record mode, you specify a note duration for each step. Each time you hit the keyboard (or your controller of choice), recording skips to the next step and waits for more data to be recorded. Step recording is helpful for creating fast, repetitious patterns like arpeggios or techno bass lines, as well as for emulating drumming techniques like eighth-note hi-hats, tom fills, or snare rolls.

Sequencer Transports

Like most other digital audio applications, MIDI sequencers adhere to the tape recorder metaphor. Most playback and recording control functions are found in a transport window. The transport often includes punch-in and punch-out recording capability, a looped playback selector, and autolocation points.

Digital Audio Integration

Most of the products covered in this chapter have integrated digital audio and MIDI playback. But each of these products continues to be offered without the digital audio option. Digital Performer, Studio Vision, and Cubase Audio are also available as Performer, Vision, and Cubase. Obviously, based on the thrust of this book, it makes the most sense to look at the digital audio features in each program. But if you just want MIDI sequencing, and are content using another audio-editing application like Deck II or Digitrax, you may not need the digital audio version of the sequencer. In fact, Deck II supports OMS, so you can synchronize the playback of tracks in Deck to a MIDI sequencer running in the background at the same time.

Some General Thoughts on Sequencing Software

We lay no claim to having the widest global view of where sequencing software has come from and where it's going; we leave that up to the folks who make their living by either creating the programs themselves or tracking features for reviews in the major industry magazines. But few would argue the point that major MIDI sequencing applications have been pushed to a level of "featuritis" that can overwhelm the beginning user. You know the pattern. When Company A implements a feature, Company B has to add that feature, plus two more to leapfrog Company A. In the end, you have a huge array of menus, windows, and dialog boxes.

Note: *Not that I'm complaining, mind you. I invariably find myself in one of two positions when working with MIDI: either I need a tweaky feature and am gratified when I find the programmer anticipated my needs; or I don't find the feature I need and wish the programmer would add yet another dialog box or menu item. The main reason I raise the foregoing issue is to warn the uninitiated. If you just need to open a standard MIDI file and make a few edits, these programs may leave your head spinning. They're starting to make Macromedia Director look simple and intuitive.*

The trend toward feature build-up has an obvious cause: spirited competition between the dominant software developers. For a long time, the leadership position for top sequencer seesawed between Opcode's Vision and Mark of the Unicorn's Performer. This struggle took on the semblance of the graphic community's "Freehand Versus Illustrator" debate, with most people falling squarely into one of the two camps. Performer was slow to catch up with the integration of audio into the MIDI environment. Although Digital Performer version 1.0 had been available for several years, it was less stable than Studio Vision. But with their release of version 1.6, Digital Performer was right back in the fray, offering TDM support for ProTools right through the sequencer interface. In the meantime, Cubase has been building a loyal following in Europe, where the Atari computer is still a very popular platform for MIDI sequencing. And over the past few years, Logic Audio has been gaining favor with sophisticated users. As with digital audio editing software, we're fortunate to have a number of excellent products to choose from.

Sequencing Software

This section reviews several of the most popular sequencing applications that also support digital audio.

**Opcode
Studio
Vision 3.0**

Opcode's Studio Vision had the distinction of being the first MIDI sequencing program to integrate digital audio. With their latest release, they've taken that heritage one step further, implementing *Pitch-to-MIDI* and *MIDI-to-Pitch conversion*. Digital audio data can be "converted" to MIDI note information. Editing the MIDI information and applying it back to the signal, you can fix or alter practically any aspect of a performance. Figure 11.1 shows the main Track window of Studio Vision.

Especially Nifty Features

❏ New DSP audio functions let you perform EQ, normalization, and other file-processing operations from within Studio Vision. In previous versions, the only way you could normalize audio data was by mixing it to another track with "Normalize on Mix" selected.

❏ StudioVision was always nicely integrated with Galaxy Plus Editors, Opcode's editor/librarian for synthesizers. But in the latest version, you can actually launch the editor for a specific patch from within Studio Vision—an extremely handy feature.

❏ Speaking of Galaxy, the product is sold in two levels: Galaxy and Galaxy Plus Editors. Plain-vanilla Galaxy is a librarian: you can use it to organize, archive, and transfer sounds and settings between MIDI equipment and the computer. Galaxy Plus Editors includes editor interfaces for many of the most popular pieces of MIDI hardware (in my setup, for example, 8 out of 11 devices have editors). It's good to see Opcode bundling the basic Galaxy package with Studio Vision.

❏ The Track window offers a good overview of the data in your sequence, making it much easier to copy, trim, adjust, or duplicate large chunks of MIDI data. You can constrain the movement of these blocks to note values (quarter, half, or whole notes, for example) so

Figure 11.1

Studio Vision's main Track window. Program changes have been pasted into Track 4.

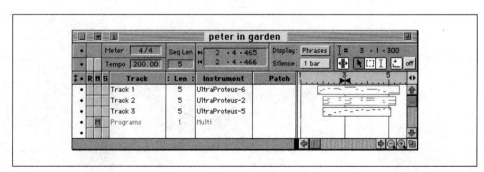

that they snap to a specific time (they can also be shifted using the Move Events command).

❏ Obviously, one thing Studio Vision has in its favor is good integration with OMS (originally the Opcode MIDI System, now the Open Music System). OMS enjoys the broadest support among sequencing and digital audio editing tools. It handles timing and MIDI communication functions between compatible applications and also provides a central "map" of all the devices in your MIDI setup.

❏ After years of looking greedily at the mixer panels available in Performer, Studio Vision now has updated mixer consoles (Figure 11.2). These are a welcome change from the old Faders window.

❏ When you've finished creating a sequence, it's very important that you also record the program changes for sounds used within that sequence. Otherwise, the next time you open that file for editing, the MIDI channel that used to play your tuba patch may have been reassigned to a piccolo. Studio Vision handles this nicely with a Copy Programs function, which automatically places all program changes into the clipboard. Simply paste this data into a track and your program change worries are over.

Not-So-Nifty Features

❏ There's one caveat to Studio Vision's Copy Programs function described in the previous section: each track can only hold 16 program changes. If you use more than 16 MIDI channels in a sequence, and you play a track with 16 program changes that was previously created using Copy Programs, subsequent Copy Programs operations

Figure 11.2

Studio Vision's new Consoles. Faders can be configured to control volume of audio files or MIDI instruments.

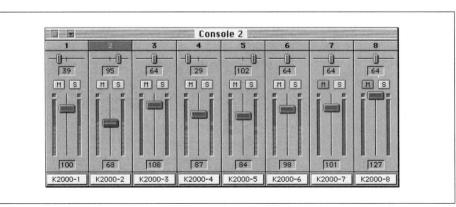

will continue to paste the original 16 program changes. StudioVision seems to be able to deal with a maximum of only 16 program changes in a track at any one time. This means that if you want to add any new program changes, you should manually insert them into a blank trank.

❑ Studio Vision lets you create a practically infinite number of MIDI tracks. If, like me, you routinely generate 30 or 40 tracks for a project, and then end up keeping just a few them, you end up with lots of muted, unused tracks. You can delete these tracks manually and drag them into new positions within the window, but a "clean up tracks" function would be nice. (Hmm, wasn't I railing about "featuritis" just a few pages ago?).

❑ You should know that there are a few things to watch out for when recording digital audio. Studio Vision is a nondestructive recorder. It keeps all of your takes unless you immediately undo the recording. So if you goof up the first four takes and decide to keep the fifth, the other four takes remain on your disk, filling up available space more quickly than you had planned. However, you *can* delete unused portions of audio from the File Management window. Studio Vision's retentivity can be a good thing or a bad thing depending on your situation.

Here's the flip side of this issue. If you record digital audio to one track, and then switch to another track to record MIDI without disabling audio recording in the Audio Record panel, silence will be recorded and appended to your previous audio. As you just read, the previous audio is still on your disk; it just won't be shown in the track window. You can get your previous track back by dragging the left edge of the audio file until your previous take is displayed or, better yet, undo the recording. If you're finished recording digital audio, be sure to turn off recording in the Audio Record panel. Stay on your toes during this process and you shouldn't have any problems.

❑ You can combine multiple audio files into the same track for faster editing. In the example shown in Figure 11.3, the data from two tracks is superimposed into a single track at the bottom of the window. This feature is a plus, right? Not necessarily. The downside is that it can become difficult to work with strip charts (graphic displays of volume or panning information). Studio Vision's power as an audio-editing environment lies in its ability to translate MIDI commands (like volume and pan) so that they control the playback of digital audio as well as MIDI. But when you combine multiple audio "instruments" into a single track (to create a multitrack audio-editing

Figure 11.3

Having multiple audio channels in a single track can be helpful for editing files relative to each other. Ideally, editing is easier when volume data (shown in the bottom track) is displayed independently.

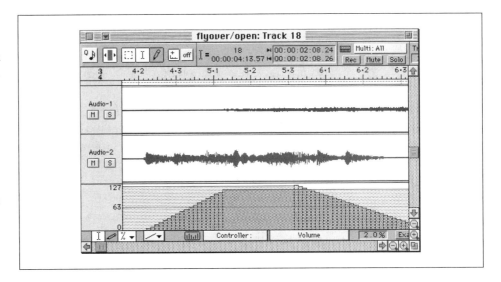

window within one sequencer track), you're given only one strip chart for modifying volume or pan. The graphic displays of pan or volume for each audio track are layered on top of each other, and it's difficult to switch the foreground priority for editing the strip chart data. It would be preferable to have multiple strip chart displays so that you could edit each audio track more easily.

❏ Digital Performer includes several features— particularly Performer's looping scheme and configurable control panels—that should really be in Studio Vision as well. For more information about these features in Performer, read on.

Who, Where, and How Much

Studio Vision 3.0

Opcode Systems

3950 Fabian Way, Suite 100

Palo Alto, CA 94303

415-856-3332

http://www.opcode.com

Suggested retail: $995

Mark of the Unicorn's Digital Performer version 1.6

Digital Performer from Mark of the Unicorn (MOTU) is another heavyweight entry in the sequencer arena. Its adherents are fanatical about its features, and it's not hard to see why. (I must confess that, after being a dyed-in-the-wool Studio Vision user for the past four years, my own experiences with Digital Performer often left me thinking, "Hmm, why doesn't Studio Vision do *that?")*

Especially Nifty Features

❏ Digital Performer lets you build custom control panels to perform just about any MIDI function you can imagine (Figure 11.4). You can choose from a selection of sliders, buttons, faders, and knobs, and then assign each object to a particular MIDI function (for example, volume) or, using System Exclusive, assign the object to control a function with a particular synthesizer. This level of programming flexibility lets you customize the program to your working style.

❏ Performer's Track window has a great mechanism for looping. In most other applications (including Vision and MasterTracks), once you set a track to loop for a certain number of measures, it just plays

Figure 11.4

Digital Performer's Console Control dialog box lets you build practically any tool you need if you can't already find it in Performer.

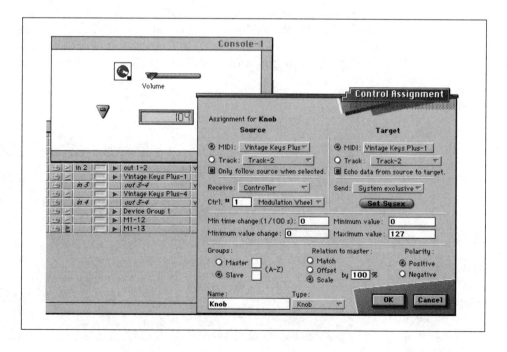

looped. In Performer, on the other hand, a segment can start looping in the middle of a sequence, loop for a specified number of times, and then stop looping and continue linear playback. This is the kind of functionality every looping algorithm should use.

❏ Performer has a built-in QuickTime window, which comes in handy if you need to score to video or QuickTime.

❏ A special MIDI monitor window lets you see the status of MIDI input and output in real time. The status monitor is especially helpful when you're trying to track the source of a problem, which in MIDI systems can be anything from a disconnected MIDI cable to a disconnected audio cable. The MIDI Monitor helps take some of the guesswork out of the troubleshooting process.

❏ Performer's program select function is built right into the main Track window. This represents a more streamlined design than the pop-up program list that Studio Vision provides at the top of its Track window; in Performer, the active instrument is automatically selected at the same time.

❏ Performer offers a processor for controlling those out-of-control synthesizer sounds. It's a compressor that affects the key velocity of MIDI data without altering the sound itself (Figure 11.5). Imagine that you play a track using one instrument sound (with its own articulation) and then switch the track to another instrument sound (which may require a different articulation). With Performer's processor, you can

Figure 11.5

Performer's Track window with views of the MIDI Compressor and MIDI Monitor

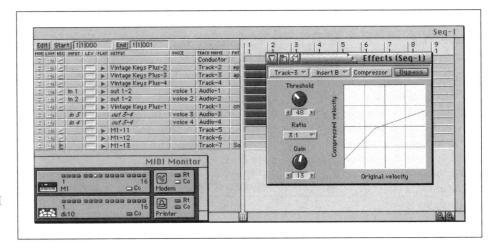

run that track through the "compressor" instead of actually changing the velocity data.

❏ An add-on to Performer is MOTU's Unisyn editor and librarian. Unisyn supports a very wide range of hardware and uses an interface similar to that of Performer, so users can jump between the two applications without becoming disoriented.

Not-So-Nifty Features

❏ Performer's artsy interface is a bit overdone for our tastes. It's too lumpy, the windows are nonstandard, and the controls for resizing and closing windows are nonstandard, too. Many people find this interface creative, warm, and inviting, but to us it seems contrived.

❏ It's unfortunate that the graphic event editor (the area below the piano roll display where continuous controllers can be edited) doesn't display the giant waves of data that can be found in some other programs. Performer's use of small iconic dots lets users see multiple data types at once but makes the tracking and editing of volume and pan information difficult.

❏ Performer ships with MOTU's FreeMIDI, a tool similar to Opcode's OMS. FreeMIDI is much more painful to set up than OMS is, though. The set-up routine is supposed to query the user's equipment and create the proper configuration automatically. Alas, it was not to be! I practically had to rebuild the document from scratch, thanks to my MIDI patch bay, which threw the poor thing for a loop. After a few phone calls, I learned that the simplest solution was to "pretend that the patch bay didn't exist" and to chain all of its associated hardware directly to one FreeMIDI port. That's hardly the most elegant solution, and it left me unable to send program changes to reconfigure the patch bay. (Granted, my system may be a bit more complex than the setup procedure was designed to handle.) Users with small systems may have no trouble whatsoever. But be prepared to spend some time tinkering when you first introduce your system to FreeMIDI.

❏ FreeMIDI doesn't automatically disable and reenable AppleTalk when you launch Performer. This is a function that OMS handles transparently. With FreeMIDI, on the other hand, your only option is to cancel launching Performer, turn off AppleTalk, and then relaunch Performer. If you use ethernet or just send MIDI through the modem port, this needn't be a problem; it's a concern only for those who use the printer port for AppleTalk.

Who, Where, and How Much

Digital Performer

Mark of the Unicorn

1280 Massachusetts Ave.

Cambridge, MA 02138

617-576-2760

http://www.motu.com

Suggested Retail: $895

EMagic Logic Audio 2.5

One of the latest products to ascend the throne of sequencer greatness is Logic Audio. The product has gained a devoted following over the past several years among high-level MIDI users, and it's easy to see why: Logic Audio is perhaps the most powerful application covered here.

Especially Nifty Features

- Logic has an extremely deep set of features. It uses *objects,* applying concepts of object-oriented programming to the use of MIDI devices, audio clips, and data files.

- Logic has a great implementation for controlling ProTools TDM systems. In fact, several well-respected sound designers we know have confessed that they prefer to do all their audio editing from within Logic, completely bypassing Digidesign's ProTools software.

- Logic lets you take advantage of all the digital audio hardware at your disposal. If you have an AV or Power Mac, you can play audio through the Macintosh outputs using Sound Manager. If you also have dedicated audio hardware (Digidesign's products, for example), Logic will play audio simultaneously from both the Sound Manager and the dedicated hardware. Most other programs make you choose one route or the other, but Logic provides extra tracks that you may need in a pinch.

- Logic also has a powerful set of tools, the Digital Factory, which apply complex processing functions to audio files. One of these, the Time Machine (Figure 11.6), has a great interface for time-stretching and pitch-shifting sound data.

- Logic has many of the audio-editing tools you expect to see in a dedicated sound-editing program like Sound Designer II. Most other integrated MIDI/digital audio products let you change how the data is played but then direct you to a separate sound-editing package to actually change the sample data (Figure 11.7). Logic lets you perform

Figure 11.6

Logic Audio's Time Machine has a unique interface for handling the related tasks of pitch shifting and time stretching.

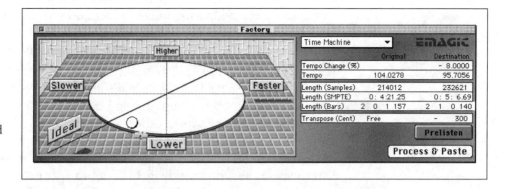

Figure 11.7

Logic's audio editing approaches the functionality of Digidesign's Sound Designer II.

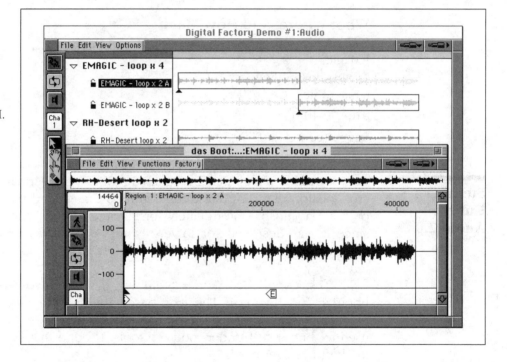

destructive editing functions (fade-in, fade-out, gain change, and so on) from within the application.

Not-So-Nifty Features

❏ With Logic's power and depth of features, you may end up spending more time than you'd like plowing through windows, dialog boxes, and the interface. Notice in Figure 11.7, for example, that each window comes complete with a menu bar, in addition to the main menu bar at the top of the screen. These can be helpful for quickly accessing a particular function, but one can easily get lost in the system. If your needs are relatively basic, you might want to consider a product with less clutter. Power users, on the other hand, will thrive on this feature.

❏ Logic has an extremely steep learning curve. It takes a different architectural approach from most other sequencers. For example, if you know Performer, it's not too hard to figure out Vision or Master Tracks. But Logic is a radical departure from previous sequencers. Plan to spend several months getting up to speed. Those who make the journey will be rewarded, but it *will* be a journey.

Who, Where, and How Much

Logic Audio 2.5
EMagic
13348 Grass Valley Ave.
Grass Valley, CA 94945

916-477-1051

Suggested Retail: $799

**Steinberg
Cubase
Audio 2.0**

Cubase Audio, developed by Steinberg GmbH in Germany, is one of the cross-platform kings. Cubase runs on the PC and Atari platforms as well as on the Macintosh. Unfortunately for Macintosh users, the interface suffers, since it was designed for lower-resolution platforms. But the software isn't limited in terms of features; you simply have to look for them in a different way.

My first experience with a Steinberg product involved an M1 editor/librarian for the Atari. The icon-based interface (a natural approach to overcoming language barriers in the European market) took some getting used to, but once I understood the tools, I found that editor to be among the best I've ever used.

Especially Nifty Features

❏ Cubase's main window (the Arrange window, shown in Figure 11.8) has a handy display called the Inspector. From here, you have quick access to most of the functions you need during a session. The standard ones you'd expect include output port (modem 1 through modem 16), channel, program, volume, and transposition. But you

Figure 11.8

The Arrange window in Cubase Audio offers control of many functions. The Controller is at the bottom of the window and the Inspector is to the left.

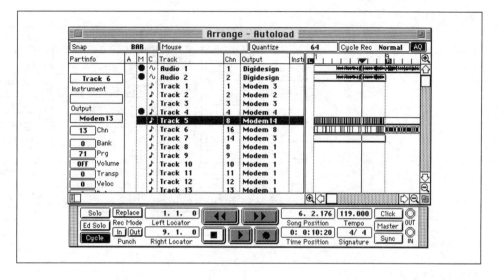

also get extra goodies. *Bank select* lets you switch banks in a synthesizer; *velocity* adds a specified value to all velocities; *delay* shifts the track back or forth in time; *length* changes the note duration; and *compression* changes velocities by a percentage, not to exceed 127. Having this much control in one area is evidence of good interface design.

❏ Combining computers with MIDI sequencing opens up tremendous number-crunching possibilities. Think of MIDI information as data streams rather than simply as musical notes, and you're on your way to unlocking your imagination. What happens when you use one type of value—key velocity, for example—to modify another type of value, such as pitch bend? You can create some really interesting effects by following this train of thought. Cubase includes a powerful MIDI processor called the Phrase synthesizer (Figure 11.9). It applies values from an existing phrase of MIDI notes to MIDI data in another channel. This type of processing can be especially effective for rhythm and percussion tracks; it can generate music that you might never have thought up by yourself, even though it's based on forms and parameters that you specify.

❏ Cubase has a built-in link to Time Bandit, the company's audio processing program (discussed in Chapter 10). One advantage of using the two in tandem is that you can specify processing for short segments of audio within a larger file. If you're not running Time Bandit from within Cubase, you have to process the entire file.

Figure 11.9

The Phrase
Synthesizer
window in
Cubase Audio

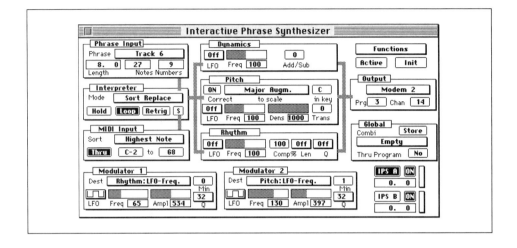

Figure 11.10

Cubase's Pool
window helps
you keep track of
the audio
associated with
a file.

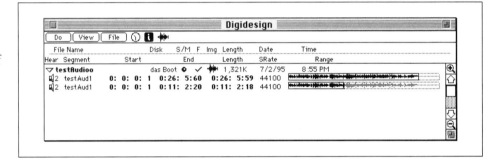

❏ The Pool window in Cubase (Figure 11.10) offers a convenient interface for audio file management. From this window, you can see waveform displays of audio files along with all their pertinent data. You can also play the files directly from the window (it's worth it just to see the animated speaker icon).

Not-So-Nifty Features

❏ For purists who are accustomed to neatly standardized Macintosh graphical interfaces, Cubase Audio may be a bit difficult on the eyes. Considering that Cubase supports three platforms in multiple countries, it gets the job done quite well. But whether Macintosh users are willing to accomodate the limitations of the interface is something you'll have to decide for yourself.

❏ Cubase supports multi-port interfaces (like my own Studio 4), but there's no way to assign your own names to the ports. As a result, you have to know whether "Modem 4" is connected to a K2000 or a Proteus. If you don't have lots of instruments, this may not be a problem for you, but I found myself constantly referring to a slip of paper that served as my personal Rosetta Stone for deciphering ports and instrument names.

Who, Where, and How Much

Cubase Audio 2.0
Steinberg Jones
17700 Raymer Street, Suite 1002
Northridge, CA 91325

818-993-4091

Suggested Retail Price: $799

**Passport
Master
Tracks Pro**

Look to the
CD-ROM

Master Tracks Pro is the first product we've covered that doesn't incorporate digital audio. It's also linear rather than pattern-based. At first glance, Master Tracks Pro seems to have scaled down quite a bit from the lofty heights occupied by Studio Vision and Digital Performer. But depending on your circumstances, simpler can sometimes be better. If, for example, your main goals in a MIDI sequencing application are only to record, edit, and playback MIDI, Master Tracks may be all you need. Its interface is straightforward and easy to use. You'll spend less time plowing through manuals, menus, and commands and more time making music. If you're just getting into MIDI, Master Tracks is a great place to start (we're speaking from personal experience here). And if you find you need more bells and whistles in time, at least you'll have a good grounding in MIDI and sequencing concepts. You'll be well prepared for the switch to a more complex environment.

Especially Nifty Features

❏ Master Tracks Pro is the first product to ship with a great set of MIDI file test utilities. These files were created by Craig Anderton, a well-respected author on MIDI and music. Use the sequences to test various synthesizer capabilities—how they'll respond to MIDI volume, for example, playing all the notes from 1 to 127, or stepping through all the programs on a synthesizer for easy previewing. The sequences even include tuning references for guitar and bass. These files are a really nice touch.

❑ Master Tracks is OMS compatible, so if you have other programs that support OMS (such as Deck II or Sound Designer), they can share timing information and play back in sync with each other.

❑ The resizeable columns in the Track Editor (Figure 11.11) give you flexibility in your working style. You can choose to display every column at maximum width to see a text description, or you can shrink column width by double-clicking the column heading so that only a numerical value is visible. Once you become familiar with MIDI controllers, you don't always need to see a text label to know that controller 7 is MIDI volume. The resizeable columns let you see all the information you need, while leaving more room for the display of MIDI data in the tracks themselves.

❑ Although Master Tracks can be classified as a linear sequencer, it does have a playlist feature that lets you string together a number of songs. You could create several musical "building blocks" and link them together this way.

❑ Master Tracks displays "ghost notes" in windows that show graphic information about controllers. These grayed-out notes can't be edited, but seeing them when you're editing continuous data is really helpful (Figure 11.12). Other MIDI sequencers would do well to include this feature.

❑ Above all, the main attraction for Master Tracks Pro is that it's relatively easy to use but still has all the basic functions you need in a sequencer, including quantization, tempo mapping, and list views of data.

Figure 11.11

The main windows in Master Tracks Pro. The columns in the Track Editor have been reduced to their minimum size.

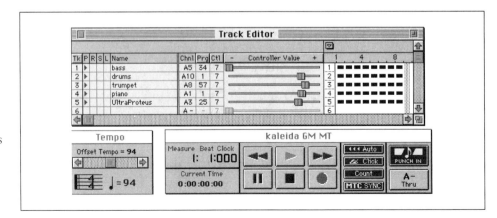

Figure 11.12

Ghost notes
displayed in the
Pitch Bend
window of Master
Tracks Pro

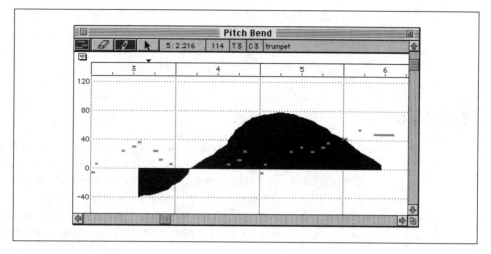

Not-So-Nifty Features

❏ Master Tracks uses a different window for each controller type.
There's a pitch bend window, a modulation window, a velocity window, and so on. This interface strategy makes controller editing much
more complicated than it needs to be. Ideally, a single window
should be able to display different types of controllers (perhaps
selecting them with a pop-up menu as in Studio Vision).

❏ There's no central location for setting preferences in Master Tracks.
Instead, the program saves the current settings for functions and window displays. Unfortunately, many of these settings are buried inside
different dialog boxes, so if you want to change several different preference settings, you'll have to root around a bit. Master Tracks should
consider offering one main preference area so that users can quickly
adjust settings based on their needs for the current project.

❏ Master Tracks has rather limited features compared to several other
high-end sequencing products. It's not really a weakness in the program; as long as you know these limitations in the beginning, you
won't be disappointed.

Who, Where, and How Much
Master Tracks Pro
Passport Designs
100 Stone Pine Road
Half Moon Bay, CA 94019

415-726-0280
http://www.mw3.com/passport
Suggested retail: $149

MIDI Tools

There's more to MIDI than merely sequencing to create digital audio mixes. Earlier, we discussed the value of MIDI as a multimedia playback device, and as a data stream that can be altered on the fly for interactive applications. In this section, we'll survey some of the tools that can help you use MIDI in real time, without a net. *Do* try these out at home, especially before you try it in a real-world product or in front of an audience.

Ear Level Engineering's HyperMIDI Tools

HyperMIDI is a HyperCard XCMD for controlling MIDI data streams. You may recall that XCMDs can be used by HyperCard, SuperCard, Director, and Authorware. Since none of these products has any type of MIDI implementation, it's a darned good thing that Nigel Redmon of Ear Level Engineering has stepped in to fill the gap.

HyperMIDI provides basic functions for opening and playing standard MIDI files, but its capabilities extend far beyond these. It lets you input, route, monitor, modify, and output MIDI data streams. It also supports six independent input and output ports. With 16 channels on each port, that works out to 96 MIDI channels.

Especially Nifty Features

- ❏ Currently, HyperMIDI is probably *the* best commercial tool for controlling low-level MIDI functions in Director, SuperCard, or HyperCard. In fact, it ships with several Director example movies (see Figure 11.13) that walk you through the process of using the XCMD in Director.

- ❏ You can use HyperMIDI to build tools for MIDI equipment that isn't supported by other manufacturers. Two examples that ship with HyperMIDI are editors for the Roland D50 and the Yamaha SPX90.

- ❏ HyperMIDI doesn't just read standard MIDI files; it can write them, too! Use it to make your own MIDI file builder.

- ❏ HyperMIDI ships with excellent documentation. The manual even includes tips on HyperTalk programming, and there are example scripts like the ones in Figure 11.14. There are also a bunch of good example HyperCard stacks on the disk to help get you started.

Figure 11.13

HyperMIDI's KeyStrummer example movie takes MIDI notes held down on a keyboard and "strums" them as they would play on a guitar.

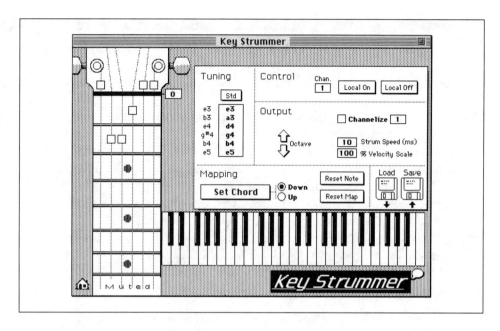

Figure 11.14

Example Lingo scripts for calling HyperMIDI from within Macromedia Director

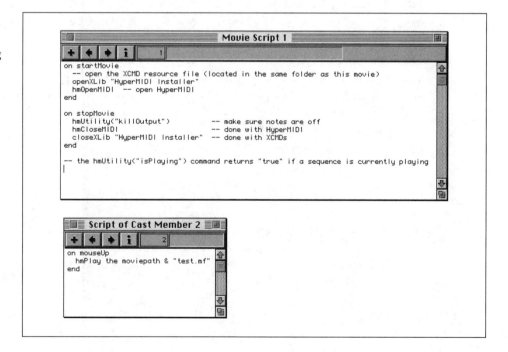

SOUND AND MUSIC IN HYPERCARD

by Kevin Calhoun, Acting Engineering Manager for HyperCard

HyperCard is a popular software development tool from Apple that enables people to easily organize text, graphics, sound, and video into "stacks" of electronic cards for custom software solutions. It's widely used by commercial and in-house developers, software consultants, educators, and multimedia authors.

HyperCard 2.3 introduces automated Button Tasks, which enable stackware authors with little or no scripting experience to easily integrate all elements of a HyperCard stack, including sound, speech, and music.

The Movie task is the most useful of the Button Tasks for authors who are integrating sound and music with their stacks. The Movie task makes it very simple to play sound and music in a variety of formats (including WAV, AU, AIFF, and MIDI) from HyperCard stacks. Try the following steps:

1. Ensure that QuickTime 2.1 (or later) and Sound Manager 3.2 (or later) are installed on your system. These versions are available with System 7.5 Update 2.0.

2. Make sure that Automatic Document Translation is turned on in the Macintosh Easy Open control panel.

3. From HyperCard's Button Tasks dialog box, select the Movie task. For information on how to open the Button Tasks dialog, see Getting Started with HyperCard.

4. Click the Choose... button in the Movie task and select the sound or music file you want to play, regardless of its format. Files in WAV, AU, or MIDI formats will automatically be converted to QuickTime format. You can find the converted files in the Translated Documents folder, which is in the Preferences folder within your System folder.

5. Click Assign Tasks. That's it. Your button will now play the sound, music, or movie file you selected.

Similarly, HyperCard's Speech task automates the process of adding speech to your stacks.

Of course, you can use HyperCard's scripting language, HyperTalk, for fine-tuning control over sound and music. See the entries for HyperTalk's play and speak commands in HyperCard's Script Language Guide and the QuickTime tools stack for more information.

Not-So-Nifty Features

❏ This should come as no surprise to anyone, but you have to be a bit of a propellor-head to use HyperMIDI. Some people jump at the chance to do programming. Others would rather not get their hands dirty. If you haven't already programmed in Director, HyperCard, or SuperCard, you'll need to spend some time learning the basics of the language before you'll be ready for HyperMIDI.

❏ HyperMIDI works only with MIDI Manager, not with OMS or FreeMIDI. Apple doesn't officially support MIDI Manager any longer, but it still works reasonably well for most applications. Support for QuickTime Music Instruments is in the works. Users of OMS or FreeMIDI will have to use MIDI Manager drivers to work with HyperMIDI.

Who, Where, and How Much

HyperMIDI

Ear Level Engineering

21213-B Hawthorne Blvd., Suite 5305

Torrance, CA 90509

310-316-2939

72736,753@compuserve.com

Suggested retail: $195

InVision Interactive's CyberSound VS

CyberSound VS is a new, improved set of instrument voices for QuickTime Musical Instruments from Invision Interactive, the company responsible for CyberSound FX. After listening to Apple's QuickTime Music Instruments all I can say is, thank you! CyberSound VS turns your computer into a full-fledged synthesizer. Now you can compose MIDI sequences without any external MIDI hardware (Figure 11.15).

Look to the
CD-ROM

Especially Nifty Features

❏ CyberSound VS is General MIDI compatible. It also supports Roland GS, a superset of General MIDI.

❏ CyberSound VS works with OMS and FreeMIDI as well as with MIDI Manager. You can use it from the sequencing application of your choice.

Figure 11.15

The Options window within the CyberSound VS Control Panel lets you configure the amount of system resources available to the synthesis engine.

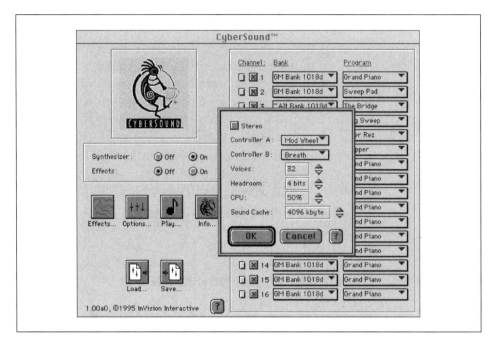

- ❏ The playback engine automatically scales its performance to match the capabilities of the current machine. You can also customize these settings, as shown in Figure 11.15.

- ❏ There's more to CyberSound VS than just sampled wavetable voices playing from RAM. It also performs several different types of synthesis and is able to create a broad range of tones.

- ❏ On a Power Mac 9500, CyberSound VS supports up to 128 simultaneous voices! You can audition them easily using your computer keyboard, as shown in Figure 11.16. Granted, not many people have that much processor power on their desktop right now, but faster machines will continue to move into the market.

Not-So-Nifty Features

- ❏ The power of CyberSound VS comes at a price. CyberSound VS can take a big bite out of your processor. Depending on the application, you might not be able to get by, particularly if you're playing QuickTime video or lots of animation. If your product is shipping to the mass market, this consideration could spell trouble for end users on older machines.

Figure 11.16

CyberSound VS's Play window lets you quickly switch between sounds, banks, and MIDI channels. You can even play chords from the QWERTY keyboard.

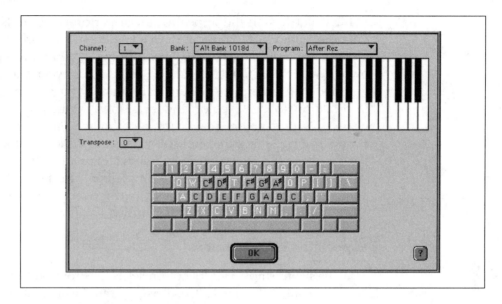

❏ CyberSound VS's distribution strategy is unclear at the time of this writing. If the manufacturer is unable to establish a workable licensing strategy to allow the distribution of the sound playback engine, your MIDI files might be played back using QuickTime's limited sounds.

Who, Where, and How Much

CyberSound VS
InVision Interactive
2445 Faher Place, Suite 102
Palo Alto, CA 94303

415-812-7380

http://www.cybersound.com

Suggested Retail: $249

BlissPaint

Look to the
CD-ROM

The use of MIDI in live performance is a subject that has been explored in many different ways (see the D'Cuckoo interview in Chapter 12). In most such cases, MIDI has been used to trigger a sound source, to switch between video sources, or to alter the movement of graphics or playback of a Director movie. Most of these installations required quite a bit of technical gimmickry: wireless mikes, video switchers, and audio-to-MIDI trigger converters.

BlissPaint has all the appeal of these performance tools, but it requires only one audio or MIDI input device (a CD or keyboard, for example) and a color Macintosh. Well, actually it doesn't *require* any input. Left on its own, it will create fabulous kaleidoscopic color cycling imagery. But when you hook up an input, the fun really starts. You can map audio or MIDI information to drive color and brightness values so that the graphics change as performers play harder or higher on their instruments (see Figure 11.17). Setting thresholds for audio input causes the main beat of a song to make the screen pulse in time with the music. It's a real visual treat.

BlissPaint is the brainchild of Greg Jalbert, a true renaissance guy who excels in traditional painting, music performance, and computer programming. These talents are all evident in Bliss Paint.

Especially Nifty Features

❏ BlissPaint ships with lots of preset effects for you to use in your own "paintings" (Figure 11.18). This program has lots of subtleties, so the starter files are especially helpful.

❏ You can save your paintings as PICTs or export them as QuickTime movies. BlissPaint is a great texture generator.

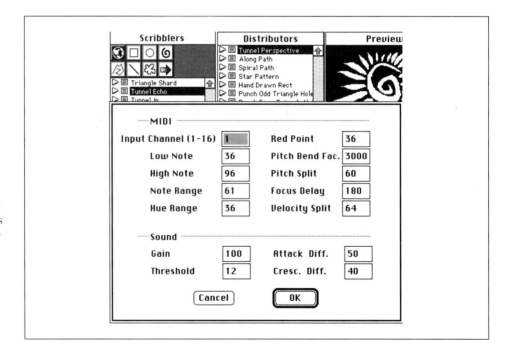

Figure 11.17

The Configure MIDI dialog box in Bliss Paint lets you control how MIDI data will affect screen graphics. It's also where you set sound input options.

Figure 11.18

BlissPaint ships with many preset effects that determine how various MIDI data types will map to the behavior of graphics.

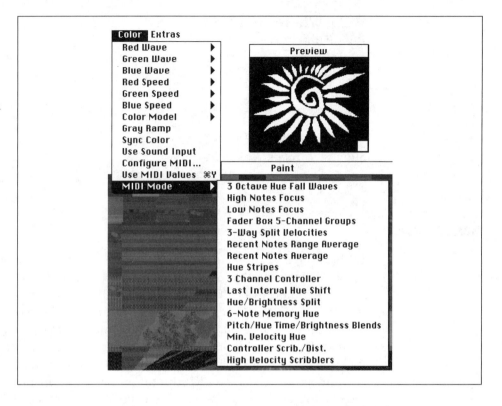

- ❏ BlissPaint has several companion products, including BlissSaver (a screen saver that also accepts input from audio or MIDI) and BlissGallery, a collection of custom "paintings" by Greg Jalbert (well worth the investment to see what the program can do).

- ❏ You can add your own graphics (such as logos or text) to Bliss paintings by placing them in the clipboard.

Not-So-Nifty Features

- ❏ You should have a two-monitor system if you plan to see full-screen paint images while still having all the windows open. If you plan to use the program for performance work, you'll also need a projection system.

- ❏ There's a *lot* going on in BlissPaint—so much so that it can be difficult to keep track of all the variables. It's also easy to make visual hash if you get carried away. With BlissPaint, simpler is often better.

Who, Where, and How Much

Bliss Paint

Imaja

P.O. Box 6386

Albany, CA 94706

510-526-4621

http://www.imaja.com

Suggested retail: $79.95

Summary

In the twelve years since its inception, MIDI has become an integral part of the musician's toolkit. When multimedia came into its own over the past five years, there was already a well-established set of tools and technology for creating high-quality music quickly and easily. Considering the fast-paced production environment of most multimedia products, it would be practically impossible to compose and edit original music without having the power and flexibility afforded by MIDI equipment. MIDI sequencers with integrated digital-audio support are at the heart of a MIDI studio, and we're fortunate to have several excellent products to choose from. There are also several products that multimedia producers can use to play MIDI music files instead of digitized audio.

Up to this point, Macintosh-based multimedia developers have been hesitant to embrace MIDI for playing music. There was no cross-platform play-back solution in software, and you couldn't depend on anyone having MIDI hardware. But as MIDI playback in software becomes better implemented on the Macintosh and Windows platforms, this is destined to change during the next year. Finally, we can look forward to long, continuous passages of music—without loops! We'll have MIDI files playing back over the Internet, on-line jam sessions, and on-line interactive games with "live" music. Perhaps MIDI will finally assume its rightful place as the optimal solution for multimedia music playback.

Part Four

LOOKING
AHEAD

12

Future Directions

The pace of change in computer technology is enough to overwhelm even the most rabid technophile. Nary a week goes by without some major announcement about processor speeds, operating systems, or new standards for this protocol or that file format. It's like having to keep track of political scandals, celebrity trials, and the NBA playoffs all at the same time.

But you won't hear me complaining about progress when it comes to audio. Within the past year, a crop of great new technologies has surfaced. Taking into account the lag time between the adoption of new technologies by developers and the arrival of real products on the market, it looks as though ground-breaking products will just begin to hit their stride in 1996. In this final chapter, we'll explore new possibilities for audio coming up in the next few years.

Software Synthesis

One major trend coming down the pike is the transition from hardware synthesizers to software-based "virtual" synthesizers. There are several different points of view on how this technology will shake out. Currently, the main method for playing back MIDI files is through hardware, whether it's an external synthesizer (often a General MIDI device like Roland's SC-7 or Korg's 05R/W) or a wavetable synthesizer on a sound card (as found in most recent-model PCs). Here's an area in which the Macintosh has fallen behind the PC in terms of built-in MIDI playback capability, since very few Macintoshes have sound cards. As a result, developers working on cross-platform titles have been unable to take advantage of the benefits of MIDI, in particular its smaller file sizes and reduced load on the CPU when compared with digitized audio.

It's likely that synthesis will move toward software playback because software is usually more flexible and less expensive than hardware. One of the main arguments against such a move, however, is that the cost of a high-powered CPU and additional RAM is greater than the cost of a sound card with a wavetable chip. If software playback requires a 100 MHz Pentium with 20 MB of RAM, users might prefer to spend $200 on a sound card instead.

This argument may hold water for a year or so, as the installed base of computers migrates up to Pentium and PowerPC processors. But by 1997 we should expect to see basic audio capabilities (inputs, outputs, and digital-to-analog converters) built into the motherboard of Windows computers. As processor speeds continue to advance, the sound card market is likely to fade away. Let's look at the current crop of contenders for the next generation of MIDI playback.

QuickTime Music Architecture

Apple's first implementation of MIDI from within QuickTime was limiting for composers. Perhaps you recall the reaction of video professionals to the quality of QuickTime version 1.0: "It's so small," or " It's choppy and too slow." By the time version 2.0 came along, the quality had improved dramatically and most users were more than satisfied. In a sense, QuickTime 2.0 did for MIDI what QuickTime 1.0 did for video. Although it wasn't an ideal solution yet, it was a proverbial foot in the door.

With QuickTime 2.2, the door swings open much wider. Apple has opened the QuickTime Music Architecture (QTMA), giving third-party developers the ability to create their own synthesizers or to create custom instruments for synthesizers. This development is taking place just as this book goes to press, so it's not possible to determine all the repercussions of the move at this time. But here's a sampling of what we can hope to expect.

First, QuickTime 2.2 makes it much easier to use custom sound libraries with QTMA. Several high-quality synthesis engines are already available, and new instrument sets may soon be on the market. Some of these conform to the General MIDI set of instruments; it's also likely that custom subsets of instruments will be created for specific projects. For example, imagine having 1 MB of storage for instrument samples on a particular project. If your title uses only orchestral music, you could "spend" your storage on high-quality orchestral samples and not waste space on high-tech synthesizer sounds that you don't need at all. On the other hand, if your tracks lean toward techno, you may want to delete a standard accordian patch and replace it with Minimoog.

As they have done with stand-alone synthesizers, major MIDI software developers will create editor/librarians for designing custom sounds. Ideally, they may also enhance their sequencing applications to save files as music tracks directly into a QuickTime movie, and to extract music tracks from movies for additional editing. Along these lines, QuickTime 2.2 supports drag-and-drop so that users can easily move files within music tracks.

Another significant feature in QuickTime 2.2 is the ability to store instrument sounds within movie files. Once you have created custom sounds, you can distribute them with your movie so that the music track plays exactly as you intended, rather than playing a different instrument sound that happens to be available in the user's machine. Other new features include support for 16/44 Music Track output on Power Macs and the ability to render to file—converting the data in a music track so that it can be saved as a 16/44 AIFF file. For the latest information on QTMA, check out Apple's QuickTime web site at http://quicktime.apple.com.

CyberSound VS

Given the new opportunities for QuickTime audio, third-party software-based synthesizers will become increasingly popular. At this point, CyberSound VS is the only game in town. InVision Interactive will ship a QuickTime driver for CyberSound VS to make configuration easier.

One major issue for developers regarding CyberSound VS is distribution. In order for people to hear the better quality of CyberSound, they'll need to have the software. The manufacturer, InVision, says it's committed to working out a licensing strategy so that its synthesis engine (perhaps a run-time version) can be shipped with titles. In an ideal world, InVision will eventually open its editing architecture so that composers and developers can create custom sound sets for different presentations.

SoundFonts

If it's synthesis editing capability you're after, you should investigate Emu's SoundFont technology. SoundFonts are a combination of sampled audio data and a set of synthesis parameters that control the articulation of that sample. The parameters you can control include most of the standard functions found in synthesizers—frequency cutoff, resonance, LFO speed and depth, reverb depth, and chorus amount, as well as attack, decay, sustain, and release for two different envelopes (one is amplitude, the other can control filtering and pitch). You can change these settings in real time using MIDI control values for non-registered parameters (98 for LSB, 99 for MSB) and data entry (controller 38). By changing effects over time, you can make reverb depth increase on footstep sounds as a player enters a cave, for example, or make the brightness of a sound change with distance. A great advantage of SoundFonts is their ability to work on both sample data and the ROM samples on a wavetable synthesizer. The main drawback to SoundFonts is that they're currently available on only one sound card: Creative Labs' AWE32. Considering that the sound card market probably doesn't have a long life span, it doesn't look too good for SoundFonts. But if Creative Labs can port their technology to software (and continue supplying digital-to-analog converters for PC motherboards), then SoundFonts may eventually find their way into the mainstream. Their availability would give every composer tremendous flexibility to reconfigure synthesizer patches to fit particular styles or arrangements.

SeerSynth

SeerSynth, a virtual software synthesizer created by Stanley Jungleib of Seer Systems, was discussed briefly in Chapter 3. Although an earlier incarnation of SeerSynth shipped on several Turtle Beach audio products, it hasn't captured a large share of the market yet due to the economics of relatively inexpensive sound cards versus more expensive CPUs and RAM requirements. But it may be poised to dominate the market by the end of 1996.

Object-Oriented Audio

As object-based authoring tools like mFactory's mTropolis, the Apple Media Tool, and Apple's ScriptX become a greater force in the marketplace, you can expect to see object-oriented audio become more viable. The issue of object-oriented audio forces us to address and resolve the dilemma of linear media (music) versus random access interactivity. One approach is modular, composing blocks of audio that can be arranged in any number of ways. Todd Rundgren's "No World Order" is a great example of an early effort in this direction. (An interview with Todd Rundgren appears later in this chapter.) Another approach is to modify or modulate data streams on the fly. Potentially, the flexibility of MIDI can help in this situation, with MIDI data being filtered so that it changes in response to the current situation.

Another interesting solution promises for interactive audio to be AVRe (pronounced "aviary"), an object-oriented music engine under development from Thomas Dolby's sound design company, Headspace. (See the interview with Thomas Dolby in Chapter 8.) Originally demonstrated with mTropolis, it appears that the goal of AVRe is to provide a toolkit for interactive composition, in which various musical themes and motifs could be attached to different "actors" (that is, to code objects and their associated media and behaviors). One could also imagine scenarios in which musical attributes such as tempo, loudness, density, or pitch range could also be varied according to the circumstances.

INTERVIEW: TODD RUNDGREN

For more than 20 years, Todd Rundgren has remained at the forefront of music and technology. In addition to his musical pursuits, he has programmed computer applications, produced videos for RCA from his own video studio, held interactive concerts broadcast over TV and radio with satellite hookups, and created the first interactive record, "No World Order", which lets listeners build their own songs. To top his string of firsts, at the end of 1995 he released The Individualist, *the first official Enhanced CD recording using the stamped multisession format. Rundgren also hosts his own Music In(tr)Action Forum on CompuServe (GO IMUSIC).*

How did you get involved in using computers with music?

I always had a technical bent as a kid. I was always disassembling things and reassembling and modifying to suit an extended vision of what they were supposed to be. I have this fixation to apply technology to some fantastic other end, functional or not—always designing robots and rocket ships. I'm not atypical in that sense, but when I got into my high school years, I started hanging out in the local Bell Telephone billing office. Phone companies were a public utility, so you could just walk into the office where they did the data processing, and I used to go in there and just watch what was going on. And I learned early on the basic concepts of computing—"and" gates and "or" gates, which later served me well when I was learning computer programming. But I was also interested in music at the time. When the choice came to go back to school and become a computer programmer or get in a band, the choice seemed obvious—I went into music.

   Becoming a musician gave me lots of latitude later in life; I had a lot of control over my own time, and eventually I developed the financial stability to buy a computer and take a year off to learn programming hands-on. It was something that just got put on hold for a while. It was something that always interested me; the opportunity simply wasn't there until personal computers appeared.

Had you been thinking about musical applications of computers for a long time?

No, I kept up an invisible wall between the work I do with computers (principally graphics) and the work I was doing with music. Even in the case where you use synthesizers, I rarely even used sequencers. Then I realized that this division of my interests was artificial, and that there might be a way that I could merge them into something that wasn't the typical application of computers—something that

TODD RUNDGREN *(continued)*

wasn't creating another sequencer or some hardware devices with MIDI. Most musical tools were software versions of MIDI functions. And I wanted to alter the *experience* of music, not just the way of making it. So I got this interactive music idea. And it turned out to be one of the few times in my life that one of my crackpot ideas had some synchronicity with the way the culture was moving as well. Even though the story of interactive music is still unfolding—what it will be like and how everyone will experience it—everyone accepts that it will *be*. It is something that will happen in one form or another.

There is a debate between those who feel that music is something audiences want to interact with, and those who say that people want to be entertained as passive listeners rather than having to make selective choices about it.

There is always a segment of the audience that will prefer one extreme. Some people will not consider any entertainment option that doesn't include interactivity. Other people, ideologically or out of fear, may just not want to get involved in those issues. But most people already exist in some middle ground where there is some degree of interaction in what they do.

You can certainly say that when you always switch between the same four radio stations, you are crafting for yourself a personal musical experience based on limited available input. If you take a bunch of your favorite records to have a party or go on a trip, and you excerpt the parts of the music you like and build a personal album on a cassette tape, it's an interactive musical experience—just not in real time. You can't make a snap decision and have it happen.

Real time is what computers are supposed to add to the mix. You can make your decisions extemporaneously and have very tight feedback. Interactivity is not something that appeared out of nowhere; it's just that we've crossed certain threshholds, sort of like still pictures versus movies. At a certain point, you start moving those pictures past fast enough, and it's a movie, not a still picture anymore. Interactivity isn't separate from normal day to day human interactions; it's just that we've crossed a time threshhold. The gap between the time you ask for something and the time you get it keeps getting narrower and narrower until suddenly, you're less conscious of that gap.

People are already interacting. As for the opportunity to interact, people will take advantage of it to a greater or lesser degree. Interactivity does not remove the possibility of having a noninteractive experience. Most interactive experiences are drawn from material that was not originally interactive, but which has other undiscovered

TODD RUNDGREN *(continued)*

aspects that expand your consciousness when experienced in an interactive environment. It's the same thing as people who collect outtakes of the Beatles' *Sergeant Pepper* album. They don't want *Sergeant Pepper* to be any different, but they do want additional parts of the experience.

As part of this process of drawing an audience in, interactivity changes the nature of the relationship between the performer and the audience.

To some degree, it can make the relationship more intimate. Just because an artist doesn't allow you to screw around with his or her music doesn't mean that you are incapable of forming some form of intimate relationship through the music to what the artist is saying. But the artists themselves often don't know exactly what they are trying to accomplish, and art in general is driven by commercial demands. People are willing to change what they do to satisfy those commercial demands. That relationship is bound to change if audiences decide that they are enjoying themselves. Then commercial artists will say, "If that's what you want, I'm certainly going to give it to you."

At the same time, interactivity also creates an opportunity for someone who has a more classical or philosophical attitude about art, one that isn't necessarily connected to commercial success. All these technologies allow people to escape from some of the rigid structures that popular music imposes on people. Songs are four minutes long because that's what the radio wants to play. Albums are essentially based on this evolutionary form. No one ever stood back and said, "Let's rewrite the rules." They are based on this evolutionary form and were limited by some physical factor (how much wax was on the cylinder, and so forth) that made it impossible to record a complete symphony. A whole genre of music evolved that was tailored to fit into that presentation size.

Even though we have removed those physical limitations, everyone continues to think in the conventional terms. If you can destroy that structure, you can give artists who feel cramped by it greater freedom to express themselves in greater or lesser chunks of music, or on different levels—that sort of archiving thing that recordings do—a crystalization of the performance. More people hear recordings than any other interpretation of the performance you give, and so they measure you according to that version of the performance the rest of your life. With the concept of interactive music, you can bring back the idea that music is a dynamic form, that music changes. Until we had recorded music, that's what it was. It did not stay the same all the time.

TODD RUNDGREN *(continued)*

Since we developed the ability to record audio, we've had a 70-year gap in the organic life of music. It's as though you poured liquid nitrogen over everything and things just came to a stop. Now, there's a possiblity that popular culture will rediscover the fact that music is a dynamic form, not dependent on some artist's two- to five-year project of 15 pop songs. And in a sense the artists don't even trust the music enough, so at the concert you have to have all these giant, 80-foot-tall images of yourself that actually detract from the music. People don't even have enough confidence in that form anymore.

Because music is being preserved rather than evolving, we're starting to discover that there are an awful lot of similarities musically, and people are imitating each other a lot. These essentially recurring motifs are something that you can't remove from the process. And the problem is that the more we lionize a particular performance of that motif, the more likely it is to be directly imitated rather than radically reinterpreted. To my mind, interactivity—particularly as we go on-line—will bring back the idea that music is constantly subject to reinterpretation.

Do you have an interactive component for The Individualist tour?

Not currently. As the tour evolves, there are things I could do, but not to the level of the last interactive show where everything was interactive to an extent, where the music was reconfigured in real time, and where the audience had the options of where they wanted to view it from and to what degree they wanted to participate in the show. That show was different every night.

That's a hard thing to take on the road, and that's why I'm not doing it now. There are just endless venues you can't get into. We figured what we are doing in part is promotion of the new music, as well as exposition of it. Now we're just proving something here. It will be tough enough just to pull it off. And *No World Order* (the previous interactive tour) was also done to prove something. It's still there, and we can take it out of mothballs and take it on the road again. The problem we discovered is that we were limited in the venues we could take it to because of the configuration of it. A lot of places cannot support the weight of the set and the audience all in the center of the floor. So venues have to be specially built in order to have the ideal interactive performances, and that may happen; the concepts there are really applicable. Interactivity would also be much more effective in an environment where you have a little more control, where a maintenance crew comes in every day, tweaking, making sure that everything's working.

TODD RUNDGREN *(continued)*

Tell us about the experience of producing an Enhanced CD title, and what differences you ran into producing it.

The other titles that I've done are principally music-oriented, basically a listening experience. Now we're giving it another vector where there is an accompanying visual experience and an interactive experience that don't have anything directly to do with the music that's on there. And in that sense, the experience has been an opportunity to evaluate other technologies. For instance, I've learned to be a Director programmer in the last few months. You can get used to anything. I learned how to use the Apple Media Tool and actually produced a title in only three weeks. But we only used the bottom-line capabilities of it. So in that sense I was already prepped. I knew the concepts and even though it was another kind of interface, another way of addressing it, it was at least sufficiently simple that the most difficult thing was keeping the concept straightforward.

How were you using audio in Director, and what kinds of compromises were forced on you?

You're probably talking about sampled audio that would be in some relatively low-resolution format, and we haven't done any of that. The Enhanced CD project uses only RedBook audio, except in the part that uses QuickTime movies. So synchronizing the sound or trying to reproduce it with sufficient quality is not our problem, at least not on this particular title. In our interactive music titles we manage sound compression and cueing and everything at a relatively low level. We don't use any authoring tools, mainly because we have to have 100 percent control of the resources of the machine in order to create a seamless presentation.

Director is a "polite" application in the sense that other things in the machine's environment can interrupt it and cause its timing to be off. We have a completely different attitude. We are entertainers. We are not required to be polite to anybody in the course of presenting our entertainment. If you want our entertainment you will get it, and if you want something else, then go get that; but don't ask us to play while you eat dinner! If you are going to run some process, we will not compete with it to give you a seamless presentation. We take over the entire resources of the machine. If what we had to do didn't take up the entire resources of the machine, we would think up something that would take up the rest of the machine. It's more of a game machine attitude. To tell the truth, I have a greater leaning toward entertainment titles; the game machines are more practical for that kind of implementation than computers are. Computers require you to sit in an office chair while you

TODD RUNDGREN *(continued)*

watch a movie or listen to a record, and people really want to lounge around on the couch while they are being entertained. So until that dichotomy is adequately addressed, I'll continue to think that people are mostly listening to my records in places other than the office two feet away from a computer screen. Having said that, the computer is an ideal way to define what you'd like to have happen in terms of the experience, because you have greater flexibility in terms of what can be implemented.

What's on your wish list for the next few years?

This on-line thing is really where it's at and I think everybody knows that. And the things that are necessary to make that happen are things that are really being dealt with. My wish list at this point is not so much technical as attempting to create clear choices for people in terms of what kind of content they can get under a particular categorization.

My biggest problem right now is that the term "interactive music" is used pretty loosely for things that don't redefine the musical experience—things that just tell you more things about the artist. While a lot of people have a technical wish list, the hardest part is sociological, cultural, market-oriented stuff where all of that connectivity is for naught, because we are unable to change the rules of the game, the rules of engagement between creators of art and audiences. If it simply becomes the equivalent of Blockbuster or Tower Records in your home, without any movement toward redefining the experience of music (or the experience of making music as well, because I have expectations as an artist), none of that will matter. So my whole crusade at this point is really to get everyone's expectations as realistically high as possible, so that if someone tries to pull a low-ball move and corner the market, they will be justifiably embarrassed. Essentially someone tries to impose an inferior standard on everyone because they can, and this is the biggest problem.

My solution to that problem is to keep everyone's expectations realistically high, so that inferior implementations will not gain hold and so that we can all benefit from the best that this industry has to offer.

Size and Speed

Faster, faster, faster! The never-ending climb toward putting the equivalent of a Cray supercomputer on every desktop shows absolutely no sign of slowing down. It's a good thing, too, since there's never a problem figuring out how to use the extra horsepower. I don't know about you, but I find that every increase in speed satisfies me for about a week. Then I start wishing that progress bar would move just a *little* bit faster. Each boost just serves to raise expectations for even better performance.

We know that digital audio can be a real roadhog when it comes to commandeering system resources. Files consume tremendous amounts of disk storage. High-fidelity compressed audio puts an additional load on a processor when decompression takes place on the fly. And synthesis in software can really tie up the CPU if you use many voices and real-time processing with reverb or chorus effects. To top it all off, many digital audio editors and processors that require dedicated DSP hardware are being redesigned to work without hardware DSPs—redesigned to do all the work in software. This wasn't really feasible a year ago, but it will be commonplace a year from now.

Size and speed will continue to increase in several different categories: CPU speed, network speed, and storage speed. By the end of 1996 we may see processors running at well over 200 MHz. This means more horse-power for demanding audio-processing applications, multi-track playback and mixing, and real-time manipulation of audio data. The main bottleneck for audio content creators, however, will continue to be the base platform in the consumer market. Thankfully, by the end of 1996 it will be safe to assume that consumers will be purchasing PowerPC and Pentium processors, making high-quality audio more feasible.

Not only will we be able to play more complex audio; we'll also be able to move it around faster. Network data transfer capabilities are likely to see huge speed gains if cable modems become available. This technology will make it possible to download data more than 100 times faster than existing 28.8 kbps modems. Data can't be uploaded at nearly the same rates, however, so it's likely that cable modems will facilitate the consumption of content more than the sharing of content. This may not be the best technology to use for sending massive audio files to other locations, but it will be a great way for people to download big audio files.

Disk storage capabilities and playback speeds will also continue to increase. In 1997 we can hope to see the introduction of the first Digital Video Disks (DVD), based on a standard recently set by Sony, Phillips, and

Matsushita. DVD promises to hold over 4 gigabytes of digital video data on a double-sided recordable disk. To what extent this technology can be applied exclusively to audio remains to be seen, but this amount of recordable storage will certainly be helpful when dealing with large, multitrack audio files.

Faster transfer protocols (like FireWire) and more affordable RAID systems will make working with large multi-track audio files faster and easier. For many uses, 8-track digital recording will become more feasible with a computer than with a Modular Digital Multitrack (MDM) like the Alesis ADAT or Tascam DA88.

Speaking of large audio files, you may recall that one minute of mono 16/44 audio requires more than 5 MB of disk storage. One of the topics currently being bandied about by high-end digital recording experts is the need for 24-bit audio rather than 16-bit audio. Processing a 16-bit file requires that the sample data be converted up to 24 bits (for greater precision) and then converted back to 16 bits after the operation is complete. Dithering is usually applied to the file as it's converted back to 16 bits, so if you process a file too many times, the dither noise will begin to become noticeable. Moving the standard sample rate up to 24 bits will help to alleviate this problem. For final delivery, 16-bit sound will continue to be sufficient. For processing and editing, however, it's likely that professional-grade audio editors will move to a standard of 24-bit support. Looks like we just found another way to swamp whatever performance gains we might be seeing from CPUs in the next year!

Internet Distribution

Of all the new technologies coming in 1996, the hardest ones to predict are those associated with the Internet and the World Wide Web. On-line was the hot new medium of 1995, and at the time of this writing, the growth of the on-line community shows absolutely no sign of slowing down. This is one fast-moving target!

In 1995, a wave of new tools were introduced to allow the integration of multimedia content into Web pages. Netscape Navigator continues to dominate as the web browser of choice and is well-positioned to offer the most multimedia-rich environment. Navigator now incorporates Sun Microsystems' Java technology, with "applets" that can be launched from within Web documents. With Java, the Web becomes more than just browsing through text and graphics. It becomes a gigantic, dynamic multimedia environment. One of the current bottlenecks for people wanting to use Java is the level of programming knowledge required to make it a useful tool for creating applets.

To facilitate the creation of multimedia content for the Web, Macromedia has released Shockwave, a player for Director documents embedded into Web pages. Like Java, the Shockwave playback engine is incorporated into Netscape Navigator, so that users can simply click on a button to launch an interactive Director movie. The great thing about Shockwave for multimedia developers is that it allows them to draw from existing content, and it leverages off a well-established pool of creative and programming talent.

Of course, the *real* story for audio on the Internet is real-time playback of sound, using technologies like RealAudio from Progressive Networks and IWave from VocalTec. These methods rely on heavy data compression, and the result is fidelity that approaches 8-bit 11 kHz. RealAudio's newest version (2.0) is designed to deliver FM quality through 28.8 modems (frankly, I found it a bit less stellar on my system, but it's certainly a step up from the previous version). Real-time delivery of audio across the Net is likely to have far-reaching implications. Real-time "phone" conversations using the Net may change the business model for traditional telephone companies. High-quality speed compression algorithms like VoxWare (from VoxWare in Princeton, New Jersey) will also make speech more feasible across the Net. VoxWare can achieve 50:1 compression levels. In this scenario, radio stations will have to compete with on-line "broadcasters." In fact, one Web site, IRock, has been granted broadcast licenses from ASCAP and BMI, the two major music publishing organizations that oversee music use and distribution of royalties.

It's difficult to predict how well these new technologies will be received by consumers if they're forced to view and hear Web-based multimedia over 28.8 KB modems. It's to be hoped that the much higher speeds of cable modems will make Web browsing a real-time interactive experience. Otherwise, the "click-and-wait" experience of CD-ROMs will look blindingly fast by comparison.

Enhanced CD

One of the biggest stories of 1995 was the advent of the first CD-ROM titles to combine multimedia content with traditional RedBook audio on CDs. A regular audio CD can contain up to 74 minutes of music. But few recordings actually last that long. The common length of conventional LPs was about 45 minutes. As audio CDs began to dominate the market, that length could technically be extended, but it's still uncommon to find discs with more than 50 minutes of audio. That still leaves roughly 200 MB of space for interactive (also called "YellowBook") data on the disc.

One of the main stumbling blocks to the creation of integrated CDs was combining different types of data on a CD and still having that disk behave like a regular audio CD. Record company executives aren't too eager to be dragged into the format battles and hardware configuration wars that continually rage in the software industry. From their perspective, they've had a pretty good deal. With audio CD and cassette titles playable on standardized equipment, they haven't had to worry about users having the right operating systems or enough RAM. They don't need a technical support staff to tell people how to connect all the cables on a stereo system. Enhanced CD has the potential to drag record companies into the dark pit of techno-configuration insanity. So a basic rule for Enhanced CDs is that they need to look and respond exactly like a regular audio CD when placed in an audio CD player. They also need to be very easy to configure and use when played from the CD-ROM drive of a computer.

The first-generation approach toward this new generation of disc is often called *mixed-mode,* since it combines YellowBook and RedBook data on the same disk. The downside of mixed-mode discs is that the YellowBook data needs to be placed on the first track in order for the computer to find it. The common industry name for this phenomenon is "the Track One problem." When a mixed-mode disc is placed in a regular audio CD player, the user has to manually skip the first track— otherwise, a wail of digital noise may come streaming from the speakers. (If you've ever wondered what a PICT file sounds like, this is your big chance!)

A second-generation attempt to integrate audio CD data with multimedia content, called the *pre-gap* solution, was introduced on several major Enhanced CD releases in 1995. This approach relies on the fact that small regions of data encoded onto regular audio CDs are always read before the actual audio data starts. These regions usually include program numbers that appear on the display of a CD player and the silence that separates music tracks. Each region is bracketed by headers and footers, which tell the CD player that it is in a data area rather than an audio area. Since audio playback is disabled in each pre-gap region, it seemed an ideal place to hide multimedia data.

Using the pre-gap regions solves the Track One problem, but there are still some pitfalls. For example, it is still possible for someone to scan backward manually into the pregap data, resulting in the same speaker-destroying scenario as with mixed-mode disks. To avoid this, the industry came up with an ingenious solution—the equivalent of the reversed signs on the front of an ambulance that read correctly in a rear-view mirror. By recording a warning message and then reversing the recording, the warning is intelligible as the disc scans backward.

There's another major limitation to the pre-gap approach. Several competing proprietary technologies have appeared on the market, so there's no standard method for creating pre-gap discs. Most of the companies that have developed pre-gap solutions have chosen to keep the technology to themselves. You provide them with the audio and multimedia material and they deliver a finished disc back to you. This approach doesn't really lend itself to the establishment of a standard means of production.

A breakthrough came in mid-1995, when a new, standard format was defined by major players in the recording and software industry, including Sony, Philips, Apple, Microsoft, and the Recording Industry Association of America. The new standard for creating Enhanced CD titles using a *Stamped Multisession* technique has been dubbed the BlueBook format.

The BlueBook format uses *multisession-capable* CD-recording technology—the ability to write data to a disc in multiple sessions (recording passes) rather than all in one session. CD audio data is written on the inside tracks of the disc in one session, and multimedia data is written on the outside tracks of the disc in a second session. Since CDs read data from the inside toward the outside, the disc looks like a standard audio CD to an audio CD player. It reads through all the music data, and when it reaches the end of the RedBook audio portion it encounters a data "footer" that tells the CD player that there's no more audio on the disc. The CD player thinks it has reached the end of the disc and so never reads onward into the computer data. No Track One problem here!

BlueBook discs place a few additional requirements on the computer. You need a compatible driver so that your CD player can recognize multiple sessions on a single disk. When seen on the Macintosh desktop, multiple sessions look like separate volumes or partitions on a hard drive. The latest CD drivers from Apple can be found at http://quicktime.apple.com You also need a compatible CD-ROM player. All the double-speed (or faster) Apple drives fall into this category.

BlueBook discs also place new demands on multimedia developers. The standard bottlenecks inherent in CD-ROM delivery become even more complex when creating an Enhanced CD. Longer data retrieval times are a problem: the multimedia portion of the data is written on the outer tracks of the disc, resulting in slower access times as the CD drive head reads further out on the platter. Another potential bottleneck is the memory available on the end user's machine. Multimedia content must fit entirely into memory when songs are playing, because there's no way to read new multimedia data from the CD when you're in the RedBook audio portion of the disc (unless you're willing to interrupt the music). This limitation places a premium on using small images or reusing images in interesting ways.

A great example of how a real-world product works around potential BlueBook limitations is Todd Rundgren's *The Individualist*. The multimedia portion of the disc was created by ION, using Macromedia Director. Some pieces (the title track, for example) use 4-bit grayscale images to reduce memory requirements. The graphic design uses black and white to its best advantage. The CD also reuses images creatively in a style that is reminiscent of MacroMind's first visionary artist, Stuart Sharpe. For example, several copies of the same small graphics or animations can be displayed at the same time, each with a different ink effect, so that each copy has a unique appearance. As a third solution to the problem of getting the most mileage out of limited graphic material, the ION team created a custom XObject for Director that has powerful graphics handling capabilities, including the ability to scale, zoom, and pan across images. The XObject was used both for simple graphics and to create the *Doom*-like 3-D game environment seen in the track "Cast the First Stone."

As of this writing, several tools for creating BlueBook CDs are available, including Apple's Enhanced CD Toolkit and ION's CDoptION tool, created in conjunction with Macromedia. To succeed in the marketplace, the Enhanced CD format must bridge the gap between the software industry and the music recording industry. Each of these industries has developed product development cycles and distribution schemes that work for their particular media. But although there are similarities in the types of content they produce and the audiences they serve, there are many differences to be resolved. To get a better perspective on this topic, we asked two experts, Norman Beil and Ty Roberts, to share their experiences and ideas.

If the Enhanced CD format takes hold in the marketplace, the volume of work will swamp the current development community, creating many new opportunities for multimedia developers. But as we've seen, the medium has many performance limitations; it's an add-on to an audio CD rather than a standard CD-ROM title as we've come to know it. Some multimedia producers may find this too limiting. But it's certain to create a new class of creative artists who are looking for innovative ways to combine visuals and music.

Three-Dimensional Sound

Although 3-D sound technology has been around for quite a long time, it has been available for playback on desktop computers for only a few years. Currently, there are four main solutions for creating 3-D sound: QSound, CRE's Protron, the RSS10 processor from Roland Corporation, and Spatializer.

How does 3-D sound work? There are several competing technologies currently on the market, but they all derive from the same basic models. These models are based on the work of researchers who placed very small, very sensitive microphones into people's ear canals and measured the changing character of sounds from different directions.

Humans determine the location of a sound in three-dimensional space based on a number of cues. One cue is the subtle differences in the volume of a sound as it reaches one ear rather than the other. Obviously, a sound that occurs directly to your left will be loudest in your left ear, while the right ear will hear mostly sound that has been reflected from other surfaces. Another cue is slight changes in timing between sound that enters the ear canal directly and sounds that are reflected into the ear. In fact, the shape of your ear and its ridges help you determine whether a sound has originated from behind or in front of you: the timing of the sound is slightly different depending on which part of your ear has reflected the sound into your ear canal. Finally, there are also frequency differences when a sound hits each ear, because your head itself casts a "sound shadow" on the ear farthest from the source. This ear picks up sounds that have been reflected from other surfaces such as walls, floors, or ceilings. The frequency content of reflected sounds changes, based on the material of the reflective surface, in the same way that singing in the shower (where tiles reflect most of the high frequencies) sounds different from singing in a theater (where upholstery and clothed patrons soak up more of the high frequencies).

There are two primary approaches to delivering 3-D sound. The first uses special hardware to create the spatialization effects during the recording and mixing process. The result is mixed to a stereo file that can be played back on any stereo system. The second approach is to rely on either a dedicated DSP or a powerful CPU to generate 3-D audio effects in real time. This second method is far more flexible, since the sound can be altered in direct response to user input, rather than simply playing prerecorded content.

For cross-platform developers, one of the main limitations to offering 3-D sound is bandwidth. Many products ship with mono sound, but 3-D sound requires stereo. If your product uses two separate audio tracks (one for effects and the other for music, for example), you could be tying up four playback channels. Even at 8/22 rates (or 16/44 with 4:1 compression), you're looking at 88 KB per second, or more than half the practical bandwidth on a double-speed CD-ROM. The primary appeal of 3-D sound is in gaming. Microsoft's new DirectSound technology is built to support 3-D audio in software.

Although increased CPU horsepower will help pump more audio data through the system, it's doubtful that many developers will dedicate that much bandwidth to audio (unless, of course, they're creating a product in which audio has priority, like Laurie Anderson's *Puppet Motel)*. We all hope that this state of affairs will change in 1996, but be prepared to hunker down until 1997.

Interactive Performance

The potential for interactive performance, and the integration of multimedia technology into performance, are likely to continue developing over the next few years. Many music performances—including the hardly-new medium of opera—already take on aspects of graphics and visuals associated with theater. But multimedia technology may be a way to create interesting links between performers and audiences.

Summary

Audio tools and technologies have been improving in synch with the phenomenal growth of the multimedia industry over the past five years. Digital recording studios have been reduced to the size of a Macintosh PowerBook, and anyone with a modem can start their own radio station on the Internet. If past experience is any indication, the rate of change is likely to continue accelerating into the next millenium. New markets will open as computer-savvy children grow up to become computer-savvy consumers. New methods of distribution will appear through the Internet and interactive TV. And multimedia is likely to develop into new forms of creative expression as our current limitations and bottlenecks are eliminated.

It's impossible (if not foolhardy) to predict the state of our medium a mere ten years from now. The computers of tomorrow will probably make our most powerful systems seem as high-tech as an Etch-a-Sketch. But as much as the tools and technologies will continue to change, at least one thing will stay the same: there will always be a need for people who can master the tools and create compelling works of art and music.

INTERVIEW: NORMAN BEIL

Norman Beil is one of the pioneers of the so-called "Enhanced CD" (he even coined the phrase in a Billboard article) and claims to be the first music executive to lose money for his company with this evolving format. As the former Vice President of Business Affairs at Geffen Records, he approaches new technology from a managerial perspective and has been advocating a radically different approach. He's also the creator of VidGrid, *an engaging CD-ROM puzzle game that features scrambled music videos by Van Halen, Soundgarden, Aerosmith, Peter Gabriel, and other major recording artists. During the past year, he has been working as a consultant for Microsoft on their development of Enhanced CD titles and Enhanced CD specifications.*

How will Enhanced CD affect record companies who are used to plug-and-play technology?

Enhanced CD titles must be plug-and-play, or else you can forget about them. Listening to music is supposed to be relaxing. Consumers won't put up with technical problems. And the music industry doesn't know jack about technical support. Record company margins can't accommodate the costs of providing technical support. Music retailers can't deal with it and won't carry the product if there are too many returns.

What's been frustrating for me is that I keep hearing *Enhanced CD* proponents recite the "plug-and-play" mantra, but they're not doing anything about it. The good news is that there is a solution. It has to do with the basic architecture of *Enhanced CD*. So far, everyone has just assumed that *Enhanced CD* means using the extra space on a CD to create a mini-multimedia show: hire a multimedia developer for each title and have him design and code an interface for that artist's content. This approach just has to result in coding errors, consumer installation headaches, and interface confusion problems. Think about it: for every individual music album, some software program has to be installed on the user's computer. And each one uses a different way to find lyrics, play a video, you name it. You couldn't make things tougher for the consumers if you tried.

The approach I've been advocating is to have the labels put just the raw data on the disc: the lyrics, the liner notes, the music, the videos, photos—stuff that record labels already own and can drop onto a disc with no incremental costs. This makes it real cheap and easy to make these titles. No interface, no coding.

The interface that reads this content is a separate product and is developed, published, and supported by third parties. Consumers could buy just one program that

NORMAN BEIL *(continued)*

can read every CD that the record industry releases. Use of a label's data could be protected by encryption and licensed for use with a particular interface program.

Once such an *Enhanced CD* player applet is installed successfully, it will run every *Enhanced CD* flawlessly. Once the consumer learns how to access lyrics on one *Enhanced CD*, he knows how to access lyrics on every title.

Getting philosophical for a moment, the entire economic world works on this same basic concept of separating content from interface. Look around. Your water company delivers "raw" water to your home cheaply and reliably. Third-party developers provide the human interface of heating it, filtering it, timing it for lawn sprinklers, and so on. It's the only way it can possibly work. I don't understand why the new media executives at the labels just don't get this basic concept. I just picked up the book *Being Digital* (by Nicholas Negroponte). One paragraph sums up the concept: in the future, for example, the weather report is delivered as raw data to the home. The interface for viewing that data would be the choice of the individual homeowners. One person could be looking at a map, whereas the next would be looking at a chart, or a cartoon, or a robotic human.

Maximum efficiency and progress can be achieved only when content is separated from the human interface and each is allowed to develop on its own.

You're talking about the equivalent of browsers for the World Wide Web. It seems that so much of the work in multimedia titles comes in the design of the interactivity, in the way that you can create the experience for the user.

That's the chief criticism I've been hearing: a standard "browser" will not give the artist enough creative control. Putting aside the creative debate for just a moment, there just won't be this creative outlet for the artist unless the business problems are solved. And the business problems of creating mini-multimedia shows for every album release are legion. I already mentioned technical support. The production cost of $50,000 to $100,000 per title is prohibitive for the labels. There's not enough shelf space at retail to add a new SKU. A real biggie is how much more time-sensitive release schedules are in the music business compared to the software business, where most release dates slip as the product is being refined and debugged. This can't work in the music business, where the release of an album has to be timed precisely with release of the single to radio, the MTV video, the appearance on Letterman, the cover of Rolling Stone, the tour, etcetera, etcetera. The first time a record label president is told that a ship date on a big release was missed because the multimedia show wasn't ready, heads will roll.

NORMAN BEIL *(continued)*

I also don't buy into the current blather that multimedia creativity is all about interface design. And consumers seem to agree with me. If you look at what's selling, it's not the "click and watch" multimedia software. Macromedia Director and similar tools that are being used for these titles were designed to create kiosks and sales presentations, not consumer titles. Who thinks it's fun to have to hunt for the "backstage pass" before you can watch the video? If kids want to play a game, they'll play a real game like Doom or Rebel Assault. If they want to watch a video, they just want to watch a video. The creativity is in the content, not in how you navigate through the content.

People listen to the same album for decades. Computer software gets old in months. I don't get what is so creative about marrying the two. It seems to be a formula for disaster for an artist to tie his classic music to an interface design that will look dated to his fans before the next tour. What's exciting about developing the interfaces separately is that they can be updated over time and use the content from previously released albums in new and more creative ways.

I love your Web browser analogy. When *Enhanced CD* was in its infancy, so was the World Wide Web. One has languished while the other has taken off wildly. Why? The architecture. Do you remember that before the Web, there were all these bulletin boards you could call for different sorts of information? Each bulletin board had its own interface, its own protocols, its own programming. It was hard for the information providers to set up bulletin boards, and it was hard for the user to install and learn different software for each BBS. The on-line information business did not happen until the browser architecture made it easy for information providers to create web sites and for information users to access them. This is what I've been saying all along.

What ideas do you have about hardware delivery of Enhanced CD titles?

If you build a *Enhanced CD* title complete with interface and coding, you have to build it for a specific platform. So you are generally limited to the personal computer. By separating the content from the interface and putting the content in some standard file structure, you can build interfaces for a multitude of hardware platforms, including game machines and platforms that haven't even been invented yet. At my urging, Sony, Phillips, Apple, and Microsoft extended the specification for *stamped multisession* (called BlueBook) to include a standard format and set of addresses for certain types of data. This will allow audio CD hardware manufacturers to inexpensively add a chip that can read this data. You won't need a computer to see a

NORMAN BEIL *(continued)*

video or read lyrics; you'll just need a video out port on an "enhanced" audio CD player. The hardware manufacturers are excited about this possibility, especially for the new DVD players.

If, how, and when computers, stereo systems, video players and game machines will converge is hard to predict. But recording artists can be assured that the *Enhanced CD* titles they release today will be technologically obsolete tomorrow unless they use a standard data specification.

What about on-line distribution of audio? How might that different distribution scheme affect the current record industry?

Well, remember, I'm the guy who did it first. We released a full-length Aerosmith single on CompuServe, in full 16-bit, 44.1 kHz stereo—the same specs as an audio CD. We compressed it, so I can't really say it was true CD quality. It took the average guy with a 14.4 modem about 40 minutes to download and ate up about 50 MB on his hard drive—so the total cost to the end user was about $20 and the artist and the label didn't get a dime. We got a ton of publicity, but not many downloads. So you can see we are far away from online distribution becoming a threat to retailers.

Is that just because of bandwidth and data rates?

Bandwidth is only part of the problem.

I commissioned a Harvard Business School study on this. There are two basic models. One is the "virtual jukebox," where you download and listen to whatever you want at the time and there is no in-home storage. The other model is having the album delivered to your in-home storage device.

With the virtual jukebox, you need incredibly huge bandwidth. You need fiber to the home. Plus, you need super servers that cost thousands of dollars per home. There's no economic incentive for anyone to spend that kind of money. It could never be recouped at the $2 per hour consumers are willing to spend for in-home entertainment. The real money for interactive television is in home shopping for higher-end merchandise—cubic zirconium rings, for example—and this can be accomplished with a simple "BUY" button on your remote control. After that technology is in place, you'll stop hearing talk about video and audio on demand.

The other model, storage in the home, is very expensive for the consumer. The raw cost of stamped CDs is pennies. Recordable CDs are about $10. Again, the economics are just not there. So I don't see it happening for a long time.

NORMAN BEIL *(continued)*

Bands are excited about Web sites like the Internet Underground Music Archive (IUMA), where people can completely bypass the established recording industry and distribute their products directly to the consumers. Do you have any feedback to a guerrila approach of people getting their music on-line?

I can see a market building up where a record label could be a Web site, with sound samples, and you learn about the band, or talk to other people on the site with you. And then you order a CD the traditional way, after you've heard the samples.

When the bottleneck of distribution is eliminated and suppliers go directly to the consumers, the consumers will have an incredibly wide choice of products. How are they going to filter it? Brand names, such as the major record labels, may take on increased importance.

What about the actual delivery of music as a finished product over the Web?

That's not going to happen, but why can't it be a promotional tool? Someone comes out with WebSite Records, signs a few bands, kids listen to it. Some will be very successful. There have always been the independent labels that figure out a niche and can make a buck on it. Why not through the Internet? If someone can sell a few thousand records, that may be enough to get things going. Then a label like Geffen comes along that says, "Hey, this WebSite Record label has had three hits. Let's either sign those bands or let's buy the independent."

The established record labels will still play an important role. Their brand names can help consumers sort through the barrage. Their ability to get on radio and MTV will still be important. They can finance expensive recording projects. They can help artists creatively. And they can support bands financially in their early years.

Where do you think the Enhanced CD format will be in five years? How many years will the format exist before it gets supplanted by something else?

We're already seeing the demise of *Enhanced CD* using the mini-multimedia show concept. Label heads are getting fed up with how much trouble this has been and how abysmal sales have been. But out of these ashes will come the "browser" approach to this technology. When the labels and the artists start sticking to what they do best—creating content—and let the hardware manufacturers and software developers come up with innovative and evolving ways to get at that content, you'll see some exciting developments. Three or four years from now, all the titles will be *Enhanced CD* **Interview: Liz Heller**

INTERVIEW: TY ROBERTS

Ty Roberts is one of the co-founders of ION, a CD-ROM production and publishing company that focuses on music products. ION's titles include Jump Interactive *(David Bowie),* Gingerbread Man *(The Residents),* Headcandy *(Brian Eno),* The Individualist *(Todd Rundgren), and* Tales From the Punchbowl *(Primus). ION is a central player in the Enhanced CD development effort and helped to create the BlueBook standard for stamped multisession discs.*

What are the major roadblocks and limitations in adding multimedia to audio CD products? How have you had to work around these problems?

The major limitations involve defining the goal of an Enhanced CD disc, and that goal has a couple of different fronts. The first is informational, the second is actual entertainment, and the third is to convey music. The first goal, the informational part, is very good. Computers are good at distributing information, putting nice graphics up on the screen, outputting data, and showing text. The third one, playing music, is also very easy and CDs do an excellent job. You get good-quality music from a CD, it's easy to use, you plug it into a computer and it works.

The problem is really the one in the middle: providing actual entertainment, particularly providing entertainment that's not in short little dribs and drabs. Most computers have a tendency to load a bunch of data into memory for a really long time and then give you a really short burst of actual entertainment. But it's tough to stretch it out more, to give you something that's more like a record. With a record, the overall experience is entertaining for 40 minutes.

To provide 40 minutes of actual entertainment on an Enhanced CD disc is an amazing feat. That 's really the toughest thing. When we try to do that, we're trying to figure out how we can provide entertainment that is somehow drawing you into or relating to the musical experience, because that's the concept behind a record. I can provide 40 minutes of *Doom*-like entertainment for anyone, because *Doom* is a very entertaining thing, but it probably doesn't work very well with any music except the music of a few bands (I will not mention any bands that *Doom* may be perfect for). Most bands have a storytelling style of music that's not *Doom*-related. How do you provide entertainment for that?

I believe we have actually managed to achieve "coolness" for nearly the length of a song—about four minutes right now. I hope that we can improve on that and build to the point of entertaining continuously, without big gaps when the computer

TY ROBERTS *(continued)*

loads a bunch of stuff. When quad-speed CD is the standard, the outlook will be a lot better.

One concept I've been exploring with people is that it seems as though the nature of being a musician is evolving to the point that we're now becoming hackers.

That's right. Technology has changed and has put more control in the hands of the musicians. That's overwhelming to some musicians, but it's empowering to musicians who can adapt and deal with it. The thing that has really changed in the last five years is that the recording studio has changed from something you had to do in a big, expensive room to something that can happen on the desktop.

Luckily, a combination of two things occurred just in that realm—the listeners evolved in two different directions from the types of music they were listening to previously. The type of music kids were listening to has changed dramatically. It used to be that the way to make a pop record was to go into a studio with as many tracks as you could get—a 48-track studio, for instance—camp in there for a month, hire the best studio musicians, bring them all in there, work out all the parts, have an orchestrator come in, and bam!—you had Barbara Streisand's record. That was the way people made records.

Somewhere around the time of Milli Vanilli, there was a real change in the orientation of kids towards music. The orientation was a generational shift.

The new generation revolted against overly produced music and went to one of two extremes. One is totally computerized music (like ambient and rave music), and the other direction is back-to-basics rock'n'roll, which is the "grunge" phenomenon.

That stuff is all recorded on someone's living room floor, potentially with old analog equipment strung together in a haphazard manner and recorded with a real raw power and feel. What was important for the kids in that music was the angst of a tortured musician pouring his soul out onto the floor of his living room and into the tape recorder and really connecting with the listener, regardless of whether it really sounded that good technically. A lot of the records that were put out in those days really don't sound that good, but that wasn't what was important. What was important to those kids was that the listenters knew it was recorded by a real (tortured) human being pouring his soul out onto the tape recorder, not in some studio with a bunch of executives sitting around saying, "I think that bass line could be a little bit louder."

TY ROBERTS *(continued)*

On the other side is the completely computer-oriented direction of ambient music made by and large with MIDI, effects, computer digital sound processing, sampling—100 percent computer technology. It's combined a little bit with analog, like turntables, but really not to extremes.

In both instances, these two movements have brought the studio into the hands of the musician. He's creating the stuff in his own living spaces, and he's able to work on it longer and perfect it more with less cost. Then multimedia CD-ROMs came along, and what happened is a migration toward greater focus on the creative ideas and content in CD-ROM, especially the direct contributions of the musicians.

The problem is the technology; there's an investment in time—at least three to six months spent learning about computers—for a rock musician to learn how to do that. You have to work on it, buy the computer, get the software, and learn how to use it. You have to understand what's possible. And at that point, you don't have to make it all yourself; you just have to understand how it's possible so you can come up with ideas and forms that fit with the medium. That's what ION is about. We know how to work with music artists, to get the ideas out of their head and out on the computer screen in some form that's entertaining. That process is what the production of the record of the future is all about. It will still involve audio creation and mixing, but the record of the future will have both the audio component and the visual component on one disc. I think we clearly understand the computer side of it; we're learning about the audio.

Do you have a wish list of things you would like to see in an authoring tool?
We use Macromedia Director. The primary orientation of authoring tools has been general-purpose. There are no authoring tools that were specifically designed to do interactive records, because there's no real generalized description of what an interactive record is. If there was one, it would be designed to preserve the playback of the audio tracks on the audio CD and allow you to do that at the same time while you retrieve media elements from the hard drive where it's cached. The basic idea of an interactive audio album is that the audio continues to play; autobuffering would have to be involved. That doesn't really exist right now.

We would also need a tool that was absolutely cross platform because these days, the playback is on both Windows and Macintosh, while the authoring side is pretty much Macintosh. One problem in dealing with the two platforms is video. We make two copies of our video on every CD. We can generalize and make lousy video that plays on Windows machines, which would be lousy on the Macintosh, or

TY ROBERTS *(continued)*

we could make totally awesome Macintosh video that won't play under Windows. So we do both—make a totally awesome video for the Macintosh and an okay video for the Windows machines. That's about as good as we can get right now.

It's not the computer that's the problem in Windows, but the interface to the CD-ROM player (most PC sound cards incorporate a SCSI interface to the CD-ROM drive). The interface is inefficient, primarily because it's communicating to the CD-ROM player across the PC bus at the same time that the computer is talking back to the bus, displaying video on the screen, and outputting audio to the sound card. I really think it's the audio that's killing it. The data coming back to the audio card is killing the bandwidth of the machine. You can do this test. Play video at 30 fps with no sound. It's awesome. Then add sound, and it plays terribly. You're trying to read a mass of data from the CD-ROM player and output it back through the sound card, which may be the same bus. We spend a lot of time judging what data rate we're using for audio and video files to try to reach the broadest number of computers and meet the minimally acceptable standards that the musicians want.

Do you stay in the general range of 120 KB per second on the PC?

It's between 120 KB to 150 KB per second in video. In audio, we like to do at least 16-bit 22 kHz on the PC side because almost all PCs have 16-bit sound cards. But the real problem is trying to do 16/44; the PCs are capable of it, but it takes all the bandwidth on the bus. You can play it, but you can't do move video around on the screen or do anything else.

On the Macintosh, we now use the new IMA compressor, and it decompresses to 44.1 kHz. It's awesome in Macintoshes. Macs with 16-bit hardware sound like a CD. On the Windows side, the technology is available so we try to use it, but doing it the same time as video restricts your video size to a really small size—potentially 240 x 180 pixels. So if you want 240 x 180 with awesome 16-bit sound it's great.

What's ION doing now with Enhanced CD?

We're creating a tool set so that Enhanced CD disks are easier to create and play more reliably. We realize that recording artists will put out between 30 and 50 of these things this year, but that next year they'll put out between 500 and 1500. If that's really going to happen, it would employ every single person you and I know. Where are those people going to come from? I don't know.

TY ROBERTS *(continued)*

We're doing our tools in partnership with Macromedia. We intend to get some Macromedia developers to get on board with us, learn to use our tools, and then open it up to the Macromedia developers. I intend to both expand and cleave off a portion of the Macintosh media developer base and take it into the record industry. We hope to do that with a basic tool such as Director 5.0, combined with some tools that we are developing—tools that will be specific to creating a kind of remote control that accesses audio CDs and basic technologies that relate to interactive lyrics on audio CDs and even on-line connections. At the same time, ION is working on several projects that will demonstrate some of these capabilities.

We will continue to add more features and enhance them. We're hoping we can get a lot of people to use it and do records with it. We are a pretty small company, but we realize that there will be so much interesting work out there that we would much rather be helping the developer base learn how to do what we now know how to do than to make our company grow to 2,000 engineers. We know that these products will be created by a wide array of a small groups of individuals, just like the music industry. Small amounts of creative artists will create music that giant corporations sell.

That's who's knocking on the door—people who have the skills to do this stuff. What they don't have are specialized tools to fix, patch, and adjust and deal with all the problems arising in trying to make an Enhanced CD disc. The problem with the recording industry is that experienced but unaware developers are meeting with the totally unaware record companies.

We know about software—bugs and slipping shipping dates. But in the record industry, everything ships on time. Late is unacceptable. And it works on every platform. How does that relate to what we do in the software business? Not at all. We make products that are mostly late, products that work for only a little while and then only on a few platforms. Everything has to be just right, or you have to have a human on the other end of the line to talk you through the problems.

The tool set that we will give the record companies is a standard methodology for creating these things at the lowest level, which will help them deal with tech support issues. If somebody is using their tools, it will work the same way as someone else using the tools, even if they are completely different developer groups. So the tech support department will be able to deal with a common installer paradigm, and a common remote control paradigm, and a common RedBook track access paradigm.

TY ROBERTS *(continued)*

The record companies will be able to use different rock groups—or, rather, not really rock groups but programming groups, which will create these things along with musicians—and the products will be similar enough that they can deal with the tech support issues. It's probably not that interesting to a rock star. He cares that he can pick and choose among a hundred different developers to find one that fits his particular lifestyle. I feel pretty confident about that. David Bowie is a lot different from Primus. Developers will have to adapt across a broad range. What music artist would be more perfect for the *Doom* game? He'll have to hang out with developers who are into the *Doom* game. At the same time, somebody who is a well-respected mainstream artist, like Sheryl Crow, isn't going to hang out with a bunch of guys with pierced heads.

Then, too, the music industry is probably the most ethnically balanced industry there is, more so than film. In fact, black entertainment artists have 50 percent to 70 percent of the dollar volume. That is amazing. There is a great opportunity in the computer industry to bring in more people of color into the computer industry. A lot of these events are white and boys, and this is the opportunity to crack that open. It has cracked open in the graphic arts area. That area is more balanced with women and the artistic community. The music industry is an artistic community and I see these developments helping out a lot in that area, if it's not entirely generated by people who live in Seattle and Cupertino.

This takes us into the discussion of two classes of people: technological haves and have-nots.

It's a big problem regarding the cost of computers and what is available. But it is totally driven by the perception of the public. People listen to what the stars do. Their perception of who they are is potentially what their favorite star is. If their favorite music star is on a computer disc, he or she might drive a lot of people to listen to the product and interest them enough to just poke their head into a computer store. If Michael Jackson would do an optimally incredible interactive CD, a lot of people worldwide who never looked at a computer would be interested in finding out what the heck it was.

How will we handle someone sitting and listening to an Enhanced CD on their living room stereo, but wanting to read liner notes on the computer in the office?

The standard for Enhanced CD is going to include the ability to have the media elements accessible on disc without running Macromedia Director as an authoring tool.

TY ROBERTS *(continued)*

Those media elements will be categorized by text files on the disc, which will say where they are located and how to get to them. That text file will be read by consumer electronics products that Sony will come out with in the next couple of years. So you are going to see it from both sides. The computer will become the television set, probably because the computer will be able to scan CNN and do e-mail. The other side is that the audio player is going to become more intelligent. Consumer electronics manufacturers have realized that a typical CD player with lots of buttons is confusing, but wouldn't it be interesting if the interface came through your television screen as a bunch of sliders and controls, and you just sat back on your couch with your remote control. What if you had a visual graphical interface to your stereo system?

Enhanced CD will be the first medium that a device like this will read, and it will drive the creation of this kind of hardware. Consumer electronics companies are thinking about all this. They showed this type of device in two places. One was at the Consumer Electronics Show; it was called the Video 2000, and all of the components—the VCR, the CD player, the tapedeck, even the turntable—were represented visually on the screen of the TV set. And no buttons were on the device except the insert and eject buttons. All the controls were on the screen. That is how it's going to develop. I don't know how big it will be and how soon. But Enhanced CD will definitely be part of that effort.

INTERVIEW: DON WAS

Don Was is one of the top record producers in the industry today. He came to prominence co-leading his own band, Was Not Was, and then went on to produce a string of hits including Bonnie Raitt's Grammy-winning comeback "Nick of Time" and the Rolling Stones' "Voodoo Lounge." He's also active in directing and producing films, having recently completed a well-received documentary on Brian Wilson, the creative but troubled leader of the Beach Boys, entitled Brian Wilson: I Just Wasn't Made for These Times.

In the last thirty years, we've seen music becoming more visually oriented with formats like MTV. Now technology and computer literacy are issues for musicians, too. How has the definition of being a musician or a technologist changed for you over the last couple of years?

A musician is a musician; that really doesn't change. They are using a really specific palette to express themselves. But what has happened is that technology has created a new medium—a virtually untapped medium that combines elements of film, story structure, and cinematic techniques with musical expression and computer programming. You are right that musicians have become judged on their visual abilities, and that's not a good development.

I think that's the way it's done to make a video. First you create a piece of art. When a musician is doing his job right, he's thinking about where to leave space, where to leave room for the imagination, and where to flesh out the details. Ostensibly, when you complete an audio song the right way, you've given people as much information as you want them to have and left as much room for impressionism as you want them to have, so that they can own the experience themselves.

But usually, a video is a bizarre growth on the entity of the musical piece—someone comes in and juggles issues of aesthetics with issues of playability on MTV. It's really an unsatisfactory art form, and it's unfair to judge music on this afterthought. The challenge is that you have a generation of art fans who have now grown up "looking" at music. So it's really important to address these things on equal footing. You don't want to have a music-driven film, any more than you want to have film-driven music. You want to have an organic entity. Maybe you can't quite articulate what it is and label this medium in a high-concept short sentence, but you want the music and the visual/dramatic content to be inextricable and organic.

DON WAS *(continued)*

To me, that's how the industry has changed, and making the medium organic is how we can address this challenge. If it's going to be a self contained situation, the musician's got to build room for the visual content into the audio content. That's why some of the best videos are for bad songs. The songs need help and the video enhances it.

You recently completed a documentary film on Brian Wilson. Are there any plans to use that material for a CD-ROM?

Make an interactive piece? There's talk of that. There are 35 hours of film, and I think that you could certainly include more detail, be more specific, and arrange it more thematically. Todd Rundgren and I are working on something right now with Brian, which involves his great unfinished album, Smile, maybe the most legendary missing album in rock and roll. He beat the Beatles by about a year to this technology-driven album. It was high impressionism. Unlike anything that anyone had been making, without anyone from him to borrow from, he created some very new music, but on the eve of completion he never released or completed the record.

He was making music in 45-second modular pieces and editing them together. And because the techniques were so primitive, he would take home a stack of acetates (pre-production masters), play them one after another on a turntable, and try to imagine how it would all fit together. He had seven or eight hours of music (some engineers say 30 hours) in these little 45-second fragments, and it was too massive to keep track of, a daunting task. If you listen to "Good Vibrations," the one song that was successfully completed from that period, you can hear the edits. You can buy some longer versions of Good Vibrations and you can see the way he was putting pieces together, experimenting. But he could never get the bulk of the album together. Some of the songs have been released, but there are still tons of fragments.

This unfinished work lends itself perfectly to Todd's software engine (the one he used in No World Order). In a way, Brian says, "I don't know how to finish it, you finish it." And you do basically what collectors have been doing, making Smile the way they think it would have been done. In reality, he doesn't remember whether he had anything in mind at the time. It's fair game. You aren't dealing with something that's sacred. No one ever put it together. What we are going to do now is lay out something very similar to what Todd did with No World Order and allow people to make their own versions. On Todd's record, my role was to do my version of

DON WAS *(continued)*

Todd's record, and a few other people did that. Once Brian sees how cool it is, he'll put a version of Smile together. It's certainly easier than stacking acetates.

What are your thoughts on the development of Enhanced CD?

Well, what I'm working on now deals with this issue of organically linking film and music. It's based on the premise that when you start to write a film, it's a good idea to let the songwriter and screenwriter develop an idea together so that it is linked and inextricable from the beginning.

I had an idea for a screenplay, and I began incorporating Hank Williams songs into the screenplay with gaps in the narrative so that the song can come in. It really stems from something that Francis Ford Coppola is doing. I'm hoping that he will produce this movie that I am making. He has a series on VH-1 and he is making twenty-minute short films for "video-unfriendly" artists. He used an album by Joe Jackson and made a dramatic short film that incorporated as much music from the album as the sound track. And I said to him, "It's too bad that Joe Jackson didn't know you were going to make this movie while he was making the album, because he could have done something differently." And he agreed. I said, "I have a record deal, let me do something with a short film in mind."

So we not only wrote this screenplay that involved Hank Williams and this lead singer on the album as himself, but we also chose Hank Williams songs that very specifically advanced the narrative, and we left space in it for these songs to be heard. As we started recording the songs, certain things occurred so that the music changed. And the screenplay changed as a result. For example, Hank Williams goes back to a lounge in the bowling alley to drink away his troubles, but the music for that scene did not come out sounding like a bowling alley; it was a little more chaotic and disturbing. So we made it an opium den, which made a little more sense. That's a case of the music affecting the screenplay, and certainly the screenplay affected the choice of the Hank Williams songs and which sections of the songs we would be using.

So my plan is to direct a film and release it as an Enhanced CD, so that it's multimedia but not interactive. The film comes out one way, but you get the full, unexpurgated version of the music. If you are driving in your car, you just bypass the film. It should stand alone as a film or an album. It was created to be a combination of the two.

DON WAS *(continued)*

It sounds like a lot of work jumping back and forth between the two media and constantly adjusting one to the other.

That's fine; it's like working with clay. There's just more clay out on the table! But at least it's making room in the music for the visuals and making room in the visuals for some music. They're not just appendages scotch-taped together.

Do you do much digital editing of audio?

I bought eight tracks of (Digidesign) ProTools about two years ago, but I've never used it once. I've rented it out. I've worked with people who do use it and love it. It sounds great. I think my problem was that it required me to take two months off to really learn to use this intuitively without picking up the manual, and I just didn't have time. I recently traded it for a 20-year-old two-track tape recorder.

It sounds like you're not using a computer very much at this point.

I have a Macintosh and CD-ROMs, but I rarely turn any of them on, and I never go on-line. Every so often I check them out, but there's nothing I find that compelling yet. I just don't have time. And so far I've found nothing on the Internet that would really address my needs to make me sit up late at night and play with this toy. As for CD-ROMs that have been music-related, I'm glad someone did them. They are pioneer works, but they're not emotionally engaging. I don't like to play video games, so I don't know why musical information should be turned into a game. This is an assumption that some people are making that is really off-base—that people want to get dropped into some space and have to figure out how to get to the information they are looking for, like in the Bob Dylan *Highway 61* CD. I just want to see him play at Newport—cut to the chase.

Interactive pieces are fine; they let me select from a list of things. But I don't want to play a video game. It reminds me of when synthesizers were first released at commercially affordable prices. Initially, having a little Minimoog on top of your piano became the province of jazz pianists to spice up the act at the Holiday Inn. You played it the same way as the piano, but it sounded like a very bad cello, and it took about five or six years before people grew into the instrument and thought of themselves primarily as manipulators of waveforms. They weren't piano players and they weren't B3 (Hammond organ) players. They were guys who were creating and expressing themselves. When these guys starting coming into the picture is when great organic things began to happen in synthesis.

DON WAS *(continued)*

And I suspect that CD-ROM is the same thing. It's very difficult for people who have been making audio-only music for 25 years to empty their minds, pick up a whole new medium, and start creating with no preconceptions. I think that it's the domain of people who are still in school. I think that forming a band ten years from now will not be three guys and a drummer, but instead a musician and a cinematographer and a hacker and a star—someone who can visually communicate. And if you put together these creative collectives with young people who aren't jaded or forced into the pigeonholes that 20th-century music has created, they will come up with something new. They won't give you the Sergeant Pepper genre in the first two weeks. Everyone is trying to dazzle. Everyone's trying to create the ultimate masterpiece. But we haven't even seen the Howling Wolf (that is, the traditional roots music) genre yet.

What you have to do is go and do your best work. Artists should be looking to communicate, to express themselves in an original and personal way. I don't see any of that changing. I think an audience is still people on the receiving end of the artistic contract. You can go to basic definitions of art in Art History 101: it has to do with communication. Someone has to get the point in order for the artistic process to be complete. So regardless of what the technology dictates, regardless of what new mediums develop, you are still converting emotion into some storage medium. It's an emotional transducer. And you are storing it in a painting, a poem, a song, and 100 years from now someone will pick up that signal and feel what you felt at that moment in creation. I don't think that changes at all. If you can't appeal to people emotionally, you are a bad artist. It doesn't matter what your medium is. You are simply putting a few new colors on the palette.

For the artist, these times are very exciting. The process changes tremendously with new language and colors. It's a great gift. I think that in music we are getting to the point where we should be asking, "How many times are we going to recycle Miles Davis, the Beatles, and James Brown?" It may be that we've really tapped those fields, and that the frontiers lie in this new medium.

INTERVIEW: LAURIE ANDERSON

Laurie Anderson has been at the forefront of multimedia throughout her entire performance career, combining graphics, video, and innovative styles of electronic music. In 1995 she released her first CD-ROM, Puppet Motel, *through Voyager. It's a refreshing alternative to many CD-ROMs in the rock-and-roll genre, with particular attention being paid to the audio environment. It also lets the viewer explore a very broad range of her creative work, from early books to spoken word pieces, to models of her electronic violins.*

You have quite a reputation for mixed-media performance. What was enticing to you about the CD-ROM format?

There were a couple of things. First, the obvious one is that it's text, music, *and* images and I'm interested in how they can be combined. That's been the case for 20 years of work now. So this was a fantastic opportunity. The second factor is really the interactivity (I suppose it's my least favorite buzzword in the CD-ROM world, second only to "user"). But of course that is an attraction, or it *was* the attraction for me. But when I think of the word "interactive," it's hearing a piece of music that changes my life or reading something that I'll never forget that really does change me. I think in a lot of CD-ROMs that I've played around with, it's sort of think-work, sort of thinking interactive. You can only do *x* number of things, and it's pretty much been laid out for you by the program. I think that's pretty unavoidable in a number of ways. That's the first thing that Hsin Chien Huang, my collaborator for "Puppet Motel," and I talked about trying to do. How can we make this something where people can really make their own experience? Obviously, there are limitations to that too, but at a certain point you can give them Photoshop or (Macromedia) Director and just go, "Hey, this is fun". So it's somewhere in between.

Do you feel that you achieved that with this project? And if not, what were some of the shortcomings of the current technology that you would like to work around?

I would like to have more places in which the audio and the text think what the "user" or player is doing and change the program a little more drastically. And it seems that this is one of the world's fastest CD-ROMs—not in terms of the speed that it works at. I wish it were faster than it is and that there weren't so many waiting moments. I'm the type of person who has a couple of computers running at

LAURIE ANDERSON *(continued)*

once, so I'm waiting for this and doing that. I guess I wish that the technology were a little more responsive, but it was done so quickly that I'm very pleased with it in those terms.

What was the total development time?

We started in November and it was out in March.

That's truly amazing.

Yes. It started out being a much simpler project. It was going to be some spoken words that were just sort of performances, but I saw how that looked, and I really don't love tiny human beings bouncing around on a computer screen. It's too much the size of mice, I think, kind of creepy. The more I talked to Hsin Chien about how to do it, the farther away it went from that idea of the performance, and it became much more about trying to have other people be co-writers of stories. It was also a question of what you can learn from games without doing one. Because I'm not a competitive person and I can't stand keeping score. It's not fun for me—it makes me too crazy. So I wanted to make something with no scoreboard. It 's about people's curiosity, not points.

One thing that was really nice in **Puppet Motel** *was hearing better fidelity and real attention paid to how audio can smooth the way between different areas of the experience.*

I was pleased by that, too. The first few tests that we did in terms of the audio were so horrifying to me. They sounded so bad that I just wanted to shoot myself. I said, "Let's not do this project, please. I don't even want to do this if it sounds like that."

How has producing a CD-ROM altered your perception of what constitutes an audience?

In terms of doing live things, I do feel thinking and responding going on at the moment. And even though I'm not looking over the shoulder of the user, that's the idea. It's not applause and it's not that kind of performance bonding. It's somewhere between the two kinds of things—listening to a record and being at a show—because I think there is something asked of every audience in a live situation. I

LAURIE ANDERSON *(continued)*

think it's always a conspiracy between the performer and the audience. I think there's a little bit of that in being a CD-ROM player.

Puppet Motel *is one of the first CD-ROMs I've seen that lets people log onto your Web page.*

Well, we are doing this "Green Room" project in conjunction with our tour. We have several people from Voyager (the publishers of *Puppet Motel)* who have come on the tour. We set up a bunch of computers in the lobby and have a Web site so that we post things from every city we're in. And the idea of a green room is the hospitality room in a theater, and it's the type of place where record executives come in and go—"Hey, great concert"—it's a schmooze room. You have a few beers and sit around after the show and talk. So, we decided to do a kind of room like that on the Net, and it really has worked out great. Usually for me it's: do the show, thank you, good night, goodbye, I'll come to your city years later. This is the way of keeping up a kind of real dialogue with people. Actually, we're planning a more elaborate green room for our European tour that starts in a couple weeks. It will be not just about the show and other related topics; it's going to expand a lot more. For example, we have put things in categories that people can add to and subtract from—things like the theme park that I've been working on with Peter Gabriel and Brian Eno, and synthetic voices, so that people can write in about things that are merely suggested by the show but get elaborated on the Net. It's really a wonderful kind of working notebook that I share with a lot of other people.

INTERVIEW: D'CUCKOO

D'Cuckoo is a San Francisco-based band that fuses technology with traditional African music. Inspired by the complex polyrhythmic arrangements of Zimbabwe, they built their own custom MIDI marimbas to trigger synthesizers and samplers. In the tradition of African cultures, where the entire village participates in music and dance, D'Cuckoo invites listeners to join in the music making, blurring the line between audience and performer. One example is the MIDIBall, a large sphere studded with wireless MIDI triggers. As it bounces through the audience, it gives everyone an opportunity to add to the song. The band also includes a virtual member, RiGBy, who joins shows thanks to combined the power of SGI workstations and the RasterMasters, a team of real-time video artists. In addition to performing, members of D'Cuckoo have scored several multimedia projects, including The Little Mermaid *for Sega and* The Vortex *for Hyperbole. For a convincing demonstration of the band's abilities, investigate their QuickTime movie on the CD that accompanies this book.*

How do you describe your use of interactive multimedia in live performance?

We never actually set out to "do" multimedia performance. We were really just interested in ways to involve the audience in the music. And it turned out that this technology allowed us to do that.

One main difference between us and other artists is that they are involved in the whole field of multimedia and interactivity. Ways to be interactive come as an afterthought for them. People are trying to figure out how they can take what they do and make it become interactive. We came from the other end of the spectrum. What we are about is being an ensemble, bringing in other people. Having our own experiences in other cultures where that was happening was what inspired us to get into multimedia in the first place. We want to use multimedia as a complement to enhance those kinds of situations in the world.

To what extent do people in your audience want to interact with a band as opposed to just be entertained?

Some people are into it in theory, but not in practice. Other people totally love it and enjoy the opportunity to play with us. One reason I think people find it difficult is the problem of sound levels in the audience. The sound of people playing drowns out the sound of what's happening on the stage and the balance of the mix doesn't work. That's something that we're finding out about as we're experimenting. It's a function of how many people are in the audience, how many people have drums, how loud the drums are, indoors versus outdoors, and so on.

D'CUCKOO (*continued*)

This is a problem that we found out about a long time ago. We wanted to get a performance space that's specifically geared for this so that we can get the balances between the electronic and acoustic instruments. Speaker placement is essential. If those problems were resolved it would be a much different situation.

How do people react when they see your band for the first time?

A lot of people initially have inhibitions that they need to overcome. They're self-conscious about doing something they've never done before. Once they abandon those feelings and embrace what's going on, they have a much better time.

For example, recently we did an interactive thing which had an audience full of resistant people, because it was their company party. Most people don't want to let their hair down in front of their coworkers. But once you get them involved, you can see this massive change in their attitudes. After fifteen minutes they were totally into it. People have to overcome the whole cultural thing.

People who don't get involved tend to be more critical. It's not a listening situation; you have to be part of what's happening to get what it's all about. That's why we'd like to get a space specific for us, so that people would know they're coming to see an interactive show. We'd advertise it as Bring Your Own Drum (BYOD). Actually, for one show we advertised "Bring a Drum." People were calling the club trying to find out when the band "Bring a Drum" was playing!

How do you really have an interactive performance with your audience? Can you interact with the audience to the point that you let them drive the musical direction?

The musicians are really important. Poise and stage presence are an integral part of the experience while the audience is still being guided and becoming familiar. Most people want to be guided; they want the structure. And most people want to be a part of the process. There is a lot of room for spontaneity if every response comes back to you and keeps you on your toes.

It's frustrating to go to a concert where a band simply sits there and plays, barely acknowledging the audience. You want to feel that they are paying attention to you. Performing should be a dialog with the audience, musical as well as mental and emotional. People are expecting that now. It's not just about being entertained; it's about participating. Entertainment isn't just about music anymore.

D'CUCKOO *(continued)*

When are we going to see venues that are specifically for interactive performance?

In the last two generations we have seen the emergence of interactive museums, and this will move from science and education into the arts. All the libraries are using the Internet. It would be a natural evolution.

Clubs are starting to have on-line kiosks installed so that concerts are happening in real time from all around the world. Five years ago that was not happening. Now there are on-line clubs like the Kitchen in New York, the Electronic Cafe in Santa Monica, and the House of Blues in Los Angeles. It's becoming more acceptable and will continue this direction, just like all clubs have video monitors now.

In some ways it's scary, because isolation is getting worse and worse. Our plans are still to use technology to bring human beings together, not drive them further apart. Really interacting with each other is essential for the health of everyone.

INTERVIEW: HERBIE HANCOCK

Herbie Hancock is among the most revered jazz musicians of the twentieth century. But he also has made forays into other musical styles and was one of the pioneers of jazz fusion. His blend of synthesizers, turntable scratching, and bata drum combined to make "Rockit" a big hit on the radio. The video version, with a jumble of robotic machines, was an even bigger hit on MTV. Herbie's been heavily involved in computers through MIDI sequencing, digital recording, and now, the Internet (he has a T1 line running into his house). Aside from music and multimedia, he also has a lot to say about the role of technology in society.

You've been involved in technology for a long time. Are you interested in remaining in music and sound, or are you moving toward exploring graphics, authoring, and programming issues as well?

The latter, absolutely. I foresee musicians getting more involved in graphics. MTV started this trend. Music video started as an artistic promotional tool for the record, but now it has become more than a promotional tool; in some cases the music video and the music have been synonymous.

Also, I think that there is going to be more of a concentration of art and graphic software available that can be accessed through MIDI and through the keyboard. In the future, I think there will be music software that can be accessed by graphics people, graphics tablets, and so forth.

You've been such a ground breaker, integrating technology into music. Do musicians now have to be hackers and programmers in order to write a good song and perform on their instrument?

I used to program all my keyboards myself, but not any longer, because I don't have time to do that and create. The things that you want to do take away from the creative process. If you have the means, you have to have someone else or something else to take care of the processes that don't require as much creativity but are more craft, such as the programming. As a performer, I have to tell the programmer whether I like the quality of sound. I can always suggest how things can be done because I used to program, so I understand how it is done. Now there are so many instruments that I can't keep up with them. I have a guy that does the programming for me. I tell him what I'm looking for and he gives me a bunch of choices.

I have to guard against getting caught up in features that an instrument has, because they are always new and different. I have to forget about whether the choice that I made makes it musical or not. I always try to keep that in mind.

HERBIE HANCOCK *(continued)*

How does one person create a piece of music while someone else overlays graphics without detracting from the experience of the listener?

I just had an experience like that. I've done some things with a group, the RasterMasters. (The RasterMasters are real-time video artists using MIDI, audio, and video inputs to process and project images from SGI workstations.) One of the problems that people have with the RasterMasters is they don't know whether to look at the images or listen to the music because both are so powerful. You go into overload. When we started doing this, I hadn't done anything like that before. A synergy happens between them and me.

It's most effective when we don't know what we're doing. We both improvise, but there's a lot of work. The audience is blown away. The audience needs training to be able to experience and process all that at once. It's really interesting.

What would you like to be doing with this technology four or five years from now?

I would like to be in an organization that uses technology directly for the advancement of humanity, and I'm establishing a foundation to that effect. It's called The Rhythm of Life Foundation, and there are several concerns we'll try to address. One is that there are a lot of creative people out there who could have a wonderful impact on the rest of us but who can't afford the technology. Another concern is that the state, country, and world are not in the best shape. The United States is in particularly bad shape; the infrastructure is badly in need of repair, but there's no money to fix it up. People are out of jobs because events in history have caused us to change a lot of the structures that were keeping people in jobs. It's interesting that organizations that were designed to kill people kept us in the job market. That's really a shame. Now that threat (Russia) is gone and they've cut back on jobs.

Politicians are doing less and less. They don't represent us anymore. They are more interested in their own jobs than in the people who elect them. It has nothing to do with ability and everything to do with how much money they can raise, how much of a show they put on. There should be one fixed price that they are allowed to spend so that there is an even playing field. Obviously, the person with the best commercial is the best candidate.

HERBIE HANCOCK *(continued)*

Look at the school system. Quality education? It doesn't exist in America, except maybe in some private schools. And the class system is starting all over again. There's too much violence, students are not attending, they're bored. Students don't have a dream to carry them into the future. They don't think they'll live past their twenties, what with AIDS and violence.

We can see that technology is growing; the kinds of tools available are vastly increased compared to just a year ago. And now we have the Internet, a wonderful thing, and the convergence of education, entertainment, games, and computer technology. The signs of the kind of future you see are already here.

We are going to depend on technology; if you don't have a computer in the future, it will be like not having a telephone. For the people who live in the city in that situation, the division between "them and us" will be staggering. Self-worth and values will be nonexistent, because there is no future as far as young people are concerned. We have to turn technology toward humanity and the uplifting of the human spirit—not in the religious way, but the society needs to be revamped.

We have to do something. We have the tools to do it. All it takes are the ideas, execution, money, dedication, and the development of a sense of responsibility among the people who do have the means and technology. The Rhythm of Life Foundation is about using computers to work toward re-establishing hope, particularly for our young people.

INTERVIEW: LIZ HELLER

Liz Heller is the Senior Vice President of New Media at Capitol Records. She oversees Capitol's Hollywood and Vine Web Page, produced the Beastie Boys CD-ROM, and is also moving ahead with Enhanced CDs, starting with Bonnie Raitt's "Burning Down The House." We spoke about the potential of Enhanced CD and how the World Wide Web may change the way music is distributed and sold. (Note: keep in mind that where the word "artists" is used, it usually refers to recording artists)

Is Capitol working to bring recording artists in and get them up to speed on Enhanced CD?

We're always seeking out artists and signing them. But the music still has to work on its own. There are a number of smaller companies that are defining the same turf. I think that they are further along with less concerns about making it work within a big corporation. There will be a rise in independent artists setting themselves up and conceivably selling a lot of records.

The recording industry has been put into the position of dealing with hardware and software issues, whereas up to this point everything has been plug and play. How will Capitol implement Enhanced CD in a way that doesn't create a burden in hardware or software support?

That's one of the issues that people in the industry get upset about when there are complaints of the rising costs of CDs. People don't realize that this is one of the costs that we must deal with. We have to budget that into the costs, and that's tough.

Right now there is more interest and support from hardware and software applicationcompanies to help. If we work with Microsoft or Apple then they'll help us more. Nobody wants to put a driver on their audio CD. They don't want to alter anything, they want the CD to be the same experience it would be without the multimediia track. You have tech support issues. There are a lot of people discussing these issues and they are changing daily

There have been a lot of meetings to come up with industry standards. At this point there is a unified feeling, that there will be a standard format that works and there'll be a market for it, with an industry wide marketing campaign on the whole format.

LIZ HELLER *(continued)*

Will Capitol try to build a big production staff in-house to create this kind of content?

There are a lot of things we need to learn to do in-house, but they have as much to do with art design as programming. We toss around the idea of a lab, but it's a lot of maintenance. If we can make it work in our situation, I'm up for it. Or if we can tie in Capitol Recording Studios and places where there is ongoing research, that's great. Just to go out to buy a lot of computers, I'm not sure yet. I know there are people in our company who could make an Enhanced CD in half an hour provided they have the content. That's kind of still open. When people say they want to do an Enhanced CD disk, I ask why. We should be doing this in house with our art department, once standards are set.

What excites artists is the graphics content, and it really should be done hand in hand with packaging very early. You're talking about areas that artists haven't even thought about yet. That's why I'd like to see it in-house, but I don't know if that means a lab, programming and a staff. I want to get as many of those people up to speed as possible so that we can do it in-house. We won't eliminate the need for outside programmers because no matter how big our lab gets, we will not be dedicated to the R&D aspect of the hardware and the tools.

Is Capitol planning to take existing content on the shelf and repackage it in an Enhanced CD format?

To date, we haven't spent a lot of my time repurposing. I don't think that takes you into the future the way that this medium can. If interactive liner notes become a standard, sure, we'll release catalogue in this format. But right now they are more costly to make and develop than they will be in the near future, because the medium is new. I think that there has to be a feeling from the consumer that there is a perceived value. I don't mean an added price but an added momentum to want to buy them at whatever price. I don't know that we're there yet.

What about online distribution? A lot of artists are hoping to distribute their music online and bypass the major record companies.

Absolutely, people can't wait for that to happen. The record companies, retail outlets, MasterCard and Visa, are also all working on it at the same time. I think the record companies will need to have more of a partnership with their artists. I don't think online will ever replace retail at least in the near future. It may make a dent. Will people eventually be downloading an album without ever buying the packaging?

LIZ HELLER *(continued)*

I'm not saying there won't be an underground network for everything, I hope there will be. But I don't know that it will replace a record company. I think there will be both, but retail will not disappear. There will be a huge catalog of content. You will have to have ways to break artists. And you will have to have all the perks that being with a major label brings in terms of breaking an act. I don't know if online will help new artists in the near future to get to 25,000 or 100,000 units. You still need the big muscle. But there will be examples where it isn't necessary. That's how New Age music started.

I think that the idea is that you might be able to break an artist or create momentum with online distribution in partnership with some other distribution to make sure you are penetrating retail. It's a great idea for us to sell records that way.

Where do you see the music market going, and how do you want to position Capitol during the next 2 or 3 years?

The online arena is one thing we want to really pay attention to. The Internet is revealing an incredible amount of information about a demographic that's important to music, because that's our buyer. We also want to maximize and inspire awareness about artists and therefore sales, and we don't have any ongoing research about this. Now we are finally dealing in that world. That's something for us to really be involved in.

A little over a year ago who had heard of the World Wide Web? Now, entertainment companies can't imagine not having an online presence. The same with videos a few years ago, you weren't "important" if you didn't have one. Music videos "broke" a whole new generation of artists, (brought them publicity) and now that will happen with interactive artists. It will all be part of the package - the music will stand, theoretically, on its own - but it will be part of the experience you are having in listening or interacting with that particular project. The way in which it is distrubuted will most likely change as well.

We need to help the artists of today get into this new world world by exposing them to the tools and educating them. Looking at and signing "intereactive" artists is mportant. I think, that helping artists' create projects and think about interactivity is a big challenge. We have just ifgured out how important it is to create the right teams. People know that in software, but it's just coming iinto the entertainment business.

INTERVIEW: THE RESIDENTS

The Residents are a San Francisco-based band with a 20 year history of combining theatre, visuals and their own darkly tinged flavor of rock and roll. In 1994, they emerged as CD-ROM artists as well, starting with their groundbreaking title "Freak Show," then following in 1995 with "Gingerbread Man" and "Bad Day on the Midway." In all these efforts, the integration between story, music, graphics and sound is phenomenal. The Residents are setting the standard for what can be achieved by a "traditional" rock and roll band in the new CD-ROM medium. The identity of The Residents has long been shrouded in mystery, but their manager, Homer Flynn of the Cryptic Corporation, was able to speak on their behalf.

What is it about multimedia that appeals to The Residents as a recording group and a theatrical band?

The Residents have always been as much visual artists as musical artists. But in a lot of ways they have not been able to fully realize the visual complement to what they do. They have done videos successfully, but at the same time, as the music video market matured, they were less and less interested in what MTV sees as carved out categories like punk or heavy metal.

The Residents have never fit into any of those categories. Music videos are more expensive to produce and on the other hand, there is less opportunity to actually show a venue for expression for the Residents. And in a way, live shows have gone the same way. It has gotten a lot more expensive to produce a live show, and no matter what you do live, it is more limited than what you can do in film or video or other media that have more tools for expression. So as CD-ROM came along, The Residents saw this as a huge opportunity to get in and create more detail and new worlds without spending millions of dollars to do it.

With music video for instance, you can't sell music video, it only works as a commercial for your product. That system works for the people it works for, but the Residents are not part of that system. CD-ROM is more of an extension of what The Residents have always done. It is just a more sophisticated album. In Gingerbread Man it's very obvious that's what that is. Freak Show is more like Eskimo (an earlier recording), in that it is only in terms of sound that a whole world is created there. There's stories, there's characters, there are very visionary things happening, but all in terms of sound. With CD-ROM and someone to work with like Jim Ludtke, here's the whole visionary world too. In 20 years of performing, CD-ROM has proven to be one of the most satisfying media for The Residents.

THE RESIDENTS *(continued)*

What are some of the big limitations?

Sound is the biggest limitation. Sound seems to be the stepchild of the multimedia industry, as to how everyone thinks of it. Everyone thinks of how much picture information they can get in there, how fast, how big, how much animation. Nobody's thinking of how we can also utilize all the tools that exist for sound. For The Residents, it has been over 20 years developing the vocabulary and techniques, most of which are very underutilized in multimedia. For them it has been a trade-off as far as they are getting the visual side of it in, while the music or sound may be very compromised compared to if they were doing music or actually scoring something. They didn't figure "well an album may come out of this." And if some-one really wants to figure out where the musical part is, buy the album. With Freak Show most of the songs are in the CD-ROM but they are edited more toward story content. Rather than full CD quality, it's 8-bit sound. They say "well, okay this is what we can do with this. This time it will spin out in the other direction, the album will spin out of the ROM rather than the ROM spinning out of the album."

On "Gingerbread Man" are you actually jumping to RedBook on the CD or is the audio in Director?

It depends on if you are listening to the Mac version of the PC version. On the Mac version, you are not listening to the RedBook audio, but what you are listening to for the most part is a new compression routine, the IMA compressor, which I understand is the same compression Sony uses on their minidisks. It is certainly not CD quality, not RedBook, but it's much better than 8-bit sound.

   With the Mac version, everything is on there twice, once as RedBook and once as IMA files. They couldn't do that with the PC version, so what they actually do with the PC version is access the RedBook files and play them along with the graphic stuff directly from disk. It couldn't actually have actually done that with the Mac, whereas they couldn't do the IMA with the PC. Bill Schulze at ION handled most of that programming, and he deserves all the credit.

Do The Residents involve themselves in the technical issues and processes, or are they more interested in the result?

They are interested in the process because they feel like there is a lot of creativity going on in terms of: 1) which compromises you're going to make that most com-plement what you are doing; and 2) a lot of times the limitations that you have will affect you creatively.

THE RESIDENTS *(continued)*

You can fashion what you are doing to work with that limitation. They have never been one to say this is what I want to do, you figure out how make it work. There is always a coming together of how to make things work. You can't be oblivious to the technology and expect to have good results. They are very interested in the process, manipulating what they do to the process without being overly compromised by it.

What feedback has The Resident's audience had as to seeing a product such as Freak Show?

Who is and isn't The Residents' audience is a constantly evolving thing. The Cryptic Corporation has consciously tried to create an audience from a PR standpoint since around the end of the 70's, and this was successful from a marketing point of view. A lot of people embraced The Residents at that point, and then in the 80's the audience changed, with things happening in their lives, or whatever, has come back as well as a new generation joining in as The Residents have become known more as multimedia artists. The Cryptic Corporation is working like crazy to let these people know that there is a 20-year backlog of material available. At the same time there is this whole new audience. Something is perceived as new periodically and where there is a feeling of newness (whether there is or not), doors open.

What directions might The Residents take with what's evolving in the online world?

It's something that they are keeping an eye on, more than being directly getting involved in. For one thing, they have enough to do right now, and on the other hand they don't really see where it applies to what they are doing right now. They are online, but as far as really approaching it as a medium, they have ideas. The idea of a virtual Freak Show online is something they've discussed. To me, that's a reality of the future. Whether it's The Residents' Freak Show or somebody else's, it will happen. If you think of it from the point of view that most people have looked at what they're calling interactive TV is actually continuing development of the Internet and on line services. They talk about the shopping malls of the future, making decisions in the most obvious, boring applications. The technology applies itself directly to something like Freak Show, where you can explore, that's the difference. Creatively that idea is out there in the future. Whether it's The Residents doing it or someone else doing it, it will exist. They're always playing around with these ideas.

THE RESIDENTS *(continued)*

Do you have a wish list as to what you'd like to be working on 3 to 5 years from now?

What The Residents are interested in particularly with Freak Show and now Bad Day on the Midway, is that they have developed a very substantial group of characters and situations that could grow a lot further than what has happened in multimedia or music or comic revivals or whatever, and they are interested in the possibility of TV. They generally feel that they are in a good position in that there are more opportunities. For the first time in 20 years, they have their first real budget and an appropriate amount of money to work with. With the success of this, the opportunities are there, if they can do it in the ROM, that opportunity will be there, as well as other ones. They potentially see a half hour animated TV series on Bad Day on the Midway, or a feature length film out of Freak Show on the lines of Nightmare Before Christmas. These are exciting possibilities.

Appendix A: Suggested Reading

One of the best resources for books on music, recording technology, and MIDI is Mix Bookshelf. It's a good place to start when searching for audio reference works. Get a free catalog by calling 800-233-9604.

Books

Audio and Music Education. comp. Cardinal Business Media. Mix Bookshelf, 1995.
Listing of programs in the United States and Canada that offer instruction in music recording, audio production, and electronic music.

Bartlett, Bruce, and Jenny Bartlett. *Practical Recording Techniques.* Sams Publishing, 1992.
Covers basics of professional recording and production, including MIDI and digital audio.

Chapman, Gary. *Macromedia Animation Studio.* Random House Electronic Publishing, 1995.
Packed with tutorials, real-world techniques, and software, this book/CD-ROM has everything you need to create professional-quality animation.

Clarke, Cathy, and Lee Swearingen. *Macromedia Director Design Guide*. Hayden Books, 1994.
This book/CD-ROM contains all the tools, tricks, techniques, and samples you need to get the most out of Macromedia Director.

Mash, David. *Macintosh Multimedia Machine*. Sybex, 1994.
A good review of audio and MIDI in Mac multimedia, particularly well-suited to users of HyperCard or Premiere.

Jungleib, Stanley. *General MIDI*. A-R Editions, 1995.
Everything you could ever want to know about General MIDI, written by a recognized MIDI pioneer and General MIDI founder.

Lehrman, Paul, and Tim Tully. *MIDI for the Professional*. Amsco, 1993.
A more in-depth treatment of MIDI and its applications for serious users. Highly recommended by Mix Bookshelf.

O'Donnell, Craig. *Cool Mac Sounds*. Hayden Books, 1993.
A thorough review of the audio capabilities of the Mac, with lots of tips for customizing Mac sound playback.

Peterson, George, and Steve Oppenheimer. *Tech Terms: A Practical Dictionary for Audio and Music Production*. Mix Bookshelf, 1993.
Explains 300 of the most commonly misunderstood terms in the fields of studio recording, digital audio, and electronic music.

Pohlmann, Ken. *Principles of Digital Audio*. Mix Bookshelf, 1995.
Technical review of digital audio concepts including sampling, DAT, CD formats, and digital audio workstations.

Roberts, Jason. *Director Demystified*. Peachpit Press, 1995.
This friendly, yet comprehensive review of Macromedia Director covers the basics as well as the intricacies of Lingo scripting.

Rona, Jeff. *The MIDI Companion*. Mix Bookshelf, 1994.
An introduction to MIDI aimed at beginners. Lots of pertinent details presented in a way that isn't overly technical.

Thompson, John and Sam Gottlieb. *Macromedia Director Lingo Workshop.* Hayden Books, 1995.
A hands-on guide to learning Lingo, written by Lingo's creator.

Trubitt, David, ed. *Making Music with Your Computer.* Mix Bookshelf, 1993.
Hands-on guide through the process of selecting and configuring a computer-based music production system.

Warner, Josh. *Enhanced CD Fact Book.* Apple Computer, Inc., 1995.
A comprehensive guide to the new Enhanced CD format, complete with case studies, interviews, technical tips, useful contacts, and more.

Yavelow, Christopher. *MacWorld Music and Sound Bible.* IDG Books, 1992.
An exhaustive compendium covering music hardware and software for Mac-based audio production. If it isn't here, it wasn't invented yet.

Periodicals

Electronic Musician

Keyboard

Mix

EQ

Interactivity

New Media

Glossary

ADPCM   Adaptive Differential (or Delta) Pulse Code Modulation. A method for compressing the amount of data required for audio files. ADPCM stores values for the differences between *samples* rather than the value of the sample itself, using mathematical modifiers and multipliers to reduce the number of bits. With this approach, sounds can be represented using 4-bit values rather than 16-bit values, resulting in a *compression* ratio of 4:1.

AES/EBU   Audio Engineering Society/European Broadcast Union, the groups responsible for defining the AES/EBU digital audio format. The AES/EBU format supports transfer of up to two digital audio channels through a single cable, usually a specially designed *balanced* cable with *XLR* connectors.

AIFF   Audio Interchange File Format, designed for transferring audio files between computer platforms. The most common format on the Macintosh, but also used by PC and Sun computers. The AIFF format can contain multiple audio *channels,* can be either 8-bit or 16-bit, and supports a wide range of *sample rates.*

Aliasing   Noise that can be created when an *analog* signal is converted to digital information. When the high frequencies in a signal are more than one-half the sample rate, they can be misrepresented, appearing as frequencies that were not present in the original signal. Most audio digitizers use anti-aliasing filters to remove high frequencies that could cause aliasing.

Amplitude   The strength or level of an acoustic or electric signal. Amplitude is measured in *decibels.* Amplitude is directly related to the perceived volume of a signal. As amplitude increases, volume increases as well.

Analog   An electric signal which is analogous to the acoustic soundwaves that were detected by a microphone or other type of *transducer.*

Balanced lines   Audio cables that use three conductors to reduce noise and interference that could otherwise be picked up by the cable. Balanced lines carry the same signal on two lines, but with reversed polarity. The third line is ground. When the signal reaches its destination, the polarity of one signal (and its accompanying added noise) is reversed back to its original state, and the two signals are added back together. During this process, the two copies of noise from each conductor take on opposite polarity. When they are added together, they cancel each other out and the noise is removed. Thanks to this process, balanced cables can be run for several hundred feet without picking up noise.

BlueBook The specification for stamped multi-session CD discs containing both an audio portion (similar to *RedBook)* and computer data (similar to *YellowBook).*

Channel Has a number of meanings depending on the context. In relation to MIDI, see *MIDI Channel*. In common audio usage, channel refers to a discrete pathway for a monaural signal. For example, a 16-channel mixer can control 16 independent audio signals. A stereo signal requires two channels, usually referred to as left and right. Audio file formats like *AIFF* and *WAV* are capable of containing multiple channels of audio. Finally, in a completely different usage, the network of distributors and stores for selling computers and software is often referred to as "the channel," shorthand for "the sales and distribution channel."

Clipping Occurs when the peak amplitude in a signal exceeds the maximum possible level. When this happens, the top of the waveform is "clipped" off, creating distortion.

Compression Can be considered in three different contexts: lossless data compression, which reduces the amount of redundant data in a file to save storage space, but does not discard information; lossy audio compression schemes (such as *MACE* and *ADPCM)* which actually lose some file data; and dynamic compression, using a dynamics compressor to reduce the dynamics (variations in volume) of a signal.

CPU Central Processing Unit. The processor chip which is the main "brain" of the computer. Also commonly used to describe the entire computer itself.

DAT Digital Audio Tape, a recordable format that offers quality comparable to audio CDs.

Decibel One-tenth of a Bel, a unit of perceived sound loudness originally developed by Alexander Graham Bell, who named it after himself. When a sound is perceived as being twice as loud, it has increased by one bel. A decibel is one-tenth of this unit. The average listener usually cannot notice changes of less than three decibels. The decibel expresses the strength of a signal on a logarithmic scale, usually abbreviated as *dB*. Acoustic signals are measured in decibels (Sound Pressure Levels or *SPL*), while electrical signals may be measured in dBv, dBu (both 0 dBu and 0 dBv equal .775 Volts), or dBm (power referenced to 1 mW).

Downsampling The process of converting audio files at high bit depths and sample rates, such as 16-bit, 44.1 kHz, to smaller, lower-quality formats, such as 8-bit, 22.050 kHz.

DSP Digital Signal Processor. Specialized computer chips capable of performing extremely rapid and complex mathematical tasks, ideally suited for processing digital audio.

Dynamic Range The difference between the loudest possible signal (short of distortion) and perceptible background noise, usually expressed in *dB*. For example, the dynamic range of audio CDs is quite good (96 dB), allowing for loud passages of audio as well as very quiet segments that contain no perceptible background noise. On the other hand, the lower dynamic range of standard cassette tapes (roughly 48 dB) means that quiet segments of audio may contain noticeable background noise.

Enhanced CD Used to refer to a range of techniques for combining standard audio CD data (*RedBook)* with multimedia data that can be read by a computer to simultaneously play multimedia data and CD-quality audio.

Envelope The contour of a waveform as it might apply to *amplitude, frequency* content, or pitch. Often associated with editing functions for shaping tones in a *synthesizer*.

FM Synthesis   A method of synthesis that generates tones using Frequency Modulation (FM), that is, using one waveform to modify (i.e., modulate) the characteristics of another waveform. This type of synthesis is often seen on older, inexpensive PC sound cards, and is of limited quality.

Frequency   The number of times a waveform cycles between high and low peaks within a given period of time. Frequency is often measured in *Hertz* (Hz), or cycles per second. In audio, frequency is directly related to the pitch of a sound. Higher frequencies are higher in pitch. The human ear can typically detect frequencies from 20 Hz to 20,000 Hz.

Gain   The ratio between the input power and output power of a circuit. In common audio terms, increased gain provides a stronger signal, resulting in increased volume.

General MIDI   A specification describing a standard set of instrument sounds and patch *mapping* for the program numbers assigned to those sounds, sometimes abbreviated *GM*. General MIDI also defines basic *synthesizer* functions needed to qualify a synthesizer as GM-compatible. Devices that support GM provide "plug-and-play" support for MIDI file playback, making the distribution and playback of MIDI files easier and more predictable for multimedia developers.

Hertz   Cycles per second. A measurement of the *frequency* (speed of vibrations) within a waveform. Usually abbreviated *Hz*. Often counted as thousands of Hertz, or kiloHertz, and abbreviated *kHz*.

IMA   The Interactive Multimedia Association. Also refers to a standard for 4:1 *ADPCM* compression of 16-bit files. Playable by Macintosh computers using Sound Manager 3.1 and Windows computers using the Microsoft IMA ADPCM Audio Compression Manager.

MACE   Macintosh Audio Compression and Expansion. Lossy audio *compression* scheme built into the Apple *Sound Manager*. Supports 3:1 and 6:1 compression ratios.

Mapping   Assigning relationships between data streams or data sources, often within the context of *MIDI*. For example, a particular sound (also called a program or patch) within a *synthesizer* can be mapped to a value within a program change table. Issuing a program change using that value calls up the desired sound. Data streams can also be mapped to perform other functions. In another example, a pitch bend controller usually changes the pitch of synthesizer tone. One could map the pitch bend controller to MIDI control #7 (volume), so that moving the pitch bender affects volume rather than pitch.

MIDI   The Musical Instrument Digital Interface. A serial communication protocol for exchanging data between devices, particularly synthesizers and computers. Using MIDI, a computer can record performance data played on an instrument, then send that data back to the instrument to recreate the performance. This is the modern-day equivalent of a player piano.

MIDI Channel   A discrete pathway for sending *MIDI* data to a particular MIDI device. MIDI transmits on 16 channels simultaneously through the same cable, sending data in "packets." Certain data types contain an identifying number from 1 through 16. The data is ignored by devices set to respond to other channels, and is recognized only by devices set to receive on that specific channel. This allows for simultaneous control of multiple synthesizers from one computer.

MIDI Manager   Apple's discontinued system-level software for sharing *MIDI* data between multiple software applications. MIDI Manager consists of a system extension (the Apple MIDI

Driver) and a utility for routing MIDI data streams (Patch Bay).

MOD File format that combines *sampled* instruments and instructions for playing the samples at the proper time and pitch. MOD files are usually created on Amiga computers, but can be played back on properly equipped Macintoshes and PCs as well.

Normalize A function available in many sound-editing programs that maximizes volume without *clipping*. A normalizing routine searches through sound data, finds the sample with the greatest amplitude, and calculates the multiplier value that should be applied to that sample to make it the highest possible value short of clipping. Then it applies that amplification multiplier to all the data.

OMS The Open Music System (previously the Opcode *MIDI* System), a system-level architecture for sharing MIDI data and timing data between multiple applications.

Panning The ability to control the location of a monaural signal within a stereo field. Signals panned to the left will play from the left speaker of a stereo. Signals panned to the center will play at equal volume from each speaker, thus giving the illusion that the sound source is directly in the center of the two speakers.

Quantization Occurs when a smooth waveform is broken into a series of discrete steps, usually during the digitization of an analog signal, or the conversion of high-resolution sample data (16-bit, for example) to lower resolutions like 8-bit. This creates quantization noise, distortion which results from the smooth curve of a waveform being transformed into a rough-edged, stair-stepped signal. Quantization is also a function in *MIDI sequencers,* which can shift the timing of notes to the nearest even value, rather like a "snap to grid" function in a drawing program.

QuickTime Apple's system-level technology for managing and synchronizing the playback of dynamic digital video, audio, and MIDI data on Macintosh and Windows computers.

Phone plug A 1/4-inch connector, usually *unbalanced.* Often used to carry audio signals from musical equipment like guitars and *synthesizers.*

RCA A type of *unbalanced* connector for carrying audio signals. Commonly used on consumer stereo equipment. Also known as a phono plug.

RedBook The specification for audio CDs, established by Sony and Philips. Often used to differentiate traditional audio CDs from CD-ROMs.

Sample A numeric value assigned to the *amplitude* of an *analog* signal when measured at a specific point in time. Also used as a verb, meaning to digitize an analog signal.

Sample Rate The rate at which an analog signal is measured and stored as a digital value. Sample rates are often expressed in kiloHertz (*kHz*), or thousands of samples per second. For example, an 11.025 kHz sample rate results in 11,025 sample values being stored every second. Common sample rates include 11.025 kHz, 22.050 kHz, and 44.1 kHz. Older Macs support rates of 11.127 kHz and 22.254 kHz. In digital sampling, the sample rate should be twice the value of the highest frequency to be represented within the audio signal to avoid *aliasing.*

Sample Resolution The number of bits available to represent a sample value. Common sample resolutions are 8-bit and 16-bit. As a rule of thumb, each bit of sample resolution provides 6 dB of additional dynamic range.

Sequencer A software application for recording, editing, and playing MIDI data.

SMPTE (pronounced "simp-tee") The Society of Motion Picture and Television Engineers. Usually refers to the time code standard established by the Society to reference individual frames of videotape. With sequencing software and a compatible *MIDI* interface, SMPTE allows synchronization of MIDI and audiotape devices. SMPTE is displayed as Hours:Minutes:Seconds:Frames (HH:MM:SS:FF), with one frame usually being 1/30th of a second.

snd Sound resource file format, found only on Macintosh. snds are commonly used in HyperCard and as Macintosh System sounds.

Sound Manager Apple's system-level software for controlling the playback of audio, including decompression of compressed sound, automatic sample rate conversion, and the ability to access third-party hardware.

S/PDIF (pronounced "spuh-diff") Sony/Philips Digital Interface, a "consumer-level" subset of the *AES/EBU* standard for transferring digital audio between devices using *RCA* or fiber optic cables.

Synthesizer A device that creates tones electronically, either by playing back *sampled* audio data or by generating new waveforms using software. Synthesizers combine and control the playback of audio waveforms to create new and different types of sounds.

Transducer A device that converts energy from one form into another. For example, microphones and loudspeakers are both transducers. A microphone converts acoustic energy into electrical energy, and a speaker does the opposite.

Unbalanced lines Audio cables that use two conductors (also sometimes called coaxial). One carries signal, the other is ground. Includes standard *RCA* and *phone* (1/4-inch plug) connectors. Unbalanced lines are susceptible to added noise, and should be less than 20–30 feet in length.

WAV (also represented as "Wave") An audio file format common on Windows PCs, supporting multiple channels of audio, 8-bit and 16-bit sample resolution, and a variety of sample rates.

XLR A three-pin connector, usually used for cables carrying *balanced a*udio or *AES/EBU* digital audio signals.

YellowBook The specification for CDs containing computer data (CD-ROMs), including Macintosh HFS and (for PCs) ISO 9660.

Index

You don't need a crystal ball
to see where multimedia is going.
What you need is a box.

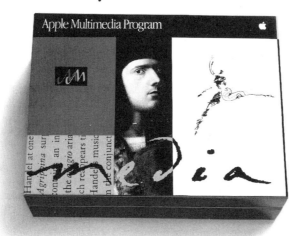

Actually, what you see here is more than just a box. Our Starter Kit is your link to the world of multimedia. An annual membership fee connects you to the best minds of the multimedia community, whether you're an educator, designer, publisher, in-house developer or marketer. You'll receive market research reports, technical and how-to guidebooks, co-marketing and networking opportunities, discounts and much more. For worldwide program information, call (408) 974-4897. That way, the future can't happen without you.

The Apple Multimedia Program.